A Bishop's Tale

✛

✛ A Bishop's Tale ✛

Mathias Hovius Among His Flock
in Seventeenth-Century Flanders

Craig Harline and Eddy Put

Yale University Press ✛ New Haven and London

Published with assistance from the foundation established in memory of
Philip Hamilton McMillan of the Class of 1894, Yale College.

Designed by Sonia Shannon
Set in Adobe Garamond type by Tseng Information Systems, Inc.
Printed in the United States of America by R. R. Donnelley & Sons,
Harrisonburg, Virginia.

Library of Congress Cataloging-in-Publication Data
Harline, Craig E.
A bishop's tale : Mathias Hovius among his flock in
seventeenth-century Flanders.
p.   cm.
Includes bibliographical references and index.
ISBN 0-300-08342-4 (cloth : alk. paper)
1. Hovius, Matthias, 1542–1620   2. Catholic Church—Belgium—Bishops—
Biography.   3. Catholic Church—Belgium—Flanders—History—
16th century.   4. Catholic Church—Belguim—Flanders—History—
17th century.   5. Flanders (Belgium)—Church history—16th century.
6. Flanders (Belgium)—Church history—17th century.   7. Flanders
(Belgium)—Religious life and customs.   8. Counter-Reformation—
Belgium.   I. Put, Eddy.   II. Title.
BX4705.H7645 H37   2000
282′.092—dc21
[B]   00-036810

A catalog record for this book is available from the British Library.

The paper in this book meets the guidelines for permanence
and durability of the Committee on Production Guidelines
for Book Longevity of the Council on Library Resources.

10 9 8 7 6 5 4 3 2 1

Contents

✛

A Word Before

✞

While he was Archbishop of Mechelen, from 1596 to 1620, Mathias Hovius kept a daybook, in which he recorded his countless appointments, triumphs, and defeats. Though the daybook ran to as many as ten volumes, only the last survived. On a muggy August afternoon in 1987, we found that precious volume and decided, together, to write a book about the world it laid bare—the busy, messy, colorful world of a zealous Catholic bishop and his flock.

During our many years of writing, we were shaped by at least four hard-earned (though hardly original) lessons, which readers may find useful as well before setting out. First, contrary to expectations and the laws of simple calculation it took the two of us twice as long to finish this book as it might one of us, while the pleasures were more than double. Second, though we envy still the novelist's total freedom of invention, we were consoled repeatedly by encounters with characters and events more improbable than we ever could have imagined ourselves. Third, in seeking to understand a world long past, we found it highly illuminating to begin with a single human being rather than a large abstraction such as "society." And fourth, while it is impossible to recapture the full complexity of this or any other past, we found it most illuminating of all to try to see the world of Mathias Hovius as he himself saw it.

Again, we did not try to see that world in its entirety: the archbishop's days numbered in the thousands, his acquaintances even more, and the towering piles of documents he left behind are, though overwhelming, still imperfect. Hence we picked out just a few of those days, which in our minds illustrated most memorably some of the challenges and themes in a bishop's eventful life. This decision to limit ourselves certainly had its drawbacks: it caused us to exclude, often painfully, even some of our favorite stories. It caused us to devote less attention to certain sloppily preserved topics (such as marriage and witchcraft) than Mathias Hovius surely devoted himself. And it caused us to worry ourselves very little over the question of his legacy. But our decision also offered at least one great advantage: the chance to sense more intensely than otherwise the drama and immediacy of a bishop's cluttered, unfinished, often exotic world—a world in which he moved by horse and coach around his diocese, regarded other-believers as outright heretics, considered the nagging fevers of his old age the result of imbalanced bodily humors, and pondered how fitting it was that a corruptible earth should rest motionless at the center of the universe while an eternal God sat exalted on a throne just beyond the fixed stars.

Notes on Documentation and Usage

✟

To avoid encumbering the text with references or numbers, we have noted all of our sources at the end, organized by chapter. The notes also include, when necessary, further explanation of how we arrived at various conclusions, or of how we constructed this scene or that.

These sources naturally reflect the languages of the area in which they were composed: the southern, or "Spanish" Netherlands—or as foreigners called it, "Flanders," after the important province of that name. The northern provinces of these Spanish Netherlands spoke dialects of Dutch, the southern provinces spoke dialects of French, and churchmen of either tongue wrote mostly in Latin. Hence we prefer to leave names in their original Dutch, French, or even Latin rather than Anglicize them—thus to leave Jan, Jean, and Joannes as they are rather than change them to John. One exception is Hendrik, which in some cases we leave in the Dutch but in others render as Henri. If there is a commonly used English place-name, such as Brussels or Antwerp, we use it, but in most cases place-names are given in Dutch or French according to the dominant language of the town in question.

Many of the Dutch words in this book will seem more foreign and formidable to English-speakers than the French. Yet English has more cognates with Dutch than any other language, and the rules of pronunciation are simpler for Dutch than either English or French. As in Spanish or Italian, every letter in every syllable in Dutch is pronounced; the trick is simply to learn those sounds that are different from English. These have their nuances, but the following general guide is a starting point.

> a and aa and ae – as in *yawn*
> e – as in *set* or *say*
> ee – as in *say*
> i – as in *bin* or *bean*
> o and oo – as in *so*
> u – as in *put*
> au and ou – similar to *house*
> ui – between *mice* and *mouse*
> ij, y, ei – between *rice* and *race*
> oe – *ooh*
> ch and g – soft sound in back of throat
> j – as in *yes*
> v – as *f*
> w – as *v*

Thus, in English approximations:

> Hovius is HO-fee-us
> Van de Vinne is fawn-de-FIN-ne
> Jansonius is yawn-SO-nee-us
> Boels is BOOLS
> Groenendonk is GROON-en-doank
> Tienwinkel is TEEN-vink-el
> Opwijk is close to OAP-vike
> Schagen is SCHAW-gen
> Goosens is GO-sens

Specialized terms are defined in the glossary at the end of the book.

✝ O N E ✝
The Canon's New Clothes

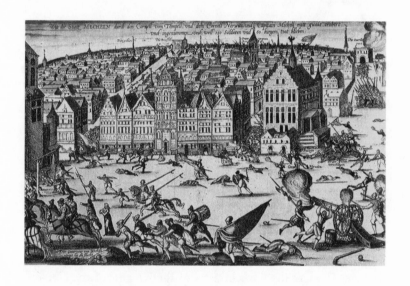

AN OLD WORLD

The eighth of April, 1580, Mechelen, the Cathedral of St. Rombout.

At the end of morning Mass the thirteen canons of the cathedral chapter filed deliberately from their heavy wooden stalls in the choir. Because it was Friday, they continued in two lines to the cathedral's chapter room, just north of the choir, for their weekly meeting.

Behind a stout wooden door, surrounded by familiar painted arches, wrapped in customary robes of black, white, and red, and seated as usual according to seniority, the canons proceeded quite as always. They invoked the aid of the Holy Spirit. They listened as a brother canon read the minutes of their last uneventful meeting. They chose for discussion, from a typical and limited supply of chapterly concerns, an item discussed at least a dozen times before.

When it was over, the canons rose and departed. While crossing the cathedral's tiled floors they had no cause to glance twice at the choir, where 160 coats of arms of the Knights of the Golden Fleece still hung proudly, and where murals of favorite saints embellished gray stone walls that soared a hundred feet high. They had no need to strain necks to study lavish stained windows, which featured dead heroes and benefactors who grew ever more illustrious with time. They had no reason to stop and ponder the luxury of the cathedral's exquisite music, paid for dearly by their long-absent bishop, who now lived in Spain.

Instead all canons could take quite for granted the forty-three resplendent altars that filled every empty space along the cathedral's massive walls and pillars, and that burst with pious triptychs, painted statuary, luxuriant tapestries, the pleasant odors of incense, and legions of burning candles. All could practically ignore the intricately carved stone rood screen that separated the clergy's choir from the people's nave, or the large mural of St. Christopher above the cathedral's high front doors, or the painted banners and lamps that brightened the interior, or the dark palls that still shrouded memorial tombs of the newly deceased.

It wasn't that the canons were indifferent toward their church —to the contrary. Each lamented deeply the current shortage of priests at its altars, the recent difficulties encountered in acquiring sufficient numbers of candles, and the makeshift wooden reliquary now holding the bones of the church's patron saint, Rombout. It was rather that the cathedral's very immensity and self-assured activity, its glorious sights, sounds, and smells, conveyed such an illusion of permanence that almost nothing about the place required a second thought at all. Here, despite momentary deficiencies, was still a magnificent edifice of worship. Confidence, not indifference, would have explained why any of the canons failed to linger one last time in St. Rombout's before leaving, each to his own concerns.

On his way out the door, Mathias Hovius, one of the junior canons, removed his precious choral robes and handed them to a servant boy: first came a waist-length mantle of black-and-white-striped ermine, then a long black velvet cloak lined in red and worn open in the front, and finally a white lace surplice that reached past the waist. These the boy carried home, holding them safely above the dirty streets of Mechelen while walking behind his master. Once outside the cathedral, Canon Hovius wore only his everyday black cassock, which buttoned to his neck and reached to his ankles. He avoided any French-styled ruffles on sleeves or collars. He maintained on top of his head the distinguishing clerical tonsure, or shaved crown, which proclaimed as much as his clothing his priestly status. And he kept his beard properly trimmed: no fussy waxing and twisting, lest he appear vain, and no protruding hairs over his upper lip, lest while celebrating Mass he obstruct the blood of Christ.

Thus did the canon clothe himself the rest of the day, which went quite like many others. He attended to matters in the parish of St. Peter and Paul, where he was still pastor. He endured several meager meals brought on by these lean times. He sang Vespers and evening prayers. And when all was accomplished, he removed his cassock and pulled on his nightgown. Though aware of recent threats to the city, he never would have imagined while snuffing his candles and retiring to bed, or even while waking during the night to fill his pisspot, that this world he knew so well, this order so familiar, would by morning be gone forever.

AN ENGLISH FURY

The bells of Rombout's sounded the alarm in the darkness of early morning, around four, but too late. After conquering the disorientation that attends all rude awakenings, Mathias Hovius hurried to his feet and understood: it was an invasion of rebel troops.

The surprise was nearly complete. True, everyone knew that neighboring towns had recently capitulated to the rebels, but until today there had been no amassing of rebel troops near Mechelen's walls, no suspicious movements around its fields, and little doubt that the city was still overwhelmingly Catholic and royalist, loyal to its overlord the King of Spain. What then could have happened? At the moment there was no time for the canon to sort things out. For now he could do only two things: hope that Mechelen would hold, and decide where to hide or escape should it not. Surely he, like other clergy in these times, considered clothing himself in something that would obscure his identity as a priest—but where to find it? Outside, the growing cries of panic and resistance blended with gunfire and clanging to form a single, loud rumble across the five parishes of the city. Inside, Canon Hovius prepared to plunge into the night.

If at that moment his vantage point had been not the confusion of his modest home but instead one hundred yards high, atop the enormous stone tower of St. Rombout's, the canon could have seen the battle's progress more clearly. More than twelve hundred rebel troops, filled with drink and Protestant zeal, unpaid since December, and intent on booty and conquest, were pouring over the southwest wall near the Brussels gate, abandoned just moments before, according to prearranged plan, by treacherous guards. Nicolas Vanderlaan, captain of the watch and belated discoverer of the treachery, was doing his best to ignore various wounds earned in previous service to the King of Spain and rallying what was left of his small cohort to counter the invaders. But soon after engaging his foe, the overmatched captain turned in retreat and won his latest reward: pieces of shot in the buttocks. Comrades carried him to a safe house, where he lay for days in peril of his life.

Now rebel troops were scaling the northwest wall as well, near the equally abandoned Cow gate. Startled members of the local civic militia, still loyal to the king, quickly assembled in the Grand Market, the cobblestoned and gabled heart of the town, and began brawling. But other Mechelaars, betting on the rebels, joined in the treachery and ran to open the guard-forsaken Brussels and Cow gates, so that invaders would not have to bother using ladders. Now the intimidating force of 150 rebel knights on horse poured inside, like water through a burst dike, to support the rebel infantry. In the face of overwhelming numbers and modern weaponry, tenacity alone was insufficient, and dozens of royalist militiamen began to fall.

While the official, strategic fighting continued, the more traditional side of war began: most rebel troops now threw their energies into rounding up persons and items of greatest monetary value, proving once more their unswerving loyalty to the old soldier's creed that looting was preferable to fighting. Some of these

mercenaries were Scottish, most were English, nearly all were Protestant, but every last one believed in plunder.

Now all Mechelaars, not just militiamen, were at risk, for
even the poor had some heirloom stashed away, and would be
threatened or tortured until they produced it. Wealthier burghers
feared not only robbery but being held for fortune-depleting ransoms. And members of the clergy could expect, in addition to
these unpleasantries, the wrath that accompanied religious war.
Rebel troops ransacked everything with practiced efficiency, but
they went after churches and monasteries with emotion as well. To
please weapon-hungry captains, they knocked bells, lead, and iron
from towers. To please their purses they stuffed valuable chalices
and other liturgical ornaments into just-emptied mattresses. But
to please their preachers and religious sensibilities they smashed
altars and statues inside Rombout's, as well as the pathetic wooden
reliquary holding the saint's remains — and they accosted any priest
or nun they could find. They wounded a canon of St. Rombout's,
who died days later. They abused, or held for ransom, dozens of
monks and nuns. They captured near the Grand Market a Franciscan named Suetens, whom they dragged to a nearby house and
hanged by the cords of his own habit. They murdered the subprior of the local Carmelites, who lay ill and defenseless in his cell.
And they would capture or slay Mathias Hovius as well, if they
found him.

On the bending street that ran past the rectory of St. Peter's
and Paul's, where he resided, the canon could not see every assault
on terrified burghers, or every purge of churches, but he could
guess them. He could also see the growing crowd of people running his way, and soon learned the reason why: they were heading
toward the Nekkerspoel gate, a short block or two beyond the rectory, and just opened by a handful of royalist cavalry. Here at least
was one gate not yet controlled by rebels: those many Mechelaars
who preferred escape to confrontation recognized that for the moment this was the only way out of town.

Leading the flight to the Nekkerspoel were fearful magistrates and merchants, who in the early light of day hastened through the gate and beyond, in the direction of nearby Leuven and Aarschot, towns still true to the king. Close behind were hundreds of monks, nuns, beguines, and pastors. At least one monk, however, an old classmate of Canon Hovius at university, halted in his tracks. This was the Carmelite Peter De Wolf, a popular but troublemaking thunder-preacher, defender of all things Catholic and nemesis of all things Protestant. In recent crowd-pleasing sermons, everyone had heard Father De Wolf's stirring exhortations to defend city and faith to the death, and so when several in the crowd saw him fleeing they uncharitably reminded him of his own words—much as Jesus asked a Rome-fleeing Peter, "Where goest thou?" Like the apostle himself, a chastened Peter De Wolf instantly turned about to face his martyrdom: putting on helmet and mail, he dashed back to the Grand Market and fought with inexperienced clerical hands to his last breath.

Mathias Hovius, like most of the clergy, at last chose discretion rather than arms, and now hastened toward the Nekkerspoel gate as well. At thirty-eight he ran better than he would in his corpulent years, but still too slow: for before he could get out the gate, rebels took control of it, too, just as they had the other six of the city. And they were not about to let any priests pass through. Had something besides indecision delayed the canon? Had he paused to conceal the treasures of St. Peter's and Paul's? Had he rousted the caretaker to ring the church's bells, thus spreading the general alarm? Had he stopped to see the corpse of his brother, already slaughtered by rebels? Hesitated and considered taking the same reckless path as Peter De Wolf? Sought a disguise? Whatever slowed him, with every gate in rebel hands, the canon's only choice now was to hide.

Just inside the Nekkerspoel gate stood the imposing palace of Hoogstraten, of the noble Lalaing family, occupied in recent times by the countess Lalaing herself. Though she was royalist and

Catholic, not even the most hardened rebels were likely to molest an unresisting noblewoman—plunder did have a few rules after all. Here, therefore, was a convenient place for the canon to hide. Still it was hardly foolproof: during a previous invasion, Protestant troops had dared to enter the countess's bedroom to ask whether she was sheltering any priests.

Perhaps Canon Hovius entered through a secondary door of the palace, prearranged in the event of troubles. Certainly he was quickly led inside by hosts who knew the secrets of their own dwelling place, and then shoved inside a wooden wardrobe. Over the next three days, as the palace was searched, as the sacking showed little sign of abatement, and as English troops particularly distinguished themselves in plunder and cruelty so that this whole bloody "Fury" came to be called after them, the canon crouched in apprehension.

Years later he told the story of the wardrobe to friends, who repeated it to others. Willfully or otherwise he may have embellished it, prodded in his imagination by recent tales of fellow clergy who had likewise suffered the horrors of religious war. He may even have distorted his length of time in confinement, to fit the favorite Christian motif of three—including Jonah's three dark days in the belly of the whale. But there was no question at all that his terror was absolutely real.

There must have been little sleep, much anxiety, and whispered communications in and around that wardrobe. There must have been temptation to compose clever, incomplete recantations of his faith, which might save his life should soldiers find him inside. Yet this temptation must have alternated with braver reflections on how to steel himself for death. And certainly while he waited there were a thousand images and memories—some rushing to the surface but most embedded in his soul—of a past that had gone so terribly wrong.

INSIDE THE WARDROBE

When Mathias Hovius was born, in 1542, Mechelen still glittered.

Its prince, Charles V, was still greatest of all: emperor of Germany, King of Spain, so forth and so forth, not to mention overlord of the seventeen provinces of the Netherlands.*

Its cultural glory, though seriously challenged by Brussels, still shone, evident in such monuments as the majestic Renaissance-styled palace where Charles spent much of his boyhood, and from where for years Charles chose to rule his Netherlandish domains.

Its robust trade was by 1540 subordinate to Antwerp's, but leather, copper, and cannon industries still prospered, and a highly urban population of thirty thousand still impressed. (In all the Netherlands were nineteen towns with populations greater than ten thousand; the British Isles contained only four.)

Above all else, Mechelen's Catholicism still seemed sure, with scarcely a heretic in sight. It boasted twenty-four confraternities of pious laypeople, five parish churches, dozens of convents, religious statuary on seemingly every house and bridge, and famously eye-pleasing processions. During Holy Week, trumpeters positioned atop St. Rombout's announced the business of celebration, prompting streets below to groan with scores of floats on which the stories and heroes of Catholic Christianity came alive for young Mathias. There in the flesh were the Four Evangelists. The Holy Family. The Holy Sepulcher. The entire city of Jerusalem on a single

---

* Throughout the book, we use the terms "Netherlands" and "Netherlandish" to refer to the entire area occupied by the original seventeen provinces, or what is today approximately Belgium, the Netherlands, and northwestern France. The word "Netherlands" is a rendition of "Nederlanden," which simply means Low Countries, so that "Netherlands" and "Low Countries" are interchangeable. Today in the western world "Netherlandish" tends to be more closely associated with the Kingdom of the Netherlands than with Belgium, but when used alone the term properly refers to the culture and geography of the entire region, north and south.

float. The predictable Jonah float of the Fishsellers' Guild. The Virgin Mary in countless variations. Near the end rolled the main float, the Ascension of the Virgin, replete with organist, prophetesses, towers, and a camouflaged giant wheel rotating on a vertical axis to help the ascent along. Last of all came the reliquary of St. Rombout, not only the cathedral's patron saint but the city's. Mathias knew from his youngest days that Mechelen was for the Virgin, and for St. Rombout.

When Mathias Hovius was a boy, learning his Latin nouns and verbs, the omens of ruin appeared.

Or so it must have seemed in the darkness of the wardrobe, where thoughts raced. There had been the August night in 1546, with Mathias barely in breeches, when lightning penetrated a gunpowder-filled tower of the Zand gate, abutting his own neighborhood. The explosion obliterated the tower, sent stones rocketing up to two miles away, flattened houses, damaged churches, killed 300 people, wounded 150, and decapitated fish in the river. Catholic pamphleteers concluded that this was a divine reminder to Mechelaars that they ought to be better Catholics, while Protestants suggested that this was God's way of telling the town's populace to renounce their old religion in favor of the new. Soon after the explosion, the last stragglers of the royal court moved to Brussels for good.

In the 1540s and '50s came the grain shortages and diseases, the first burning of heretics on Mechelen's main square, the ever heavier taxes for Charles V's eternal wars with France, and the decline of Mechelen's wool trade. Then of course there was the anxiety that reigned in all the land in 1555, when the weary, occasionally heavy-handed, but nevertheless legendary Charles abdicated. Upon his dramatic announcement in a densely bannered hall in Brussels, all the audience cried. But no one of them ever felt so sentimental about Charles's heir and son, Philip II.

Charles was a native of the Low Countries, but Philip was Spanish first and last. Too many Netherlanders soon felt that a distant Philip trod upon local political customs. Too many, including among the vast Catholic majority, soon disliked Philip's version of Catholicism, especially his plans to improve orthodoxy through new, smaller bishoprics and even—said well-grounded rumors—a more efficient and powerful Inquisition. Most vocal in opposition was the Protestant (especially Calvinist) minority, which began to grow in disturbing numbers during the 1560s. Thanks largely to them, the war of words soon became the real thing.

Long before Philip II, Netherlanders had complained to princes about trampled customs and capricious taxes. Long before Philip, they had resorted to armed defiance. Long before Philip, Netherlandish fields had been burned and ruined, Netherlandish peasants forced to huddle in shelters, and Netherlandish buildings transformed to piles of timber and dust. But by the time of Philip there was a new incentive behind all the havoc: the proper version of Christianity. Ever since the split of the ancient faith during the 1520s into Catholic and Protestant confessions, Europeans could add to their old-fashioned motives for war—dominion, booty, revenge, boredom—the quest for the one true church. For some, here was another version of the Crusades, within Christianity rather than without. It was a motive first exhibited by Charles V when he set out to conquer Lutheranism in his German lands. And it was a motive about to be continued by his son Philip in the Netherlands. Though more willing to compromise than the various Black Legends about him would soon have it, Philip did absolutely insist that his dominions be wholly Catholic.* Religion was not his only motive for war, just as it was not the only motive for Crusaders, but it was the leaven. It gave the new age its passion.

This was a time when a Catholic father could threaten to

---

* The Black Legends, developed largely in England and the Netherlands already by the second half of the sixteenth century, portrayed Philip as a reclusive monster who murdered his son Don Carlos and sanctioned all sorts of cruelty against his own subjects; the legends included as well exaggerations about the Inquisition.

smash his son's head against the wall for even thinking of converting to the new faith. The schoolboy Mathias therefore heard less the restraint of his fellow but discredited Netherlander Erasmus and more the zeal of the Netherlander Titelmans, a Catholic Inquisitor, who roamed tirelessly, paid ubiquitous informants, and arrested triumphantly at any hour, in any weather, to purify the flock of Protestant heresy. The student Mathias heard tales of nearby Catholic clergy whose skulls were cracked, ears and noses cut off, tongues cut out, heads placed in hot waffle irons, bodies run through, and corpses tossed casually into rivers by irreverent Protestants. The grown Mathias heard talk of the dreaded William Blois van Treslong, a Netherlandish pirate turned Calvinist zealot who sailed into cities and strung up Catholic clergy, no questions asked, and his partner in terror, William van der Marck, lord of Lumey, who ignored the orders of his more clement superiors and hanged nineteen priests in a barn near the riverside town of Gorcum. The canon therefore knew that such a fate might await him too should he be found in this wardrobe.

When Mathias Hovius was preparing for ordination, in the summer of 1566, the work of ruin began.

Bands of Netherlandish Calvinists decided then to do what Protestants elsewhere in Europe had done in decades past: smash the "idolatrous" statuary and paintings of Catholic churches, thus striking a blow against faith and king at once. The Iconoclastic Fury, as it was called, reached Mechelen on 23 August, while Mathias was home from his studies at the university. He avoided the mob, and the city suffered relatively little. But the larger damage was done: mighty Antwerp was threatened by Calvinism, scholarly Leuven was nearly emptied of students, and, worst of all, King Philip of Spain was furious.

When Philip and his ministers heard that iconoclasts were, in the name of Protestantism, stomping on sacred hosts, obliterating relics, burning crucifixes, cutting off heads and arms from statues of the Virgin, and murdering priests and nuns, they lost patience with all Netherlanders, not merely the guilty. Now little effort was made to distinguish between mildly protesting Catholics on the one hand and openly rebellious Calvinists on the other: now most anyone who expressed dissatisfaction was suspect, as a traitor, a heretic, or probably both. Influential Spanish voices urged Philip to immediate retaliation, or even a personal, authority-confirming visit. To make things safe for his arrival, Philip turned loose on the Netherlands his longtime *mayor domo,* the Duke of Alva, with ten thousand Spanish troops.

Alva arrived in Brussels in the spring of 1567 not with reconciliation but with a fist. His Council of Troubles, popularly called the Council of Blood, moved unforgettably from town to town, burning books, conducting eight thousand trials, executing a thousand people (including Catholics), and alienating just about everyone. Most Netherlanders still claimed loyalty to Philip but felt no obligation to extend that sentiment to Alva. Some subjects, including Catholics, joined the ranks of rebel armies opposed to the duke. Sixty thousand other subjects, including still other Catholics, quit the land altogether, crippling commerce and industry, and demonstrating once and for all that Alva earned his nickname "the Iron Duke" not for any prowess in trade. From where Canon Hovius sat, in the wardrobe, it was easy to blame Alva for the entire mess.

When Mathias Hovius was a new pastor hearing confession, in 1572, the ruin reached Mechelen at last.

It was the work not of Calvinists or other rebels, but of Alva. During the summer, the duke had marched his armies to the southern borders of the land to ward off a rumored invasion from rebel-supporting France. While Alva was away, Mechelen and various other cities displeased with his regime decided to play: they opened their gates to rebel troops, in anticipation of allying with the invading French against Alva. But the possibility of French aid collapsed in late August 1572, when that nation plunged into civil war. Free once again to turn his attention to matters Netherlandish, a seething Alva marched back north, determined to make all rebel-friendly cities pay.

Most of the newly installed troops in these cities fled before Alva even arrived: now defenseless, these same cities had little choice but repentantly to open gates and let the duke back in. When Alva reached Mechelen, the guilty city put up a show of keeping its gates shut, but it capitulated without a fight on that lamentable morning of 2 October. Pastor Hovius was part of the banner- and cross-bearing delegation that trudged out to meet Alva, then knelt and begged his forgiveness for having entertained rebels. Had he been in a better humor, or had his troops been satisfied in sacking other towns en route, Alva might have listened. But instead the troops felt cheated, having just days before been left empty-handed outside Mons, which escaped by paying a huge fine. Hence Alva ignored the delegation that stood before him now, and gave his soldiers Mechelen.

Here was another Fury for the city, the Spanish Fury, to go along with the Iconoclastic Fury that had threatened Mechelen in 1566, and the English Fury that would ruin it in 1580. The Spanish version lacked some of the religious enmity of the other two, for Catholic Spanish troops at least left untouched the massive gilded reliquary of St. Rombout, and they were less inclined to kill priests. But dissimilarities ended there: after all, these Spanish troops would loot just about everything else, even in churches, and they had no qualms about assaulting and robbing priests—as Mathias Hovius learned firsthand.

Having taken refuge inside the church of Our Lady, along with many other frightened Mechelaars, Canon Hovius sensed that many in the crowd wished to confess. Putting on surplice and stole, he sat in a chair and began hearing penitents one by one. The scene was upset when Spanish soldiers, ignoring the custom of church sanctuary, pushed violently inside and began their work of destruction. These brave soldiers heroically conquered altar cloths, drapery, poor boxes, chalices, and any other object of value. They even desecrated sacred hosts. One soldier brazenly interrupted the confession of a kneeling woman by putting a dagger to the chest of Mathias Hovius, who was listening to her, and demanding money. The pastor wisely complied, handing over "six or seven" *daelders*— enough to satisfy the soldier, who ran off to finish his work.

The Spanish Fury removed the last coat of shine from medieval Mechelen. Now even more people emigrated from the city. Sympathetic parishes in Brussels sent alms. City after city opened its gates rapidly to Alva, and paid him generous fines, in order to avoid Mechelen's fate. As far as Mathias Hovius could see, only one bit of good came from this most recent round of war: Alva and his soldiers were now so despised in the Netherlands that Philip recalled him to Spain the next year, in 1573. And Philip decided that the Netherlands were too dangerous to visit personally after all.

There was one other consequence of Alva's ruin: the armies of the rebels now swelled even larger, bolstered not only by native Netherlanders but especially by Protestant adventurers and mercenaries from abroad.

When Canon Mathias Hovius was asleep in his bed, just hours before, Mechelen was ruined again.

Thanks especially to Alva, the land was divided in two during the 1570s, between those loyal first to King Philip and those loyal first to the States General (a "national" assembly of representatives from each Netherlandish province).* Though the Royalist party was wholly Catholic, the States party at first included both Catholics and Protestants, much like the *politiques* of France, who subor-

---

* Each provincial assembly was called a "States," as in the States of Brabant, States of Flanders, States of Holland, and so forth, because they were made up of representatives from the traditional three States (or Estates) of society: the clergy, the nobility, and the towns. Hence the national assembly was called a States General. A fuller depiction of the political structure of the land under the archdukes (1598–1621) appears in the figure on p. 45, but the basic institutions were much the same before and after their time.

The Spanish Netherlands Before 1629

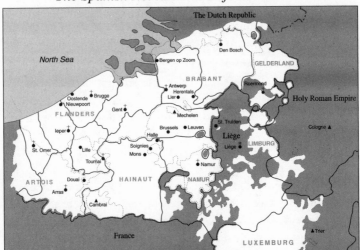

The Spanish Netherlands before 1629, with featured towns

dinated religion to the peace of the land. Canon Hovius watched anxiously as a largely Catholic Mechelen, along with many other Netherlandish towns, wavered in its allegiance between king and States. In 1578 Mechelen sided with the States and its growing armies, and even complied with orders to raise money for defenses by selling off precious religious ornaments—including the once untouchable reliquary of St. Rombout, which was temporarily replaced by a simple wooden chest. Then in 1579, unhappy with the increasingly Calvinist States party, Mechelen returned to King Philip, apparently for good. But by early 1580 the city was again ripe for change: States armies had by this time captured cities and forts all around Mechelen, thus turning the city into a perilous royalist island. Moreover, Mechelen was poorly defended, for though loyal to King Philip it still smarted from the Spanish Fury of 1572 and thus refused to accept the king's offer of a Spanish garrison to protect it. Recognizing Mechelen's precarious position, the decidedly Calvinist leaders of the States hurriedly met in Brussels in early April 1580 and concluded that the city could be taken again for their side—this time without the Catholicism.

Only days later Mechelen was falling, burghers and troops were running, and priests were squeezing themselves into wardrobes.

A BLESSÉD SMOCK

There was no question that the canon would have to escape: the States army, now full of Protestants, was absolutely against Catholic priests and planned to settle in Mechelen for good.

When on the third day the English Fury began to lose momentum, limited passage through the city's gates became possible. Someone in the palace of Hoogstraten brought Canon Hovius a peasant's smock, in which to disguise himself. Who had more innocent reason than peasants to move in and out of town? An exit through the nearby Nekkerspoel gate was the obvious choice. Perhaps suspicious eyes were cast upon this unlikely peasant, or perhaps not: several days in a wardrobe would have roughened his appearance. In any case, he finally walked safely through, then continued on to Leuven, a journey of several hours by foot.

As he stepped through the ruined buildings on the outskirts of Mechelen, the smell of gunpowder and smoke still in the air, it was easy to turn and see the tower of Rombout's. Its baptized bells, Libertus, Carolus, Rumoldus, Maria, Maria Magdalena, and the eight-thousand-pound Salvator, rang no more. Within days all but Salvator were melted down, to be forged into Protestant cannons. Sixty to a hundred burghers would be left dead by the fighting. A stripped Rombout's was soon host to Calvinist sermons attended by up to a thousand people. Despoliation would last a month.

During the terrible journey to Leuven, Canon Hovius must have wondered whether he would ever see his native town again. Not only Mechelen but the entire Netherlands were torn asunder. The seven northernmost provinces would within the year declare independence from Spain. The southernmost had already declared allegiance to King Philip. For many decades everything north, south, and especially in between—such as Mechelen—would be contested, bringing all the Netherlands to its knees.

Spanish authorities offered little consolation to exiles from Mechelen, telling them they should have accepted a garrison when they had the chance. On the other side, the States cities of Antwerp, Brussels, Lier, and Herentals lit bonfires and rang bells to thank God for bringing about Mechelen's fall and the enlargement of territory controlled by the States, for surely God had done it. But to the biblically astute Canon Hovius this disaster was certainly not a divinely assisted Protestant triumph: it was instead Mechelen's punishment for not being Catholic enough. It was the lamentation of Jeremiah. It was the desolation of the land prophesied by Joel. It was the shaken heavens, removed earth, chased roe, fleeing people, spoiled houses, ravished wives, and wrathful Lord of Isaiah. It was the apocalypse itself, and the beast seen by John was loose.

One chronicler of these events wrote in consecutive sentences that Canon Hovius left the city dressed as a peasant, and became a "great defender of the faith and an enemy of heretics." Whether the chronicler intended a connection between the two sentences or not, he was right: the flight of the young Mathias Hovius was indeed the nourishment for the zeal of the old.

The Third Man

A ROMAN DELIBERATION

The twenty-fifth of September, 1595, Rome.

O n one of Rome's seven hills, called the Quirinal, in the midst of sprawling gardens and ancient ruins, stood the sparkling new palace of the Congregation of the Consistory. For the twelve cardinals who made up the Congregation, and the throng of clerks who served them, it was simply another meeting, another agenda full of prime ecclesiastical appointments to be made all around Catholic Europe. But for the ravaged Netherlands one item on that agenda was of the highest importance: approval of a new archbishop for Mechelen, first in rank of the seventeen bishoprics in the land yet also among the most troubled.

Outside the palace, the ancient Colosseum lay in view to the south, and the Vatican to the northwest. Inside, venerable members of the Congregation listened as the designated cardinal-protector of the Low Countries presented the case for the latest nominee. The customary inquest, or Scrutiny, into the nominee's life had been conducted in Mechelen on 18 July, under the direction of the senior bishop in the Netherlands, announced the cardinal. Four honest clerics and two honest magistrates had offered testimony about the nominee, whom they knew well. Each witness had recounted the miserable state of the archdiocese. Each had confirmed that the previous archbishop was dead, for they saw him die. Each had assured the interviewers that the nomi-

preceding page: Lucas Franchoys, *Mathias Hovius,* in his early years as bishop
Beguinage Church, Mechelen, © IRPA-KIK, Brussels

20

nee's pious mother Elisabeth and his long-deceased father Andreas legitimately procreated him. And each had attested that in the nominee's past and present duties as pastor, chaplain, and canon he proved himself diligent, sober, modest, reputable, and in possession of all "other qualities demanded of bishops by the Council of Trent and the Apostle Paul." Finally, each witness had sworn that the nominee always behaved "irreprehensibly," at least "as much as human fragility permits."

The cardinal-protector, fully mindful of gifts already received for his patronly efforts, did his best for the candidate, invoking all the reassuring clichés required for the occasion. In addition, the cardinal displayed notarized certificates of the nominee's baptism, ordination, and university degrees, plus the usual profession of faith. If it all seemed formulaic, it was supposed to be, for there was a particular way to do things in Rome. Most formulaic and persuasive of all in the cardinal's pile of documents, however, was the stately letter of nomination, dated 20 April, and signed by King Philip II of Spain.

This deliberation by the Reverend Congregation was, after all, a formality, a stamp of approval affixed to a decision already taken in Madrid. Since the early part of the present century, the kings of Spain, like many other Catholic princes in Europe, had owned the right to name bishops within their dominions. The pope and the Congregation made the "canonical conferral" and might dispute unworthy nominees, but in practice it was King Philip who made bishops in the Netherlands.

For long there were only four bishops to be made there, but by 1559 Philip succeeded, after much resistance, in increasing the number of Netherlandish bishoprics to seventeen, with the new archbishopric of Mechelen as *primus,* or head. Philip's first appointment to Mechelen proved less than felicitous: it was the controversial Antoine Perrenot de Granvelle, chased out of the Netherlands in 1564 and resident ever after everywhere but the archdiocese, until he finally resigned the position in 1583. The second archbishop of Mechelen, Jean Hauchinus, proved more virtuous than his predecessor but no more successful as bishop, for he began his reign in exile and ended it with a broken death in January 1589. Ever since, during six long years, King Philip had been unable to persuade anyone to come to Mechelen and fix things.

It was not for want of trying: no one could blame the delay this time on Philip's usual indecision. For after Archbishop Hauchinus' death, Philip decided on his new man with lightning speed, by November 1589: it was William Allen, exile from Elizabeth's Protestant England, who had spent his university days in the Low Countries and still considered it his adopted home. The fit seemed perfect: Rome would surely go along, and Allen seemed to say yes. But by late 1589, William Allen was a cardinal in Rome and showed no sign of actually extricating himself from the city's endless attractions and intrigues—thus giving yet another meaning to the label "Eternal City." While he delayed and wavered and stayed put, the leading diocese of the Netherlands continued to languish.

As the weeks became months, then years, as Netherlandish notables pleaded with a lingering Cardinal Allen to at last take up his post, a weary Philip finally turned to a second candidate, closer to home: Laevinus Torrentius, bishop of Antwerp, collector of rare coins, connoisseur of fine art and tasteful accommodations, and accomplished composer of neo-classical Latin poetry.

Upon hearing the news, Bishop Torrentius put his talent at composition to good use, thanking all concerned, in the loveliest letters, for their consideration. Yet his determination to take up the post proved no more genuine than Cardinal Allen's had been. The only difference this time was that the reluctant nominee at least explained why: the honor of being named to the archbishopric would be far greater, hinted Bishop Torrentius, were the office to include a respectable income as well.

Here was what ailed, and why no one would come to Mechelen: this chief bishopric in all the Netherlands was in practice among the worst endowed. It was one thing for Philip to have won his thirteen new bishoprics back in 1559, and quite another to furnish them with incomes. Philip's plan was to provide each new bishopric with the income of a nearby abbey, but the predictably fierce resistance of the abbeys, along with the outbreak of war, seriously complicated that plan. Neither of the first two archbishops of Mechelen were able to solve the puzzle of steady revenues. The Archbishop-Cardinal Granvelle was too long absent to effect a lasting arrangement, so that his vicars got by on temporary solutions and the cardinal's own deep pockets. Jean Hauchinus fared more poorly still, for he had no private wealth to sustain himself—rumor said that he even died of melancholy brought on by staggering debts.

Laevinus Torrentius wanted no part of such a scene, and not merely because it violated his standards of comfort. As he wrote to one friend, "Poverty is holy, but a great obstacle to administration." The diocese of Antwerp was of lesser rank than Mechelen, but by 1589 it fed and housed its bishop, it had no huge stack of unsettled lawsuits, and its cathedral possessed sufficient ornaments for worship—all in contrast to Mechelen. And so Bishop Torrentius quietly held out for more, even wondering—discreetly of course—about the possibility of royal subsidies to bolster the archbishop's income. But no one in Madrid budged, and the string of complaints from the Netherlands lengthened: want of bishops, especially this bishop, caused "unspeakable damage" to the faith, and for "pregnant reasons" would His Most Dread Majesty please find someone to accept?

That Philip felt as desperate as Netherlanders to find a new archbishop of Mechelen was evident in his next move: in early 1594 he tried Cardinal Allen once more. But the cardinal died in October, irresolute as ever about moving from Rome. Astonishingly, Philip even considered Bishop Torrentius again, but soon the humanist-bishop too lay in a grave. This tragicomedy in many acts convinced Philip that none of the great would come to a penniless Mechelen. After still more months of gentle prodding from his governor-general in Brussels, Philip finally signed the document now before the cardinals, which bore the name of his third choice, the low-born, battle-scarred Mathias Hovius.

The nominee certainly knew about the king's decision by the time it reached Rome. It could not have come as a great surprise, for the name of Mathias Hovius had already been tossed about for other bishoprics in the land. Still, such a lofty position was far more than he long could have imagined possible for himself, given his recent sorrows, and of course his lowly birth.

EXILE AND RETURN

Most obvious was the sorrow of his exile.

After his smock-abetted escape from the English Fury in April 1580, Canon Hovius stopped briefly in Leuven, but continued eastward when that city was threatened by rebels as well. He finally stopped in the politically neutral but decidedly Catholic prince-bishopric of Liège, a temporary home of choice for a host of other refuge-seeking, income-free priests from around the Netherlands, including many of his fellow canons in the chapter of St. Rombout's.

Like most exiles, this one was bitter. Mathias Hovius wondered whether he would ever return to Mechelen. He watched as the longtime dean of St. Rombout's chapter suffered death in Liège. And he scraped to support himself by lecturing on theology in a local monastery. Yet exile also brought spiritual resolve and the attention of the great. For while in Liège the displaced Canon Hovius was offered the important pastorship of Breda, next door to rebel Holland (he refused, surely out of hope that Mechelen would soon be free). He was offered the prominent position of archdeacon in the cathedral chapter of St. Rombout's-in-exile, and accepted. And he accepted appointment as the vicar-general-in-exile of the archdiocese of Mechelen. Still, for the moment this was all wishful thinking and musical chairs: none of these offices in the chapter or archdiocese would mean anything unless those who held them could someday return to a Catholic and royalist Mechelen.

In July 1585 that finally became possible. For in that month the Calvinist regime in Mechelen fell at last, partly because of temporal troubles, partly because Mechelen never became fervently Calvinist, and largely because of the political and military gifts of King Philip's latest governor-general in the Netherlands, Alexander Farnese, Duke of Parma. When the rebels' leader, Prince William of Orange, was assassinated in 1584, Parma began picking off rebel strongholds in the southern Netherlands one by one. Over the next year he recovered the medieval jewels of Gent and Brugge, then Brussels, and then Mechelen—all quick and astounding. Though the Duke's *reconquista* came to a halt just above Antwerp in late 1585, he put the southern half of the Netherlands back in Spanish hands once and for all.

No one knew then that war would rage on and off in the Netherlands until 1648, or that Parma's campaigns of the mid-1580s virtually fixed for good the boundaries of the entire region: the southern provinces would by the end still be Spanish, and thus called the Spanish Netherlands, while the northern provinces would become a new, independent state, the United Provinces of the Netherlands, or Dutch Republic. All anyone knew in the summer of 1585 was that guns still roared, and that for the moment Antwerp, Brussels, and Mechelen were again Spanish and Catholic. This last was what mattered to Mathias Hovius and hundreds of other priests, monks, and nuns who set out jubilantly on dusty roads from exile in Tournai, Cologne, or Liège for their rightful homes.

There was also the sorrow of Mechelen's ruin.

Canon Hovius' joy at arriving in his native city was tempered by the sight of desolation, for Mechelen still had not recovered from the English Fury of 1580. It was an unpeopled and ghastly Mechelen that greeted Mathias Hovius in July 1585.

Only eleven thousand people remained. The immense stained-glass window in St. Peter's and Paul's, which with proud anachronism once showed Christ and St. Peter and Charlemagne

and Charles V together in one happy group, had been smashed
to pieces. Pastors had no income. Foundations for Masses and the
poor were in shambles. Convents were flattened, their scattered
stones used to refortify city walls. Weeks later, when the new Archbishop of Mechelen, Jean Hauchinus, arrived from exile in Tournai, some must have wondered whether it would not have been
wiser for him to continue on to Brussels, permanently, with the
rest of the great. For old Mechelen was gone.

Spiritual ruin accompanied the physical. Canon Hovius lamented the heresy, impiety, immorality, and atheism now in and
around the city. In the 150 diminished parishes of the western archdiocese, most had no pastor at all, and more than a third of the
churches were piles of rubble. Rural parishes that did have priests
rarely saw them, for they had fled to the relative safety of towns.
Churches left standing were often the only shelters around in the
countryside, so that they became crowded, stinking places of eating, sleeping, dying, birthing, "even coupling"; some rural pastors
took up residence in church towers.

Though the task of rebuilding city and archdiocese was overwhelming, there were glimmers of hope. Processions were soon res-
urrected in Mechelen, if without past splendor. The Grand Council, supreme court for all the Netherlands, returned to the city,
though the king's governor-general and the great courtiers did not.
St. Rombout's was still sound in structure, even if the music never
was quite as heavenly as before 1580, even if the whole was still too
bare for proper Catholic services. Then of course faith-promoting
stories about the English Fury abounded. The priceless coats of
arms of the Knights of the Golden Fleece, hidden by clever canons,
miraculously survived. Irreverent Calvinist brewers who used the
twelve wooden Apostles inside St. Rombout's to make a new batch
of beer saw with horror that the beer turned to blood. Calvinist
soldiers who climbed on the roof of the church of Poor Clares
to begin its demolition were said to have fallen to their deaths, as
divine punishment. Hans de Grafmaker and Gommer van Hou-
vorst rescued from Calvinist soldiers the sculpture of the Mount

of Olives near St. Jan's church. And brave persons scooped up the relics of St. Rombout moments after they were scattered on that first night of the English Fury, then concealed them during the entire Calvinist regime.

Such stories helped Mechelen gain determination. Unlike Archbishop Granvelle, who rarely set foot in the city, Jean Hauchinus was adamant about remaining there, and he threw himself into the rebuilding and reconsecrating of damaged structures. He also convinced magistrates to supplement pastoral incomes. And he was gratified that the aged but still dexterous Michel Coxie signed a flurry of contracts to paint new altarpieces. But the heaviness of the task soon vanquished Archbishop Hauchinus.

In fact during the years of recovery the greatest promise for the old faith proved to be not the archbishop but his vicar-general, Mathias Hovius. When a demoralized Jean Hauchinus died in January 1589, the chapter elected Canon Hovius as temporary administrator of the archdiocese. He had helpers in Brussels and Leuven, but the burden of rebuilding rested largely on him, especially as one nominee after the next politely refused to come to Mechelen and become its third archbishop.

Year after uncertain year, six in all, a younger Mathias Hovius shouldered willingly the burdens that had worn down Jean Hauchinus. He diligently inspected damaged roofs, defiled altars, and unsteady walls in churches and monasteries. He ordered the razing and rebuilding of the church's kitchens and barns. To renew spiritual life, he visited nuns, parish priests, canons, and laity and issued decrees regarding schools and the Sabbath. His efforts were hampered in part by his interim status as vicar-general, his less than episcopal powers and budget, and of course the lingering threat of rebel invasion. But he never stopped.

One sign that his efforts were bearing fruit, and that Mechelen was returning to health, came during the early 1590s when magistrates and clergy recommenced their long custom of arguing with each other over this right or that, a custom put on hold during the years of crisis. But the biggest sign that Mathias Hovius

The Archdiocese of Mechelen, 1596-1620

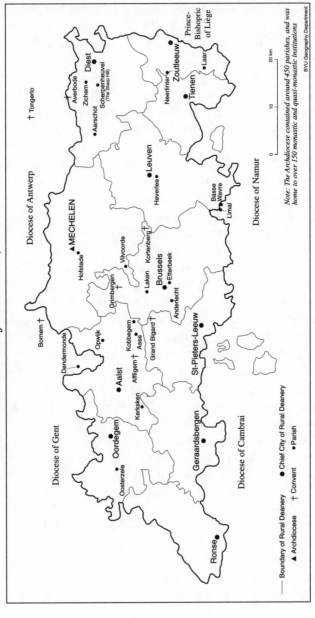

Diocese of Antwerp

† Tongerlo

Averbode
Zichem • • Diest
• Aarschot
Scherpenheuvel
(The Sharp Hill)

Prince-
Bishopric
of Liège

Zoutleeuw
Neerlinter •
• Laar
Tienen

Leuven
Heverlee •

MECHELEN
Hofstade •

Vilvoorde
Grimbergen †
Laken Kortenberg
† Kortenberg
Brussels
• Etterbeek

Basse
Wavre
Limal

Diocese of Namur

Bornem †

Dendermonde •

Opwijk •

Kobbegem
• Asse
Grand Bigard †

Anderlecht

Aalst
Affligem †

St-Pieters-Leeuw

Kerksken •

Oordegem •

Geraardsbergen

Oosterzele •

Diocese of Gent

Diocese of Cambrai

Ronse •

Note: The Archdiocese contained around 450 parishes, and was
home to over 150 monastic and quasi-monastic institutions

0   10   20 km

BYU Geography Department

—— Boundary of Rural Deanery   • Chief City of Rural Deanery   • Parish
▲ Archdiocese   † Convent

The Archdiocese of Mechelen, 1596-1620

had made an impression was his nomination, however belated, as archbishop in 1595.

THE EQUALIZER

Surely one reason King Philip took so long to consider Mathias Hovius for the archbishopric was the matter of his birth.

His father, Andreas Hovius, had belonged to the humble Fuller's Guild, whose members lived in only a modest quarter of town. Even if the family was better off than some and Andreas respectable among guildsmen (which no one bothered to record one way or the other), this was hardly the easiest path to high office in the church. But the boy Mathias was fortunate three times: his city had a new school for boys (especially poor boys), he showed ability at that school, and academic ability was one of his world's only levelers—especially when it was put to use within the church.

Like other towns, Mechelen realized early in the Reformation that growing up Catholic could no longer be taken for granted, and so it expanded instruction for its children. Young Mathias learned his religion first socially through scores of communal rites, and he learned it last emotionally through the scars of war, but he learned it most systematically at Mechelen's new Standonck College for poor boys.

The deepest premise and highest object of this elementary schooling was religion—or more specifically, the orthodoxy of the moment. In a roomful of benches, among children of all ages, he learned reading and writing through mastery of the Ten Commandments, the Seven Penitential Psalms, the Benedicite and Gratia, the Our Father, the Ave Maria, other basic tenets of Catholicism, and of course the "good manners" so prevalent in many new manuals on the subject.

In early adolescence he learned to sing psalms. He learned better the language of Catholicism, Latin, through reading sanitized versions of classical authors. And he learned even more deeply the substance of Catholicism through precept. He discovered that

Truth could be divided in four: Faith, Prayer, the Commandments, and the Sacraments. He added the Athanasian and Nicean to his repertoire of creeds, and the Magnificat and Nunc Dimittis to his array of prayers. He expanded his knowledge of fear, hope, virtue, and sin through mnemonic and conceptual devices that connected the seven mortal sins to the seven dispensations of time and the seven devils that tempted Christ and the seven lions of Daniel's den and the seven bloodlettings of Christ. He memorized the four cardinal virtues and four last things. He could recite the sins of the heart, the sins of the tongue, the sins against God, neighbor, and self, as well as the sins of omission and commission. At last he mastered such pithy and useful sayings as "the devil suggests, the flesh takes pleasure, the spirit consents."

At the Standonck College young Mathias drew the attention of the priestly rector, Martin Duncan. So impressed was the rector, or so willing Mathias' parents to further their son's education, that the rector even took Mathias for a time to Holland, to study at a school there. More certain was that when Martin Duncan moved yet again, to become rector of the Standonck College in Leuven, the teenaged Mathias, encouraged by one of his sisters, went along as well.

These days at the Standonck College were surely crucial. Not only did the college furnish Mathias with the usual training in the now standard liberal arts (grammar, rhetoric, logic, mathematics, geometry, music, and astronomy), which would prepare him to move on still further to Leuven's renowned university, but its clerically inspired regime of strict living also nudged him toward the priesthood: Erasmus was not the only student to decry the cold air and unimaginative food of such schools, he was simply the most famous. Students at the Standonck College arose early, dressed in somber gray tunics, attended Mass, studied long, lived in bug-infested rooms, fasted often, suffered meager meals all year round, and distanced themselves from the spirited night life and extraordinary drinkers of the university town.

Despite these hardships, or because of them, Mathias de-

cided after all to study for the priesthood—a step that would inci-
dentally provide him yet another critical boost up the ladder of
mobility. Upon completing his training in the arts in the early
1560s, he entered the Pope Adrian VI residential college, an institution reserved for boys who intended to become priests. He also
chose to pursue a degree in theology, one of the two disciplines
(along with canon law) recommended for prospective priests.

And so, after taking the usual oath of obedience to the university's statutes and the special fourth oath repudiating Martin
Luther "and all other heretics," Mathias began his theological
studies at Leuven. He listened in early years as professors commented on the Bible, then on commentaries on the Bible. He
studied on his own the most famous commentary, the twelfth-
century *Sentences* of Peter Lombard. But under the influence of his
mentor, Michel Baius, he surely paid more attention to the Bible
itself and to the church fathers than he did to the traditional logical exercises imposed on these sources by scholastic theologians,
who still dominated most faculties of theology in Europe. However he came by his knowledge of the Latin Bible, he certainly
learned it well. All his life, his letters, notes, sermons, and decrees
were peppered with far more biblical citations than they were with
quotations from relentlessly rational scholastics, whom Erasmus
liked to call "the Leuven jackasses." *

---

* Scholasticism, as it came to be called, emerged in the Middle Ages and continued to thrive in Catholic universities and seminaries long after the Reformation.
Though there was no single version of scholasticism, its overarching goal was to prove
the truth of Christianity (and more specifically Catholicism) through rational means,
especially the sort espoused by Aristotle. Its relentless systematization of theology, and
its reliance on authority and logic rather than a focus on biblical texts themselves,
proved distasteful to those influenced by the new humanism of the fifteenth and sixteenth centuries, which urged direct study of the Bible in the original Hebrew and
Greek. At Leuven some professors of theology, including Michel Baius, were influenced by humanism, but most were not; indeed most still blamed humanism for the
Protestant Reformation.

In December 1566, still in the midst of his university studies, Mathias Hovius was ordained a priest and appointed underpastor of his home parish in Mechelen, St. Peter's and Paul's, where his quarry now was no longer abstract theology but mastering the tangible duties of a pastor: how to administer the sacraments, calculate movable feasts, bless holy water, purify women who had recently given birth, cast out demons of all kinds in all places, administer extreme unction even to people who had no hands or feet to anoint, sort out among lovers those who were distant and near relations and thus who was allowed to marry whom, plus every other highly desired ritual.

In 1569, the year he finally graduated from the University of Leuven, the canons of St. Rombout's, in charge of ecclesiastical appointments within Mechelen, recognized his abilities once more by naming him head pastor of St. Peter's and Paul's. In 1577 they even made him, in addition to his duties as pastor, one of their own: canon of the elite cathedral chapter. He had taken all the steps, displayed all the abilities, that helped him to conquer his rank. Or at least almost.

That he was not King Philip's first choice as archbishop must have been tied to his rather common birth and his lack of personal resources (even in healthier dioceses, bishops were often expected to possess enough money to offset the heavy expenses of the first years in office). That he would for some time feel wary around the great was also no doubt rooted in social anxieties: he lacked not only the desired four generations of nobility on either side of his family, but any nobility at all. But that he finally was nominated reflected that here was one of those rare moments and places in European history in which merit seemed to matter nearly as much as birth. Indeed for the next two decades more non-noble than noble bishops would be appointed in the Spanish Netherlands. Or was this image of merit an illusion? For these appointments most likely grew from practical considerations rather than any kind of new social idealism: who in society except the ill-propertied, with nothing to lose, would ever be tempted by such poorly endowed bishoprics as those which dominated the ecclesiastical map of the Spanish Netherlands?

Whatever the reasons for his getting a chance at high church office, Mathias Hovius was glad to have it.

BISHOP AT LAST

The cardinals understood the situation well enough.

The nominee was less learned and eminent than both Laevinus Torrentius and William Allen, and perhaps even Jean Hauchinus. And he was certainly no Cardinal Granvelle, with an international education and renown, a trendy illegitimate son, "easy morals," three episcopal palaces, a barrel of benefices, excessive power, and little regard for pastoral responsibilities. But the nominee did possess merit, including a social inheritance mean enough to survive on less income than required by the great, and a Catholic zeal born of schooling and war. Above all else, he was the choice of King Philip.

In truth the cardinals in Rome, or even King Philip in Madrid, hardly knew Mathias Hovius and the depth of his faith. None of them knew the story of the wardrobe or his encounters with soldiers or his struggles as a parish priest. They knew much less, for instance, than the nominee's good friend and noble neighbor, Jan van der Burch, *chef-président* of Philip's privy council in Brussels and the man who had probably recommended Mathias Hovius to the king. And so, dependent on the opinions of others, the cardinals routinely confirmed Philip's third choice as third archbishop of Mechelen.

The cardinals also approved the more sensitive, oft-rejected request that the impoverished archdiocese be granted dispensation from the usual fees and gifts owed the papacy upon the installation of a new bishop. The candidate's agent soon brought back from Rome all the symbols of the archiepiscopal office, and a month later the unhurried cardinals finally sealed and sent the official documents as well. All less theatrical than some elections, as in an upcoming papal conclave when Cardinal Avila would run desperately down the hallway of the papal palace, shouting wildly that his master the Catholic king of Spain did not want so and so as pope! Though the Catholic kings lost that battle in Rome, they almost always got their way with bishops in the Netherlands — including this one.

With documents and symbol safely together, and the candidate fitted out in new quarters and even more new clothes than he had needed in his colorful past, he was consecrated and took possession of his throne on 18 February 1596. There was a long procession through the city. Much bell ringing, incense, and singing. The usual yards of festive drapery around the pulpit. Longwinded preaching and welcoming by the cathedral chapter. Heartfelt thanking by the nominee. Abundant sprinkling of holy water. Deep genuflecting. Solemn promising to preserve the cathedral's laws, immunities, and privileges. Luxurious robes. Hushed consecration with holy oil, by three brother bishops. Dramatic enthroning in a chair near the high altar. A final blessing by the new archbishop upon the audience, which included the usual throng of dignitaries from church and state. Still more parading. A closing, echoing Te Deum of thanks.

It must have been a day of wonderful paradoxes within him, of sweetness and bitterness accumulated over many decades now melting together, unfettered by the precise chronology of his fifty-four years. In gratitude for his appointment, Archbishop Hovius hosted the customary dinner with as much grace and finery as he could muster. He was surely assisted in this by his loyal older sister, Catharina, now sixty, who so long ago had encouraged him to study, and who now would run his household. Though the dinner inevitably fell short of the standard set by Cardinal Granvelle at his consecration in 1561, this archbishop would stay in town beyond the last course, rather than leave immediately — and forever.

To those attentive to such things, his choice for the traditional motto was more provocative than the dinner. It was close to the motto of a near contemporary on the religious scene, which read "Patience Conquers Fortune," and which the archbishop might well have used to interpret his own long rise. But instead he chose something more self-conscious: "Patience Conquers the Mighty." Surely this referred to soldiers he had outlasted in unpleasant places, but it suggested as well his tenacity in comparison to noble and great candidates who had refused the post of archbishop while he labored steadily in the trenches.

In truth patience, along with circumstance and timing, had done much to win him this new position. He was as aware as anyone that his biggest asset was his own steadfastness, along with the reluctance of every other candidate to take on the challenges of a debt-ridden, spiritually impoverished diocese that in theory was the cornerstone of the Netherlandish church, but which in fact was sand.

✝ THREE ✝
Isabella's Dowry

Early August 1599.

F or the archbishop, here at last was a season of hope: the Spanish Netherlands were to have resident princes of their own. Surely this was the antidote to the plagues of war, ruin, and false religion.

It wasn't as if Mathias Hovius had, since his memorable consecration three years before, sat idly by, waiting for a deliverer. Rather he took a leading role in rebuilding his corner of the land. He scraped together florins to buy three adjoining burgher homes on Mechelen's Wool Market, near St. Rombout's, and shaped them into the archdiocese's first official residence. He restored, for his private use, a crumbling chapel inside Rombout's. He pestered towns and villages everywhere to fix churches. He became chaplain of Spanish armies in all the Netherlands, and instructed his sub-chaplains to refuse absolution to soldiers who persisted in robbing people and holy places. He shepherded some 450 parishes, 75 convents and hospitals, and more, surprisingly often in person, trying to shape them according to his vision of religious life, based especially on the monumental reforms of the church's universal Council of Trent (1545–63). To this end he also took special care to appoint trusted helpers in his diocesan hierarchy: a seal-bearer to dip the episcopal ring in hot wax and secure official documents; a vicar-general and vicariate (or council) to run everyday affairs; a

opposite: Jan Luyken, Anna Utenhove buried alive
National Archives Belgium, Topografisch-Historische Atlas, 711/103

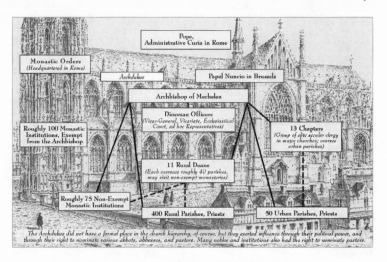

Basic ecclesiastical structure of the Archdiocese of Mechelen

judge, prosecutors, defenders, and bailiffs to staff his newly organized diocesan court; 11 deans, with more than 40 parishes each,
to tend clergy and flock in reorganized rural deaneries; secretaries
to care for mounds of documents; messengers to deliver them;
stewards to guard precarious temporal interests; standard-bearers
to walk before him; servants of all kinds to attend him.

It was simply that even these efforts were not enough. The
archbishop's ecclesiastical army could do little to repel the fighting
sort of army. It could do little to secure him a stable income. Alone
it could not even achieve his vision of proper religious life. For all
these the archbishop required the muscle of the state, especially
from the very top. And now the type of muscle he needed seemed
on its way.

The old system of rule in the Spanish Netherlands, with
governor-generals in Brussels taking orders from Madrid, had
proven erratic. The archbishop must have hoped that resident
princes would work more energetically for peace. He must have
hoped that proximity to their subjects would promote more effi-

cient, sympathetic rule. And more than most he certainly hoped that resident princes—especially these particular princes—would help to establish a proper Catholic society.

THE SPANISH ROAD

The objects of the archbishop's hope were at this time somewhere in the Alps.

Carriages were useless on the steep, uneven roads up and down St. Gothard's pass. Members of the winding noble entourage therefore had to choose between a litter, shouldered by carriers who in summer months made their living on alpine highways, or a mule. Many settled on the former, and sat with legs dangling, but Princess Isabella preferred to ride, for she rode expertly. She also loved nature and was thus free to inspect at her leisure the renowned flowers and plants of the pass, which she saw now for the first and last time. She was free as well to observe her companions in travel, and would hardly have failed to notice, with her characteristic mirth, that a nun in a litter required four carriers while a canon required at least six.

Inquisitive though she was, this eldest daughter of Philip II had never before in her thirty-two years traveled outside Iberia, but honed her myriad talents at home while awaiting the fate her father had in mind for her. Philip had long dreamed of putting Isabella on the throne of France, or England, or wedding her to the next emperor of Germany. Candidates came and went. Furious wars were waged with the destiny of not only nations but Isabella in the balance. For a while it appeared she might even succeed her father in Spain, since her older half-brother, Don Carlos, died tragically in 1568, the year of Isabella's birth, and since her younger half-brother, Philip, was sickly.

But politics alone was not why King Philip kept his daughter close by, a pawn in a chess game. Isabella was also his favorite. Born of Philip's third wife, Elisabeth Valois of France, Isabella possessed the same zest for living as her mother, and thus

avoided the better-known traits of her father's side: excessive so-
briety and madness. Yet for all her fire Isabella was at the same time
devout. This began with her conception and birth, the result of
a vow, believed many, by her long-childless mother Elisabeth. It
continued with her name: Isabella in honor of her pious grandmother, Clara in honor of the saint on whose day she was born,
and Eugenie in honor of the saint to whom Elisabeth had made her
fruitful vow. And it ended with Isabella's upbringing in the heart of
Spanish Catholicism, where she learned the flagellations of Holy
Week, where she heard reverberating all night long the chanting
of Philip's royal monks as they prayed for the king's armadas, or
where most of all she was sobered by death. Elisabeth Valois died
when Isabella was only two, then came Uncle Don Juan, who had
held Isabella at baptism, then six siblings, and still more. By adult-
hood, Isabella had endured a dozen deaths among close family—
none of whom, remarked cynical French ambassadors, were helped
by the notoriously furious bloodlettings and purges of Spanish
doctors.

      And so Philip and Isabella were united by flesh, affection,
and tragedy. With his daughter, the king showed a side never mentioned in the dark English and Dutch legends about him. In frequent letters to her and her younger sister Catherina, Philip told of
his travels, his judgments of morals, the fashions of court, and how
the nightingales did not sing as they did when his young daughters were nearby. He offered fatherly advice on what to eat, teased
Isabella about her fear of thunder, and humorously recounted
the most recent tantrums of the aging, demented courtly servant
Magdalena, who in public loudly criticized Philip, the king before whom all the world was supposed to tremble. He held balls
and masquerades for his daughters, so that they might learn social
graces in addition to French, Latin, riding, hunting, shooting, and
prayer.

      As an adult, Isabella's bond with her father strengthened,
for sister Catherina was now married away in Savoy, half-brother
Philip was still young, and the last of King Philip's four wives died

in 1580. It was to Isabella's room that the king ran, in the middle of a night in 1585, with news of a victory, exclaiming, "We have Antwerp!" It was Isabella who sat alone with Philip in his office and learned affairs of state while he corresponded with all corners of the empire. It was Isabella who carried his portable writing table, with ink and paper and secrets, for after a recent betrayal Philip no longer trusted any secretary. It was Isabella who, when Philip's fingers grew stiff, took up the royal pen. And, at the last, it was Isabella who sat next to Philip's sore and putrid body, reading aloud ascetic works, until his final breath.

Some thought Philip would never let Isabella go. Some thought she wasted her best years living like a nun, and blamed Philip for it. But when Philip finally sensed his end, when plans for a French alliance and marriage collapsed, when all four of his armadas against England limped home in failure, and when young Philip proved healthy enough to succeed in Spain, then a marriage for Isabella was arranged at last. Not to any far off prince, but someone she knew well: her cousin Albert of Austria. And not as a courtier at some foreign palace, but as virtual sovereign with Albert of her own land: the Netherlands. The couple would be given the title of Archdukes.

The idea of establishing sovereign princes in the Netherlands, rather than mere governors-general, had been raised before, in the hopes of quieting unrest there. But Philip, determined to leave his entire empire intact for his successor, long resisted the idea. That in the end he changed his mind in favor of Isabella said much about his regard for her—and for Albert.

Fourth son of the German emperor, Albert was raised at the Spanish court from age eleven and became, like Isabella, one of Philip's favorites. Indeed Albert seemed more like Philip than his own Austrian family. He was studious rather than sociable. He was somber rather than witty. He showed courage in battle, but was too short and thin and disinterested to cut the figure of a commander. He was as pious as Isabella, but without her liveliness. He was inclined to the priesthood and even became a cardinal and

archbishop, but put off ordination in the event the family's interests required him to rule. In fact he gained political experience as
Viceroy of Portugal, and then in 1596 as governor-general of the
Netherlands. Finally, while Philip deteriorated and Isabella aged
and all other suitors faded away, it was decided that Albert, nearly
forty, should renounce at last his churchly career, marry, and become a prince. Isabella and the Netherlands were his reward.

And so in 1598, in August, the Act of Cession was read
in Brussels at a colorful gathering of the States General, in the
same hall where Charles V had bidden his tearful farewell four decades before. Albert was present at this August drama, already in
the land as Philip's last governor-general of the Netherlands. Also
present were representatives from every provincial States, including Mathias Hovius, chief ecclesiastical dignitary in the States of
Brabant. It was Archbishop Hovius who, on the second day of the
ceremonies, bowed deeply to Archduke Albert, then, clothed in
sumptuous new robes paid for by the States of Brabant expressly
for this occasion, held out the missal on which Albert swore an
oath to respect the customs of the land. And it was the archbishop
who became the first representative to swear loyalty to Albert in
return. Soon after the swearing-in, Albert left Brussels to fetch Isabella in Spain. Before Albert arrived, however, the elderly King
Philip died, thus missing the wedding he had so badly wanted to
see. It was not until April 1599, after long detours through Austria
and much inclement weather, that Albert finally landed in Spain,
at Valencia, where he was met by Isabella and where their marriage
was confirmed.* A month later, in May, Albert and Isabella began
the return journey to the Netherlands, leaving Spain forever.

By sea they traveled to Genoa, the closest Spanish posses-

---

* The couple was actually married by proxy in November 1598 in the Italian
town of Ferrara, where the pope himself performed the ceremony, to bestow extra
dignity on the match and to hasten its achievement. In Valencia the marriage was
therefore only confirmed.

sion in Italy. Then overland to Milan, for several days of festivities. And finally northward with purpose in late July, before summer passed them by. They reached the lakes at the base of the Alps within days, moved upward through the tranquil valleys of Ticino, and then further up the St. Gothard's pass, where they now admired the wonders on this part of the trail that reached all the way from Genoa to the Netherlands, and which contemporaries simply called the Spanish Road.

ANNA AND A THOUSAND OTHERS

Despite the archbishop's great anticipation at the arrival of the new princes, he knew there was much anxiety in the land as well.

Some of his new subjects grumbled that Albert, though he had helped bring about peace with the French, left in the middle of a military crisis with the Dutch. Many wondered how truly independent the new princes would be, given their not quite sovereign title of "archdukes" and their subordinate role to Spain in foreign policy. And who could avoid asking whether the archdukes, sovereign or not, would exhibit any more understanding of Netherlandish political and religious customs than had Madrid—especially on that delicate question of religious orthodoxy? For who could forget the case of the servant woman just two years before?

In July 1597, in a field outside Brussels, forty-five-year-old Anna Utenhove was, with the consent of Albert and Archbishop Hovius, buried alive.

Anna's troubles began in the late 1580s, in the parish of Kapellekerk in Brussels, where she worked as a servant girl for two sisters called Rampart. For years Anna neither confessed nor communed. The local pastor, Francis Eland, eventually concluded that Anna and her mistresses were tied to the heretical Family of Love, a group he reckoned among the despised Anabaptists. It was more likely that these women belonged to one group or the other rather than both, or more likely still that the outwardly Catholic sisters

were of the Family while the openly delinquent Anna was Anabaptist (especially because she was later openly celebrated as an
Anabaptist martyr). But fine distinctions between heresies mattered little to Pastor Eland: both groups ultimately believed that
the ever-listing, uncontrollable Holy Spirit was a personal guide
superior to the visible church, and hence in his mind they were
united in error.

For long the pastor worked patiently with all three women.
But by the cold of 1594 his patience expired, and he finally urged
secular authorities to arrest the unrepentant, uncommuning Anna.
On the night of 21 December, while she was leaving her new quarters to go dine with her friends the Rampart sisters, bailiffs of
the Council of Brabant, highest civil court in the province, seized
and imprisoned Anna, with the intent of putting her on trial. The
Rampart sisters, who had already testified against Anna, were soon
detained as well—despite their sixty-eight and seventy years.

That the Council of Brabant, a civil body, participated in
the arrest of Anna and her friends was no surprise. Heresy was
both a civil and a religious offense, and church and state often
cooperated to oppose it. In this case as in many others, the archbishop's ecclesiastical court therefore conducted Anna's trial, while
the state provided the muscle necessary to arrest and, if necessary,
punish her. Within weeks, the ecclesiastical court declared its verdict: Anna was indeed an incorrigible heretic. Her judges gave her
the usual opportunity to recant, which had she accepted would
almost certainly have limited her punishment to penance and a
fine, but she refused. Thus the ecclesiastical court called upon the
Council of Brabant to carry out the full punishment prescribed by
law. And that was where the case bogged down.

In a world quite accustomed to capital punishment for an
assortment of crimes, and rife with belief in the temporal and eternal necessity of true religion, it was not terribly surprising that
incorrigible heresy should have been punishable by death. In fact,
since the 1550s, the punishment in the Low Countries for incorrigible female heretics was death by burial. After the collapse of

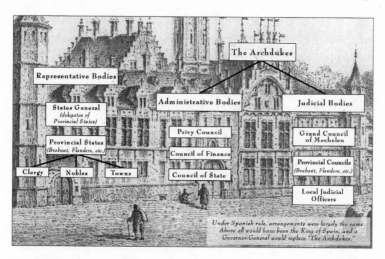

The Archdukes

Representative Bodies

States General
*(delegates of
Provincial States)*

Administrative Bodies

Judicial Bodies

Provincial States
(Brabant, Flanders, etc.)

Privy Council

Grand Council
of Mechelen

Clergy   Nobles   Towns

Council of Finance

Council of State

Provincial Councils
(Brabant, Flanders, etc.)

Local Judicial
Officers

*Under Spanish rule, arrangements were largely the same.
Above all would have been the King of Spain, and a
Governor-General would replace "The Archdukes."*

Basic political structure of the Spanish Netherlands under the archdukes, 1598–1621

Alva's regime in the 1570s, however, no civil court had shown itself willing to do such a deed, at least not for heresy: there were the unpleasant memories of Alva, there was the fear of harmful emigration that always followed executions, and there was sentiment that the penalty of death, especially such a gruesome death, exceeded the crime of even stubborn misbelief. All this explained why, after Anna's condemnation by the church's court, the Council of Brabant acted no further. She languished for weeks, then months, in the council's prison, the *Treurenberch,* or Mountain of Sorrows.

When Anna's trial began, Mathias Hovius was not yet archbishop. But immediately after his ascension in February 1596 he took a personal interest in the stalled case, determined either to reconvert Anna or to see that the state should enforce the church's verdicts rather than implicitly mock them. Thus he, along with several other prominent clergymen, braved the prison's gloomy confines to visit Anna. They reasoned with her, and gave her opportunity to recant. But when Anna would not budge, and instead showed herself ever the "rebellious and unteachable heretic," these men saw only one alternative: imposition of the punishment required by law. Still the Council of Brabant did nothing. Which was when Albert got involved.

Albert first discussed Anna's case with Archbishop Hovius in December 1596, then again in March of 1597. In the meantime he also sought direction from Spain. Everything he heard moved Albert to urge full punishment—or in other words execution—of Anna Utenhove, and in March 1597 he wrote harshly to the foot-dragging Council of Brabant to say so.

It was not clear who was the driving force behind this decision—Albert or Philip II. It was no more clear whether Archbishop Hovius necessarily sought Anna's execution. For even while insisting on proper religion, even while insisting that the state enforce its decrees on heresy and carry out the sentences of the church's courts, the archbishop urged the release from prison of such repentant heretics as the Rampart sisters: after their initial stubbornness they became contrite, and their explanation that the wars of the 1570s and '80s had caused them (and many others) to be confused about religion was persuasive enough. Moreover, the archbishop's latest complaint about the unrepentant Anna was that the longer she sat in her cell, the more opportunity she had to infect visitors and other prisoners with her heretical ideas. His goal at the end, therefore, was to get Anna out of prison. But since she would not repent, it just so happened that in her case the only way legally to get her out was to bury her alive.

Still, even if the archbishop's chief intent was not Anna's execution, even if he wished to wash his hands of the deed and leave it to Albert, he knew the consequences of his efforts. And if he left no judgment about the nature of Anna's punishment, it was likely because he assumed it reasonable after all. For although he gave offenders many chances, this was the same Mathias Hovius who as a boy in Mechelen had seen heretics burned alive on the town square, who as a new priest heard of fellow clergy suffering odious deaths, and who as a canon was forced to hide in a wardrobe to save his life. Like most people of his time, the lesson he seemed to learn from having suffered religious persecution himself was empathy not for all sufferers, but for those of his own kind.

And so while the archbishop stood by and watched, Albert pushed the Council of Brabant harder. Soon the state's prosecutor advised Anna that if she did not recant she would be executed. Again she refused. When she refused yet again, at a last meeting on 20 June 1597, she sealed her fate, for now the state was out of patience. When she finally proposed to the prosecutor that she be allowed to leave the land, it was too late: like the church, the state had its pride. She had behaved as if she wanted death, and now she would get it.

The deed was done in the early morning of 17 July. The unusually sparse, almost private crowd—chancellor and judges from the Council of Brabant, plus a few clergymen—reflected the sense of organizers that this would hardly be a popular act: most executions were deliberately public, after all, and well attended. Along the way, and while the grave was dug, chaplains repeatedly asked Anna whether she wished to recant, but she declined. When she was laid into the grave they asked again, and she declined again. After each shovelful by the executioner they asked once more, and she declined once more, until her lower limbs were covered, and then everything except her head. A final chance, but the same answer, and she was under. The executioner packed the dirt with his feet to shorten her suffering.

Word spread quickly from Brussels. Criticism was strongest over the border, in the Dutch Republic—not that Anabaptists were so beloved there, either, but here was an opportunity to attack. Songs and verses likened Albert to Cain, Pharaoh, and Nero in his lust for righteous blood. Brabant should lament with bloody tears what was now shouted abroad about it, Brussels should be ashamed for betraying one of its own, simply because she would not partake of "the Bread-God," or Eucharist. Mass-produced engravings and prose told of Anna's execution in the most gruesome detail, and then some.

Within the Spanish Netherlands, the response was more subtle. The thousands of friends and neighbors who preferred a new faith to the old, but who wished to stay in the land, simply grew more careful. In years past they had, like Anna, been bold enough to cease communing or confessing at Easter, to tell authorities they were content to "pray at home," to deny the Virgin birth, to boast to authorities that they had read the entire Bible but seen not one word in it about the Mass, or to claim they feared neither pastor nor archbishop. But for a time right after Anna's death, dissidents watched their tongues, or sought absolution; some were frightened enough that when summoned by church courts they fled across the Dutch border, expecting the worst.

Yet who could have known, in the summer of 1599 while Albert and Isabella drew closer to their new land, that within a very few years, even months, the very manner of Anna's death and the reactions to it would actually have a softening effect — including upon Albert and the archbishop? The two men still opposed heresy, as promised in their oaths of office. Each still agreed with the final acclamation of the Council of Trent, "Anathema to all heretics." And Albert would still insist that he would rather have no subjects than heretical subjects. But Anna was the last of a long line of executed heretics begun in 1523 in the Netherlands; by the time of her execution in 1597 even she was practically an anachronism, the victim of an attempt to instill discipline by resurrecting the stern methods of the past. Soon Albert would, like Netherlandish courts, refuse to execute for incorrigible heresy, and be content with banishment: execution on religious grounds would be reserved for witches. Soon, as archduke, Albert would prohibit altogether execution by burial. Soon Spain would complain that Archduke Albert was being soft on heretics. Soon the archbishop's diocesan court would hand over another Anabaptist to the state, with no talk of execution. Soon some pastors were overlooking many forms of misbelief in order to avoid driving parishioners into the waiting arms of Protestantism.

But in the summer of 1599 there was no knowledge of the

future. On Netherlandish minds were the pride of having new princes and of Albert's recent triumphs against the French, or the hope of peace with the Dutch—and somewhere in those minds the less pleasant memory of the servant woman Anna Utenhove as well. Her legacy, and thousands of her kindred spirits still at home in the Spanish Netherlands, were part of Isabella's dowry too.

A JOYOUS ENTRY

August through December 1599.

Over the pass and down through the Reuss valley the eight hundred travelers continued, braving chilly winds and precarious descents, and accepting profuse welcomes and gifts, even in the village of Altdorf where William Tell was supposed to have refused homage to another Habsburg. Clearly the Swiss were working hard to keep their promise that the journey of Albert and Isabella through their lands would be as pleasant as possible.

The greetings and obstacles along the way slowed progress enough that word soon came from the Netherlands to speed things along, for the crises there continued. There was no time for amusements in the charming villages around Lake Lucern, or for long discussions in Colmar, where Isabella lodged with a heretic whom she tried to convert. Only one obligatory stop remained, at Nancy, at the palace of the Duke of Lorraine, where Isabella tried to repress her laughter at the giant hoops courtly ladies wore, with much toil, beneath their dresses.

Finally on 20 August the princes reached Thionville, southernmost town in their new lands. Crowds cheered and threw flowers into the coach. Chroniclers insisted that old men and women wept, and pressed forward to touch the archdukes. If there were still hesitations in private about the new rulers, for the moment they were in public conquered by joy.

And so it went all the way to Brussels. In Namur, Isabella laughed herself silly at sixty men who jousted on stilts and spilled

into the audience—much different from bullfights in Spain, she
wrote. At the southern boundary of Brabant, a delegation that included Archbishop Hovius greeted the princes. At last they entered
their new capital, on 5 September, astride two white horses, fully
aware of the old Netherlandish prophecy that said peace would
come when two princes on white horses rode into Brussels.

So satisfactory was their reception that the archdukes decided, despite the onset of wet autumn weather, to tour their lands
immediately. Now was the moment, while all was fresh, to perform the traditional "Joyous Entry" into every major city, during
which subjects and rulers promised mutual loyalty and respect.
Albert himself had pledged once before, at the reading of the Act
of Cession, but he was eager to pledge again, with Isabella.

And so they began in Brussels the Noble, where Isabella sat
on a jeweled saddle worth thousands of florins and marveled at
tastefully dressed women on the crowded balconies of the Grand
Market. Then to Leuven the Alarming, where rebel troops, in a
purposeful show of strength, brazenly pillaged nearby villages to
put a damper on the festivities. Then Tournai the Amusing, where
Isabella went snow-sledding for the first time in her life. Then Gent
the Comical, where during the ceremonies a nervous churchman
accidentally girded Isabella rather than Albert with the legendary
sword of Baldwin With the Iron Arm. But for Mathias Hovius,
who witnessed several of these entries, the most memorable took
place in Mechelen the Beloved. His native city's recent past had
been so unsettled and upsetting that the prospect of powerful
Catholic rulers here to stay, and come to declare sovereignty and
loyalty, surely overpowered him.

The date for the entry into Mechelen was finally set for
5 December. In preparation, the city on the Dijle spared neither
expense nor effort. For the moment, ruin was forgotten: here was
a rare chance, through color, image, statuary, lighting, verse, song,
and spectacle for the city both to pay respect and to proclaim that
it deserved respect in turn.

On the appointed day, members of the magistrate, dressed

in black velvet robes lined with blue taffeta, rode out to greet the princes. Next came the city's five guilds, whose robes and flapping banners bore the archducal colors of blue and white. Just outside the Brussels gate, on a raised platform, waited Mathias Hovius in pontifical robes, flanked by the clergy of Mechelen.

Albert and Isabella rode to the gate, stepped out of their carriage, and ascended the platform. Kneeling on purple cushions provided for them, they kissed the silver cross in the archbishop's hands. All the bells in the city began to sound, while guns fired in salute. Climbing aboard brightly decorated horses, the archdukes situated themselves under a silken canopy borne by six noblemen, and began to move, with the whole procession, through the Brussels gate.

The city overflowed with the torches, garlands, tapestries, floats and poems reserved for such occasions. Passing under a first triumphal arch, nearly twenty feet high and adorned with the inevitable allegories, the archdukes proceeded to the steps of St. Rombout's, where they were greeted for a second time by the archbishop, who had gone ahead. After descending from their horses, they were sprinkled with holy water, then followed Archbishop Hovius to the high altar, where they knelt again as the mighty organ accompanied the choir in the Veni Creator Spiritus. The archbishop sang a prayer and welcomed the archdukes with a stumbling speech that betrayed his nerves. This might have surprised some, since the archbishop was by now accustomed to being at the center of crowds, but it was no surprise to those who understood how much this particular ceremony meant to him. Then the princes, like their predecessors, swore with hands on the Bible to respect the rights of the church. When it was over, trumpets blared, and the archdukes exited the cathedral.

It was on to the neighboring Grand Market, where Albert and Isabella viewed another huge triumphal arch bursting with allegories. A panel depicted Religion holding a cross in one hand and in the other an open book labeled "The Word of God." Religion was attacked by Heresy, Sacrilege, Civil War, Envy, and other besiegers. But from a cloud descended Albert and Isabella, bound together by the Holy Spirit. For those who somehow still failed to grasp the allusion, an accompanying verse in large print clarified things: let us hope that the archdukes end the horror of decades past.

And so it went for two days. Another solemn Mass was celebrated, more oaths were exchanged, and throngs of people watched, even from rooftops. It poured rain that night, but Burgermaster Nicolas Vanderlaan, the hero of the English Fury back in 1580 who had survived after all his memorable wounds, ordered Mechelen's muddy streets covered with long rolls of white cloth. Hence noble boots stayed clean. Further rain was ignored. At last a herald ended the ceremonies by yelling from the balcony of the town hall, "Vive the Archdukes and Their Majesties!" then throwing handfuls of gold and silver coins among the crowd. Barrels of pitch on the street and torches on every home blazed into the night to keep the city bright. Albert and Isabella retired to the palace of Hoogstraten, where twenty years before the archbishop had spent so many uncomfortable hours in a wardrobe. The next day most everyone left by barge, for Antwerp, to do it all over again.

To the archbishop, whose participation ended in Mechelen, all of the Joyous Entries seemed a huge success. True, a few observers wrote that Albert and Isabella came across as rather Spanish in the land of Bruegel. Admittedly, the archdukes soon showed in their treatment of provincial States, and especially of the States General in 1600, a desire to rule without the inconveniences of pesky Netherlandish councils: they never bothered to call another States General again, despite pressure from their subjects to do so.*

---

* The various provincial States of the Netherlands rotated responsibility for presiding over meetings of the States General. First to preside during the gathering of 1600 was the States of Brabant. Since the clergy held the first rank in the States, the first presider was therefore the first clergyman, and thus Mathias Hovius. Though some delegates (surely Mathias Hovius among them) were disappointed that the gather-

And granted, the happy crowds evident at the Joyous Entries were perhaps due as much to the license of celebration as to genuine joy. Yet even if opinions varied in the details, even if shadowy memories and suspicions remained, even if Anna Utenhove gave Albert and Archbishop Hovius reputations for severity, who could deny in the winter of 1599 that hope seemed triumphant and anxiety was flee-ing away? When Albert had left the year before to fetch Isabella, rumor said that he would never return again, that the land would be snatched away from him by a covetous King Philip III (who had never wanted to give up the Netherlands in the first place), and that the couple would get Portugal instead. But Albert and Isabella were now here in the Netherlands after all.

The archdukes were happier than they would be for years. Isabella's virtue and good humor were soon evident and endearing. Subjects seemed willing to concede a period of grace to the new princes: Anna Utenhove was temporarily forgotten, swallowed up by the promise of a new beginning, or at least obliterated by a bar-rage of other troubles. And the archbishop benefited as well: his pile of troubles hardly disappeared, but with the archdukes nearby he at least found new energy to confront them.

---

ing produced little fruit and that the archdukes decided not to call another, Albert and Isabella still managed over time to earn the good will of most of their subjects—thanks in part to such happy events as the Joyous Entries.

✝ F O U R ✝
Mathias' Pence

The twentieth of March, 1600, the Grand Market of Mechelen.

When there was no invasion or celebration going on, the city was at night empty and dark. The occasional footstep or torch of a passing watchman only accentuated the stillness.

This night seemed quite like most others until at the Grand Market the watch came upon a monk, in alb and stole, holding a copper cross before him and staggering around the square. Though the sight of drowsy priests carrying sacraments to the dying was a familiar one, this monk surely was on some other sort of errand. When the suspicious watchmen approached and asked the monk's business, there came an unexpected reply: he was, he said, on his way to exorcise the Archbishop Hovius, whose residence stood just two blocks farther.

AN OLD, OLD QUARREL

This small drama had actually begun earlier that day, when the same monk stood before the same archbishop and suffered a most unpleasant rebuke, and then, said brother monks, lost his mind. That was why he went wandering on the Grand Market tonight. But there was a much larger drama behind this one, a drama that

opposite: Pieter Bruegel, *The Battle of the Piggybanks and the Strongboxes,* detail
© Royal Library Albert I, Brussels (Prentenkabinet)

preceded both archbishop and monk, for it reached back to when the archdiocese was born.

Forty years before, when Mathias Hovius was at school and the dazed monk a tiny boy, King Philip II decided that the Benedictine abbey of Affligem should become the official milk cow of the new archdiocese of Mechelen. The Archbishop of Mechelen would assume the title of abbot of Affligem, occupy the abbot's coveted chief seat in the provincial States of Brabant, and use the abbey's enviable income to run the archdiocese. The monks would receive an allowance from what remained and continue to live in their monastery, but the archbishop would be in charge.

Naturally the monks were incensed. Like all other abbeys designated to support new bishoprics, Affligem opposed the very idea of incorporation. But if it was inevitable, then why them? Why not, from dozens of other candidates within the archdiocese, a smaller, more easily subdued monastery, one without five hundred years of independence and thousands of acres of income-producing land? But it was precisely because of its greatness, precisely because of its wealth and position in the States of Brabant, that Affligem was chosen for Mechelen.

From the start, the monks of this venerable abbey, situated in the hilly terrain between Aalst and Brussels, fought incorporation with all the lawyers they could muster. They enlisted as well the support of great nobles, who treated great monasteries as private hosting centers, and as suitably dignified careers for their surplus sons or daughters. And they surely mobilized for good measure supernatural aid from the abbey's patron saints. With such allies, Affligem managed to delay incorporation until 1569. Thanks to the leveling of the abbey by rebel troops in 1578, and the subsequent scattering of monks and income, the incorporation was confused and weakened. In the 1580s, when other Netherlandish abbeys attached to bishops succeeded in undoing their incorporations, the arrangement was truly threatened, causing monkish hopes for an independent Affligem to soar.

They all came crashing down with the arrival of Mathias

Hovius as vicar-general of the archdiocese in 1589. He recognized that although war and ruin had indeed disrupted the incorporation of the abbey, they also made the monks more vulnerable to decisive action: in their exile in Brussels the monks were easier to subdue than they had been when operating from their once-magnificent grounds. Hence, the vicar-general, sorely in need of money to keep the still young archdiocese running, decided to assert his authority over the abbey, prompting a bevy of complaints from the monks. Vicar-General Hovius, said monks, seemed disturbingly indifferent to their having been chased from one refuge to another. He displayed, they continued, little interest in rebuilding the abbey. He forbade the entry of new members. He had seized the abbot's staff and seal. He was impudently suggesting that this wandering, unsupervised community of monks-on-the-dole was bearing the rotten fruit of moral decline. He had even tried to force remaining monks to dissolve their abbey altogether and join themselves and their comely allowances to the underfunded cathedral chapter of St. Rombout's. When this plan failed, the vicar-general took another offensive step: in February 1595 he forcibly conducted an official visitation of the monks, something that had not been done in decades!

Frantic at these assaults and especially the visitation, the eleven monks who still made up the dwindling abbey suddenly recalled that many decades before they had subjected themselves to a congregation of fellow Benedictines, headquartered at an abbey in Bursfeld, Germany. To the monks of Affligem, this loose, distant, and almost forgotten subjection to a congregation of fellow Benedictines was far preferable to the aggressions of a nearby bishop. Hence the invitation went out: would the congregation of Bursfeld care to send a delegation of monks to Brussels, conduct a visitation of their own to counteract the recent visitation of Vicar-General Hovius, and renew their claim of jurisdiction over Affligem? The monks of Bursfeld were only too willing to comply, and a delegation was sent as requested in April 1595. But the counter-visit by Bursfeld was countered just weeks later by Mathias Hovius, who listened with less amusement than he might have as each monk of Affligem came forward to solemnly declare newfound loyalty to their long lost Benedictine brothers from Germany who before last week had not visited in twenty-five years.

In the middle of this arguing and maneuvering, in April 1595, came news that horrified Affligem: Mathias Hovius was to be the next archbishop of Mechelen, and thus their new abbot. He was no longer merely vicar-general, advancing the interests of the archdiocese generally and temporarily, but now had a deep and personal interest in the subjection of the abbey. By June 1595 he felt strong enough to impose his will: all jurisdictional ties with other Benedictines were to be severed, he declared, and the community was to move from Brussels in order to save money. Each monk was given a choice of residence: they could move to one of the abbey's two priories (in Bornem and Lower Wavre), or to Leuven, or right near him to a palace in Mechelen.

And so Affligem scattered again, diminishing its identity further. Four or five monks, including the prior, finally settled in Mechelen and constituted a frail, dejected core. Unappeased by their spacious quarters in the Keizershof, one-time home of Philip the Fair and Margaret of York and Charles V, they recalled to one another with great nostalgia the deferential treatment shown them in the good old days by their previous archbishop-abbot, Jean Hauchinus.

Ironically, it was a memory of the same Jean Hauchinus that inspired Mathias Hovius to act so aggressively against Affligem. But this memory was far less pleasant than that held by monks: Archbishop Hovius' image of Jean Hauchinus featured a pitiful death, thirty-six thousand florins in debts, hounding by creditors, and no permanent residence—all because Archbishop Hauchinus was ever the uncertain master of Affligem. Jean Hauchinus never understood fully that along with a well-appointed hierarchy and a cooperative state, a steady income was the third essential pillar of a strong church. He never grasped that in the new tenuously endowed archdiocese a steady income meant the unconditional subjection of Affligem. And he never could forget his penchant for courtesy long enough to carry out the occasional impolite but necessary deed.

Mathias Hovius had no such qualms. In late 1595, just after his confirmation as archbishop, he sold, without the tiniest bit of consultation, two of Affligem's buildings in Leuven and Dendermonde; he then used the proceeds to pay for his new official residence in Mechelen. When Affligem's prior, Livinus Mulder, protested, the archbishop dismissed him from office and sent him from Mechelen to the Benedictine monastery of Vlierbeek, near Leuven, as a common brother.

This was not as arbitrary as it seemed, for the archbishop had a long list of embarrassing goods on fifty-six-year-old Prior Livinus. The most damning came from the convent of the White Ladies near the monks' former quarters in Brussels. Nuns there reported that the prior had long been overly familiar with a Sister Linken, walking in and out of cloister as he pleased, giving her silver thimbles, all the bread, beer, and fish she needed, and even a large tray of sausages. In return she gave him a gold ring with a turquoise stone. One night at dinner Sister Linken yelled at Sister Grieten, "You're a public whore, you've had so many children," to which Grieten responded, "You've done the same with the prior of Affligem." Some sisters said it was all in fun, a "peasant game," but this hardly impressed Mathias Hovius. Neither did news that Prior Livinus spread his familiarity around to nuns in the convent of Grand Bigard, outside Brussels. When these tales were added to reports that the prior was still conspiring with Benedictines from Bursfeld to come and claim jurisdiction over Affligem, it was easy for the archbishop, in October 1597, to remove him.

Yet Affligem was not broken, and Livinus Mulder least of all. Though the archbishop considered his punishment quite restrained and still addressed the ex-prior as "Most Dear Mulder," Brother Livinus was unmoved. From his new, sober quarters in Vlierbeek, situated at the foot of rolling hills outside Leuven, he wrote all who would listen to say so. He griped to dispersed brother monks. He protested to the archbishop his barbaric treatment, invoking the usual memory of a kindly Jean Hauchinus, among others. Most serious of all, the prior told the saga of Affligem to friends in much higher places, including the papal court: by the middle of 1599 an anonymous letter was circulating in Rome, describing at length the foibles and unsuitability of Mathias Hovius as Archbishop of Mechelen.

While all these letters raced in and out of Leuven, Archbishop Hovius summoned one of the monks of Affligem, Brother Joannes Houbraken, to an audience at the episcopal residence in Mechelen. Because the monks were now few, the archbishop's strategy was to win them one by one to his version of incorporation. But the interview ended in disaster when Brother Joannes, to the archbishop's surprise, declared that he was prepared to give his life for the independence of the abbey. Mathias Hovius exploded and Joannes crumbled.

Which explained the poor monk's state when the watch found him that night on the Grand Market. Though detained only briefly, Brother Joannes' disturbed condition lasted for months. Livinus Mulder, upon learning Joannes' state, said he was not surprised: he claimed that others had similarly lost their spirits after chats with Mathias Hovius. Brother Joannes recovered his senses only in December, and then just long enough to receive the last sacraments. He died at forty-five years of age. A few years later, when the abbey of Affligem was finally rebuilt, brother monks moved his remains to an honored place in their new church, making him almost a martyr.

THE MEDIATOR FROM NAPLES

January and February 1601.

However undignified his methods in attacking Mathias Hovius, Livinus Mulder was quite right about one thing: the abbey's only hope for independence now lay in Rome. For in their own land not only was the archbishop against them but so were the new archdukes, whose vision of a national church in their own image somehow failed to include local monasteries run by foreign monks from Bursfeld.

Hence, besides circulating anonymous letters in Rome, the monks of Affligem employed more conventional means as well, such as appointing agents to intervene with the right people in the papal curia. In public these agents stated that they simply wanted Archbishop Hovius to cease overstepping the boundaries of incorporation. But in private their intent was to destroy incorporation altogether and return the abbey to its former state of independence, subject to Rome alone.

In fact the monks had good reason to hope: though Affligem's incorporation into the archdiocese had occurred four decades before, Rome listened with perked ears whenever anyone started claiming direct subjection to it. All Catholics were of course ultimately subject to the pope, but an important minority—such as many monasteries—was *directly* subject, thus removing all authority-diluting layers of jurisdiction in between. Any addition to the number of directly subject institutions strengthened papal authority. Any loss weakened it.

The most famous threat to papal authority had long been the secular state, which liked to meddle in affairs Rome considered its own—such as the naming of bishops. Certainly the state's gains in this regard diluted Rome's control. But there was a more subtle threat as well to papal authority, and it came from within the church itself: namely, the decision of the Council of Trent to give bishops, not Rome, the role of implementing the council's reforms. Though the council's proceedings had been controlled by Rome, though some observers believed that the council promoted the papacy's universalist aspirations, and though many at the council willingly accorded to the pope the right to proclaim doctrine for the universal church, the decision to empower bishops in the area of reform posed a potential problem. Almost everyone recognized that reform of abuses worked best at the local level, under the watchful eye of bishops. Yet many of the local institutions in greatest need of Trent's reforms—such as monasteries—claimed to be "exempt" from those bishops and subject only to preoccupied, faraway Rome. For Trent to work fully, Rome would have to cede some of its authority over these institutions to bishops.

There was the rub. Rome was not necessarily against reform, but it was religiously against any loss of central authority. Without such authority, the pope, as bishop of Rome, was simply greatest among equals rather than prince of the church. The demands of local reform and central authority did not always clash, but when they did Rome had to choose, and it often chose the latter. That was why even soon after Trent the papacy was still granting dispensations and protective titles to some who blatantly violated Trent's reforms, such as great churchmen who wished to hold more than one office, or scandalous chapters and monasteries (including even certain concubining clergymen) wanting to escape the jurisdiction of local bishops. It was not that the popes approved of scandalous practices, but that the very seeking and granting of dispensations was a recognition and confirmation of Rome's authority at the expense of bishops. It was a matter of priorities: to bishops Trent was especially about the church local, but to the papacy Trent was mostly about the church universal.

These lofty abstractions came crashing down to earth in such tangible cases as Affligem's. However much the abbey needed reform, however badly the archbishop needed the abbey's income to run and reform the archdiocese, the papacy would not ignore an appeal that touched upon its own jurisdiction. After all, before that lamentable bull of incorporation in 1559, Affligem could claim centuries of direct subjection to Rome. It was enough to move the papal secretary of state to promise Affligem's agents that three cardinals would indeed study the abbey's request of subjection to Rome alone.

Cultivating favor in Rome also meant cultivating favor in Brussels—at the court of the new papal nuncio, Ottavio Frangipani. By early 1601, both archbishop and abbey turned to him as the most important local mediator of the dispute. The attractions were obvious: he was nearby, and possessed more influence in Rome than any hired agent. And the gifts of this particular nuncio in the delicate task of mediation were many.

Ottavio Mirto Frangipani had been born in Naples in 1542, and was thus an exact contemporary of Mathias Hovius. A bishop at age thirty, he then followed the more sure path of promotion in the Italian church: succeeding his uncle, who was in the papal diplomatic corps. His first major post came in 1587, as nuncio of Cologne. There he honed his distaste for combat and his desire to please all sides. But a shadow developed as well: some in Rome regarded his passion for moderation as weakness, his caution as inaction. Upon hearing such criticism, a weary Frangipani acted his usual unruffled self but soon afterward asked for reassignment back to his own bishopric in Italy.

He was indeed reassigned, but to Brussels, in 1596, as the first nuncio of Flanders. Some might have regarded it as a demotion, but the post in Brussels had its importance: rumors were already circulating by now about the imminent appointment of Albert and Isabella, and good relations with them had to be established early. Moreover, few posts were situated in the convergence of such rich gossip lanes as those that ran by way of Brussels between England, France, the Dutch Republic, and Germany.

And so Ottavio Frangipani reluctantly set out from Cologne, arriving in Brussels in September 1596, only months after Albert became governor-general and Mathias Hovius archbishop. His health was gouty. He bore northern climates poorly. He was still in debt to German bankers, thanks to his irregular salary from Rome. And he was still being spied on by his own superior in Rome, the papal secretary of state. Nevertheless, Ottavio Frangipani carried out his duties diligently, including immersing himself in such unpleasantries as the dispute over Affligem.

Soon after his arrival, the nuncio could already recite by heart Livinus Mulder's litany of woes against Mathias Hovius. But the most impressive recitation of the archbishop's sins, sixty in all, was

compiled by two other monks in a document that reached the
nuncio in January 1601.

Archbishop Hovius, began the monks, had forced them from
Brussels, taken their archive, sold their property to build a fine
palace for himself, and provided them a paltry allowance. Their
shoes and clothing were handed to them by a "little old lady." The
archbishop also scared away new recruits, so that now only eight
monks remained—where there once had been forty! Under Cardinal Granvelle no one had surpassed Affligem in hospitality, in
alms, in numbers, in celebration of the divine office. But now the
church was a stall for cows and pigs, and neglect had damaged the
buildings more than any soldier. When monks asked about returning, the archbishop gruffly told them to chase the thought from
their heads.

So serious were the charges of the monks that the nuncio sent
a copy to the archbishop himself, and requested a response. After
years of initiative against the abbey of Affligem, Mathias Hovius
suddenly found himself on the defensive. Not only had he recently
been forced to explain to the papal secretary of state why he did
not wish to rebuild Affligem (it would cost three hundred thousand florins, explained the archbishop), not only had he recently
found it necessary to solicit from brother bishops glowing testimonials about his character (to be forwarded to Rome), but now
he was having to vindicate himself to the nuncio as well.

Each of the sixty points the archbishop answered with a
thoroughness Ottavio Frangipani would have appreciated. Forcing
the monks to move from Brussels, began the response, was neces-
sitated by the unseemly behavior of Livinus Mulder, and nothing
else; had times been less troubled in past years, even Archbishop
Hauchinus would have acted against the man. As for the charges
of frugality, Mathias Hovius knew no other way to remove the
archdiocese's crippling debts: the only reason creditors had not
already stripped the robes from his back and forced him to sell
all the abbey's lands was that the archdukes had protected him.
His plan was to rebuild the abbey's farms gradually, and steadily

increase annual income to a modest twenty-three thousand florins, far short of the thirty-six thousand once enjoyed, and certainly too little at the moment to rebuild the abbey. If there were cows in the ruined abbey church, it was a common sight in the countryside during war. If recruiting had not gone well, it was because the abbey's future was unclear, and because novices were scandalized by the laxity of current monks. If he had a new official residence, it was because a bishop needed one: besides, the monks were the only ones who called it a "palace," and their own lodgings in the Keizershof were not exactly plain. As for the "little old lady" belittled by the monks, this was, as the monks knew perfectly well, the archbishop's pious sister Catharina, manager of his household: she distributed goods to the monks as part of her regular duties. More than any other accusation was this surely the reason for the archbishop's demand that all monks who had signed the sixty points kneel before him and ask forgiveness.

Although the nuncio was sympathetic to Affligem's claims that the archbishop at times went too far, he was at last weary of the monks and persuaded by Mathias Hovius. This may have been a simple, classic bias: the nuncio belonged to the "secular" clergy, who served the laity, and monks to the socially withdrawn "regular" clergy. But even more likely was that the nuncio detested the anonymous letter circulated about the archbishop in Rome, for Ottavio Frangipani too had been the victim of unfair letter-writing campaigns in the Eternally Rumoring City.

And so the nuncio decided to defend Mathias Hovius to the pope. At the moment it was no easy thing, for the archbishop was hardly a favorite in Rome. The anonymous letter, and the horror stories still being whispered by Benedictine agents, were having their effect. So were still other unflattering rumors murmured in papal ears by still other malcontents from the Spanish Netherlands. Then there were reports, this time from the nuncio Frangipani himself, that the archbishop had lately discouraged Netherlandish bishops from making their required quadrennial *ad limina* journey to Rome, supposedly because one such bishop had been coldly received there. It was a rumor the papal secretary of state wanted the nuncio to investigate and squelch. Hence, under the circumstances, the nuncio thought it best to bide his time and await just the right moment to tell Rome of his support for Mathias Hovius against the upstart abbey of Affligem.

If the famously cautious nuncio was willing to wait, Archduke Albert was not. He had seen enough: as long as this increasingly scandalous dispute went unresolved, as long as the Archbishop of Mechelen stood on shaky financial ground, the local church could not move forward. Affligem had to be subjected, and now. Rather than sitting by while the nuncio and Rome did nothing to solve the dispute, Albert decided that he would settle it himself.

UNA BELLA CONCORDIA

At the end of March 1601, Albert sent two members of his privy council to the nuncio's residence. Together all three men were to draw up an "agreement" between abbey and archbishop, then impose it.

Fortunately for the archbishop, the terms of this agreement supported him in almost every way. Incorporation was irreversible, it declared, fixed forever. Hence the abbey was to cease its appeals to Rome. Of the abbey's twenty-three thousand florins in income, the archbishop was to have fifteen thousand (a rather average income for Netherlandish bishoprics) while the rest was for the monks. The congregation of Bursfeld was excluded forever. Albert's only concession to the monks was a big one: the abbey was to be rebuilt and the now scattered monks were to return. Affligem would survive after all.

Not one monk or archbishop was present at the drawing up of this agreement sponsored by Albert, but the nuncio Frangipani sent it on to Rome anyway, along with an unmercifully long explanation of why the pope should confirm it. The papal secretary of state grew weary reading the nuncio's details and said so in the margins. But more important, the secretary saw in the agreement what all the pages in the world could not hide: the monks were not a party to it, and had therefore agreed to nothing. Neither had the archbishop, of course, but he hardly needed to, since the agreement was quite in his favor. The secretary sneered that here was *"una bella concordia"* indeed.

This was true for not only the archbishop but the archdukes as well: strong bishops were more to their liking than strong monasteries. Like princes, bishops tended to identify with a local or "national" church, while monasteries looked to Rome. Strong bishops therefore meant not only strong religion, which suited the archdukes, but a strong state, which suited them as much. In fact it would not take Mathias Hovius long to realize that in the triangular contest for religious authority among archbishop, archdukes, and Rome, he often had stronger ties with the second than the third—including on such matters as reform. In Brussels the archbishop, despite his mediocre French, sat on Albert's Council of State. In the archdiocese the archdukes were his biggest supporters of reform. The archbishop had no such intimate links with Rome, and no Italian at all.

In spite of the desirability of regaining direct jurisdiction over Affligem, and in spite of its willingness to hear Affligem's appeals, in the end Rome had reason to support the bella concordia as well. Though it did not like princes interfering in the church's affairs, for that very reason it was important to maintain good relations with the archdukes and make concessions to them when possible. In this case, because Rome's jurisdiction over the abbey had been officially relinquished so long before, it was not as if Rome would suffer a new loss by finally acknowledging it; moreover, efforts to recover papal jurisdiction over Affligem, at this late date, would surely damage relations with the archdukes and lead to even more damaging attacks on Rome's authority. It was better to yield this time, saving energies for more winnable cases. By June, Rome let the nuncio Frangipani know that it would reluctantly go along with the archdukes' (and thus the archbishop's) subjection of Affligem.

With that, the nuncio, Albert, and Archbishop Hovius proceeded as if all were decided, not only preparing to take more forceful command of Affligem than before but also laying plans for rebuilding it. Albert's private builders and two privy councilors led the archbishop and nuncio on an afternoon excursion to Affligem to inspect the ruins and estimate the cost of repairs—which turned out to be much less, noted the astute Frangipani, than the three hundred thousand florins the archbishop had once suggested it would cost. Because it was spring, the party ate a lovely picnic before the portal of the ruined church, under a roof of new foliage, and discussed the order of the building.

But someone told the monks about this picnic. Though gratified by the news of rebuilding, they were mortified to learn it was part of an agreement they knew nothing about. Affligem's lawyers in Rome started flinging papers once more. Now that the truth about the "agreement" was in the open, the papacy had little choice but to announce that there could be no agreement until the monks actually did some agreeing.

The nineteenth of February, 1602, a monastery in Brussels.

In the Benedictine priory of Our Lady of the Chapel the tension was thick as blood.

The nuncio had arranged the meeting in order to obtain what Rome required: the consent of the monks of Affligem to the agreement. He had even left Albert's side at the siege of Nieuwpoort just to attend. But things were not going as planned. The first problem was obvious: all six remaining monks were present at the meeting, but the archbishop was not. He had sent instead Henri Costerius, a powerful and shady priest just returned from Rome. The absent Albert was represented by his architect and universal man,

Wenzel Coeberger. Later the architect became famous for bringing the Italian Baroque to the Low Countries, but today he was a
compeller of monks.

That was the second problem with the meeting. The representatives of the archbishop and the archduke were there not to
discuss but to get signatures. Master Coeberger was an imposing
presence, yet on this occasion he left the work of intimidation to
the priest, who was even better suited to the task. Indeed there
was no better evidence of the archbishop's desire to win at all costs
the struggle with Affligem than his designation of Henri Costerius to represent him today. Here was a man of unbounded ambi-
tion who had begun as a simple parish priest, then climbed to his
present position as canon in the prestigious chapter of St. Goedele
in Brussels. Yet the canon's impressive collection of benefices only
began to describe his intriguing spirit: he was also exorcist, trader
in dubious relics, worker of supposedly miraculous deeds, author
of suspect books, and possessor of a mercurial personality. That
the archbishop decided to employ such a one was due not to merit
or trust, but politics: Henri Costerius sat at the bargaining table
because, for reasons that still baffled everyone, he happened to
enjoy the favor of the pope, and the archbishop needed that favor
right now.

The man had catapulted to Rome's attention, in 1596, during
a local Netherlandish lawsuit involving papal interests, in which he
astutely took the side of the party that backed Rome. Emboldened
by the good fortune and attention this lawsuit brought him, he
decided to go to the Eternal City and present himself. From 1597
to 1600 he mongered gossip among prominent people in Rome on
the awful state of the Netherlandish church, on the weakness of
Ottavio Frangipani, and on the mistakes of Mathias Hovius. Naturally Henri Costerius had brilliant suggestions to fix everything.
He was so convincing as the resident expert on the Low Countries
that the pope himself granted an audience and bestowed upon
Costerius the title of apostolic protonotary, thus giving visible evidence of his enviable ties to Rome. Still it was not enough: Henri

Costerius wanted to return to his native land as a bishop. The pope even asked Ottavio Frangipani to intervene directly with Albert on the matter, who since becoming archduke had inherited the right to appoint bishops. But Albert, already wise to the machinations of Protonotary Costerius, would not go along.

This embittered the protonotary, but only briefly. For when he returned to Brussels in the summer of 1600, he was eager to flaunt his Roman connections and to exert influence one way or another. He even possessed a letter from the pope recommending that Archbishop Hovius heed his own particular proposals for reform. Surely such a letter made the archbishop shift in his throne, for he may already have known, as the nuncio did, of the protonotary's unsavory gossip at the papal court. But uneasy as everyone in Brussels was with Henri Costerius, there was no doubt that someone with the papal stamp of approval might be useful against Affligem. So there he sat, facing the monks.

The monks made the mistake of assuming that this was a negotiation in which they might add a bit of water to admittedly strong wine. Hence they arrived at the meeting with several proposals of their own. But Henri Costerius simply swept each one from the table, no doubt surprised at the optimism of the monks. Only the nuncio Frangipani, nominally in charge of the pathetic scene, understood why the monks were still hopeful: Affligem's agents in Rome were still brashly and wrongly asserting that incorporation could be completely broken. In truth, knew the better informed nuncio, the monks' only choice was whether to accept the proposal now or later.

After rejecting every suggestion, Henri Costerius then placed the agreement on the table and asked the monks to sign. When they requested time to consider, the protonotary responded that he would grant it, on one bizarre condition: that they promise now, in writing, to sign the agreement as soon as they had finished their considering. They refused. For a few moments the protonotary tried the subtle method of bribery: a pension to this monk, a desirable parish to that. Several were moved. But when some still refused to sign, he finally resorted to what he knew best: yelling threats, of imprisonment and exile.

The bombastic gifts of Henri Costerius had their desired effect: after four days the monks broke. All but one signed the hated agreement. Three days later all gathered at the archbishop's residence in Brussels to hear it read aloud, and to swear obedience to Mathias Hovius, in person. Though the archbishop stopped short of forcing each monk to kneel and beg forgiveness, as he had once required, the very setting of the scene was a final insult: this residence in Brussels had once belonged to Affligem, until it had been appropriated by Archbishop Hovius.

After the meeting, the monks made last cries for help. They claimed they had signed under duress. They appealed again to local nobles. They sent a plea to the congregation of Bursfeld. But all too late. Papal ratification came in May 1602, and the signature of the archdukes in September. Affligem was at last and for good incorporated under its bishop.

And so Mathias Hovius won. And it was no mean victory, for Affligem was the only abbey in all of Brabant to remain incorporated under its bishop: Rome went along with the unincorporation of all others. But the archbishop won this contest only with much help and at much cost.

The nuncio, whose support of the archbishop in Rome mattered greatly in this affair, felt neglected. He complained that the archbishop had put all his trust in the nearby archdukes while the monks had put theirs in Rome, so that in the end all ignored him. He asked again to return to Italy.

Archduke Albert, whose support the archbishop appreciated, had not only aided the cause but taken it over. If Henri Costerius dominated the final meeting, it was because the archduke allowed him to. Moreover, that Affligem survived, as Albert insisted, rather than withered, as Mathias Hovius seemed to prefer, was a painful reminder of who was really in charge.

The steepest cost was the archbishop's unfortunate alliance with Henri Costerius. Within a few years, Mathias Hovius would regret having ever been associated with the man.

The final cost was ill will from monks. The archbishop began trying to redress this in the year of the agreement, by appointing a new prior, continuing the rebuilding, and finally accepting new novices. Then in November 1605 he even moved a group of ten new monks from their temporary quarters in Mechelen to the partially rebuilt abbey itself. But he kept the old monks away. The archbishop had decided that they, like Moses, would never see the promised land. Not one of the old guard returned to Affligem. They lived out their days scattered in other monasteries, telling stories of Mathias Hovius.

The papal secretary of state was right: this was a harsh agreement. But the archbishop would have responded that there was no other choice. The secretary of state did not have to run the archdiocese. He had no stake in it. He had no cause to see that it must come before even proud abbeys. And he had never known the polite but impoverished Jean Hauchinus.

FIVE

Rumor Mill

Two figures trudged up the stairs to this least desirable room in the archbishop's residence. One, a sixteen-year-old boy named Paul, carried a tray of food for his uncle, incarcerated just that morning. The other, prosecutor Ludolph vande Bossche of the diocesan court, was there to lead the way and keep watch.

As they neared the landing, both saw that the small opening in the jail's door, through which they intended to pass the food, was stuffed from inside with a woolen blanket. "O Lord, what will we find here," muttered the prosecutor. Rapidly he and Paul dislodged the blanket, then peered inside: the prisoner, clothed in ecclesiastical raiment, was hanging from the neck by his own fully stretched garters.

Moving as fast as his fifty-five years allowed, the prosecutor bolted down the stairs, through the brewery, then into the kitchen, where the keys were kept and where the archbishop's sister Catharina was directing the preparation of the household's midday meal. Grabbing the keys, he yelled, "Dear lady, it's a disaster, the man has hanged himself!" Then he ran back upstairs. Despite the grief this prisoner had caused her brother the archbishop, Catharina hesi-

preceding page: Unknown artist, *The Canon Cornelius van der Haeghen,* ca. 1600. The figure in pontifical robes (St. Cornelius) behind this canon suggests the strong relationship between Rome and chapters.
Gent, Sint-Baafskathedral

tated not at all but sent for a pastor, grabbed wine and vinegar, and told a servant girl to accompany her to the prisoner's cell.

Meanwhile, Paul continued to peer fitfully through the opening, looking for a sign of life in his uncle, whose feet barely touched the ground. Suddenly there was movement, causing Paul to cry out, "Hurry he's still alive!" Seconds later the prosecutor arrived, unlocked the door, and flung it open. Inside the room, he held the prisoner upright while Paul hacked at the suspended garters with his knife. Catharina and the servant girl came just in time to see the prisoner being eased to the ground. His hands and knees were already cold, his throat gurgled, and froth poured from his mouth.

The four witnesses pleaded for the prisoner to respond. One covered him with a blanket while another wiped his mouth clean. Catharina poured wine through his lips and sprinkled his face with vinegar. More onlookers arrived. After an hour, the prisoner finally began to stir, but so agitated was he that three men in the room could hardly restrain him. Then he began to speak imperfectly. The only words anyone could make out were *"Pasquil, pasquil"*—libel. Those present wondered: was the prisoner confessing at last that he had written after all the scandalous leaflet against Archbishop Hovius, which had started this unpleasantness?

Up from the growing crowd in the cell went cries to God, to Mary His Dear Mother, and to all the blessed saints. The prisoner too began to shout "Mary, Mary," then all in unison "Mary, pray for me, miserable sinner." But some present said that when the prisoner heard the name Jesus, he changed his demeanor, shook his head angrily, and defiantly summoned every devil he could think of—Beelzebub, Balial, Astarot—while imploring, "If you have power or authority, show it," and "O Archbishop, if there's no power in heaven, then let it come from Hell: devils come and rescue me." All the while he looked at the window and waited for darkness, explaining that the devils had promised to take him away at nightfall—however many locks, bolts, and chains secured him.

Now the prisoner sought his garters—around his neck, on his thighs, in his pockets, but no luck. He gestured wildly with the blanket, asking someone to cut a piece of it so that he might hang himself again, pleading, "Devil, couldn't you make a strong rope from this?" More than once he grabbed a nail from the wall and tried to plunge it into his temple, but those around him prevented it. This talk of devils terrified some, especially since the prisoner was a clergyman. But the archbishop's resourceful sister kept working, placing before the prisoner's face a small image of Our Lady of Loreto, in Italy, where the prisoner had once celebrated Mass. These helped him to relax, as did the arrival of his brother-in-law and a pastor.

With the prisoner calmed, the prosecutor asked him why he had done such an awful deed. The answer stunned one and all: Archbishop Hovius had come to the cell and told the prisoner to kill himself. This was impossible, said the prosecutor, for the archbishop was out of town. Now it was the prisoner who was surprised: then who, he asked, was the man in pontifical habit, wearing choir robes just like the archbishop's, and with a bishop's miter dangling from one of his horns? To the prosecutor it was obvious: this was the devil. If nothing else, the horns were the giveaway. But how, said the prisoner, could the enemy from Hell change himself into the shape of the archbishop, with his stature, color, and voice? The answer was simple: you know well what the Apostle Paul said about the angel of darkness appearing as an angel of light.

Desperate, the prisoner invoked the devils once more, reminding them of their promise to free him when it was night. But the crowd urged him to look outside: the disturbances had gone on for so long it was already dark, and no devils had come. In anguish, the prisoner struck his chest and collapsed, lamenting his vision of the false archbishop.

Days later the archbishop returned to Mechelen and sister Catharina told him everything.

THE MAN IN THE GARTERS

The garters, worn only by nobles, were the clue that this prisoner was not accustomed to jail cells. In fact he was Franciscus Pussius, nobleman, son of a councilor of the Grand Council, graduate in law, canon of the chapter of St. Rombout's, and for the past three years the sworn enemy of Mathias Hovius.

As if it were not enough that monks and lawyers and protonotaries were busy darkening the name of Mathias Hovius in Rome, this canon in the garters had from much closer by waged an assault of his own on the archbishop's precious reputation. Though now embarrassingly immense, the conflict between the two men had begun quite small.

Franciscus Pussius joined the chapter of St. Rombout's in 1593. Like most clergymen of his stature, he was attended in his household by several servant boys, placed there by parents who expected the canon to provide education and patronage in return for the boys' work. Trouble began in the summer of 1598, when the parents of one of those boys removed their son, named Andreas, on grounds of mistreatment. This alone insulted the canon. More insulting still was news that Andreas' parents had acted with the approval of Archbishop Hovius. Most insulting of all was that the archbishop had then accepted Andreas into his own highly visible household, where everyone who mattered would see.

The loss of a single servant might have seemed trivial to some or gone unnoticed by many. But to Canon Pussius the intervention of the archbishop was blatantly public. By placing the reclaimed boy at his conspicuous side, the archbishop might as well have declared to all the world that Franciscus Pussius had failed in his duty as patron and priest. The canon could not bear such things being thought of him; as a nobleman and churchman, his reputation meant everything, especially among fellow canons, fellow nobles, and his family. Yet these were precisely the people most likely to find out about Andreas, for they moved in social circles that intersected with the archbishop's, and they knew one another's households. Since it was too late to get the boy back or even to stop word from spreading, the canon's only recourse was to try to shape opinion by getting his version of events into parlors first.

Surely emboldened by superior social rank, Canon Pussius in the autumn of 1598 sent two "uncivil" letters to the archbishop, demanding a servant in compensation for Andreas and suggesting that the archbishop was to blame for the entire mess. Over the next weeks the canon also planted seeds of gossip: canon lawyers at the University of Leuven, he claimed, assured him that the archbishop had sinned against the tenth commandment, especially the part about coveting a neighbor's servant. Still this was not enough for the canon, for in March 1599 he found it necessary to take even more drastic action: he forged a confession that supposedly came from the hand of Mathias Hovius.

On the morning of 14 March, a Sunday, when it was the turn of Canon Pussius to celebrate High Mass in St. Rombout's, this confession was found beneath a bench in the archbishop's chapel, not far from the high altar. On the outside of the document was the archbishop's seal. Inside was a Latin text in a blockish hand. "I MATHIAS HOVIUS," it began, unjustly removed the boy Andreas from the household of Franciscus Pussius, who, by the way, had just outfitted the boy in expensive new clothes. "I did so," it continued, "because I was wrongly persuaded by various ambidextrous men," and so forth. So remorseful was the archbishop, so eager was he to repair the good name of Canon Pussius, that copies of this same confession were affixed to the doors of churches in Leuven and Brussels.*

Those who saw the document recognized immediately that it was a fraud and thus deserved the derisive label *pasquil*, or libel. The canon was just as immediately the prime suspect, based on motive, hand, and trademark grammatical errors. But for a long while he denied everything, and the investigations dragged on.

---

* A translation of the full text of the forged confession appears in the Notes.

PROFILE IN PATIENCE

During these attacks on his name, the archbishop showed unusual restraint. Forgery was a serious matter, punishable by penance, imprisonment, or even branding. Yet to the canon's impolite letters, rumor-sowing, and suspected forgery Mathias Hovius offered but a single, mild, written response. Perhaps the archbishop was heeding his motto: Patience conquers the mighty. Or perhaps he was, as Canon Pussius claimed, rendered immobile by a guilty conscience over his role in the removal of the boy Andreas. But the best reason for the archbishop's calm was that the canon was no mean adversary and thus required no mean response.

There was first the canon's powerful family to consider, which like most such families was attentive to every blot—even deserved blot—on its name. This explained why Archbishop Hovius' initial plan was to put the matter in the hands of the canon's eminent father, Adrian Pussius: let the father read for himself the son's "uncivil" letters to the archbishop, investigate himself the origins of the forged pasquil, and then discipline in private as he saw fit. It was an excellent plan. The father possessed a reputation for prudence and the family would surely appreciate the archbishop's discretion. There was only one snag: Adrian Pussius never saw his son's letters or even knew that the archbishop intended him to see them. For when the archbishop sent the letters, and an explanatory note, to the father and mother of Pussius, their son the canon fortuitously intercepted the bundle on the doorstep. Hence the father did nothing.

As the spring of 1599 dragged on, and the family still did nothing, the archbishop turned to a second possible instrument of discipline for the canon: the chapter of St. Rombout's. Here too the archbishop chose wisely, for chapters were as fierce as noble families in defending their reputations and rights—including the right to discipline their own without interference from outsiders—and it would not do to step on their toes. It was much safer for the archbishop to work through the chapter than to try to levy discipline on his own, especially since his relations with the chapter of St. Rombout's (unlike his relations with the other twelve chapters of the archdiocese) were excellent, praised be God. These good relations came about largely because Archbishop Hovius employed most of the canons of Rombout's in his diocesan hierarchy—including the judge and prosecutor of the diocesan court, his private seal-bearer, his vicar-general, and the members of his vicariate. Such double service in both chapter and diocesan hierarchy gave participating canons extra prestige, extra income, and something to do besides cause trouble or wage lawsuits against their bishop. But most important, such service strengthened the bonds between these canons and Mathias Hovius. The archbishop had yet another bond with the chapter: its dean, or leader, thirty-two-year-old Henri van der Burch, not only doubled as the archbishop's vicar-general but was son of the royal councilor who likely suggested Mathias Hovius as archbishop in the first place. In short, as long as the archbishop showed these leading canons proper respect and observed their rights, he could expect their support when he needed it. And in the summer of 1599 the time seemed right.

By now the chapter was already weary of their confrere Franciscus Pussius. They had grown weary of him first in March or April 1599 when he recklessly threatened to sue Mathias Hovius for libel. They grew weary of him again in May and June when he performed arm-waving, head-shaking public tantrums in the cathedral, on the street, and in private homes, denouncing the chapter for not defending him. They grew wearier still one day in June when during the divine office Canon Pussius violated all the customs of the chapter by crossing the choir, walking past the archbishop's throne, bowing sarcastically, and saying, "Bona Dies," or good day. And they were weary at last when Canon Pussius took to bounding about the choir to chastise canons who had fallen asleep, as if to point out that others in the chapter were hardly without sin. By July of 1599, the sentiment had arisen among canons that Franciscus Pussius suffered from "turbation of the brain." Now the archbishop could be sure that the chapter would act, and thus he turned the whole sordid affair over to them.

FIVE DAYS THAT SHOOK A WORLD

On 10 July 1599, Archbishop Hovius appeared unannounced at the chapter's weekly meeting. Unaware of his looming humiliation, Canon Pussius started badly by arriving at the meeting wrongly clothed. Warned several times to put on his proper robes, he replied that white did not suit him. Finally he complied. When all were properly seated and clothed, the archbishop made his surprise entrance and took the floor.

He began by recounting his thirty years "in public office" in Mechelen. There were many present, he noted, who could attest to his peaceful and decorous behavior throughout those years. But for the past year, "our confrere Pussius, here present," had treated him with contempt. For the first time the archbishop revealed his version of the story of the servant Andreas. He had never pursued the boy, he explained, but instead the boy's parents had for long pressed him to take their son into his household. The archbishop had persistently refused, but eventually the father gave compelling reasons why Andreas should not remain with Canon Pussius, and so the archbishop relented. As for the pasquil: the archbishop could not say for sure that the canon was the author, but he could say unequivocally that the canon's rude personal letters of recent months violated his oath of obedience to the archbishop. Because of this, the canon was to be stripped of his license to preach in the archdiocese, effective immediately. In truth, concluded Archbishop Hovius, the canon deserved formal prosecution in the diocesan court, but he would leave discipline to the chapter rather than undertake it himself, partly to avoid the appearance of partiality, and partly because he did not wish to tread on the chapter's rights. Then he walked out.

Canon Pussius hardly enjoyed this speech. He interrupted

more than once, despite being ordered to silence. He also refused to show proper reverence and take off his hat, despite reprimands. And he would not budge when the chapter asked him to leave the room so that they might discuss the archbishop's proposal. When Dean van der Burch threatened to levy a fine of fifty florins, the well-to-do canon simply responded, "You may say one hundred, you may say one thousand, my father will pay it, even if he must sell his coat." There came a third and a fourth warning and several canons yelling, "Leave, leave." This only made him more determined to stay. Finally the canons rose and left instead.

As they did, Franciscus Pussius began ranting loudly enough for everyone in the church and the surrounding neighborhood to hear. He threatened to take vengeance on the traitorous chapter with crimes so memorable that they would be talked about a hundred years hence. If the canons were so intent on punishing him, then why not take a cup of his blood right now? He angrily grabbed a metal cup and demanded a knife so that he might cut into his arm. He also clamored that he wanted to climb the tower of St. Rombout's and from there tell the entire city his story.

News of the scene in the church spread quickly, causing both father and mother Pussius to come running, along with the canon's brother-in-law Maillard de Vulder, a prominent lawyer in the Grand Council. When the latter urged him to act peaceably and respectably, the canon responded, "Get out of here, I renounce you." When the lawyer held his ground, the canon raised the metal cup as if to strike and forced him to recede into the church with "quick steps."

That evening Adrian Pussius sought an urgent meeting with the archbishop.

The two men apparently still had not discussed the behavior of Franciscus in any detail. But whatever larger conclusions Adrian Pussius had reached on the subject, his purpose tonight was simply to explain his son's outrages of that afternoon in the cathedral. It was the banishment from preaching that hurt most, said father Pussius, especially because Franciscus was scheduled to preach tomorrow in Rombout's. How would it look? After a long discussion, the archbishop relented and agreed to let Franciscus preach as scheduled.

When the canon heard the news, he was not assuaged. In choir the next morning, 11 July 1599, he jumped from his seat, ran to the front of the choir, genuflected, and with raised voice yelled: "Good gentlemen, yesterday between three and four o'clock I was banned from preaching. Last night between seven and eight the ban was lifted. But I say that neither now nor later, and neither here nor twenty miles around, will I preach. Tell it forward." Despite the dean's command to sit down, Canon Pussius ran to the wooden reliquary of St. Rombout, placed his hand on it, and swore an oath not to preach.

The chapter needed no more convincing: they would do as the archbishop requested and discipline their brother canon. On 12 July they voted to place Canon Pussius under house arrest in the home of his father. If the canon refused, then he was to be imprisoned among the Cell brothers, a religious order devoted to the keeping of the terminally ill, and infamous for its austere cells. After a messenger brought news of the chapter's vote, Canon Pussius immediately violated his house arrest, ran to the cathedral, climbed into the pulpit, and asked his confreres, busy singing Vespers, what right they had to treat him so. All stood to leave, but the angry canon followed them into the street, demanding to know who had voted to arrest him and saying that if he was so terribly guilty then why not take him to prison this instant?

Dean van der Burch had finally heard enough and ordered it done: guards led the canon away to the Cell brothers. Inside their prison, Canon Pussius raged, telling brother canons who came to calm him, "I do not know you!" Later he decided he wanted the chapter to come fetch him after all, but they would not have to: the canon had in the meantime become so disorderly that the superior of the Cell brothers, fearing the ruin of his prison, released him at midnight. Immediately Canon Pussius ran to the houses of his confreres and started yelling once more, alarming not only the canons and their neighbors but the watch, who arrived soon after to take him home. Franciscus Pussius was determined to misbehave just as badly now as before.

Two days later, on 14 July, this woeful scene repeated itself. During yet another dramatic chapter meeting, the canons of St. Rombout's voted yet again to place Franciscus Pussius under house arrest. Again he yelled that if he was worthy of arrest he wanted jail, not his parents' home. Though his father, mother, sister, and brother-in-law attended this meeting to urge him to submit to this lesser punishment, he ignored them. This caused an exasperated Adrian Pussius to jab at his son's chest and exclaim, "Listen well son, I insist that you not blame me for what may come of this."

    And so once again guards led Canon Pussius away to the Cell brothers, this time in daylight and in shackles, for the Cell brothers, said the dean, would take him back only on that condition. But within hours Adrian Pussius decided that he could not bear after all the thought of his son in such a place: not for nothing did a neighboring (and noble) bishop declare that no honest man would dare enter the order of the Cell brothers. Besides, their cells for prisoners were suited better to dogs and beasts than canons of the metropolitan church. That night Adrian Pussius therefore visited Dean van der Burch, recounted the damage already done his family's reputation, and asked for his son's release. The dean relented, once again putting Franciscus on the street. But all the dean got for his troubles were more threats from the newly freed canon (who started yelling in public that he might have to "do away with two or three" in the chapter), plus a bill from the Cell brothers for damages to a certain cell.

THE ETERNAL CITY

Over the next year, public confrontations ceased, as Canon Pussius finally accepted his house arrest. Energies therefore turned on both sides to letter writing and evidence heaping.

The canon sent long epistles to the chapter, officially in charge of his fate, and even longer epistles to the archbishop, holder of the true keys. He sounded deeply penitent. He pleaded that the archbishop be too light rather than too severe. He thanked the archbishop for benevolence toward such a little soul, for embracing him paternally just as Jesus embraced the Magdalene and publican. He prayed to avoid that hostile enemy of salvation, the devil, who lay in wait. He explained that his misdeeds sprang not from malevolence but a disturbed mind and cloudy spirit, caused by the ban from preaching and by all the canons shouting at him as if he were the lowest beast on earth. He accepted the archbishop's demands that he sign a confession and pay a fine should he lapse.

But the canon would not admit to the pasquil. Neither would he admit that the chapter's punishment was just. The canon had once said of Mathias Hovius, "what is light to others is heavy to the archbishop," but now he was more inclined to say this of the chapter. Treated with a bridle rather than a sword he would have acquiesced, but from the chapter it was "all flames, iron fists, iron breasts, steel hearts, laughing and scoffing." His banishment to the Cell brothers, where he lay shackled and suffering from fever, had pierced him more deeply than anything else the chapter might have devised. And their house arrest was little better than the real thing: people in town did not see him in church and thus spread rumors that he was still with the Cell brothers.

Joining vigorously in the canon's defense were his father, Adrian Pussius, and his brother-in-law Maillard de Vulder, who abandoned their former policy of cooperation with chapter and archbishop and instead began to criticize them. Though they recognized that the canon deserved punishment, the two men believed that the dean had gone too far in sending him to such a despicable place as the Cell brothers' prison, and in allowing him to be led away in chains. The dean, charged these men, had also attempted to intimidate the canon when the latter hinted that he might appeal his case to the nuncio: "Why would you do that?" replied the dean. "We have the nuncio in our back pocket, for he seeks to please the bishop; we'll accomplish more with one letter than all of you in a full-blown lawsuit." Most seriously of all, Dean van der Burch was also supposedly spreading rumors that the servant Andreas had been taken away by his parents because Canon Pussius had engaged in carnal relations with him.

The lawyers of the chapter of St. Rombout's, in anticipation of a full-scale lawsuit before the diocesan court, gathered evidence to refute each of these charges. The dean had sent the canon to the Cell brothers because the canon requested it. No one had ever heard the dean say the nuncio was corruptible. And no one had ever heard talk from the dean about "nefarious and detestable" acts between the canon and Andreas.

Despite these denials, suspicions on especially this last count must have entered people's minds. There were after all actual cases and many rumors of sexual misconduct among the clergy, includ- . ing with servant boys. There was also the manner in which the archbishop had proceeded throughout: in the vaguely recorded, obscurely worded, within-the-house style that typified cases of sexual scandal. In all the voluminous records made, never did the archbishop note specifically why Andreas had to be removed from the household of Franciscus Pussius, except to say that the reason was "compelling." And did whispers of scandal help to explain a bizarre document that suddenly emerged, in the same idiosyncratic hand as the canon's forged pasquil? In this second document, the unidentified author wrote that he had recently seen Canon Pussius and a young woman embracing passionately in a chapel and then heard them agree to meet later in the churchyard. Was this genuine evidence of more unclerical ways, or was it the canon's attempt to tell everyone that he preferred women?

Whatever the truth on this matter, the chapter's lawyers understood well that though rumors about the canon and Andreas may have worked to their advantage on the street or in respectable parlors, more solid evidence was required in court. Hence they dug deeply into the canon's past, focusing on his behavior with other servants. They found, for instance, nuns in the convent of Thabor, where the canon had once lodged and taken his meals, who were prepared to testify that Canon Pussius had regularly beaten a servant, once hitting him in the face with a strap of large keys, which caused many in the convent to conclude that the canon was not sane.

After arming themselves with piles of evidence, both sides in the dispute finally decided that compromise was better than a lawsuit. The family surely dreaded the thought of more witnesses, facts, and rumors, while chapter and archbishop detested the spectacle of lawsuits between churchmen; by making known the sullied deeds of one, they might arouse sentiment against the clergy in general. No doubt this explained the motivation behind the next offer of the Pussius family, and why the chapter accepted it: let the canon leave town.

And so the chapter released Canon Pussius from house arrest so that he might make a short trip to Antwerp, for devotional purposes. Other trips followed, as rewards for good behavior. In the summer of 1600 the canon asked to take his biggest trip yet: a pilgrimage to Rome for a full year. The chapter agreed. The canon, after promising to return a new man, left sometime in the autumn of 1600.

Was it possible that by traveling to Rome the canon hoped not only for relief but the chance to spread tales against Mathias Hovius or the chapter? After all, Henri Costerius, suspected of telling tales himself in the Eternal City about the archbishop, returned from Rome in June 1600, weeks before Franciscus Pussius decided to travel there. The two canons certainly moved in the same circles, and may have known each other. But Canon Pussius left no account of events that transpired during his trip to Rome, save two: first, while the canon was still away, a heartbroken Adrian Pussius died, in April 1601; and second, while at the shrine of Our Lady of Loreto, Canon Pussius celebrated Mass and purchased an image of the Virgin.

FALL OF AN ENFANT TERRIBLE

As promised, Canon Pussius returned to Mechelen within a year, around July 1601. In fact he seemed positively eager, for he returned weeks ahead of schedule. But great expectations only made disappointments all the greater.

His return seemed to begin quite well, including the granting of a long-sought audience with Archbishop Hovius on 10 September. But the archbishop meant the audience as an interrogation, not a reconciliation: he still wanted to know the truth about old events. After hard questioning in the presence of Dean van der Burch, Canon Pussius finally admitted that he was, as the archbishop always suspected, indeed the author of the pasquil. He had forged the seals from genuine seals on various decrees. And he had not sent copies of the pasquil to Leuven and Brussels, but said this only to strike terror in the archbishop's heart.

According to friends, the archbishop accepted the confession, expressed willingness to grant the canon grace, and promised to counsel him for his soul's salvation. But on one condition: that the canon repeat his confession in the presence of two other members of the chapter so that the archbishop's reputation, "badly damaged," might begin to be restored. The canon agreed and the confession was arranged for five o'clock that evening.

But the canon changed his mind. Fearful of losing honor, he simply could not bring himself to admit to a wider public that he had committed such a grievous sin as forgery. He would admit only to speaking irreverently and telling lies. The archbishop must have fumed. He fumed even more over the next two days when Canon

Pussius fell back into his old habit of lying by running to nearly every religious establishment in Mechelen and declaring that the archbishop had cleared him: "I bring you good news, thank and praise God, the Lord of my ways, truth has won out, the author of the pasquil has been found; let this be a lesson to superiors not to be too hasty in punishing and a lesson to subjects to have patience and await their time."

Hearing this, the chapter, still legally responsible for the canon, met hastily and voted to arrest him. They handed the warrant to Prosecutor Ludolph vande Bossche of the diocesan court, who decided to see to the arrest himself. He found the canon on the street near St. Rombout's.

After the two men greeted each other, the canon spoke next. "Why are you so troubled? You look so upset."

"It's because I'm always saddened when any priest comes into trouble," explained the prosecutor, who now revealed his commission.

The canon stayed calm; "I feel no trouble at all," he said. "This is the day I've awaited, for I desire nothing but justice." He asked the prosecutor to read the warrant aloud. But the prosecutor declined to do so on the street. And so the two men walked to the residence of the archbishop and went in the front door. There the prosecutor handed the warrant to the canon, who read in silence. Afterward the canon stated simply, "At least it's more honest here than with the Cell brothers," then followed the prosecutor up the stairs to the jail. Before going inside, the canon took out a letter he wanted delivered to the chapter. He also asked the prosecutor to tell his brother-in-law, the lawyer Maillard de Vulder, what had happened, but please not to tell his distressed, widowed mother. The prosecutor agreed and added that he would also arrange for the prisoner's nephew to bring food and drink. The canon went inside the cell, the prosecutor locked the door, then took the keys downstairs to the kitchen.

Two hours later the canon stuffed the door with a blanket, removed his garters, hooked them over a beam, and hanged himself by the neck.

When the chapter's lawyers arrived at the jail the next day, they brought little sympathy and many questions.

The lawyers declared that the canon was now, at his own expense, to be shackled and guarded by three men. This infuriated him. He threw off nightcap and blankets, kissed his image of Our Lady of Loreto, and yelled, "How can you shackle me, me, me, preacher, son of a Councilor, and nobleman, and I say this without boasting?" Then as the night before he called upon devils: "What are you waiting for? Show yourself to have greater power than the Archbishop; seize, seize, the soul with the body." The lawyer-priests exorcised him, calling upon saints, sprinkling with Holy Water, and holding out the image of Our Lady.

When the canon had calmed, the lawyers began with their real work. They wanted not only to discuss yesterday's attempted suicide, which was a sign of sinister influences, but to go all the way back to the start of the case. And so went their rigorous inquiries throughout the rest of September. One day the lawyers bombarded the prisoner with forty-six questions. Another day they hinted at the old rumors of illicit relations by asking why the canon was so attached to the boy Andreas. That the lawyers dredged up everything suggested their intent not only to discipline but to compile a case strong enough to get him out of the chapter for good.

The canon did not sink easily. He evaded. He said that he would remember things better if he could go to the home of his desolate mother and examine his papers. He confessed one day and denied everything the next. He said that his attempted suicide and his invocation of demons were faked, "nothing but fantasy," and that he had merely wanted the chapter's sympathy, especially the dean's.

The questioning, the admissions, the denials, and threats by Maillard de Vulder to countersue the chapter in the court of the Grand Council lasted into early 1602. By January momentum swung to the chapter, for Franciscus Pussius admitted at last that his attempted suicide and his invocation of demons had been real. It was enough to compel his family to agree to a private settlement out of court. In exchange for a pension of 150 florins a year and the chapter's dropping of the suit, the canon vacated his prebend, paid all legal expenses, and signed a confession. "Because I have acted irreverently, strewn false libels, tried to hang myself in prison, and called upon Beelzebub, . . . I pray forgiveness from God Omnipotent and the aforesaid archbishop and dean, and I promise correction." And so he finally admitted everything after all.

It was not clear whether Franciscus Pussius moved away or remained in Mechelen at the home of his mother, but in either case he did not have long to live, for he died of unknown causes in September 1606, probably not yet forty. No more clear was the dwelling place of the servant Andreas, though it was likely that he spent much of his youth in the household of the archbishop, a physical reminder to all of old events. More clear was the legacy of Franciscus Pussius. Single-handedly he confirmed the stereotype of the old-fashioned, irresponsible canon, immortalized at some unknown date in unforgettable rhyme: big of belly, false of voice, mind of jelly. Such judgments no doubt chagrined the archbishop and Dean van der Burch, who as canons themselves had tried to exemplify a new breed of discipline suited to this age of Catholic Reformation. Whether the removal of Canon Pussius would do much to uproot the old sort of canon remained to be seen.

✠ S I X ✠

Our Dear Lady on the Sharp Hill

SISTER CATHARINA

The fourth of October, 1603, a Saturday,
the archbishop's residence in Brussels.

Since July the archbishop had heard reports of miraculous healings on a lonely, pointed hill in the easternmost regions of the archdiocese. Any misgivings he had about these reports were due not to disbelief—miracles were a sign of the true church, after all—but to discretion. Experience taught him that most cries of "miracle!" were the product of vain imaginings or natural processes rather than divine intervention. Still, as bishop it was his task to investigate all such reports and he did so dutifully, determined to separate true miracles from false.

Already there was much to persuade him about the special powers at the hill, which surrounding inhabitants called *scherp,* or sharp. First, his sister had visited there recently and been cured of a burning fever. Second, the archdukes were showing keen interest in the place. Last, a nun the archbishop had known since her childhood, named Catharina Serraerts, had just days before been healed of a lifelong affliction to her leg. At this very moment she stood waiting outside the door of his audience chamber, where she had been summoned so that the archbishop might see for himself. The door went open and Catharina entered. To the delight of Archbishop Hovius, she stood straight and walked without a limp.

opposite: Unknown artist, the shrine at the Sharp Hill. The man on short crutches in the left foreground represents Hans Clemens.
From Sanderus, *Chorographia Sacra Brabantiae*

After the greetings, he asked to hear her story, even though much of it he knew.

Catharina, now thirty-five, had since childhood been bent like a crooked tree, her left leg five thumbs shorter than her right. Her left hip was not on her side but behind her. Her left knee turned inward, digging sharply into her right thigh. Her left heel she could not set flat. She could walk, but only with strenuous effort, and then with the aid of a high left shoe. Catharina's father, the lord of Hadocht, hired the best doctors to try to cure her; one, for instance, sewed a linen harness around her lower body to pull her hip into place. But nothing worked. When Catharina was eight, her father sent her to school at the convent of the White Ladies of Leuven. Here she came under the spell of the religious life, and at age sixteen decided to become a White Lady herself. For years her cosisters saw her pain as she tried to kneel on her left knee or stood bravely in choir to sing the divine office.

Doctors kept visiting and failing. Confessors kept urging her to accept her condition. Then, just a week earlier, stories of the new shrine at the Sharp Hill reached her convent. Instantly Catharina felt that her cure lay there and thus she sought permission to go. But the vow of cloister, which bound nuns forever within their particular convent, made Mother Superior reluctant to consent to such a trip. Likewise with the convent's confessor, the Leuven theologian Jacob Jansonius, who urged Catharina to suffer her "accident" with patience, thereby increasing her humility and merits. She complied, but privately retained hope that she might yet be able to travel to the Sharp Hill.

Her answer came one week ago when the Marquis of Havré, afflicted with an ailment of his own, rode through town on his way to the hill. Hearing of Catharina's plight, he decided to champion her cause and seek permission for her to travel with him. Dr. Jansonius and Mother Superior finally consented and assigned a sister to accompany Catharina. The next day, a Sunday, Catharina stepped outside the convent for the first time in years and struggled into the marquis's coach. It was twenty miles to the hill.

Though poorer pilgrims camped right around the shrine, it as yet offered no proper lodgings for the likes of a marquis or a nun. So Catharina's party found rooms in the town of Diest, several miles away. From there they rode to the shrine on Monday, Tuesday, and Wednesday. Most pilgrims along the busy road walked or were carried. All sang and prayed as they went. When they arrived at the hill, all paid their devotions before the miraculous image of Mary, which hung in a giant oak.

The experience was primitive and exciting, so far removed from the familiar surroundings of her convent and so perilously close to the battlefront with the Dutch. Camps of rebel troops were visible just hundreds of yards away. The chapel under the tree was only six feet by five, with walls of loam and roof of straw. Catharina and the marquis took their turn to crowd inside, confess, commune, and hear Mass. On Wednesday she felt a sensation extending from her left ear down her left leg, but thought little of it.

After Mass on Wednesday, the party returned to Leuven, arriving that evening. As Catharina walked to her room, her left shoe suddenly felt strange. She removed it; to her great surprise she stood firmly on both feet. Then came a tension and pulling in her hip and then all through her left leg: the healing had begun. She wept with thanks to God and His Holy Mother and tried to pray all night, but was so weary that a few rosaries put her to sleep.

By morning the cure was complete. The entire convent saw that she walked smoothly, that her hip was in place and her legs even. Word reached the marquis, still in Leuven, who rode joyously to the convent to see with his own eyes. Now he asked to take Catharina to Brussels to show Archduchess Isabella, whose interest in the hill was by now insatiable. This time Mother Superior granted permission more readily. After her audience with Isabella, Catharina learned that the archbishop wished to see her as well, and so there she stood.

Her story ended, Catharina again walked around the room, then departed. Archbishop Hovius wrote immediately to her confessor in Leuven, Dr. Jansonius, one of his oldest friends, to ask that he go interview all the White Ladies about Catharina's case and also bring in the usual array of medical doctors required by the protocol for investigating miracles. But there was already enough to impress. The nuncio Frangipani, whose ear for news was keen as ever, reported Catharina's healing in his next missive to Rome.

Such a case would have stirred even the most skeptical churchman. It certainly allowed Mathias Hovius to let loose his unashamed—but usually restrained—belief in divine cures. After many dubious stories about miracles, here was something genuine. After diversions from unruly monks and canons, here was refreshment. After recent criticism in print from the Bishop of Roermond, who said the archbishop's hair was too short and his beardless face too bare for a Netherlandish prelate, here was something important. Rather than waste energy on silly debates over what constituted orthodox grooming, Mathias Hovius much preferred to ponder why the Mother of God was preparing to pour out an abundance of grace on a forlorn hill in the scarred, rolling wilds of eastern Brabant.

THE LEGEND AND ITS KEEPERS

In the beginning the oak tree on the hill was a pagan shrine. In the Middle Ages clergymen tried to Christianize it. Their efforts peaked in the fifteenth century when a small statue of the Virgin mysteriously appeared in the tree. Some said that the tree itself then began to grow in the form of a cross. Still others told of the inevitable peasant who removed the image to take it home for himself, but whose feet stuck to the ground as soon as he tried to walk away. Whether placed in the oak by human hands or divine the meaning was clear: Our Lady (who only in Dutch was Our Dear Lady) had made this place holy and wished to work her powers and be adored here. More and more people in search of divine aid began visiting the Sharp Hill.

That nearly identical accounts of images in oak trees were

told all over Catholic Europe hardly disenchanted believers but re-assured them. Such learned men as Archbishop Hovius preferred that such accounts be based on impeccable documentation rather than legend. But to most believers, shrines and their legends were more about faith than scholarship. They confirmed the old notion that otherworldly powers were more potent at some locations than others. They proved that the Virgin was mightier than such pagan favorites as Diana. And in the age of Reformation shrines and legends took on still another purpose: they reaffirmed to Catholics that theirs was the one true faith.

So it was at the Sharp Hill. The pagan oak was first made Christian. Then, though for centuries obscure, war with the Dutch put the shrine right at the battlefront and transformed it into a symbol of old faith against new. From 1565 rival armies in the region contested not the tiny, isolated shrine itself, of course, but the prized towns of Zichem and Diest, two and three miles away. Yet as armies passed back and forth across the Sharp Hill on their way to ruin or defend each city, they took more and more notice of the shrine. Before the royalist and Catholic Duke of Parma attacked a rebellious Zichem in 1578, he paid his devotions at the Sharp Hill first. It worked, for the invasion was a big, bloody success, and the town subjected: at its end 170 rebels were tied back-to-back and thrown into the Demer river. Two years later, while rebel troops prepared to retake Zichem, they also paid their devotions at the shrine but in Protestant fashion: by destroying the image of the Virgin. This worked too, for the rebels' conquest of Zichem was just as successful and awful as Parma's.

The person who did most to nourish the shrine during each of these disheartening assaults upon his native city was Godfried Tienwinkel, pastor of Zichem since the 1570s. During one rebel invasion, soldiers wrenched the chalice from his hands while he said Mass, then dragged him outside to hang him, but parishioners saved his life. During another invasion, rebels set the city ablaze, so Pastor Tienwinkel climbed to the safety of the church tower, only to listen in horror as two children and several horses, locked inside, screamed and burned to death. Some said no town suffered as much as Zichem. The church was razed. The rectory lay in a heap. The pastor slept at night in a decrepit stall, the sacred host by his side lest rebel troops steal or desecrate it. Even the pastor's letters of appointment, his official identity, were destroyed, so that even after years of service it was possible for Archbishop Hovius still to wonder what kind of a pastor Godfried Tienwinkel was.

This acquaintance with grief, this shedding of blood, were what motivated Pastor Tienwinkel to revive devotion at the Sharp Hill. He knew its usual peacefulness. He knew its grace, for he was cured of a fever there as a six-year-old boy. And so he decided to repair the place, and encourage soldiers and parishioners to visit. Here might they find relief from worry and slaughter.

From a widow in Diest he accepted gratefully in 1587 the donation of a new simple wooden image of Mary to replace the one ruined by the rebels. He affixed it to the tree and covered it with a tiny roof. The Virgin showed her pleasure by performing through the new image miracles just as powerful as the old. And the pastor showed his thanks by leading in Lent of 1602 the first formal procession to the Sharp Hill. Underneath the sprawling branches of the oak tree, he built with his own hands the simple chapel where Catharina Serraerts and the archbishop's sister Catharina would soon pay their devotions. To his delight, word of the shrine spread and outsiders began to travel there. In March 1603, on the eve of the Annunciation, the hill shone for miles with 750 campfires—not from soldiers but from pilgrims in search of divine aid.

The pastor did not intend his homemade shrine to become famous. That it did was due in his eyes to divine favor. Oh, every shrine was by definition holy. And every shrine might be the site of miracles. But this shrine was especially blessed, he thought: the Mother of God chose to work miracles at such an unlikely, remote place precisely because it was remote and right under the noses of the rebels.

Set against a backdrop of physical isolation and the military perils that surrounded the Sharp Hill, Her infinite grace and power stood out even more clearly. It proved to the faithful that she was up to any challenge. And it proclaimed to scoffing heretics the validity of the Catholic faith.

But not even the pastor would deny that this-worldly forces helped catapult the Sharp Hill to genuine fame (although he might well have disputed what constituted "this-worldly"). Its location at the front brought it to the attention of all the Netherlands. Its proximity to rebels made every trip there a dramatic act of courage. And most of all its patrons were well chosen, for they were none other than Albert and Isabella.

When the cheers of their Joyous Entries faded, the archdukes found themselves confronted by one military crisis after the next. By 1601 Albert's strategy against the Dutch focused on two goals: to hold Den Bosch in the north and to retake Oostende on the coast. But the siege at Oostende was going badly: three thousand troops were lost in a single attack. Grumblings about Albert rolled from councils in Brussels, from assorted provinces, and especially from Spain, which still sought to subordinate Netherlandish policies to its own. Spanish courtiers urged Philip III to replace Albert not merely as commander but as prince. The king readily heard such talk, for he wanted the Netherlands himself. There were even concrete plans to send Albert and Isabella elsewhere—no longer as Viceroys of Portugal, but now to Sicily instead.

It was Isabella who saved the couple's day. She made the siege at Oostende her concern, camping by Albert, riding on horseback to encourage the troops, vowing not to change her underlinens until the city was taken, and writing her brother the king to defend Albert. She also helped Albert turn his attentions to the Sharp Hill. In early 1603, on his way from Oostende to lead the defense of Den Bosch, Albert even vowed that if the city held then he would make a pilgrimage to the shrine on the hill. Den Bosch did hold, despite a final furious assault by the Dutch. Afterward, returning to

Oostende, Albert went out of his way to visit the shrine, as promised. He also left three hundred pounds for Pastor Tienwinkel to build a small stone chapel. Word of fresh healings and Albert's actions spread rapidly: on 8 September 1603, the feast of the Birth of Our Dear Lady, it was said that twenty thousand pilgrims covered the hill.

If Isabella was the driving force behind princely attentions to the Sharp Hill, then it was only fitting. She was born in 1566, the year of the Iconoclastic Fury in the Netherlands, and now she would be the great patroness of new religious images. But whichever archduke noticed the hill first, both became convinced—after Den Bosch, after Catharina Serraerts—that their destiny lay there. Albert and Isabella traveled to the hill together for the first time in November 1603, walking daily from their quarters in Diest. Isabella, an expert seamstress, followed the old Spanish custom of sewing clothes for the image. She wrote to friends about the countless pilgrims, about the sick rising from their beds, and called it the "most beautiful thing she had ever seen." When her brother the king lay ill, she sent him shavings from the oak on the hill, to be taken with water, for this had cured many people. No doubt Isabella gave a similar drink to her husband and herself for other curative purposes: after five years of marriage she and Albert were still childless, and time was waning.

The enthusiasm of the archdukes for the Sharp Hill ensured its fame. Laypeople and plain priests such as Godfried Tienwinkel were quite capable of establishing shrines or of moving around the countryside on their own to visit one newly potent holy place after the next. But when the great lent their prestige and resources, a shrine's chances of attaining lasting fame increased. Signs of the enduring renown of the Sharp Hill were becoming unmistakable: by late 1603 and early 1604, Catholics great and small limped, rode, and walked to the hill as never before, even from across the border, while Dutch Protestants paid it the ultimate compliment: they made the shrine the chief target of their ridicule.

TWO CROWNING MIRACLES

July 1604.

The defense of Den Bosch, the crowds of pilgrims, the forty-nine documented miracles of 1603, the piles of crutches, trusses, and high-shoes left behind at the shrine as tokens of thanks for cures, all impressed Archbishop Hovius as they had the archdukes. But the shrine's two most famous miracles occurred this month.

The results of the first the archbishop saw himself in yet another interview with a healed person. This man the archbishop knew less well than he knew Catharina Serraerts, but the man's story was easy to confirm. Hans Clemens was born in Lucern in 1581, cut from the stomach of his dying mother. When he emerged, his knees were stuck to his chest and stayed that way. His legs pulled so tightly to his body that one could hardly fit a finger between his thigh and chest. As a child he learned to move by resting his hind end on the ground, leaning ahead on two tiny crutches, and swinging his bunched-up body forward.

When he was thirteen, Hans came to the Netherlands, where his father served as translator for a Polish nobleman. Two years later his father was murdered, leaving Hans an orphan. With little inheritance and no trade, Hans traveled through the land in search of charity before settling in Brussels, where he begged alms and sold crude wooden crosses. Someone sewed layers of cloth to his bottom so that he might rest comfortably. Thousands saw him near the entry to the archdukes' palace. Neighbors paid for him to learn the craft of painting so that he might quit begging. It was as an apprentice painter that he heard talk of the Sharp Hill. After dreaming twice that he stood upright there, he yearned to visit the place.

Hans's chance came this past 4 July when his master arranged a ride with an acquaintance. Arriving early, Hans scooted inside the new stone chapel to hear Mass, and he also received the host. About an hour later, he felt excessive pains in "all his members" and broke out in sweat from head to toe. When he tried to leave the chapel he became disoriented, so he stayed all day, praying before Our Dear Lady. The pains and prayers continued until evening, when he suddenly felt himself lifted from the ground—his legs had burst from their cramped position on his chest, breaking the sleeveless vest he wore in cold weather over his short body, so that he stood now on never used feet.

Finding himself in this unfamiliar position, he began to praise God and His Mother, then fell over in a great faint. People witnessing the scene rushed forward immediately, placed him in a nearby confessional chair, and covered him with blankets. Then, on weak legs, he walked unsteadily from the chapel, leaving behind his small crutches as tokens of his cure. He stayed nine more days to complete his devotions and let his legs grow stronger. People flocked to the hill just to see Hans. Medical doctors came in droves. By 15 July he was in Brussels, the star of a procession in which he walked and carried a large candle, still with much pain in his legs from the tugging of nerves and arteries. It was at the end of this procession that Hans visited Archbishop Hovius.

It was easy to be skeptical about Hans: precisely because the archbishop's society believed so strongly in miracles was the potential for fraud great. Moreover, no one could say that every detail of his story had happened the way he told it. Protestants even said that Hans had been cured naturally, by a barber-surgeon. But since at least his thirteenth year, there were hundreds who had seen Hans's unenviable condition and plenty of doctors who could testify that they had tried unsuccessfully to cure him. In the end the archbishop could not pass off the cure as the work of nature or the invention of Hans the scheming adult, and so his conviction about the supernatural powers at the hill grew.

The second crowning miracle came in September 1604, two months after the cure of Hans Clemens: Oostende finally fell to the armies of Albert. Some attributed victory to Albert's newly arrived and famous general, Ambrosius Spinola. Although the archdukes would never deny the commander's gifts, more prominent in their minds was another explanation: their fortunes in the Low

Countries had improved from the moment they began paying attention to the Sharp Hill. No matter that other port cities were soon lost to the Dutch. No matter that rebel troops near the Sharp Hill stole to the shrine by nightfall and destroyed the small stone chapel. To the archdukes these were mere annoyances. Oostende had fallen, they were sure, thanks to the Virgin on the hill. Plans for something bigger began to take shape in their minds—an entire city on the Sharp Hill, perhaps even peace in all the land.

A PROPER SHRINE

If the role of Mathias Hovius seemed rather secondary in the birth of the Sharp Hill, for a time it was. Initiative came first from Pastor Tienwinkel, pilgrims, and archdukes. But by the autumn of 1604, when it was clear that all the world was determined to visit the Sharp Hill, the archbishop grew aggressive about his particular task: making the shrine safe for orthodoxy.

Like most Catholic bishops and thinkers, the archbishop surely had mixed feelings about shrines. He believed as much as anyone in their powers and thus against Protestants would defend them to the death. But within the church they could be a nuisance and a constant source of tension. To most Catholics, the greatest attraction of shrines and all other supernatural powers offered by the church was the promise of divine aid against a host of earthly woes. That aid was real, believed the archbishop, but its true purpose was faith, not fortune: physical healing was merely a means to an end. The common and excessive emphasis on "instrumental" or this-worldly aid caused people to forget the higher purposes of divine aid, to forget the divine source of aid, or worse to use unchurched alternatives when the church's remedies seemed to fail. One such alternative, medicine, the archbishop would not have opposed: he was himself a prolific user of pharmaceutical concoctions. But he denounced magic and superstitious spells or charms, which attempted to invoke otherworldly powers without the church's authority or participation, and which focused faith on the object or the words or the healer rather than God. Such were unprofitable for genuine faith and hence for salvation.

Most objectionable to bishops were practices and remedies of pagan or even diabolic inspiration, present at shrines and elsewhere. But nearly as annoying were unauthorized rituals that drew in part upon the church's. Magical slips of papers placed in doorways for good fortune or around the necks of sick beasts contained words in the biblical languages of Hebrew, Greek, or Latin. Holy water and relics were added to magical potions, special herbs were picked on the feast of St. John the Baptist to protect homes from fire, the host was kept in one's mouth until after Mass so that it might be buried in fields to promote a good crop. And most relevant of all for the Sharp Hill, images were believed to possess power themselves, when church and archbishop taught that divine power worked *through* them.

If the dividing line between acceptable and unacceptable supernatural power was vague to many believers and outsiders, to the archbishop the test was simple: was the church in charge? To ensure his jurisdiction over the powers at the Sharp Hill, the archbishop appointed one of his own to direct it: the obvious choice, Pastor Tienwinkel. It was frantic work, given the crowds and the pastor's continuing duties in his home parish. It was also onerous, for it required more accounting than was ever expected of the pastor in asset-free Zichem.

The archbishop helped the pastor along. He drew up specific guidelines, beginning with the regulation of offer-boxes in which pilgrims dropped their coins. He stipulated how to record and store gifts of precious jewelry and clothing, including a silver cloak from Isabella. He explained how to manage generous gifts in kind from pilgrims: wax, linen, flax, fowl, and eggs. He gave the pastor permanent assistants: two priests to care for liturgical objects, watch for new miracles, report major gifts, snoop out scandalous clergymen, supervise the small store, and dress the image in proper colors. He warned the pastor to be sure only trustworthy people made and sold devotional objects — no superstitions and no blasphemous imitations, such as the heretical marionette makers across the border who earned fistfuls of money by selling Virgins on strings. He insisted that the pastor approve all confessors and see that all exorcisms were performed according to authorized rites and only after a physician's confirmation that an illness was super-natural in origin. And he visited the shrine himself regularly, miss-ing only one early audit because of an injury to his shin.

The pastor did his best not to disappoint the archbishop. He bought supplies and paid the wages of builders, priests, singers, and messengers. He lovingly composed a simple history of the hill. But as the shrine grew it all seemed a bit much for Godfried Tienwinkel. His accounts showed irregularities. Auditors forgave him because of his inexperience with such matters, but they grew weary. When at last he heard the official explanation that his pas-toral duties in Zichem made him too busy to run the Sharp Hill and that he would have to be replaced at the shrine, it must have caused him pain. Though the archbishop knew Godfried Tien-winkel's past heroics, the shrine needed more than just a "good" priest, and a new, younger man named Joost Bouckaert therefore took over in 1609.

In addition to finding the right priest, the archbishop ar-ranged for the right official history. It would include miracles, of course, but only those confirmed by authorized investigators. It would also include explanation of the purpose of miracles: to pro-mote faith in God and the church. The archbishop gave these tasks to Philip Numan, secretary of the city of Brussels, who had already interviewed a number of the cured. Secretary Numan was trained in law. He was also a poet. And his status as a layman helped ward off criticisms of clerical bias.

The secretary's official history of the Sharp Hill appeared in late 1604. It explained the standards for a miracle: cause and effect lay above or outside nature. It explained the various reasons for miracles: they happened in this particular place on the front to promote unity and peace so that Dutch Protestants might be convinced of the true church and thus end the war. It explained why miracles happened on this lonely mountain: sacred events often happened in the wild, including the Ten Commandments, the offering of Isaac, or Christ's suffering on the Mount of Olives. It explained why miracles happened at the oak: not because the tree possessed any power in its nature but because God made it holy, just as he made holy the oak where Jacob buried pagan gods, near biblical Zichem. It explained why miracles happened through the image: not because it possessed any power but because it was a prototype of the Virgin, who interceded with Christ. And it explained that miracles happened in approved ways: after a person's swallowing the host or hearing Mass or confessing, not while wearing lucky charms or chewing bits of bark from the oak or offering the equivalent of one's weight in coin or goods, all of which most people who visited the shrine often tried first. The book even prescribed rituals and rules for pilgrimage: blessings, songs for setting out and while under way, how to walk and talk, refraining from carnal relations, and so forth.

To ensure that those who could not read the histories still understood correctly, the archbishop taught in visual fashion: he had the grand oak, on which the image had rested for so long, chopped down. The practice of stripping the tree's bark, to take it home for use as an all-purpose remedy, had not only damaged the tree but blurred the lines between medicine, magic, and miracle. To discourage such vagueness, the archbishop had the oak fashioned into orthodox form: craftsmen fashioned wood from the felled tree into copies of the image of the Virgin, for display in one's home. Isabella bought several to give to friends.

Last of all the archbishop cooperated in the building of the new church and town. After the fall of Oostende, Albert proposed that the Sharp Hill be the site of a wholly separate town and parish—despite protests from battered Zichem, which would have benefited spiritually and temporally from incorporation of the shrine within its boundaries. In 1605 the archdukes granted the new town on the hill the same royal privileges enjoyed by its unlikely cousin, the faraway, worldly Oostende. They decreed that its walls would form a seven-sided star, symbol of Mary. They envisioned at the center a glorious domed church, the first in the Netherlands, covered with seven-sided stars and surrounded by a seven-sided garden. And Albert assigned Wenzel Coeberger, his architect, to develop the plan, while Archbishop Hovius saw to the hiring of stone masons who would follow instructions carefully and not get ideas of their own.

The very scale of the shrine helped it become the greatest place of pilgrimage in the Netherlands. No one could measure the influence of Mathias Hovius' regulations on the spiritual life of the place, but the tangible influence of the archdukes' campaign was unmistakable. They not only provided alms of their own but required each province to make an immodest "gift" in florins for the new church. Most provinces opposed this plan soon and long but the archdukes eventually won. Albert and Isabella still patronized older shrines at Halle or Laken, but the Sharp Hill was their favorite: it was a "national" monument to the Virgin and a symbol of the Virgin's pleasure with their rule. The shrine never gave the archdukes a child, but it did save their regime. After Oostende, never again would they be threatened by Madrid with removal from the Netherlands.

The Sharp Hill was finally a monument to peace. Victory at Oostende encouraged the archdukes to begin negotiations with the Dutch, despite opposition from courtiers in Spain. Unlike Philip III or his ministers, Albert and Isabella lived close by their Netherlandish subjects and knew the desire for peace, even if it must be had at steep prices. The fall of Oostende made the archdukes strong enough to pursue their desire, so that by 1607 a temporary truce was agreed to and talks for something more lasting were already being arranged. The cornerstone of the new church at the Sharp Hill was laid when peace finally came. For the war-weary generation of Mathias Hovius here was the last, almost unthinkable miracle.

The proper shrine, the surer circumstances of the archdukes,

and talk of peace encouraged the archbishop as well. It allowed
him to consider plans of his own for the archdiocese and for the
Netherlandish church more generally. Hence even the cautious
archbishop must have been grateful to Our Dear Lady of the Sharp
Hill. Until his final days he visited the shrine often—and not just
as administrator but as pilgrim.

So did another prominent, hard-to-convince churchman. In
1606 the nuncio Frangipani finally got his wish: he was recalled to
Italy as an ordinary bishop. But before leaving the Netherlands he
went out of his way to visit the shrine on the hill one last time, the
shrine where Catharina Serraerts and now many others were said
to have found their cures.

Pulling Up Tares

AN EVERLASTING COUNCIL

The twenty-sixth of June, 1607, the Wool Market in Mechelen.

Shortly after eight in the morning a colorful procession of clergymen favoring purple and red set out from the archbishop's residence, in the direction of St. Rombout's. As usual on such occasions they walked in order of ascending importance and brilliance. First, in surplice and stole, came representatives of the parish clergy. Then, in surplice and cope, canons of collegiate and cathedral chapters. Also in surplice and cope were the next group, delegates of abbeys and monasteries, with abbots wearing miters as well. Last and more ornate were the bishops, each in surplice, toga, cope, and miter, each carrying a staff, and each with a dignity-boosting entourage of chaplains. At the very end of the procession, greatest and most brilliant of all, walked Mathias Hovius, who had called everyone together.

These hundred or so notables were in town for a council of the church province of Mechelen (which included the archdiocese and its six neighboring dioceses). Though every province in the entire church was supposed to hold such a council every three years, to ratify the decrees of Trent and adapt them to local needs, almost none did: only two provincial councils had been held in Mechelen, for instance, the last in 1574. This was largely because of war, but here in 1607, with the whiff of peace in the air, Archbishop

preceding page: Pieter Bruegel, *The Devil Sowing Tares*
Private collection

Hovius decided it was finally time for another. His official letter of convocation had gone out in February. By today the delegates were gathered at last.

They entered the cathedral to hear the Mass of the Holy Spirit. Then they marched again, this time to the snugger confines of the chapel in the archbishop's new seminary, where most of the council's sessions would be held. Here the archbishop declared the council open and invoked the protection over it of the Holy Spirit. Plenipotentiaries were appointed to inspect credentials of all delegates. Notaries and secretaries were chosen to make notes. Messengers were selected to run errands. One delegate, Henri Costerius, caused a scene when he observed that only the pope in a general council, and not a mere archbishop, had the right to invoke the Holy Spirit. But discussion was short, the meeting disbanded, and the council moved forward.

Real work began the next day when Archbishop Hovius, full of hope, set forth in a long, echoing speech his vision of the council. It elaborated a theme already stated in his letter of convocation: "When the masses sleep, the enemy sows tares in the field of the Lord, and through this scandal and heresy take root. That is why the shepherds of the church must never sleep, but always keep alert." Surely the archbishop knew that shepherds watched sheep, not grain, but his point was unmistakable: good religion in the land was up to the clergy. It was an old clerical bias, reflected as well in the very composition of delegates to the council (clergy one and all): the clergy *was* the church. While clerks scribbled and brightly robed delegates listened, the archbishop ascended the pulpit and spoke in his best Ciceronian Latin, reserved for just such occasions.

> Most Reverend Fathers, Reverend and Venerable Lords, I give thanks for the divine bounty which in this fearful time of war has stirred our spirits and kept you safe on your journeys, so that you are able to come together to this holy convocation, convened for our sal-

vation. As it is incumbent upon me to reveal the reasons for convening this council and to propose a certain method of conducting it, I cannot do better than to place before your eyes the exhortation of Nehemiah, that most pious and zealous of prophets, whose words these are: "Come let us build the walls of Jerusalem, for even we are not beyond reproach."

Led back to Jerusalem from captivity in Persia, the tribes of Judah and Benjamin discovered that the temple had been burned, the courtyards were grown over, the Levite priests were degraded, the mouths of hoary-headed lords were closed, the rituals prescribed by sacred law were polluted and neglected, the people of Israel had mingled with Gentiles or were held captive by the godless. On all sides Israel was surrounded by enemies, of God and of themselves—all this, distressingly, because of their sins. In the words of Jeremiah the prophet, "Jerusalem has sinned, and for that reason she has become infirm."

Is our situation dissimilar from theirs? How many churches have been burned? How many convents devastated? How many altars overturned? If physical ruin is not enough, what of spiritual? How many offenses have grown up out of these unlucky times? Where is catechism still taught? There are no priests in the country and few in cities. The divine office is sloppy. Vestments are contemptibly shabby and cheap. Scholars are weak in grammar. Seeds of heresy have sprouted in many souls. Pernicious books land in unsuspecting hands. Brothers, neighbors, and friends across the border live in captivity and in peril of their salvation. And this because of our sins—as long as we remain as dried wood rather than vines which produce fruit for the Lord, as long as my soul makes me nauseous over the dust on the tombs of saints, as long as priests, who have been negligent, tremble at the filth, as long as God seems to be worshiped here by lips alone.

If we have taken long to convene the council, surely this was because of war and the advice of the reverend nuncio Ottavio Frangipani (since departed), to await better times. In the meantime all have suffered. God cast darkness on the land and it became night; and during the night the beasts of the forest came forth — those selfsame brutes, those heretics, that infest the path and that roar like whelps of lions as they snatch food for themselves because their souls have been abandoned by God. But the sun of peace now lies on the horizon and I have taken care to guard those whelps in their lairs. Now is the time for us to gird ourselves about with piety for this work. Now is the time for us to undertake to purify, sanctify, and restore good counsels, lest the Lord God upbraid us for yet a while longer on account of our negligence, as foretold by his prophet Jeremiah: "Oh idle Shepherd who has forsaken the flock!" Truly if we fix our gaze upon nothing, as an idle man does, we will not see the abuses and scandals we must correct.

Just as forty-two thousand Israelites rebuilt the walls of Jerusalem as if one man, so must this council proceed. And when this unity is achieved, we shall no longer be like those who vainly undertook to build the Tower of Babel. Instead, we will hearken to the Apostle Paul: "Brethren, I beseech you, in the name of our Lord Jesus Christ, to all speak with one accord and to have no quarrels among you." Each of you will be permitted to step forward at this council and speak to matters at hand. But such must be done in order and love. Each must identify himself. Each much await his turn. Each must speak with the good of all in mind, not merely himself. Each must remember that Christian humility requires us to submit to others and avoid being too fond of our own opinions. Remember what Luke, the blessed author of the Gospel, said concerning the nascent Church: that all the faithful were truly of one heart and mind. Let such singleness be ours even now. Let us, the wise Architects of the church, restore what has collapsed by building upon the cornerstone of piety.

Let each consider, says the Apostle, how he should build: for God ordains skillful spirits to be Priests and Pastors of the Church, as he said of Jeremiah: "Behold, I have established you this day over the peoples and kingdoms, that you may pluck out and destroy, build up and plant." Let us therefore pluck out the tares we find growing in the Lord's field and the thickets which spring up in the courts of the Lord. Let us destroy the evils produced by the licentiousness of times past. Let us plant the young shoots of sound laws and godly constitutions from divers places, whence they have produced the fruit of pious works and of true ecclesiastical life.

And because individually we cannot accomplish all things, let us follow Nehemiah's example and train many for the duties of Pastor, taking special care to build and endow seminaries, a charge the Sacred Council of Trent wishes foremost in our minds. For the harvest is great in all directions, but the laborers, alas! exceeding few. Let us plant starting with ourselves. Clearly a man must first clean out his own garden before he can remove the muck of another. Clearly each can show, by prompt obedience to the ordinances that shall be decided in this sacred Assembly, that he prizes the comeliness of the house of God. For without true and perfect obedience this council will bring forth no fruit.

For this purpose no one is to call upon any customs or privileges to resist the decrees of this council or the Council of Trent, but everyone shall pull up weeds of the past to make room for better plants. No one, as Joshua wrote, shall erect one altar against another altar. Let no one believe himself exempt from the law of God or the delegates of the Holy See. I exhort you in a few words with the Apostle: "Obey your superiors, and submit to them; for they keep vigil on behalf of your souls as though they will have to give an accounting for them." Let each man consider with soberness that no field, no garden, is so well cultivated that it requires no weeding or tilling. Likewise no house is so meticulously constructed that it does not at some time require repair. As the prophet Hosea warned the disobedient, "you will fall." Oh how fearsome are the threats of God! Oh how serious and exceedingly hateful the sin of contradicting the King of Heaven! Oh how wretched, how miserable, I tell you, those pastors of God who produce no fruit.

Let us conclude with Nehemiah's words: "We are not beyond reproach." In ages past there was a temple of astounding beauty, famous in all the world, in the royal city of Jerusalem. There was no one, Jew or Gentile, who did not stand in awe of her. But lo! she was betrayed to burning and pillaging, and mockery, and set before the reproach of Gentiles, who said: "This is the city of consummate beauty, the glory of the entire world?" So do our enemies mock us now. They mock the destruction of temples and monasteries, the impoverishment of churches, and the priestly office itself. They rule states once Catholic. Such is the shame and neglect of the Church! Such is the injury to our true faith and the blasphemy to God. As I read in a tract not long ago, our adversaries rashly say against us that their prosperity and our suffering prove the truth of their religion. This we know to be nothing if not perfidy. Oh cursed pride! Oh fearful neglect! Can we tolerate it much longer? Let us work, Fathers, let us work, I say, to make this instead an occasion of reproach for our enemies, that they may know our calamities spring not from their rectitude but from our sins, from our neglect of our spirits and duties, and from our squeamishness in reverencing God. Let us lift ourselves from within and let us secure for all men the thing for which this council was convened.

Let us pluck up the tares. Let us shun scandal and abuse. Let us mend our ways and destroy evil. Let us build the walls of Jerusalem. Let us construct a living temple. Let us plant shoots of youthful piety and dress our gardens with strong, new plants, by bettering our lives, repairing walls, and restoring reverence for the Church and the Lord. And at length let us hope that when the causes are removed, reproach will be lifted. Then will the former honor, authority, and dignity possessed by the Church return. Then will those who fled the Church in times past, who deserted it and destroyed it as they would a sinking ship or ruined house, return to a Church purified and restored. Then, in the end, will they visit, build, and adorn it with us.

In the audience were indeed plenty who, as the archbishop hinted, had come to resist rather than support the council. But for now, after this climactic ending, all peacefully submitted to the usual formalities, which meant coming forward to make a profession of faith and to promise acceptance of the Council of Trent. Then all listened again as the topics of reforms proposed by the archbishop for this council—from sacraments to clerical residence, all drawn from Trent—were read aloud. Some discussion ensued, but most was reserved for the afternoon, when delegates divided into separate groups of pastors, chapters, abbeys, and bishops, to discuss proposed decrees at length.

Thus did the council proceed for several weeks—plenary session in the morning, separate conclaves in the afternoon—until its conclusion on 20 July, the feast of St. Margaret. So lasting was its work that no Council of Mechelen was ever held again: its decrees would serve as the foundation of the Netherlandish church for generations to come.

A TROUBLED COUNCIL

The first week and before.

The bright robes, the dramatic speeches, the unexpected fits of cooperation, the seemingly eternal decrees—these were what outsiders saw of the Council of Mechelen. But to those on the inside, such as Archbishop Hovius, the council was more like a war, featuring regular skirmishes, the taking of prisoners, and confused, uncertain endings. Indeed from the participants' point of view the reason no other Council of Mechelen was ever called again (and why few were held at all around Catholic Europe) may have been not because such councils were so decisive, but because they were so much trouble.

Troubles beset the Council of Mechelen even before the opening procession. From the moment the council was announced in February, the thoughts of invitees turned predictably to precedence: which chapter or monastery or bishop should go first (least) and last (greatest) during all the marching, sitting, standing, kneeling, bowing, and cap removing that would take place at the council? Most of the time the clergy who made up these assorted institutions were never together in one place; they could therefore happily assume that they were superior to all rivals. But at the council a definite order would be established, and so anxiety set in. There could be no thought of obscuring status, such as by proceeding alphabetically. Instead all supposed that one's place in the various processions and services rightly proclaimed one's rank to the world: the first truly were last and the last truly were first.

All parties could generally agree on the basic order among groups: the lowly parish clergy first, then chapters, abbeys, and bishops. But who was first and last *within* each group? Chapters fretted most. All agreed that the cathedral chapter of St. Rombout's was greatest among chapters, and therefore last, but who should come immediately before them? Chapters from Gent, Brugge, and Antwerp all laid claim. Lawyers were called in. Angry letters flew across the land, with angry canons not far behind, on their way to attend emergency meetings regarding precedent. The archbishop proposed a solution but to no avail. Nothing was decided by the opening procession described above: the order observed there was merely temporary. Nothing was decided by the next procession, either, or the next, not even after still more committees of learned men were formed to study the disputes. Instead tempers flared hotter. By the time the council ended, the debate over precedence raged on, unresolved as ever.

A second and more serious trouble in the ecclesiastical air was anticipated in the archbishop's opening speech: resistance to the very notion of a council. All around Catholic Europe, bishops liked provincial councils while few others did. Bishops called such councils. Bishops enjoyed the highest rank at such councils. Bishops invited many to their councils but made sure only bishops had a vote. And bishops used these councils to increase their authority at the expense of all competitors: in a bishop's mind, his authority within his diocese must be supreme and indivisible. Many parish clergy might go along with this and submit to bishops without a peep. But near-equals of bishops, such as great monasteries and chapters, all of whom could wave fistfuls of ancient parchment to prove their eternal independence, wished not to submit at all.

Once again chapters led the resistance. Because the Council of Trent formally subjected chapters to the authority of bishops (while exempting many monasteries), the chapters had most to lose from a provincial council. That was why numerous chapters sent no delegates at all to the Council of Mechelen, as if to ignore it. That was why chapters that did send delegates gave strict instructions to oppose all decrees that threatened their independence or implied submission to bishops. And that was why Archbishop Hovius called all bishops early to Mechelen to discuss specific plans for subjecting chapters—at the council and beyond.

Another source of opposition to the council, albeit a more subtle one, came from another competitor of bishops for authority: Rome. Though Trent required provinces to hold councils every three years and individual dioceses to hold them every year, Rome hardly complained when few did. Provincial and diocesan councils strengthened the local church, legally and emotionally, at the expense of the universal. Provincial and diocesan councils did such things as force chapters to renounce the jurisdiction of Rome and accept the jurisdiction of bishops. No wonder Rome became, willingly, the great hope of chapters and all other institutions that sought independence from local bishops. No wonder Rome would drag out the process of confirming the council, and then only after various decrees were altered in Rome's favor. No wonder Rome told the nuncio in Brussels not to attend the Council of Mechelen, and even recalled him to Italy days before it began. And no wonder the next nuncio arrived in Brussels just days after the council ended, his sole charge in the meantime having been to keep a distant watch on the proceedings through correspondence with one of the delegates there, the old papal loyalist Henri Costerius.

Here was the final and ugliest trouble of all at the Council of Mechelen: this same Henri Costerius, ever the bosom friend of Rome, was by the time of the provincial council the bitter rival of Mathias Hovius. When the archbishop mentioned in his opening speech the need for polite conversation and the avoidance of discord, he had in mind not only stubborn chapters but this particular man.

Throughout the first week of the council, Henri Costerius appeared intent on disrupting things any way he could. He was in Mechelen as delegate of the scattered chapter of Bergen op Zoom, a Dutch town, and as such had the right to voice opinion during the afternoon conclave of chapters. But this was not enough for him. He insisted upon being heard as well during the morning, plenary sessions. And he appeared there not as a spokesman for chapters but as a lone, heroic cavalier—against Mathias Hovius.

To seemingly all of the archbishop's proposed decrees the protonotary raised loud complaint or amendment: on confession, on the profession of faith, on baptism, and more. Here was the drop that caused the bucketful of tension between the two men to overflow, for after a week of such speeches the archbishop decided he had heard enough. During the bishops' afternoon conclave of 4 July, Mathias Hovius persuaded his peers that the apostolic protonotary Henri Costerius should be locked up. To avoid scandal, the arrest would be made late that night while all the delegates slept.

FALL OF A PURPLE ONE

Like the wall around Jerusalem, that between archbishop and protonotary was not built in a day.

It may have begun in 1587, when Henri Costerius vacated his first pastorship under a cloud of suspicion, only to land, characteristically, in an even better position: vice-rector of the prestigious cathedral of Antwerp. Suspicions grew in 1590, when Vice-Rector Costerius wrote his first sensational and dubious book, on miracles, relics, and werewolves, including a self-important account of the many miracles he had worked personally by means of his jaw-dropping collection of relics. Suspicions deepened in 1595, when Henri Costerius became a canon in the chapter of St. Goedele's in Brussels, was granted the title of scholaster, or supervisor of local schools, and commenced arguing with everyone in sight about education. And certainly there was ill feeling left over in the archbishop from Henri Costerius' infamous trip to Rome, where from 1597 to 1600 he so bleakly portrayed the abilities of such current

Netherlandish bishops as Mathias Hovius and where he had intrigued so shamelessly to become a bishop himself.

But the first sure and open conflict between archbishop and protonotary occurred only in 1602, shortly after they had teamed up for their inglorious conquest of Affligem. The initial cause of the conflict was the protonotary's plan, supposedly endorsed by the pope, to open a school in Brussels for poor boys who hoped to become priests. The school itself the archbishop could hardly oppose, especially because it seemed to have the pope's support. But Archbishop Hovius detested the protonotary's flamboyant means of establishing it. In order to house his school, for instance, the protonotary, through treachery, took over part of the monastery of the local Bogards, a poor order of religious. Then, in order to pay his teachers, the protonotary sent schoolboys in packs into the streets of Brussels to beg, virtually compelling scandalized burghers to give alms. When Archbishop Hovius and the nuncio Frangipani questioned his methods, the protonotary simply responded that his school was approved by the pope: who were they to obstruct it?

Such a response hardly pleased Mathias Hovius. Neither did it please the Bogards, who bore the protonotary a heavy grudge for having invaded their convent. At first the monks simply made life difficult for the schoolboys—barricading doors, threatening boys with harm, and shortening the rope on the church's bell so the boys could not reach to ring it. But in early 1603 the monks grew much more serious in their efforts: now they decided to attack the protonotary's morals. They circulated anonymously around Brussels a pamphlet accusing Henri Costerius of forging documents, employing fake relics, performing dubious exorcisms (especially on women), violating the vow of chastity, and engaging in magic, thievery, and other crimes. Especially the female convent of St. Elisabeth, where the protonotary held the office of permanent confessor, figured prominently in the charges.

An angry Henri Costerius demanded that the Bogards appear before the nuncio to offer proof of their charges. (The protonotary might as easily have charged the monks in the archbishop's diocesan court, but he knew where his power lay.) When the Bogards thrice failed to appear as ordered, the nuncio prepared a standard letter of purgation for the protonotary and ordered all accusers to cease such talk for eternity. Now Protonotary Costerius was more confident than ever—so much that he even dared to ask Archbishop Hovius for a letter of recommendation to the archdukes. Clearly he still wanted to be bishop.

Mathias Hovius, however, was more disturbed than ever. Though the Bogards of Brussels were hardly pillars of virtue themselves, the archbishop saw enough in their claims about the protonotary's easy morals to prompt investigation. And what he found was enough to allow him to remove Henri Costerius as confessor of St. Elisabeth's, and to prohibit him forthwith from confessing and exorcising in all the archdiocese.

Humiliated, the protonotary turned again to the nuncio. Ottavio Frangipani did not particularly like Henri Costerius, but the nuncio's unstated credo was never to make enemies—especially when they had influence with his superiors in Rome—so he at least listened. How was it possible, lamented the protonotary, that the archbishop would treat him this way after he had supported the archbishop in so many endeavors? If the nuncio nodded sympathetically, for he had been present when the protonotary had so mercilessly subjected Affligem, still he did not act. Impatient for action, and sure of his connections in Rome, Henri Costerius therefore decided to do something himself: he had one of the notaries in his employ deliver an insulting tract—"a famous libel," said the nuncio—to the archbishop in person.

No record survived of the archbishop's reaction, but surely this was the deed that caused him to break with the protonotary forever. Though open conflict between the two men apparently ceased for the next several years, it was not because the matter was resolved. Rather both men bided their time. To attack someone so well connected in Rome, the archbishop would have to await the perfect moment. To conspire successfully against an archbishop, the protonotary would have to do the same, not to mention shoring up apostolic support in Rome. The moment awaited by both men seemed to arrive with the announcement of the Provincial Council of Mechelen, to open in June 1607. Here was new and genuine opportunity for each to take decisive action against the other. The protonotary decided to attend the council by any means possible, in order to wreak havoc, while the archbishop had a plan of his own.

That Archbishop Hovius decided to move against Henri Costerius at the provincial council was due not merely to the protonotary's overbearing, critical speeches delivered during the first week, nor even the fortuitous discovery by plenipotentiaries that the proto-notary's credentials to the council were forged: he had no real authority to be there at all. These were mere bonuses, added to an already sufficient pile of incriminating evidence. Rather, the arch-bishop waited until the Council of Mechelen to act because of the occasion itself.

The very publicness of the council offered specific advantages to the archbishop. If the nuncio attended, as the archbishop had invited him to do, and a conflict between archbishop and protonotary broke out, then the nuncio and Rome would have to choose sides—and the archbishop had little doubt they would have to choose his. Rome wanted to be put in no such position. Its channels of intelligence were sufficient to warn of an imminent confrontation between archbishop and protonotary, and of a growing stack of evidence against the latter: it took no genius to see the undesirability of Rome's being appealed to in public by a discredited Henri Costerius. That, as much as Rome's innate jealousy of councils, was surely why the nuncio was recalled to Italy just before the Council of Mechelen began.

Whether the nuncio attended or not, the council could work to the archbishop's advantage in another way: all fellow bishops would be present to offer him support. Despite any differences over hairstyles, all bishops could agree on their enmity for Henri Costerius, "the purple one," as the archbishop called him, in reference to his protonotarial robes. All bishops recognized that but for the grace of God any one of them might just as easily be suffering the protonotary's wrath. Hence, at the secret meeting on 4 July, when all bishops agreed to the arrest, they also agreed to send to Rome letters of justification for Mathias Hovius. Rome could hardly ignore such distinguished support for the archbishop, and such eminent disdain for the protonotary.

Finally, the council offered a third advantage: an opportunity for the archbishop to get the strong arm of the state publicly on his side. On 3 July, the day before the protonotary's arrest, there had arrived at the council — coincidentally? — Jacob Liebaert, chief justice of the Grand Council, with a letter from the archdukes offering the state's support. Though such support may have been meant in a general sense, the archbishop had a very specific purpose in mind. It was the archbishop who persuaded fellow bishops to accept the chief justice's offer, which meant allowing him, a layman, to attend the council's all-clerical proceedings. It was also the archbishop who brought Justice Liebaert to the fateful meeting of the bishops on 4 July, when the arrest of Henri Costerius was planned.

With local church and state behind him, with the stack of evidence rising, and with the international church sufficiently out of the picture, the archbishop now felt sure enough to act. On the night of 4–5 July, guards roused Henri Costerius from his bed and took him to the archbishop's jail — the same place where Franciscus Pussius had once tried to hang himself. At daybreak, the six bishops of the province dispatched their letters of justification to Rome.

FINALE

5–20 July 1607.

The archbishop must have reflected more than once on the similarities between Canons Pussius and Costerius: both brazenly attacked his name in word and print, and both were well-placed men. Yet ultimately Canon Pussius was a nuisance and little more, much like the hero of a recent Spanish novel who tilted harmlessly at windmills. Henri Costerius, on the other hand, was a foe of real intrigue with such powerful patrons as the pope's nephew, Cardinal Borghese, in Rome. Henri Costerius was therefore Pussius with a difference, and his arrest would not go unnoticed, not even in distant places.

Despite the attempt to keep the arrest of the protonotary quiet, every delegate knew about it soon after awaking on 5 July. Surely the matter weighed heavily on minds and tongues during the council's remaining two weeks, but just as surely did the council's work proceed more smoothly. With the protonotary gone, now there was virtually no debate on any of the archbishop's proposed decrees: not on sacraments, worship, preaching, seminaries, repair of churches, or ecclesiastical jurisdiction. Not even the decrees that subjected chapters, presented on 11 July, provoked any debate, but in this case it was not for want of will: it was because bishops, the only participants with a vote, simply decided that there would be no debate. They then declared that all past and current privileges contradicting the Council of Trent—including privileges granted by popes—were henceforth void. At this even the cathedral chapter of St. Rombout's, the archbishop's usually reliable ally, joined with every other chapter in protest. In response the archbishop drily reminded the delegates that they were at the council merely to advise, not vote. This was a less severe action than that of the Bishop of Cuenca, in Spain, who at his diocesan council insisted that delegates approve all decrees sight unseen. Still, Archbishop Hovius' relative lack of severity hardly mollified chapters.

For another week the bishops of the council kept approving decrees while chapters kept grumbling. And then, just like the Council of Trent, the third Provincial Council of Mechelen suddenly ended, on 20 July. All decrees were read aloud a final time, all at once. A last Te Deum was said. Archbishop Hovius invoked

the prayer "Let Us Recede in Peace." He embraced each departing
bishop but no canon. Final conclaves were held: Chapters met to
organize a protest to Rome. Monasteries and parish clergy met to
voice small protests on points that displeased them. And bishops
met to agree on the need for a uniform set of statutes for diocesan courts, and a uniform catechism for children. Last of all, the
bishops made sure to appoint delegates to seek confirmation of the
council's decrees by Rome and Brussels.

Here, despite the apparent finality of the council's closing Te
Deum, was the bishops' most important work yet: convincing the
universal church, and the central government of the land, to give
the decrees of the Council of Mechelen the force of canon and
civil law. The shaping of a godly society could hardly be left to
individual consciences alone—it required a strong dose of enforcement. And so while other delegates headed home from Mechelen, Denis Christophori of Brugge, one of the council's secretaries,
journeyed to Rome to obtain approval, while the archbishop and
two fellow bishops made an appointment at the archdukes' palace
in Brussels.

In Rome, it was no surprise that the curia showed itself not
entirely pleased with the council's decrees: a generation before,
the curia had treated the decrees of Carlo Borromeo, the age's
most famous archbishop, quite the same. Bishops such as Borromeo or Mathias Hovius regarded themselves not as mere agents
of Rome but as independent or at least intermediate authorities
in charge of their local church. To assert its own authority over
local churches was precisely why Rome took so long to inspect
and approve provincial councils: the very act of approval implicitly
reinforced Rome's supremacy in deed, while the revision of decrees reinforced that supremacy in word. And so Rome sat on
Mechelen's decrees for months, and then insisted on a number
of revisions. The process was a wearing one—so wearing that a
tired Archbishop Hovius even instructed Secretary Christophori
to drop certain decrees aimed at chapters if this would move things

along. After various concessions and the usual assortment of well-placed gifts from the Netherlandish side, Rome finally confirmed an amended set of decrees a year later, in the summer of 1608.

Meanwhile, approval of the council's decrees proceeded hardly any faster in Brussels. For all their piety, for all their willingness to assist in the arrest of such nefarious characters as Henri Costerius, for all the justifiable hopes the archbishop had of their Most Catholic cooperation, the archdukes were in truth also the final formidable competitor of bishops for authority over religious life in the land. Albert and Isabella had proven already that they would cooperate with the church when it suited their interests, as it often did, and that they would proclaim the church's laws as their laws, for this was a Catholic state. But they had shown as well that they did not wish to be told by Rome or by local bishops how actually to go about their work. In short, they wished to have the last word on policy in their dominions, including religious policy. Hence the archdukes too were slow to confirm the Council of Mechelen—so slow that the archbishop finally had to compose the official proclamation himself for the archdukes' signature, and engage in much tactful prodding thereafter. At last, in September 1608, the archdukes confirmed the decrees of the Council of Mechelen, with an enthusiasm as bridled as Rome's and with similar qualification: the decrees would be law insofar as they violated none of the rights of the archdukes or their vassals. Simple as this sounded, it in fact made the archdukes the ultimate arbiters of the council and thus of religious life in all the land. This worked to the archbishop's advantage when the archdukes happened to agree with him—as when the archdukes compelled the reluctant cities of Brussels and Den Bosch to accept the council's decrees. But when the archdukes did nothing the archbishop had little recourse.

After these assorted and faint confirmations, the provincial council was finished, at least in word. What remained was the biggest question of all: to what extent would Rome, Brussels, and even the local church enforce its decrees? The answer would only begin to become clear during the archbishop's remaining years.

More conclusive than the fate of the decrees was the fate of the council's would-be star, Henri Costerius.

When the council ended, he was still in jail, and the biggest question on minds was: would Rome rescue him? Cardinal Borghese urged the brand-new nuncio in Brussels, twenty-eight-year-old Guido Bentivoglio, to assert jurisdiction over the protonotary. For as an apostolic protonotary Henri Costerius could insist that if he was to be tried, then it must occur in a papal court rather than a mere bishop's court. Yet Archbishop Hovius was determined, more than in the instance of Franciscus Pussius, not only to bring the case to trial but to try it in his own diocesan court. In the end the nuncio, more aware of the protonotary's crimes and of local ecclesiastical realities, recommended to Rome that the case be left with the archbishop. The cardinal finally agreed, for he "could not doubt" the integrity of Mathias Hovius. Still, he instructed the nuncio to keep an eye on things, lest the archbishop allow his passion for revenge to overwhelm justice.

For the next year, while Rome watched out of the corner of its eye and while the protonotary was moved to the more secure prison of the archdukes, in Vilvoorde, the archbishop prepared his case, sending agents here and there to investigate further the misdeeds of Henri Costerius. The pile of evidence grew immense, thanks to the testimony of more than fifty witnesses, and featured tales far more serious than even the archbishop had imagined: all the signs of self-aggrandizement, all the rumors of personal corruption, proved true. Henri Costerius was nothing more than a priest who purported to work miracles through his vast collection of holy relics but who in truth forged relics and abused his position to satisfy his lusts—for power and otherwise.

It was discovered, for instance, that while Costerius was vice-rector of the cathedral of Antwerp in the 1590s, he had once presented the chapter with a gift of dubious relics that he claimed be-

longed to St. Fredegandus, and which chapter and bishops quietly
let gather dust in an archive.

It was told by Wenzel Coeberger, architect of the Sharp Hill
and the protonotary's one-time companion, that he had seen the
protonotary acting strangely in regard to certain relics in Rome.
In the late sixteenth century the catacombs were once more giving
up thousands of bones—one zealot suggested that the remains of
174,000 early Christian martyrs graced a single site. Such lands as
the Spanish Netherlands, where altars had been obliterated and
stripped of relics, were eager to have them, and Henri Costerius
was unusually eager to provide. One day the well-connected Master Coeberger arranged, at the protonotary's request, an unusual
meeting in the crypt of St. Peter's basilica, amidst the bones and remains of centuries of Christianity. At this meeting the sacristan of
St. Peter's, the under-sacristan, and a local nobleman were to attest
that certain drawings and objects in the protonotary's possession
were faithful copies of actual relics in the crypt. These drawings
included a sweat-cloth of St. Veronica (sketched by Wenzel Coeberger himself), two blood-stained iron lances patterned after the
Holy Lance that pierced the side of Christ, portraits of Saints Peter
and Paul based on the original that Pope Sylvester V showed the
Emperor Constantine, and a painting of the throne of St. Peter.
Objects in the protonotary's possession, for which he likewise
sought attestations as faithful copies, included two copies of nails
of the Holy Cross and an original silver piece from the thirty for
which Judas betrayed Jesus. Here was a hall of fame of the early
Christian church. The question implied now by Wenzel Coeberger,
to the archbishop's investigators, was this: had Henri Costerius
brought back to the Low Countries these copies of lances and
sweat-cloths and nails and other objects and claimed they were
more than copies? The investigators suspected this to be the case
indeed, for there was no documentation for the protonotary's relics
—aside from a letter signed by the nuncio Frangipani that they
appeared real. But the nuncio had signed this letter simply on
the strength of the protonotary's word and nothing else. Surely

this testimony of the architect Coeberger, as much as any other testimony, caused the archbishop's investigators to conclude that virtually all relics owned by Henri Costerius were fakes. So troubling and far-reaching was news of the protonotary's activities that keepers of the catacomb of Santa Lucina in Rome, where Henri Costerius had so often worked, henceforth allowed excavations there only with formal permission.

Evidence of forgery would alone have landed the protonotary in trouble with Mathias Hovius, who hardly wanted priests adding to the confusion of an already unmanageable universe of holy remains. But even worse was evidence of how the protonotary unscrupulously used those forgeries, especially among women. In one early tract Henri Costerius alluded to his special ability to heal "very discrete weaknesses of women toward diverse temptations of the evil one," temptations that in this context were often of a sexual nature. In another he described exorcising a possessed girl by placing a relic on her tormented body parts. But more direct proof of carnal misdeeds came especially from his former subjects, the nuns of St. Elisabeth's in Brussels. The old accusations of the Bogards were true after all, and more.

These nuns and still other witnesses testified that Henri Costerius routinely offered the host to women without ceremony and after idle rather than reverent conversation. On occasion he touched the host, or a cross, or relics, to the ears, mouth, and bare breasts of female penitents, and to other "indecent parts of the body." He sang in their presence obscene songs about relics. He pulverized relics, then mixed them with ashes and holy water to make a plaster, which he then applied to the naked bodies of virgins, under pretext of driving out devils from their unpossessed bodies. He shut himself up with married and unmarried women in suspect places and times, undressed himself and undressed them, then touched their "private parts" with relics or placed his tongue in the patient's mouth, claiming these were methods of exorcism. He compelled at least six nuns to go along with such techniques by threatening to reveal to the world secrets they had told him in confession. In addition to these charges there came from boys who had once attended his seminary whispers of sodomy, but these were not pursued: his sins against women and relics would suffice.

The archbishop's court announced its verdict on 5 July 1608, one year to the day after the arrest of Henri Costerius at the Council of Mechelen. It presented that verdict not to the nuncio but to Albert's Council of State, as if this body, more predictable and agreeable than Rome on this matter, was the final authority. The archbishop also allowed justices of the secular Grand Council in Mechelen to study themselves the entire mountainous file of evidence against the man. Both bodies quite agreed with the verdict of the archbishop's court. With no opposition from the only entities that might have saved Henri Costerius — the state or the nuncio — the verdict itself was finally read to the protonotary in his cell, and put into effect. He was forever banned from serving at the altar. He was stripped of all benefices and incomes, which were now used to pay the expenses of the trial. He was to remain in prison forever. The libel he had composed against the archbishop was torn to pieces and burned before him. And at last he was ordered to kneel before Archbishop Hovius to ask forgiveness and recant his slanders.

The verdict made no mention that the biggest crime of Henri Costerius may have been the threat he posed to the authority of Mathias Hovius. It did not address whether those who offered testimony against the protonotary might have done so out of fear, or after being prompted, or in anticipation of what investigators wanted to hear. Such possibilities required no mention, for the archbishop was sure of his cause. He therefore simply thanked the Council of State for its support. His only concern now was that the protonotary might still have nerve enough to appeal the decision of the diocesan court to Rome. "If he is allowed to appeal this sentence," Hovius wrote, "then, knowing his character, I think I can predict the outcome: for the rest of my life I'll be in a state of war." In fact, when the Antichrist appeared on earth, wrote the archbishop, it would hardly be surprising if he did not use the same techniques as Henri Costerius.

The protonotary did appeal to Rome, and to public opinion. Like the devil in a font of holy water, he sent still more tracts into the streets of Brussels. But the tracts persuaded few, and Rome did not hear his appeal after all—even if Cardinal Borghese harbored suspicions about the legal procedures employed against Henri Costerius, and even if Rome needled the archbishop by dragging out confirmation of his provincial council. In the end the nuncio Bentivoglio saw that it was not in Rome's interest to keep fighting for such a tragic figure as the protonotary. The nuncio therefore did nothing to prevent shutting up the man forever in solitary confinement, with no visitors except his lawyer, and certainly no paper, pen, or ink. There was to be no rescuing of the man who wanted to be bishop. At last this tare, sown at night in the field of the Lord, was finally rooted out.

Three Pastors

The ninth of April, 1609, the square of Antwerp.

After years of skillful bluffing, brought on by even more years of inconclusive fighting, negotiators of Albert and Isabella on one side and the rebellious Dutch Republic on the other finally agreed to peace. Amid much pomp and bell-ringing, and just before even more drink, dance, and song, both parties signed a document saying they would cease their fighting for twelve years.

Most inhabitants of the Spanish Netherlands were overjoyed at this event, but few more so than Mathias Hovius. Now that sinister protonotaries were in prison, now that demented canons were far away, now that headstrong monks were subjected, now that decrees for proper religious living were in place, and especially now that soldiers were at rest, the archbishop could turn fully to his real work as shepherd. He prepared to lay the cornerstone of the church at the Sharp Hill. He called a diocesan council in Mechelen to follow up his provincial council. He traveled without fear around the archdiocese to visit, confirm, consecrate, preach, and say Mass—far from the day in 1580 when he walked to Leuven cloaked only in anxiety and a smock. But most of all he could labor as never before for the betterment of his undershepherds, the parish priests, who moved among the flock even more than he.

From his reports to Rome, who would have known that his pastors needed betterment at all? In his report of 1606 he wrote that pastors were few but sound, thank God, and caused no last-ing scandal in any parish of the archdiocese. Later observers would confirm this, praising the "glorious diligence" of this reforming generation of pastors and concluding that the truly scandalous were few. But within his circle of trust the archbishop showed a great deal more concern. Inside this circle his point of view was not distant and clear, filtered by detail-obscuring centuries or gen-eralizations, but up-close and muddled, in the very thick of things. Early and late, young and old, in health and in sickness, hundreds of pastors paraded through the audience chambers and diaries of Archbishop Hovius. Some were there to bask in the warmth of approval, but still more were there because of troubles: the huge size of the archdiocese meant that the adage about squeaky wheels prevailed. Though at first glance these troubles were as varied as recipes for Flemish stew, decades as a parish priest and bishop had taught Mathias Hovius the fundamental ingredients in all pas-torly woes: not enough income, not enough discipline, not enough pastors.

THE PRINCE OF TITHES

In the days of peace, when the sun was August hot and fields shim-mered with gold, the thoughts of some rural people still turned to war. This was not war with soldiers, who now yielded their traditional strongholds in the farmyards and grainbins of Bra-bant and Flanders, but between priests and parishioners. Absent from the tranquil Netherlandish landscapes immortalized by three generations of Bruegels, unpictured among the groaning wag-ons, bundled sheaves, or scythe-swinging, basket-carrying, lunch-breaking, nap-taking peasants, were sharp words and outright blows over that vexing and eternal question: how much grain was owed the servants of God?

On the surface the principle seemed simple enough: all cul-tivated fields and farmyard animals were subject to the church's tithes. But here simplicity ceased, as people disputed what kind, how much, to whom, and for what purpose.

These disputes did not begin under Mathias Hovius, but it surely frustrated him that in his day they were still as fierce as any. Surely peace with the Dutch should have promoted peace within the parish. Surely pastors and flock, grateful for an end to scarcity and pillage, should have worked together toward a true Catholic community and ceased arguing over trifles of grain. But instead the very possibility of a return to normalcy, the very thought that a respectable living was within reach for pastor and peasant, raised hopes and tempers in the countryside, where nine of ten parishes lay, and where tithes constituted the single most important source of clerical income.

Many parishes experienced varying levels of strife over tithes, but of all the champions of tithes known to parishioner and bishop perhaps the most disagreeable was Hendrik Heynot, pastor of Opwijk. Though his village recovered faster than most from the scars of war, its tithes were never enough for him. Soon after his installation in 1605, he therefore began offending one and all through unbridled pursuit of what he considered his rightful portion. He was so sure of being cheated by his flock that rather than send an agent to collect his share he took to wading through sweltering fields in person, adorned in long priestly cassock, pitchfork on shoulder, to gather his due. More than once, knee deep in grain, did he by his deeds thunder the words of Malachi, "Will a man rob God? Yet ye have robbed me." During harvest and even beyond did he show himself wholly dedicated to the proposition that all fields were created to be tithed.

Pastor Heynot's aggressiveness in the fields, his countless appearances before the local tribunal of Opwijk to sue this parishioner or that, ran quite contrary to one of the roles pastors were still expected to play in villages: that of peacemaker. How could he expect to reconcile others when he himself was such a font of hostility? Tensions finally peaked during the harvest of 1611, when village magistrates decided to gather sworn testimonies about his conduct and send them to Archbishop Hovius. Surely if the archbishop knew the truth, he would never endure such a pastor. By the spring of 1612, the village's stack of damning stories was high enough to be forwarded to Mechelen.

Though the archbishop read the reports from Opwijk with his usual dose of skepticism, though events described there were hardly new, though the matter was blurred by three dozen other sorts of problems that occupied him at the same time, he saw enough in Opwijk to trouble him. For though willing to fight like a wolf in winter to secure decent livings for his pastors, he could hardly condone the aggressions of Hendrik Heynot.

There in the testimonies was the pastor marching imperiously into freshly harvested fields and demanding more than parishioners had set aside. Amid tied sheaves of flax and grain he loudly insisted on a full tithe, or every eleventh sheaf, while farmers just as stubbornly insisted that the pastor's share was a light tithe, or every thirty-third sheaf. While farmers protested, or worse while they were absent, there was the pastor loading more sheaves onto his wagon anyway, yelling that so and so was nothing but an old scoundrel who should be ashamed for stealing the church's goods. There was the pastor in the confessional refusing to grant absolution to one young farmer until the man paid a full tithe—a refusal quite contrary to the precepts of the church as well as the sacramental sensibilities of villagers.

There was the pastor bounding from field to field with a new little book in which he recorded intelligence about every tithe in Opwijk. Armed with book and pitchfork, bolstered by his father, mother, and sister, who lived with him, the pastor grew more confident still. There was the pastor's father, also with pitchfork in hand, charging an overflowing wagon, bellowing that it contained stolen tithes, knocking grain to the ground, and threatening to run the driver through. There were father and mother Heynot furtively carrying sheaves from another field, then throwing them over the churchyard hedge to their son the pastor, who waited on the other side.

There was Pastor Heynot last St. Martin's Eve (11 November) riding to the home of yet other parishioners, demanding to know where the family kept this year's harvest of flax. When the woman of the house told the pastor that it lay in the attic but there was no ladder, he simply climbed the walls of the timbered structure and began throwing down flax to his servant. When her husband arrived and asked what the pastor wanted, the pastor replied, "My flax." When told that his action required an order from the magistrates, the pastor blurted, "I care not a lick for mayor and magistrates, and have nothing to do with them." When he descended from the attic, the pastor opened his large cloak as if it concealed a weapon, put himself in a posture to fight, and yelled insults at the man "in front of his wife."

There, as the strife over tithes spilled into all else, was the entire pastoral family arguing with Jan van Hoorenbeke over the pastor's escaped pigs. Since the pigs had caused damage in his fields, Van Hoorenbeke was according to custom driving them toward the mayor's barn, where they would remain until the pastor paid compensation. But the pastor's sister blocked the way, the pastor's father took up his trusty pitchfork and shook it at Van Hoorenbeke, and Mother Heynot used a big stick to drive the pigs back to the pastor's barn. Three months later there was Jan van Hoorenbeke suffering the unholy family once more, this time over the excise tax on "foreign" beer, which he was appointed to collect. When he called at the pastor's door, the pastor invited him inside, then started hitting him in the face, saying with each blow, "This is for the foreign beer, that is for the foreign beer." When Van Hoorenbeke stumbled into the pastor's kitchen to wash himself, Mother Heynot dumped a warm liquid of unknown origin all over him.

There were Pastor Heynot and his father making deals at local taverns to cut down certain trees in someone's woods, but then cutting down larger, more expensive trees than agreed upon. There was the pastor rearranging the last will and testament of Gillis van Nieuhove, who had left a fund for the upkeep of the parish church, which fund the pastor now appropriated for his personal use. There was the pastor entering the village school and demanding to discipline a certain boy, then, when the schoolmaster's wife protected the boy, pushing the woman down into the benches of other students.

There on New Year's Day of 1612 was the pastor in the remodeled sacristy of the church, preparing himself to deliver the much anticipated New Year's Sermon in which pastors all over the Catholic world publicly offered specific wishes to the dearly gathered. There was the pastor putting his head out the sacristy door and yelling into the crowded church that he wished to see three particular magistrates. There behind the door, while everyone awaited his sermon, he insisted that the three magistrates approve his choices for new church wardens (responsible for upkeep of the church), but all refused, insisting like magistrates in most villages that this choice belonged to them alone. There was the perturbed pastor minutes later ascending the pulpit, then granting his first wish of the year to local magistrates: a serpent. Just as a serpent crawled on its belly and busied itself with every affair and sought at all costs to preserve its head, so our magistrates, proclaimed the pastor. There sat the audience scandalized, even if a few agreed.

There was the pastor tricking the illiterate peasant Jan Vermeer into a highly unfavorable written contract for the lamb tithe: twenty-six of the peasant's lambs would go to the pastor, and only sixteen to the peasant himself. When the peasant Vermeer learned his mistake, thanks to his literate wife, he and a magistrate aroused the pastor from bed. But the pastor merely said, "I have my signed document, you have yours, do your best and your worst with it."

Discomfiting as the pastor's behavior certainly was to Archbishop Hovius, just as discomfiting was how forcefully the entire dispute reminded him of every defect in the system of tithes. The problem in Opwijk was not merely about a headstrong pastor but a flawed institution.

Most problematic was that the majority of tithes collected

from a parish's fields went not to the local church but to a great, distant titheholder. In the early, murky Christian centuries of northern Europe, nobles instituted tithes to sustain newly built churches and their pastors. But it wasn't long before financially strapped nobles carved up and sold those tithes to a bewildering array of private parties—including laypeople, chapters, and monasteries— who regarded the tithes as income pure and simple. Temporal needs of parishes became an afterthought. By the time of Mathias Hovius, most parishes had three or four titheholders, some as many as ten. But whether few or many, whether lay or clerical, whether of this century or others, titheholders all over Europe had one thing in common: they kept most of any tithe to themselves and left a smaller portion for the parish.

The division of grain—the chief tithe—in the fields of Opwijk was a prime example, and hardly uncommon in the archbishop's experience. In "old fields," plowed since the parish's earliest days, titheholders collected every eleventh sheaf of grain, keeping for themselves the eleventh and twenty-second sheaves (about six percent of the total crop) and leaving the thirty-third sheaf (about three percent) for the local church. In "new fields," cultivated well after the parish's origins, only the thirty-third sheaf was collected, again only for the local church. The local church might then divide its share from old fields and new even further, among pastor, the Church Fabric (the physical church and its assets, managed by church wardens), and the Parish Poor Table. Although the pastor was in addition entitled to one out of every ten piglets or lambs, there was rarely enough at the local level, thanks to all this dividing and subdividing, to satisfy any single party. Which was how the fighting usually started.

In Opwijk as elsewhere the biggest fighting occurred in "new fields," which gave up the thirty-third sheaf only and where the local church saw the greatest potential for new income. All around the region such enterprising pastors as Hendrik Heynot wondered, "why not me?" Why should pastors not collect the eleventh and twenty-second sheaves as well from new fields, since farmers were accustomed to losing those sheaves anyway in old fields, and since the local church so badly needed the income? But villagers knew their rights and were not about to pay more than required. This was not out of indifference to religion or because they imagined that the local church had enough. Rather, villagers were already squeezed in every direction for their grain—by titheholders, by increased state and local taxes, and by additional religious contributions for Holy Wars, new shrines, new ornaments, ransoms for priests held in Holland, or even baptism, burials, and other rituals. To villagers the answer was plain: titheholders should return a larger share of their receipts to the parish. It wasn't more tithes that were needed but better distribution of existing tithes. In fact, more and more villages began taking titheholders to court to argue just that.

All this the archbishop knew. He knew that local horizontal wars (priest against parishioners) were often the result of larger and failed vertical wars (priest and parishioners together against titheholders). He did all in his power to settle the local wars, which caused alienation between pastor and flock and which made nearby Protestantism all the more tempting to the disgruntled. He labored mightily in vertical wars as well, for negligent titheholders were regularly brought before the archbishop's diocesan court and ordered to return more tithes to local churches and pastors, as decreed by the Councils of Trent and Mechelen. Most dramatically, when these same titheholders appealed their unfavorable judgments to the nuncio or Rome and won reversals, Archbishop Hovius did the unthinkable and began dragging titheholders, even fellow great clergymen, before secular courts instead: secular courts, though out of the archbishop's control, tended to favor the local church and never suffered appeals to Rome. The heyday of using secular courts against titheholders would come only a century later, but that the archbishop knowingly wounded the jurisdiction of the church by allowing cases long under its baili-

wick to be heard before lay judges reflected once more his willingness to put the local church ahead of the central, to put Mechelen
before Rome.

For all his willingness to combat titheholders, for all his awareness of the problems with tithes, for all the indelicacies of Hendrik Heynot, the archbishop nevertheless proved reluctant to take
decisive action in Opwijk.

After all, there was yet another issue at stake besides the system of tithes or the pastor's sins, and it was this: who was in charge
of pastors? The parish or the archbishop? The archbishop readily
disciplined pastors and did not ignore complaints from parishioners about them. But he preferred to levy discipline on his own
initiative and terms. If he were to comply precisely with every complaint from parishioners, then what would become of his authority
or that of any pastor? Because the dispute in Opwijk fell just short
of an obvious scandal, Archbishop Hovius would do all he could
to keep the pastor in place—even if it was Hendrik Heynot.

And so when he finally took up his pen to write the magistrates of Opwijk in June 1612, he made clear that, whatever the
crimes of their pastor, magistrates had no right to gather testimony
against him: "No lay person has any authority over a religious," he
insisted. It was a tension old as Thomas Becket and Henry II in
medieval England, a tension old as church and state themselves.
The church's longstanding position on the subject, and the archbishop's, was repeated at the Council of Trent: display no "unseemly kind of servility" to the secular arm—especially when it
consisted of small-time magistrates from Opwijk. Villagers should
have requested an inquiry by the bishop rather than conduct one
themselves.

Also objectionable to the archbishop was the smell of village
politics. Years of intervening around the archdiocese had taught
him that for every complaint in villages there was an equal and
opposite complaint. Those who had taken and given testimony
in Opwijk were obviously those who most wanted to see the pas-

tor removed, but surely there were others who felt differently. The archbishop therefore told magistrates that, although he did not possess and did not wish "the reputation of protecting any of my pastors when they are in the wrong," he found himself "unable to believe everything one party says without hearing the other." Indeed, Pastor Heynot had already sent his version of events to Archbishop Hovius, and offered "much evidence in his own favor."

The archbishop did not push this argument too far, for he was not ignorant of the deeds of Hendrik Heynot. A trusted dean had already expressed the opinion that the pastor should resign, while a second concluded that the pastor was like Ishmael: "His hand is raised against all, and the hands of all are raised against him." The archbishop would himself eventually call the pastor "intolerable." But he would say none of this to magistrates. All he would say was that he would act "in due time and manner with the help of God." "I promise you that I will do all that one may rightly expect from a good and diligent bishop."

But the archbishop moved not diligently enough for Opwijk. Six months after his promise he still had not acted, so magistrates employed a tactic the archbishop knew well: they called upon the state. First the magistrates tried the Council of Flanders, highest civil court in the province, which asked the archbishop to investigate the situation in the village. Under pressure from the council, Archbishop Hovius finally sent a representative to Opwijk in January 1613. But he also gave that representative instructions to strike an increasingly common compromise rather than release the pastor outright: over the next four years let the village collect the tithes and from them pay the pastor a fixed, respectable salary.

The solution seemed to work, for complaints to archbishop and council ceased for a time. But once this temporary agreement expired several years later, it wasn't long before Hendrik Heynot was back in the fields and the old complaints about him resumed. Added this time were comments that the pastor was so preoccupied with his business dealings in general that, among other consequences, the schedule for Mass had become most irregular. Now magistrates turned not only to the Council of Flanders but the privy council of Archduke Albert, urging it to "require the archbishop of Mechelen" to remove Pastor Heynot. Just as the Council of Flanders before had done, the privy council supported the village's request and implied to the archbishop that the pastor ought to be removed.

Such pressure from the secular arm was not what the archbishop had in mind for this case, especially not since he had already concluded on his own by now that Hendrik Heynot should resign. But because he had acted so slowly about Opwijk, the aging archbishop now suffered the indignity of having it appear that Brussels was ordering him to act. On 3 April 1618 he compelled Pastor Heynot to travel to Mechelen and resign his office, in exchange for a pension of one hundred florins per year.

Several times over the following years the pastor requested other positions from the archbishop, but each time he was refused. The man had caused trouble enough for Mathias Hovius. Despairing of ever finding a position in the archdiocese, Hendrik Heynot finally moved back to his hometown of Antwerp, where he died in 1625. It was said that everyone in Opwijk loved his successor.

THE POOR PRIEST OF LAAR

In the days of peace, when fields lay untrampled and prospects for income were bright, most country pastors still wallowed in mire. Indeed most rural priests were much worse off than the avaricious Hendrik Heynot, for unlike him they lived as miserably in peace as they had in war. Just as in the years of no sleep, when they ran from soldiers of all persuasions, legions of pastors still had nowhere to lay their heads. And though they spun and toiled they were poorly arrayed anyway.

The pastor of Laar knew this firsthand. On the northern slope of a modest hill, surrounded by fields and a few earthen houses, and close by the eastern borders of the land, stood his lowly village church. It was short and narrow, with a squat tower, no aisles, and certainly no transept. Opwijk seemed positively opulent in comparison.

Here was a parish still so defiled by war that it used stones from a few decrepit altars to rebuild its church. Here was a church so poor that though the pastor, Gendulphus van Schagen, had the thirty-third sheaf, it amounted to very little. Here was an income so tiny that the pastor was grateful for a Mass worth a paltry six florins a year. Here was a village so destitute that inhabitants could build their pastor no rectory. And here was a pastor so needy and enterprising that during his thirty-five years in the parish he felt compelled often to take temporal matters into his own hands, and support himself in ways that bishops such as Mathias Hovius deplored.

Some in the village knew that to fortify his woeful income the pastor, against all priestly propriety, hired himself out to collect excise taxes for an abbot in St. Truiden. Many knew about the pastor's attempts, against all local customs, to take over farmlands belonging to the parish's Church Fabric and Poor Table, not the pastor. Others knew that from his illicit income the pastor purchased, against all canonical rules, a flock of sheep, which he rented out to someone else. And everyone knew that the pastor, against all bishoply precepts, lived in a small room inside the church and used the churchyard to raise his own hens, pigs, doves, and vegetables.

Despite common knowledge of the pastor's temporal activities, few in Laar resented them in principle: they understood his acquaintance with poverty. Resentment surfaced and complaints to the archbishop began only when the pastor's enterprises started to threaten the livelihoods of villagers. Besides failure to perform sacraments or failure to play the role of village peacemaker, here was yet another reason for parishioners to become angry with their priest. Of late the pastor of Laar had jeopardized local livelihood in a variety of ways, but resented most of all was his recent seizure of the local parish's farmlands. Specifically, the pastor removed the tenant farmers who had long leased and worked those lands, then replaced them with tenants of his own choice. Yet the lands belonged to the parish, not the pastor. Moreover, some of the older tenants had worked their parcels of land for thirty years—long enough, said custom, for tenants to expect to continue on those lands. Especially sixty-four-year-old Gordt Coenen complained that fields "long under his plow" and tended with "much labor and fruit" were simply confiscated by the pastor. Bitter feelings between Gordt and his pastor reached a crisis one autumn day in 1609, not long after the onset of peace.

While walking past the parish church, Gordt was invited inside to the pastor's cramped quarters. There he joined the pastor, the pastor's brother-in-law Antoon, and a couple of villagers in a drink. While talking "in their cups," harsh words arose about the pastor's recent appropriation of Gordt's fields. The pastor grew so enraged at one of Gordt's insults that he sent everyone but Antoon from the room. When the door was shut, yelling commenced, blows were thrown, and in the end Gordt lay sprawled in a corner, four bloody wounds on his head.

As usual, it was trouble like this that led Archbishop Hovius to learn more about another obscure parish than he would have ever before thought necessary. As in the case of Opwijk, the villagers of Laar soon flooded the archbishop with their complaints. Unlike that other case, however, the people of Laar did not themselves undertake any investigation of the pastor, but tactfully left that to the archbishop. This deference served Laar well, for the archbishop sent to the parish in November 1609—within weeks of the complaints—a prosecutor from the diocesan court to look into things. The prosecutor's primary task was to learn about the brawl, but in the process he discovered much else.

By 1 December the prosecutor had interviewed enough villagers that he could confront Pastor van Schagen with sixteen specific charges, including not only the fight but other unpastorly conduct. The pastor denied each charge, beginning with the fight.

It was no fight at all, he explained, but a mere argument. The pastor and Antoon were not drunk, but simply enjoying a midday meal. Gordt's wounds resulted from falling down after drinking too much, not from any blows. If there were harsh words or threats they came from Gordt, who told the pastor, "I'll blacken your name with the bishop!" As for improper temporal affairs, the pastor denied any. Though he admitted living in a room inside the church, this was only to obey the archbishop's decree not to sleep within the church proper—the new walls and roof of his room made it physically separate from the area of worship. And if he kept a few hens in the churchyard, they never wandered inside the church itself.

After this interview, the prosecutor returned to Mechelen, apparently unsatisfied by the pastor's explanations and ready to move against him. But then, like so many cases, this one bogged down, thanks in large part to the pastor's lawyer, who threw up enough legal obstacles that it would be an entire year before the accusers in Laar even had a chance to attack the pastor's defenses, by which time it was surely hoped that memories would fade.*

Despite the passage of time, when villagers a year later finally got their chance to testify again and refute the pastor's explanations, they did so with enthusiasm and clarity, as Archbishop Hovius read for himself. Gordt's version of the fight, for instance, was as lively as if it had occurred the day before, and, even more important, much different from the pastor's. Gordt claimed merely to have been walking past the church, minding his own affairs, when the pastor's nephew was sent to lure him inside. The wounds on his head, explained Gordt, occurred when the pastor and Antoon hit him with their silver beer mugs. Gordt did not wish to repeat

---

* The hiring of lawyers was surprisingly common among rural people of modest means, including poor pastors; but it was also possible that the diocesan court appointed a lawyer to represent Pastor van Schagen, which occurred when the defendant was too poor to afford one.

to the prosecutor the insult that provoked the fight, but another witness did: Gordt had supposedly said to the pastor, "Maybe you wanted the church farmlands for your own tenant because you've slept with the tenant's wife."

Because the only witness to the fight, Antoon, was not allowed to testify (presumably because he was tainted and had even tried to intimidate other villagers into testifying for the pastor), the truth about the fight itself came down to the pastor's word against Gordt's. But on other topics eleven different witnesses willingly or inadvertently offered incriminating evidence against Gendulphus van Schagen. These included events immediately preceding and following the fight, the pastor's personal habits, and his material life.

One witness, in a clumsy effort to help the pastor, actually harmed him by claiming that the pastor was not drunk before the fight but merely "cheery," a fact he knew from having seen the pastor *truly* drunk. But most witnesses were eager to volunteer deliberately hurtful evidence: if the fight was not enough to get him in trouble, then other offenses would do just as well. Several recalled that Archbishop Hovius, while consecrating altars in Laar several years before, had whispered to those standing around him that the pastor must move out of his room in the church. All witnesses told—and Gordt most energetically—of the pastor's many wandering animals. The hens sometimes laid eggs on the church's three altars. Often they even flew around the small choir during Mass: once the pastor had to hold the chalice precariously with his left hand while shooing the hens away with his right. Gordt's dogs had chased the hens more than once, even bitten one to death, Gordt was proud to say. The pastor's pigs once tore an altar cloth on Our Dear Lady's Ascension Day. Sometimes, said Gordt, full of momentum, the pastor even spread the pigs' food inside the church. But worst of all were the pastor's doves, for they hit the audience with droppings during Mass or the sermon.

Just as in Opwijk, these testimonies raised the usual problems of interpretation for the archbishop and his men. Did Gordt, for instance, testify more out of concern for lost fields and wounded honor or for the desecration of the church? Did he and other witnesses truly care that the pastor lived inside? After all, the pastor's current arrangement was a much cheaper solution for villagers than a proper rectory would have been, for villages were supposed to build the rectory at their expense. And to what extent had Antoon, the pastor's brother-in-law, been successful in his tampering with witnesses?

There was at least one source of apparently objective evidence in the case: the twenty-three-year-old surgeon called to examine Gordt's wounds immediately after the fight. His expert opinion was this: the wounds could not have been caused by a fall, as the pastor claimed, for they were on top of Gordt's head, not on the side or back where one would expect to find them in such a case. Moreover, the wounds fit exactly the curved edge of the pastor's drinking mug.

If the people of Laar were angry at their pastor for economic and social sins, the archbishop had other causes for displeasure. Much as he regretted want of income among pastors, he regretted even more its usual consequence: want of decorum. Of course poor priests might be as pious as Chaucer's parson. Of course even priests with fine incomes might engage in shoddy behavior, as canons in many parts of the archdiocese were laboring to prove at this very moment. But in the archbishop's experience poverty and piety did not mix well in pastors. Poverty too easily led to moral woes—as in the pastor who could afford to hire as his housekeeper only a woman of ill repute. Poverty easily led to heresy: were conversions to Protestantism among clergy due, as some suspected, to skimpy incomes? But most especially poverty easily led a pastor to start acting the peasant, or merchant, or brawler, rather than the priest.

That, not the pursuit of mere comfort, was why Archbishop Hovius worked so hard to assure proper livings for his pastors. In such places as Laar, goading titheholders was not enough to give pastors incomes: other sources would have to be found as well. Hence the archbishop also made sure to instruct pastors on honest means by which they might supplement their incomes—such as serving as chaplain at an altar (which returned an annual fee in exchange for memorial Masses), serving as a *deservitor* (or temporary pastor) in a neighboring village, or even collecting modest fees for burials, marriages, and other rituals performed. The archbishop also subsidized some pastoral incomes from his own pocket. And of course he encouraged villages and towns to subsidize pastors as well.

Village subsidies were especially important when it came to providing the pastor a proper home. All around the land, rectories had been ruined by war, neglect, weather, and age, and Archbishop Hovius wanted village magistrates to take the lead in fixing them. The usual arrangement came to be this: the village was to reconstruct the rectory and the pastor was to maintain it. But in these early years after war, most villages, genuinely poor, dragged their feet. Although he recognized that villages could not afford everything at once, the archbishop was adamant that rectories must be a first priority. He had one strong bit of leverage at work for him: most villages were served by deservitors but wanted their own pastor. A deservitor, who usually lived miles away in a neighboring village, was inconvenient in emergencies, when the need for soul-saving sacraments was greatest, and even in ordinary times, when Masses were desired at regular hours, or when the priest's authority would help solve arguments. So when a parish asked for a pastor, the archbishop often replied that he would take the request more seriously were the parish to build a rectory first.

All this haggling among pastor, parish, archbishop, and tithe-holders about rectories and "decent" pastoral incomes was enough to give outsiders a perception of simple greed among the clergy. In fact some rich clergymen were expert hagglers, and some, despite reminders that they were called to the pastorate not to "gather money and gold" nor to "yoke their flock," succumbed to the deadly sin. But the archbishop knew that most pastors hardly died rich. And if pastors still had more possessions than many in rural society, this was not about Mammon but the decency of their station.

In the end the archbishop, prosecutor, and rural dean decided that the behavior of Pastor van Schagen was scandalous enough to warrant prosecution.

But because the lawyerly posturing dragged on for yet another year and a half, the teeth of the prosecution were dulled. The case limped to an end only in June 1612. As usual, little care was taken to preserve the documents that specified the conclusions. A simple note said that no fine was imposed. But did this mean that the pastor was not guilty or that he was too poor to pay? And was he punished for the fight, or for his room inside the church? All that was clear was that the pastor remained in office until 1634, long after the demise of Mathias Hovius.

The archbishop encountered Pastor van Schagen only rarely after the lawsuit. He would have been glad to know that the pastor's lawful income eventually stabilized at a respectable three hundred florins per year. But it would have displeased him that there was for many decades still not enough money in church or village to build a rectory, that the pastor continued to live inside the church, that the church itself was threatened with ruin, and that ornaments were sordid. As Laevinus Torrentius almost said, poverty was holy, but an obstacle to pastorly respectability and discipline.

THE CARNAL PRIEST OF ETTERBEEK

In the days of peace, when Hendrik Heynot terrorized fields and Gendulphus van Schagen bumped about a makeshift room in his parish church, other pastors disappointed Archbishop Hovius even more deeply with their crimes against parishioners and the priestly state.

One 13 April, not long after the festivities of the Easter season, two women from the parish of Etterbeek paid a visit to the archbishop in Brussels. They were come to complain about the misdeeds of their pastor, Egidius Lantschot. Weeks before this audience the archbishop had heard several alarming reports about the man. And now the women confirmed them.

Linken vanden Dale told how four years before the pastor offered to pay her in return for carnal favors. When Linken declined and said it was an ugly thing for a priest to tempt a married woman, the pastor supposedly replied that "he was a priest as long as he stood at the altar but everywhere else he was a man, like any other." The archbishop's secretary scribbled this all down earnestly. Meanwhile, Esther Coppens added that Pastor Lantschot was notorious for flirting with women, married or not, kissing them and engaging in "improper handgames." That Esther did not allude to some harmless village sport was hardly lost on the archbishop. Finally, said Esther, the pastor was drunk almost daily and justified it by saying that he could not go to sleep at night if sober. Here was a claim certain to capture the attention of Mathias Hovius, for drunkenness so often led to other priestly troubles.

Days later three other women from Etterbeek made the short trip to Brussels to recount their own woes with Pastor Lantschot. The archbishop, despite his increasingly shaky hand, even recorded parts of their testimonies himself, so serious was the matter. One woman, Sara van Ursel, testified that she had been the pastor's housekeeper for many years. During that time, she too had been pressured on diverse occasions to "sleep dishonorably" with him, but resisted and called him a scoundrel, prompting him once to threaten to smash her head with an iron. Moreover, she revealed that on Sundays the pastor sponsored drinking and dancing in the rectory—troublesome to the archbishop in and of itself but also because the pastor sold these drinks, using his tax exemption as a clergyman to undercut local traders and thus prompting even more grumbling against him.

Because it was not unheard of for parishioners to concoct stories of sexual (or other) wrongdoing by pastors in the hope of seeing them removed, the archbishop decided to hear from the pastor himself and therefore summoned him immediately, on this very same day of 18 April. It wasn't long into the interview before the archbishop decided that the charges were indeed true. In the presence of the rural dean of Brussels, Archbishop Hovius gave the pastor an unpleasant choice: resign now or await a lawsuit from the diocesan court. While he pondered his choice, the pastor was locked up immediately in the tower of the Laken gate, owned by the city of Brussels. Two days later, on 20 April, the pastor at last chose resignation. The archbishop accepted but said the pastor would have to remain in prison anyway until St. John the Baptist day, 24 June, and that the pastor needed to put his resignation in writing. In the meantime the archbishop wanted to investigate further.

Still other witnesses came from Etterbeek, including Sara van Ursel once more. She had come again because during her first interview she had, out of fear or shame, omitted an important piece of information; now her confessor urged her to come forward and reveal it. At some length Sara described how the pastor, in a drunken fury, had once raped her. After this disturbing tale, it must have surprised the archbishop when other villagers of Etterbeek stepped forward to support the pastor and asked that he not be let go, whatever his sins may have been—but they did not deny those sins. The archbishop wrote: "Several scruffy inhabitants of Etterbeek came to ask me to forgive the deeds of their pastor." Though always prepared to forgive, the archbishop told them he could not allow Egidius Lantschot to remain as pastor. The disappointed parishioners returned home.

In the end, after much sorting through testimonies and motives, the archbishop decided in favor of the stories of Linken vanden Dale and Esther Coppens. On 18 June, with the pastor still in prison, the archbishop sent a bailiff to impound the pastor's income and to notify him of his release as pastor. In September, Archbishop Hovius noted simply in his journal that Peter Cuveliers was now pastor of Etterbeek.

THE GOOD SHEPHERD

That archbishop and parishioners alike were scandalized by the behavior of a Pastor Heynot, a Pastor van Schagen, and especially a
Pastor Lantschot, revealed that the banner of the good pastor was
raised not only by Mathias Hovius but laypeople with him. After
all, it was they who initiated action against each of these troublesome pastors. Yet it was also true that the archbishop's version of
the good pastor did not coincide exactly with that of parishioners,
even if they did have many points in common.

The archbishop's good pastor was no longer a priest when
at the altar and a man when on the street. He was no longer to
stand out solely by his authority to perform sacraments but by
personal virtue. What the Council of Trent said about bishops
Mathias Hovius said about pastors: their entire lives were a "perpetual sermon" for good or ill. Nothing wounded the flock more
than a bad pastor, nothing aroused it more to piety than a good.
One churchman went further: the good pastor was "not only an
angel but a god" in his parish.

The good pastor now always resided in his parish and never
wandered or lived elsewhere.* He now showed concern for the
souls of his parishioners by, among other things, keeping accurate
records of births, marriages, and deaths. He now was free of the
slightest hint of heresy. He now carefully explained to his flock
the consecration of the Host, the definition of usury, the prohib-
ited and acceptable degrees of marriage, and all other laws of the
church. He now studied to be a priest rather than inheriting a pastorship from his uncle, and he went back to study more if the archbishop demanded it. He now delivered sermons on all feast days
and Sundays, preached while standing in a pulpit and not sitting

---

* All of the following examples of the good pastor and bad pastor are, unless
otherwise noted, from actual instances that occurred under Archbishop Hovius in the
archdiocese of Mechelen. They are similar to examples from other dioceses around
Catholic Europe.

in a chair, kept sermons free of "improper notions," preached to the understanding of his audience rather than coldly, and always stayed within the one and one-quarter hour set aside for Mass and sermon.

The good pastor no longer casually heard confession and routinely granted absolution but understood and applied the archbishop's "short and lucid" manual for confessors. In fact he no longer heard confession at all unless granted license by his bishop to do so. He certainly no longer heard confession in secluded rooms or dark corners but in new semipublic wooden confessionals, to avoid temptation. And if he had no choice but to hear confession in private surroundings, because he was nearly deaf and parishioners had to shout out their sins to be heard, then he secured his bishop's approval first.

The good pastor no longer dressed, talked, or acted in ways that degraded priesthood and church. He no longer hunted, hawked, danced, or gambled. He no longer wore short-sleeved tunics, soiled vestments, or silken hats. He no longer went without hat, cross, tonsure, or untrimmed moustache. He no longer used such worldly instruments as the lyre while singing Mass. He no longer wore silly fur hats or gloves to celebrate Mass, even in the cold of winter, even when aged, but instead lit a fire near the altar. He no longer dressed himself in a short cassock, not even when it was muddy or when carrying the Holy Sacrament late at night, but was covered always to mid-calf. He no longer used obscene language as his coarser parishioners might. He no longer was a "remarkable," "distinguished," "incorrigible," "great," or "assiduous" drinker, like many other men in the village. He no longer frequented wedding feasts, or childbirths, or taverns, and certainly he never appeared drunk at a baptism, for he might get the name wrong and have to do it all over again in secret. Unlike so many of his medieval predecessors, whose local authority came from an ability to blend into the community, he no longer did anything to blur the line that divided laity and priest.

Above all else the good pastor was now fastidiously chaste.

He no longer merely refrained from the act of unchastity but the appearance. He no longer appointed his illegitimate son to succeed him as pastor because he would have no children at all. He no longer merely refrained from fornication but avoided the "burning fire" of a beautiful young housekeeper. He no longer allowed his housekeeper to masquerade as his sister, especially when he bore no resemblance to her, thus risking rumors that she was his sister as Sarah was Abraham's sister. He no longer greeted women in public with a kiss. He no longer threatened to shoot parishioners who might criticize him for keeping a concubine, for he had no concubine. He no longer even thought of commissioning altarpieces for the parish church that included himself on one side panel and his concubine and son on the other. He no longer gave his servants any cause to whisper or talk or peek through his doors, to see what unseemly things their pastor might be up to, especially when he was a pastor at a popular shrine. And he no longer tried to sleep with his maid or play indecent games with women.

No one could say how many such good pastors there were or how many scandalous. Surely many had something of the zealous Joost Bouckaert, the new pastor of the Sharp Hill, or goodhearted Godfried Tienwinkel, or dependable Hendrik Calenus of Asse. But too many possessed as well bits of Hendrik Heynot, or Gendulphus van Schagen, or Egidius Lantschot. All that could be said was that the archbishop's version of the good or bad pastor led him to spend most of his energies on the latter, and that a number of obstacles prevented him from rooting out such pastors overnight—or ever.

Besides the eternal obstacle of human imperfection, institutional obstacles conspired against the archbishop's ideal as well. The most basic was the colossal size of the archdiocese. Most of the new bishoprics in the Low Countries contained a manageable 100 to 150 parishes, but Mechelen had an old-fashioned 450—far less than the impossible 1,338 of Rouen in France, but still unwieldy. For all the archbishop's travels and audiences, he still gave the impression of knowing few pastors well and some not in the least.

And for all the travels of his "select men," the eleven rural deans, contact was still too infrequent to enforce perfect compliance.

Given the size of the archdiocese, a better solution than enforcement was to appoint trusted pastors who did not require constant supervision. But here another institutional obstacle arose: the archbishop had the right to name pastors in only 67 parishes of the archdiocese. Everywhere else, since forever, pastors were nominated by some great patron—including monasteries and chapters as well as nobles. Trent and the provincial council tried to change these arrangements and put bishops in charge, but especially for the sake of nobles did the archdukes, like the kings of Spain, refuse to go along: lay patronage was sacred, not to mention of great political value. Ultimately the archbishop was therefore able merely to examine a patron's nominee and to remove him if truly scandalous. No wonder some pastors might feel more loyalty to their patron than to their archbishop.

But the most fundamental reason why there were not enough pastors in the archbishop's image was that there were not enough pastors, period, especially in the countryside. Priests seemed plentiful enough: Archbishop Hovius would ordain almost twenty-five hundred of them before he was through. But many went into monasteries and most avoided the parish, at least the rural sort.

Well-trained priests preferred a position with a sparkling prebend and little care—precisely what most rural parishes did not offer. Many priests fancied a chaplaincy under some great lord. Many sought a well-funded canonry in a chapter, underburdened with pastoral cares. Few were the university students groomed for the trials and undignified incomes of rural parishes, few the theology professors like Jacobus à Castro of Leuven who took his students to poor villages outside the city's gates, that they might be motivated one day to take up their cross and use their learning to confront the challenges awaiting rural pastors.

Archbishop Hovius attacked the problem of recruitment in a way typical of churchmen after the Council of Trent: he established a seminary, controlled by himself. Older methods of priestly education—tutoring by an uncle-priest, or training at the university—simply would not do. The first was erratic, while the second prompted lofty ideas about comfortable positions in church and state. The new diocesan seminary would instead turn out a specific kind of clergyman: a country priest, trained systematically, and free of charge, by the archbishop. This priest would not only be more able than his predecessors, but because his education was paid for by the archbishop he would be more obligated than university-trained priests to accept assignment to even a poor rural parish. The seminary would seek rural boys eighteen and older who had shown promise in assorted grammar schools for poor boys, who inclined to the priesthood, who could cope with the social and economic realities of village life, and who would regard their new position as a leap up the social ladder rather than a drop down. The seminary would also identify candidates early: as the archbishop put it in one letter, it was "almost impossible" to find Dutch-speaking pastors for rural parishes unless they had been "raised to it from their youngest days."

Of course providing free education cost loads of money. Though the archbishop had the seminary up and running soon after his nomination in 1595, it ran barely. He poured in "thousands" from his own purses ever after. He taxed the clergy of the archdiocese at a rate of one penny for every sixty they earned. He won from magistrates the revenues of a special tax on dairy products, plus special tax exemptions. He identified endowments that had been designated for general "pious purposes" in the archdiocese and then appropriated them for the specific purposes of his seminary. He perfected the old ecclesiastical way of raising money: fining sinners. And he was tireless in that most draining of tasks: currying at his dinner table the favor of potential donors.

Despite the archbishop's heroics, he secured enough by the end of his life to educate for free only about twenty seminarians at a time, each enrolled for three or four years. Even if one added to these twenty those students who paid their own way at the seminary, or the many Norbertine canons who devoted themselves to the service of rural parishes, the total number was still far from sufficient to meet at once the needs of all the archdiocese's some four hundred country parishes.

Ironically, the archbishop himself helped to restrict the number of priests by his insistence on quality. Like Clement VIII in Rome or Bishop Triest in nearby Gent, he preferred a "few well instructed priests to many who were ignorant" or immoral. As the archbishop informed his nephew Henri, when turning him down for a position as pastor, an unqualified priest imperiled not only his own soul but the souls of all in his care. Certainly the archbishop gave pastors second and third chances. Certainly he recalled the admonition of Trent that as a bishop he was a "shepherd, not a striker," that exhortation, admonition, and benevolence affected change more effectively than severity. Yet as his aides reported, the "peaceable" Archbishop Hovius spared neither expense nor labor to root out "the evil," not to mention "the incompetent."

He did not take this too far. Even Mathias Hovius occasionally tolerated pastors who had no official papers granting care of souls but whose presence was badly needed on account of the plague or some other exigency. Even he once told a rural dean to proceed softly against a transgressing pastor in Neerlinter, because there wasn't yet anyone to replace him. That even the strict archbishop was for practical reasons occasionally compelled to tolerate shortcomings suggested the final obstacle to a spotless priesthood: parishioners would tolerate even more than the archbishop, and more often, just to have their own priest.

Though more and more laypeople were beginning to concur with the archbishop's idea of the good pastor, many still required less than he did of priests—or at least viewed the priest's tasks differently. These many laypeople surely preferred a pastor who preached well, who was chaste and sober, or who had good understanding of rituals, but they placed even more value on his dependability in performing sacraments, on his leaving local wives and daughters alone, on his staying sober enough to allow him to play his role as peacemaker, and on his willingness to accommodate local rituals and customs. Even if the pastor fell short of these desirable attributes, parishioners might tolerate him still for his sacraments alone. The people of Laar, for all their complaining, never sought the outright removal of Pastor van Schagen. Though the villagers of Opwijk griped about Hendrik Heynot for long, their biggest objection by the end was that his business ventures caused him to perform Mass at irregular hours. Even some villagers of Etterbeek were willing to have their blatantly offensive pastor back. And they were not alone. Parishioners in Kerksken were slow to complain about their elderly, "highly sordid," tone-deaf, stammering, unlearned, non-preaching pastor because he had no other way to support himself and because they did not want to lose him. The parishioners of Kobbegem asked a nearby chaplain to serve them, without the archbishop's permission, even though the man was "completely stupid." A bad priest might inconvenience villagers. Villagers might not like confessing to him or listening to his sermons or paying him tithes. They might wish that he would deal more peaceably with them. But unlike a substitute pastor or no pastor, even the lax pastor was at least close by with the power they wanted when they lay dying.

This still common emphasis by parishioners on the pastor's authority to deal in matters supernatural was in fundamental ways quite consistent with Rome's: it was an old and quite official heresy, for instance, to believe that sacraments somehow depended on the worthiness of the priest who administered them. Parishioners did not believe this: few supposed that their pastor's sacraments were defective simply because he kept a concubine or drank too much. Indeed it was possible to argue that the efficacy of the sacraments and thus the authority of the church were even more impressive when a bad priest administered them than a good—for they were valid in spite of him! Hence, popular regard for the sacraments of a pastor worked quite in the archbishop's favor when it came to getting rectories built. But it could work against him when it came to reforming pastors themselves. Wider acceptance of his ideal would take longer than his lifetime and more than his efforts alone.

In the end, for all his labors, the archbishop simply could not enforce his image of the good pastor everywhere at all times. He surely agreed with a dean who near the end of the archbishop's life concluded that despite years of admonition, pastors under his jurisdiction still neglected catechism, rarely sang vespers, seldom confessed, often skipped meetings of the pastors, and too often dined with nuns. Not even in the control of its pastors was the church of the Catholic Reformation the monolith it was later imagined to be. But it was not for want of effort from Mathias Hovius.

✛ NINE ✛

The Trouble with Peace

SCABBY SHEEP

The seventeenth of June, 1610, a Sunday.

T he annual Sacrament Procession was winding its usual, deliberate way through the streets of Mechelen.

The highlight of the procession was the Eucharistic host itself, set in a spangled, bursting monstrance carried by Archbishop Hovius. He and his entourage moved under a canopy, meant not so much to block the sun or rain as to focus eyes on the host and its bearers. As usual, numerous groups marched before the canopy, to claim their share of the proceedings. And as usual an even greater number of onlookers lined the streets, for to observe such events was also to participate.

As the canopy approached the Corn Market, a sudden commotion broke the calm. Several Dutch sailors, standing near a house called The Little Golden Lion, were refusing to remove their hats in reverence of the Sacrament. Instead they stood snickering among themselves in ridicule of the entire affair, then finally burst out in laughter and walked away, scandalizing the crowd around them. Most scandalized of all was Archbishop Hovius, who saw everything and cried out, "Where is the sheriff?!" The sheriff, responsible for order in the city, was not immediately at hand. But a servant ran to tell him what had occurred, emphasizing the reaction of the archbishop. Soon several of the sheriff's men chased

opposite: Pieter Bruegel, *The Good Shepherd*
© Royal Library Albert I, Brussels (Prentenkabinet)

down the irreverent sailors near the wharf and threw them into the city's jail.

The archbishop certainly preferred peace to war. But he had to admit that this most recent round of peace had already brought problems of its own.

To begin with, there were many who had not wanted peace at all. The Dutch were still arguing among themselves over its desirability: war with Spain was the foundation of the young Dutch Republic, said some; surely peace would tear the Republic apart! Courtiers in Spain grumbled that Albert and Isabella had been granted the Netherlands to reunite them in their entirety: this could occur, they argued, only through reconquest of the north, not a negotiated peace. Besides, said these courtiers, war was the pastime of noblemen: surely with no fighting to occupy them, naturally brave Spaniards would become effeminate. But Albert and Isabella, cheered on by their subjects, went forward anyway: they told King Philip that if he wanted outright military victory over the North rather than compromise, then he could pay for it himself. Spain's latest round of bankruptcy made that impossible, and so peace won out.

Then, once peace was settled, there were those who threatened it. Most serious was a crisis sparked by the latest romantic adventure of King Henri IV of France. In the spring of 1609, the ever amorous, fifty-nine-year-old Henri set his sights on a fifteen-year-old noblewoman named Charlotte-Marguerite de Montmorency. When Charlotte's new husband, the young Prince of Condé, learned of these royal intentions he decided it was time for a change: in the middle of the night, Condé packed up Charlotte and fled with her from Paris to Brussels. When Albert and Isabella granted the couple asylum, Henri exploded in fury, though of course in public he could not say why. Instead he accused Condé of treason, sent diplomats to Brussels, schemed with Charlotte's family, threatened war, and even amassed troops on France's northern border for an invasion of the Spanish Netherlands. Isabella and her gifted ambassador, Peter Peckius, took these threats very seriously (even if Isabella did have a chuckle at the thought of an aging Henri chasing Charlotte around his palace), and did much to defuse the situation. At length a Homeric war, with the king in pursuit of his Helen of Troy, might still have occurred had not Henri been assassinated in May 1610, a dagger to his heart.

Yet another threat to peace was the childlessness of Albert and Isabella. Doubtful of the couple's ability to approximate the miracle of Abraham and Sarah, King Philip III was already taking steps to ensure a smooth return of the Netherlands to Spain, as stipulated in Isabella's marriage agreement. But instead of smoothness Philip's actions produced only resentment in the land. Was that resentment deep enough to produce another Netherlandish rebellion, among southern subjects grown accustomed to their own princes and emotional distance from Spain?

Surely these and other crises on the international scene concerned Archbishop Hovius, but it was another sort of problem with peace that affected him most directly: the freedom that peace afforded to heretics. In order to have peace in 1609, the archdukes had compromised much, including on religion. They had agreed to give up the old Spanish demand that the Dutch Republic return officially to Catholicism. They had agreed to allow Dutch Protestant merchants to trade in the Spanish Netherlands. They had even agreed that all Netherlanders, of whatever confession, should be allowed to move freely between north and south. This was how the archbishop's troubles started.

Inhabitants of the Republic who visited the south and subjects of the archdukes who visited the north were supposed to abide by certain rules, decreed by the archdukes on the last day of 1609. While in the south, Dutch Calvinist visitors were not to worship in public. They were not to ridicule Catholic customs and rituals. They were not to argue with Catholics over doctrine. They were not to bring with them heretical publications. While in the north, subjects of the archdukes were not to attend Calvinist services. What troubled Archbishop Hovius was that these rules were so often violated, to the detriment of his Catholic faith.

Besides the incident in Mechelen on Holy Sacrament Day, he could name countless others. He knew that hundreds of Spanish Netherlanders crossed from Antwerp into the Republic each week to attend Calvinist sermons. He knew that in northern deaneries around Antwerp, villages subject to the archdukes impudently appointed Calvinist preachers. He knew that Calvinist preachers from the Republic traveled to cities of the south and initiated public debates with Catholic theologians. He knew that ordinary northern Calvinists engaged in less sophisticated debates with southern Catholics, brawling in taverns over the question of whether Christ was present in the Eucharist. Right under the archbishop's nose in Mechelen someone deliberately smashed the image of Our Dear Lady in the churchyard of St. Rombout's, an Iconoclastic Fury in miniature. Right to his face a certain Sabina Golsius of Brussels dared to say that Our Lord was in Heaven, not in the Eucharist, that there were but two sacraments, and that it was useless to appeal to the saints—all classic Protestant heresies and all still present in the south despite the execution of Anna Utenhove.

The archbishop also saw the flood of anti-Catholic propaganda that poured from the print-rich Dutch Republic. This included such works as the phony *Sermon of the Bishop of Den Bosch*, which poked fun at Catholic shrines, featured on its cover the pope dressed as a merchant, and in mock solemnity recounted the story of a boy in a wheelchair who traveled to the Sharp Hill, offered two whole silver buttocks to Our Lady, and "immediately his bones went click, click, all his members cracked into place, and he sprang from his chair!" Or a tract that called Our Lady of Halle a puppet, a kermis-doll, a decaying, saintless block of wood. Or the ribald *New Song*, which depicted bishops, abbots, monks, canons, and friars as gluttonous, lecherous pigs. Or the Protestant chortles at the death in 1611 of Bishop Miraeus of Antwerp, who collapsed during a sumptuous dinner party: admittedly, wrote the nuncio, the bishop was "very heavy," but that heretics used his death to suggest the gluttony of the Catholic clergy was unfair, for the bishop had eaten almost nothing on the night he died.

Mathias Hovius did what he could to oppose such assaults. His diocesan court drew up proposals for no fewer than forty-eight different legal problems raised by the presence of unbelievers. His diocesan councils demanded of Catholics rigorous compliance with traditional rituals that proclaimed their faith to all: Easter communion, baptism, confirmation, professions of faith, and statements of orthodoxy. He warned pastors and deans to beware of persons who spoke eagerly about religion or read the Bible often or visited the Republic frequently, all signs of likely heretics. He even encouraged the preparation of counterpropaganda, such as *The Origin and Present State of the Calvinist Sect,* which was dedicated to him, and which was as liberal with slander and unfounded accusations against Calvinism as Calvinist tracts were against Catholicism. But most of all the archbishop encouraged secular authorities in the south to use their monopoly on force to punish all transgressors.

By yelling "Where is the sheriff?" the archbishop acknowledged yet again how dependent he was on the state to help him achieve a Catholic community. Though his diocesan court might discipline the clergy as it saw fit, laypeople were another matter. His court had the right to levy fines on them and prescribe penance or punishment, but the state reserved the right to physically enforce those penalties. The only weapon the archbishop wielded absolutely was excommunication, with its threat of separation, its exclusion from sacraments, and its promise of burial "like a dog" in unconsecrated ground. Though he suggested that deans should use the threat more often, the archbishop had to admit that "everyone merely laughs" at it—especially unbelievers from the Dutch Republic. That was why he needed the state. He no longer sought the death of any heretic, in the style of Anna Utenhove, but "to put a bit of fear into others" he wanted exemplary fines and banishment for those who failed to behave.

On paper the decrees of the archdukes against public heresy sounded stern as ever. In fact, when it suited them, all secular authorities could move convincingly against this heretic or that. Sabina Golsius, who had dared speak so boldly to the archbishop about the Eucharist, was ordered by the Chancellor of Brabant to leave the land within six days—precisely the penalty requested by Archbishop Hovius. The chancellor quite agreed with the archbishop's conclusion that this "scabby sheep" should not be allowed to infect any others. Another resident of Brussels was similarly banned because, like the sailors in Mechelen, he showed insufficient reverence toward the Eucharist. A third violator was expelled from the Spanish Netherlands soon after, with tragic results: hopeless, this woman drowned her two young children, then herself, in cold February water, all described in gruesome detail by Dutch pamphleteers.

But just as before the peace, enforcement of the decrees continued to be sporadic. The state would go only so far—partly because of practical limitations, partly because it did not wish simply to do the bidding of the church, but especially because of the politics of peace. There were far more Catholics in the religiously mixed Dutch Republic than there were Protestants in the officially Catholic Spanish Netherlands. If the magistrates of the south punished Protestant visitors and natives too harshly or often, then Dutch rulers might retaliate against Dutch Catholics with even greater consequence.

Even Archbishop Hovius conceded that this complicated the matter of enforcement in his own land: "I do not think that heretics must be banned to the last person; this would disturb peace too greatly and cause retaliation against our co-religionists in the north." But the archbishop had a lower threshold for "scandal" than most southern magistrates and wanted more enforcement than at present. To him there was an obvious solution: grant the church's courts more power over violators, including the right to exercise physical constraint. It was a solution quite similar to Archbishop Borromeo's, who requested an armed episcopal police force to implement the church's decrees in his archdiocese of Milan. But just as in that diocese, so in Mechelen was the request denied and the local archbishop frustrated: not even the pious Albert was about to share the state's monopoly on force. His only response was to call a meeting of legal dignitaries at the home of Archbishop Hovius, then repeat tired old decrees urging local magistrates to cooperate with the church.

The fate of the Dutch sailors who had mocked the Sacrament Procession confirmed the archbishop's fears about weak enforcement. In their jail cells the sailors were read the archdukes' decree on proper behavior—but there was no fine and no banishment. Two days later, they were, like so many other-believing visitors, set free without further ado.

FOUND SHEEP

In the middle of peace, in the middle of 1613, came the sad news that Mathias Hovius was dead. The nuncio Bentivoglio, an admirer of the archbishop, wrote to inform Cardinal Borghese, protector of the Low Countries at the papal court, and to recount the archbishop's reputation for incorruptibility, his defense of the church, his zeal until the end. The cardinal expressed the requisite regret at the loss and instructed the nuncio to push immediately for a successor who was in no way inferior.

Most surprised of all by this news was Mathias Hovius himself, who, though often ailing, remained busy as ever. An embarrassed nuncio soon wrote to Rome to correct his mistake and angrily blame the rumors on the archbishop's enemies. Some of these enemies were Spanish Netherlanders, but thanks to peace no doubt even more were from the north, who now came freely across the borders of the land.

Though he certainly disliked the thought of northern enemies infesting the land, the archbishop was delighted that a now-
open border brought as well a stream of Dutch Catholics in search
of spiritual relief. From the first days of peace, thousands of these
faithful crossed into the Spanish Netherlands to make the pilgrimage to the Sharp Hill, then moved on to Mechelen for the
sacrament of confirmation at the hands of Archbishop Hovius. Attendance at Catholic processions in border towns surged, including at the revived Our Dear Lady procession in Antwerp, where
visiting Dutch Catholics turned the Schelde River into "a forest
of boats." Many Catholics visited Brussels and the palace of the
nuncio Bentivoglio, who blessed the pilgrims and showed them
his portraits of the pope and the pope's nephew, Cardinal Borghese. The faithful were surprised, wrote the nuncio, that the pope
was so young, for they imagined that popes were necessarily old
and worn. And they were comforted that both pope and cardinal
hardly resembled the monstrous descriptions that were a regular
feature in the sermons of Protestant preachers.

Also pleasing to the archbishop about peace was the chance
it offered for the conversion of Dutch Protestants. But in this lay
a problem as well: the political sensitivity of conversion was now
greater than ever. Each side in the religious tug-of-war resented
more deeply than ever conversions not in its favor, yet trumpeted
louder than ever those that were. One Sacrament Procession in
Brussels featured a Dutch convert in penitential white, who was
allowed to spout prophecies that peace would bring much fruit to
the Catholic church.

One of the most sensitive conversions in the archbishop's experience was that of a Dutch teenager named Frans Boels. Frans's
father was originally from Mechelen, but during the "Troubles"
of the 1560s and '70s he converted to Lutheranism and moved
to Amsterdam. There he met his wife-to-be, Maria Schuyt, a
Lutheran emigré from Antwerp. While Maria was pregnant with
Frans, in 1596, her husband died. Maria thereafter taught school
to support herself and groomed her son for a career as a mer-

chant. Her labors bore fruit in January 1613 when she at last secured for the now seventeen-year-old Frans a position with a trading company in Moscow. Because Frans had never seen his paternal, Catholic grandparents, who lived in Mechelen, Maria decided that he should pay them a visit before embarking on his long journey to Russia. For reasons unknown—perhaps the grandparents were poor, perhaps they could not forgive their son for converting to Lutheranism—Frans lodged in Mechelen with someone besides his grandparents: Jean de Froidmont, canon of the cathedral chapter. Thanks to a cold winter, his short visit there turned into a stay of several weeks. To help pass the time, Frans talked about religion with the canon, the servant boys of the house, and no doubt his grandparents. By the end of January these talks had convinced him to become Catholic: he therefore abjured Lutheranism and received the sacrament of confirmation from Archbishop Hovius. He also wrote to tell his mother that he was abandoning not only Lutheranism but his career as a merchant, for he wished to stay in Mechelen and study his new faith.

Mother Maria, mindful of all the money and trouble and emotion she had invested in her son, was beside herself and urged Frans to meet her in Antwerp, where they might discuss the matter in person. But Frans would not budge from Mechelen, not even after Maria traveled there herself to try to persuade him otherwise. Frustrated, Maria returned to Amsterdam, where she told the city's magistrates that Frans was being held against his will. These magistrates wrote immediately to their counterparts in Mechelen to inquire about the situation. But the rulers of Mechelen, after investigation, were satisfied that Frans had stayed in their city of his own accord, and they wrote to Amsterdam to say so. They invited Maria to visit again, so that she might speak with Frans once more and see for herself that his determination to remain was genuine and unrestrained. Maria agreed and even dined in the household of Canon Froidmont, where she had a chance to see how her son lived. Still Frans would not leave.

But Maria was determined to get her son back: she had not

raised him for this. Back in Holland, she went to The Hague
where met the States General of the entire Dutch Republic, which
sent more accusations to the magistrates of Mechelen. Would the
magistrates not put an end to this "iniquitous, tyrannical, in-
human, unnatural, and unchristian situation" and return the boy
to his mother? What a pity it would be, the States General not so
subtly warned, if peace and good relations between the two lands
should be upset by such events. But the magistrates of Mechelen
insisted still that the boy acted freely.

With no cooperation in sight, a desperate Maria decided to
go to Mechelen a third time and, if necessary, use force. She came
in disguise, and fortified by a friend whom witnesses described as "a
robust Dutch woman." From their room at the strategically located
hotel the Little Windmill, the two women watched Frans's routine,
walking to and from St. Rombout's with his new master, Canon
Froidmont. On Holy Saturday, while Frans returned from midday services carrying the canon's robes, Mother Boels and friend
pounced: they ran from the hotel, grabbed Frans, and tried to drag
him to their room. But the boy shouted for help and servants of
Canon Froidmont freed him. Again local magistrates were called
in. Again they spoke with Maria and Frans. Again Frans declared
that he would not return to Holland but wished to live and die a
Catholic, God willing. Again a wounded Maria returned home.

Now Maria cut off Frans financially, refusing to send him
clothes, linens, or books, and making the classic threat of the betrayed parent that if he remained Catholic then he was no longer
her son. Yet she would not give up hope. She tried the States General once more, which this time went directly to the archdukes
with Maria's claims of forced conversion and noted especially the
"sorrows of the mother," heartbroken that Frans was "wasting his
best years carrying a canon's robes, when he had been destined for
trade." The archdukes promised an umpteenth investigation, this
one by Archbishop Hovius in person.

The archbishop therefore summoned Frans Boels and asked
him the usual old questions. After interviewing magistrates as well,

the archbishop came to the same conclusion as those before him: Frans was Catholic by his own will. For good measure, Archbishop Hovius added that it was against all "divine and natural law" that a Catholic prince would compel a subject who had reached the age of discretion to return to a land that would deny him the free exercise of the "true religion." And so Frans stayed in Mechelen, breaking his mother's heart, unlearning the tools of trade and acquiring the language of his new religion.

Whether the conversion of Frans Boels was pure as Flemish fleece or not, it combined with other similar incidents to build tensions and decrease the likelihood that peace between north and south would extend beyond the agreed-upon twelve years.

BICKERING SHEPHERDS

Peace put the Dutch Republic much on the mind of Mathias Hovius not only in regard to heresy within the flock, or the political sensitivity of favorable conversions, but the state of the Dutch Catholic Church itself. Who was in charge of it?

With no bishops in the Dutch Republic, Catholics on both sides of the political border debated this question for too long. Those believers who lived in the border-straddling bishoprics of Roermond and Den Bosch did not have to bother: they had real bishops and pastors close by who moved easily among them. But Catholics farther north belonged to the so-called Holland Mission, formed in the 1590s after every other Dutch bishopric collapsed under the pressures of war and Protestantism. Now instead of four or five bishops in these regions, as there were supposed to be, there was simply an apostolic vicar appointed by Rome, who spent most of his time in faraway Cologne supervising about seventy pastors working among the Dutch faithful. Now instead of full-fledged parishes in the north there were simply remnants and roaming priests. Now instead of worshiping openly, Catholics were forced underground and Calvinism became the "public" church of the Republic. Certainly Dutch Catholics enjoyed more freedom in practice than Calvinists who lived under the archdukes, but just as certainly were Dutch Catholics always second-class burghers in their own land, subject to denigrating laws and even persecution when convenient—such as during wars with Catholic archdukes.

The Catholic clergy in the Spanish Netherlands, beholding the vacuum of ecclesiastical authority in the Dutch Republic, rushed to fill it, thus initiating the arguing that so troubled Mathias Hovius. As Archbishop of Mechelen he had no direct authority over the Holland Mission, but as primate of all the Netherlands he felt a moral obligation to intervene—especially since the authority of the apostolic vicar was so vague.

By the time of the peace, Vicar Vosmeer in Cologne had already argued long with various clergy over who was in charge of the Holland Mission, but his biggest battle was with Jesuits, who came into the Republic from their houses in the Spanish Netherlands, determined to minister to the bishopless faithful. These Jesuits labored bravely, if in less life-threatening circumstances than their counterparts in Protestant England. But it annoyed the vicar that the Jesuits did not bother to seek his permission or to coordinate their labors with those of his seventy pastors. Like all Jesuits, they considered themselves bound to obey their own superiors above any bishop, and likely even above an apostolic vicar. The vicar and his pastors in turn regarded Jesuits as troublesome pastoral freebooters. Conflict between the two parties only intensified with the onset of peace between north and south.

When peace was announced in 1609, Sasbout Vosmeer immediately embarked from Cologne to make a turf-claiming tour of the Holland Mission. He followed this up with a visit to Brussels, where he hoped to receive moral support from the archdukes for his authority. Even more provocative, however, was the vicar's decree that visiting clergy (thus Jesuits) laboring in the Holland Mission were not to preach or administer sacraments in areas where one of the vicar's own pastors was already in place. Moreover, lay Catholics were not to receive sacraments from any unapproved clergy, on pain of excommunication. This decree the Jesuits regarded as an all-out declaration of war. A compromise between vicar and Jesuits was reached in 1610, but as usual implementation lagged behind proclamation. It wasn't long before Vicar Vosmeer was threatening to send the Jesuits away altogether. Rumor even spread that he was planning to use the Protestant-minded States of Holland against his fellow Catholics, the Jesuits, by seeking a ban on their very presence!

Archbishop Hovius corresponded with Vicar Vosmeer early on and suggested ideas for reconciliation: the work was more important than who conducted it. The archbishop also discussed the matter with the nuncio Bentivoglio and Archduke Albert, and asked as well for the intervention of his old friend, former classmate, and native Amsterdammer Jacob Jansonius, who played a large role in the affair. After all this, the archbishop concluded that although the Jesuits had certainly committed acts worthy of complaint, so had Vicar Vosmeer and his seventy pastors.

Since both sides were at fault, Archbishop Hovius thought it critical that both admit it and be reconciled. He suggested a conference, supported by Rome and Archduke Albert, for the autumn of 1611 in Mechelen. But when the time for the conference arrived the vicar did not. When the vicar died in 1614, his successor, Philip Rovenius, hauled from the ice chest the same old idea of a problem-solving conference. In fact the delegates actually gathered in Brussels in December that year, and prospects seemed bright. But then the vicar declared that he needed more time to prepare for the negotiations, and as it was nearly Christmas he and the others could hardly afford to be gone: every last priest and yes even every last Jesuit was needed to administer to the faithful in Holland. Could they not postpone the conference until the spring? The archbishop could hardly ignore such a request, and all the delegates departed.

When spring came, who was surprised that the conference did not? This time it was the weary archbishop himself who decided to postpone it: his concern now was the scandal that might result when word leaked out to Protestants that Catholic clergy were bickering among themselves. As there was little hope for true, quick reconciliation between vicar and Jesuits over the Holland Mission, why take the chance of engaging in debates sure to become public? As a later nuncio said about intra-faith disputes, "in the midst of heretics one must tread lightly against fellow religionists," because such gave cause for ridicule. Better to let the Dutch church struggle along in semiprivate, was the implicit conclusion, than to force the issue or to hang out dirty laundry for all to see.

The archbishop eventually made at least one trip to the edge of the Republic: in the spring of 1615 he traveled to Den Bosch to consecrate its new bishop and to discuss the ongoing problems of the Dutch church. But formal agreements about the operation of that church were never struck, and tensions continued. The ideal of the one, true fold proved more elusive than ever in the north, even during peace.

Or because of peace? After all, Dutch Calvinists likewise argued more violently among themselves during peace than ever before or after: the debate of the two camps within Dutch Calvinism, "Remonstrants" and "Contra-Remonstrants," ended only with spilled blood and rolling heads. Dutch Catholics did not go that far, but the failure to solve the question of who was in charge of their faith in the Republic planted seeds that a century later would bloom into outright schism: division into Jesuit-supporting "Roman Catholics" and vicar-supporting, Rome-denying "Old Catholics," a division that would have horrified Mathias Hovius even more than violence. Peace was not the great panacea after all.

A Schoolboy from Diest

The twenty-fourth of June, 1615, the Feast of St. John the Baptist, a rectory in Diest.

During his trips to Diest, Archbishop Hovius often lodged with his good friend Haymo Timmermans, rural dean and pastor of the local beguinage.

One benefit was the setting. Pastor Timmermans' rectory lay just within the gate of the beguinage itself, an attractive walled town-within-a-town for some two hundred pious women, called beguines, who were not quite nuns but not quite laypeople. And of the eleven beguinages in the archdiocese, the one in Diest was the archbishop's "glory and pearl," having somehow survived both the physical and spiritual destruction of the Troubles.

The second benefit was the company. The pastor's sense of proper religion nearly matched the archbishop's. Hence, at this tranquil rectory, with this stalwart pastor, Mathias Hovius might find not only refuge from his troubles of the moment but solutions. In the evening, with horses in stalls and gates secured, the two men could talk over a meal in a room near the kitchen or walk on the large grounds, which included a peaceful garden divided by a brook. Neither left a record of their conversations, but in the middle of 1615 topics were easy enough to guess: the Holland Mission, rumors of a new nuncio, Isabella's fabulous triumph at a recent shooting contest in Brussels, and of course the immediate pastoral work at hand in Diest.

preceding page: Sucquet, *The Way to Heaven*
From *Via vitae aeternae* (Antwerp, 1620)

The archbishop was in town to consecrate altars, confirm children, and visit the clergy. The pastor was assisting him as needed. Today's visit to the chapter of St. Sulpitius, the main church in Diest, would alone have provided the two old friends an abundance of material for evening conversation and vigorous headshaking, since the canons of Sulpitius' appeared more devoted to scandal than duty. Yet for all the impressive recent sinning of these canons, it was their role in a more distant drama that surely lay even more heavily on the hearts and minds of archbishop and pastor this night: namely, the drama of the missing schoolboy.

Two years earlier, this promising boy had been stolen away from the household of Pastor Timmermans, thanks largely to the efforts of one of the canons. Then, just two weeks before, while the archbishop was in Den Bosch muddled in the problems of the Holland Mission, the same boy was stolen away again—this time from the protection of Mathias Hovius himself. The archbishop, no stranger to the problems of household disturbances, had always heard the pastor's story of the boy with sympathy. But now he was a full partner in the pastor's tragedy, and no longer merely a listening ear.

This most recent theft, combined with the likely sight of new household boys serving at the pastor's table, were reason enough to revisit the still-unfolding saga of young Jan Berchmans, who would one day become a saint for all the church but who to Mathias Hovius and Haymo Timmermans was simply a lost protégé and priest.

STOLEN ONCE

From the time he became pastor of the beguinage in 1601, Haymo Timmermans knew the name Berchmans. He knew Jan's father, Jan senior, who was dean of the local shoemaker's and tanner's guild. He knew Jan's aunts, Maria and Katheline, who were beguines and with whom Jan came to live in the beguinage at age six, in 1605, in order to attend the beguinage's school for children. And the pastor knew Jan himself, who served as an altar boy at early Mass in the beguinage church.

The child Jan showed piety beyond his years. On the Feast of the Holy Innocents, every December, when the Catholic world was turned upside down for a day in childlike silliness, to commemorate the children massacred by Herod, and when a boy might dress as a bishop while priests might uproariously curse the audience rather than bless it, Jan stunned the audience with his gravity: instead of turning the mock Mass into the usual parody, he performed it most solemnly and properly. In addition to his piety, Jan showed unusual academic ability as well, enough that around 1608 he moved across the street from the beguinage's school to Diest's Latin School, an elite institution for boys eight to eighteen possessed of intellectual promise. It was while a student at this school that Jan received, with a crowd of other children, the sacrament of confirmation from Archbishop Hovius. And it was while at this school that Jan encountered the first in a series of crises that would affect him, Pastor Timmermans, and Mathias Hovius so deeply.

In the summer of 1611, Jan Berchmans senior announced that the family was in serious financial trouble: The recent peace was bad for the shoe business, explained the father, and there was no longer enough money for such luxuries as the Latin School. Would Jan junior consider instead the cheaper path of learning a trade, beginning as an apprentice in the home of some master? According to Mother Berchmans, twelve-year-old Jan was so distraught at the thought that he fell to his bare knees and pleaded to finish his studies at the Latin School, even if he had to live on bread and water, for a priest he wished to become.

This was the crisis that brought young Jan more intimately than before into the life of Haymo Timmermans. Somehow, perhaps through his beguine aunts, the pastor learned of Jan's plight. It happened that one of Pastor Timmermans' predecessors at the beguinage had founded a scholarship for a poor boy inclined to the priesthood, which provided tuition at the Latin School and lodgings with the pastor, an arrangement intended to help the boy absorb the clerical regime more fully. Jan's family was not truly or forever poor, but at the moment they certainly qualified. However it happened, Jan likely received this scholarship, for by the autumn of 1611 he was joyously back at the Latin School, this time living with his new priestly patron, Haymo Timmermans.

At the rectory of the pastor, Jan's virtues blossomed. This wasn't because the regime of the Latin School grew any easier: as before it was out of bed at five, early Mass and breakfast and class, frequent study and little play, always dressed in toga or coat or choir robes, and evening reading around an inefficient fire. Rather, blossoming came of new opportunity. Now Jan could pray in the privacy of his own room or the rectory's tiny chapel, rather than in crowded quarters. Now by serving Pastor Timmermans at table or otherwise, Jan could perfect that virtue beloved of all church- men, prompt obedience. Now he could let shine the quality that drew comments from all who knew him: gaiety, or "hilarity," evi- dent even in his prayers. All these, plus the boy's aptitude for Latin and Greek, caused Haymo Timmermans one evening to gesture toward Jan, who was serving at table, and declare to guests: "That boy is an angel." The pastor surely hoped that Jan would remain with him several years until finishing at the Latin School, and then move on to the archbishop's seminary in Mechelen.

But these hopes were destined to crumble, thanks to the designs of another and greater priestly patron of the Berchmans family, a patron who eventually came to decide that Jan should live and learn somewhere else. Such middling families as Jan's, in happy possession of a boy gifted enough to surmount his in- herited station, invariably required some superior patron to point the way to a more exalted life. In return for the patron's guidance and connections, the family offered loyalty and service. Thus did a patron build his influence, thus did a family improve its stand- ing. The priest Martin Duncan had played this role for young Mathias Hovius. Pastor Timmermans played it temporarily for Jan—but sometime in late 1612 Jan Berchmans senior determined

that another local patron could do even more for the family than
Haymo Timmermans: this was Frans van Groenendonk, canon
of Diest's inglorious chapter of St. Sulpitius'. Thus began another
crisis in the boy's life.

The elder Berchmans came to know Canon Groenendonk
better starting in 1609, when Jan senior became one of the
church wardens of St. Sulpitius and thus met periodically with
the canon about accounts. By gradually shifting loyalty to the
canon, the family was not necessarily being ungrateful to Pastor Timmermans for past services. Rather, they simply recognized
that Canon Groenendonk was greater. The chapter, however ill
disciplined, was the mightiest ecclesiastical institution in town,
mightier even than Haymo Timmermans. And within the chapter Frans Groenendonk was not only canon but also bursar (in
charge of accounts), cantor (in charge of song), and scholaster
(theoretically in charge of local education). Little wonder that by
1612 the canon was regarded as the family's "best benefactor and
friend." And little wonder that Canon Groenendonk was eventually able to persuade Jan's father that the boy deserved better
than the Latin School of Diest or for that matter the household of
Haymo Timmermans.

For various reasons, Canon Groenendonk was enamored of
neither one. Like most scholasters in Catholic Europe, he was in
constant disagreement with the local Latin School. Such schools,
run now in practice by secular town magistrates, three clerical overseers, and a rector, infringed upon the medieval rights of scholasters, including the long-standing right to collect licensing fees
from local schoolmasters. For years, Canon Groenendonk had
therefore argued with the current proprietors of the Latin School
over who was really in charge of it, they or he. Once, to ease tensions, the proprietors had made Canon Groenendonk rector, in
1599, but then fired him in 1603 for negligence, which only made
things worse.

The canon got on little better with Pastor Timmermans. As
one of the three clerical overseers of the detested Latin School,

Pastor Timmermans was the canon's rival in local education. As Archbishop Hovius' rural dean of Diest, Pastor Timmermans was the canon's rival in local ecclesiastical power. And as current mentor of young Jan Berchmans, Pastor Timmermans was of course the canon's rival in local patronage.

The lingering tensions among Canon Groenendonk, the Latin School, and Haymo Timmermans all merged into a single crisis in 1612, in the form of a dispute over the school's latest rector. For the first time in the school's history, this rector was a layman, not a priest. This alone infuriated the chapter and Canon Groenendonk. But what infuriated the canon even more was that Haymo Timmermans, as one of the three overseers of the Latin School, had agreed to the rector's appointment, and thus betrayed the priestly state.

That the rector, named Walter van Stiphout, refused to bow and scrape before the canons, and even openly despised them, did not improve the situation. He practically went out of his way to show that he did not need or care for them. Secure in his position, he proudly pointed to the Latin and Greek plays not only performed but composed by the boys. He pointed to a host of satisfied parents. He pointed to his beloved star pupil Jan Berchmans, the "flower of the school and the glory of the students." And he painfully pointed to his rescuing of the school from the dismal guidance of the previous rector, the dull-witted Jan vanden Brule, or the brief and equally dismal rectorship of the one before that, Canon Frans van Groenendonk himself. So confident was Rector Stiphout toward the canons that he even shouted in public, during the St. John the Baptist procession in June 1612, that the chapter of Sulpitius was full of "restless souls" and "great pigheads."

This insult brought the crisis to a peak. For here was an affront so grievous that it caused the usually bickering canons to do the unthinkable: they would cooperate. Together they devised a plan to drive the rector out. It went as follows: the rector's contract expired in several months, namely January 1613. In the meantime, the chapter would bring to Diest its own candidate for rector in

order to show him off, and do all in their power to block the renewal of Rector Stiphout's appointment.

In addition to the chapter's corporate plan, Frans Groenendonk devised a private plan of his own, one meant to personally
wound the canon's rivals, Rector Walter van Stiphout and Pastor
Haymo Timmermans. This plan went as follows: If magistrates
and overseers decided to renew the contract of Rector Stiphout in
January 1613, then Canon Groenendonk would counsel Jan Berchmans senior to move his son not only to another school but to a
household outside of Diest. Rector Stiphout would then be de-
prived of his best student, his "wonder of nature," his "crown,"
"ornament," "glory," and "hope." And Pastor Timmermans would
lose years of influence over his dear protégé.

This plan was no idle fantasy. In November 1612, while on
business in Mechelen for the chapter of Sulpitius', Canon Groenendonk paid a visit to his friend and counterpart, the cantor of
the chapter of St. Rombout's, and made a proposal easy enough to
imagine: was the cantor interested in receiving into his household
a most promising schoolboy, who currently resided in the most
objectionable conditions in Diest? The cantor of St. Rombout's
replied that he was. Everything was set.

When that great and dreadful day of 22 January 1613 finally
came, and magistrates and overseers defiantly voted to renew the
contract of Walter van Stiphout as rector of the Latin School, Frans
van Groenendonk was prepared. Immediately his plan went into
effect. As advised by the canon, Jan Berchmans senior removed
Jan at once from the Latin School and the household of Pastor
Timmermans, then announced to all that he was moving Jan the
next day to the household of the cantor of St. Rombout's in Mechelen, where the boy would continue his studies and training. Canon
Groenendonk would accompany Jan to his new lodgings.

Everyone was caught by surprise. A broken-hearted Walter
van Stiphout, despite his new contract, resigned almost immediately as rector and left for northern Brabant, where he remained
long "embittered" about life because of the theft of Jan Berchmans

from his school. The angry magistrates of Diest and the overseers of the Latin School refused to appoint the chapter's candidate as rector, instead giving it to another of the chapter's rivals in education: the local Augustinians. And a distressed Haymo Timmermans was forever "alienated" from his fellow priest, Frans van Groenendonk.

As for the canon, he and the nearly fourteen-year-old Jan arrived in a cold Mechelen as scheduled the next day, 23 January, to begin the boy's new life.

STOLEN TWICE

The only consolation to Haymo Timmermans in this affair was that Jan would be near Archbishop Hovius.

In fact, almost immediately upon arriving in Mechelen did Jan enter the world of the archbishop. This was not only because the duties of Jan's new patron, the cantor of St. Rombout's, took him often to the archbishop's cathedral, but also because this cantor was none other than Jean de Froidmont, who doubled as patron of the new Dutch convert Frans Boels, whose story the archbishop knew. Jan arrived in the cantor's household on 23 January 1613, with the visiting Frans already there. Frans converted to Catholicism five days later, on 28 January. Archbishop Hovius heard of the conversion within days and performed the sacrament of confirmation for Frans. No doubt the archbishop also heard the rumors, already spreading around town, that it was the new boy Jan Berchmans, not Cantor Froidmont, who had most influenced Frans's decision to become a Catholic.

The archbishop would have believed it, for he knew few redeeming qualities in Jean de Froidmont. To the archbishop this latest choice of patrons for the boy Jan Berchmans was as disastrous as the last, for Canons Froidmont and Groenendonk shared an alarming number of undesirable traits. Both stood ready to sling lawsuits at the slightest imagined offense. Both boasted uncles and brothers in high legal places. Both had become canons in the 1590s. Both had become cantors around 1600. And both were remarkably unwilling performers of their duties.

But the two were no mere clones. In fairness to Frans van Groenendonk, who was merely irascible, Jean de Froidmont was ridiculous, a model of the silly noble canon. Every illness known to humanity he possessed, as he recounted in exhaustive detail to those around him. Every threat to his status in choir, or his place in procession, he contested. And every penny he received as cantor still was not enough. Indeed his greatest legacy after four decades as cantor would not be his singing voice, his legal expertise, or his popular dinner parties, but rather his constant complaint that he wished not to be cantor at all, for the income attached to the office was too small for such a fat bird as he.

How Jean de Froidmont had come to accept this office and its paltry income belonged itself to the realm of the absurd. It was usual when offered any such position to inspect the account books of one's predecessor, to assess one's likely income. During his inspection, Jean de Froidmont mistakenly calculated the cantor's income at ten times its actual amount—in his own woeful words, he "made an elephant from a fly." Initially unaware of his mistake, he happily accepted the office. Soon afterward, when his first revenues came in and his mistake became clear, he quickly tried to resign. The account books were in Dutch, he explained, and his was a bit rusty—that was why he had read things wrong. But such an excuse failed to arouse any sympathy in his fluently bilingual brother canons, or in Archbishop Hovius, so he was stuck. Thus did he become and remain the reluctant cantor of St. Rombout's.

Jean de Froidmont, nobleman and licentiate in civil and canon law, had come to Mechelen from French-speaking Soignies, in the diocese of Cambrai. He left his family home for Mechelen not to become cantor or to improve his Dutch or even to remain a canon, but because he hoped to use his new position to attain even higher position—namely as ecclesiastical councilor on the Grand Council, highest legal position in the land for a clergyman.

Though finally nominated to his dream post, Canon Froidmont never came close to actually winning it, and so he fumed. Instead of dictating expensive briefs to secretaries and handing out costly legal advice, as he had imagined himself doing in his middle age, he was instead stuck for the rest of his days with a thin choir and a paltry forty florins a year. That he also had a family fortune, plus three hundred florins a year from his position as canon, plus a fief-dom in Feluy worth four thousand florins, did not assuage the new cantor.

For years he continued to ask dean and archbishop for re-lease as cantor, but always they refused: he had accepted the duties, now he must fulfill them. Cantor Froidmont grew bitter. "Behold the mighty revenues and great fruits of the cantoral dignity of the metropolitan church," he noted at the bottom of one of his ac-counts. When he refused to perform all his duties, out of protest at his incommensurate salary, the archbishop and the dean threat-ened a lawsuit, but this only animated Jean de Froidmont, who fan-cied himself in court, and he sued back. The cantor's case against archbishop and chapter was still raging even as Archbishop Hovius sat chatting with Pastor Timmermans in Diest in June 1615. Ironi-cally, one of the witnesses the cantor sent to testify on his behalf during the case, a witness whom he thought would impress any judge, was the teenaged Jan Berchmans, ever the dutiful and able protégé.

Despite the cantor and his lawsuits, Archbishop Hovius could, even more than Haymo Timmermans, find several redeem-ing qualities to the fact that Jan Berchmans now resided in Meche-len—even if it did happen to be with Jean de Froidmont. First, the boy seemed impervious to the cantor's deleterious influence, for his virtues continued to shine. Were the stories already told of Jan falling prostrate to stop arguing among his roommates? Of happily cleaning dishes and pots and sordid courtyards? Of con-tentedly wearing obsolete clothing to keep his father's expenses at a minimum? Of leaving words half finished when his master the cantor called? Of being in demand to serve at table when the cantor hosted a dinner, because of his unusual cheeriness and quickness to obey? Of praying so long, laughingly, that his knees inflamed? Indeed, though the mother of Frans Boels once complained that her boy was wasting his life away carrying the robes of Cantor Froidmont to and from the cathedral, Jan objected not at all to the task, because while waiting for his master in St. Rombout's he had opportunity to pray at an altar containing a replica of Our Dear Lady of the Sharp Hill, a place he had visited often as a boy.

Most pleasing and certain of all to the archbishop about Jan's situation, however, was the boy's enrollment and progress at the Latin School of Mechelen. Here was a place with a more settled past than the Latin School of Diest, and a place dear to the archbishop's heart besides. When a young priest, Mathias Hovius had himself taught boys at Mechelen's Latin School, and now as archbishop he considered it the main feeder for his seminary. It was logical and probable that Jan would complete his studies at the Latin School, then enroll in the archbishop's seminary, and finally become a pastor in the archdiocese. There would be a happy ending after all to the tragedy of Pastor Timmermans. But this happy ending was threatened just weeks before the archbishop's visit to Diest in June 1615: for in May Jan decided, after two characteristically impressive years in Mechelen's Latin School, to transfer to a brand new Latin School in town, run by the Jesuits. When finished there, it was still possible that Jan would enroll in the seminary. But more likely, everyone knew, was that he would enter the Jesuit order and be taken from the archbishop and his archdiocese forever. Now Archbishop Hovius too had lost Jan Berchmans.

Mathias Hovius cared deeply about Catholic education in the broad sense. He worried much about youths raised during the "Troubles," when no schools had functioned at all. He believed that "the salvation and ruin of a republic" depended "almost wholly on the good or ill instruction of the youth," who "by nature were inclined to evil." But he cared most of all about the education of pastors, which to him meant especially the Latin School of

Mechelen and his seminary. He was proud that the Latin School had produced four students who graduated "primus" from the University of Leuven, but he was equally proud that other graduates of the Latin School had entered his seminary and produced the lion's share of the 121 priests emerging from it by 1615. When the Jesuits upset this cozy arrangement, the archbishop understandably grew defensive.

Jesuits had first arrived in Mechelen in 1611 with the intent of establishing a novice house to train new Jesuits, who were to be over eighteen years old. Though nothing was said about opening any school for boys, the archbishop was wary of the Jesuits from the start. He knew that such schools were already the heart of Jesuit enterprises in Catholic Europe, that most of their thirty houses already established in the Low Countries alone (the densest concentration of Jesuits in Europe) had such schools attached to them, and that these schools were wildly successful. He also knew the reasons for this success: innovations in curriculum and the practice of charging no tuition. And he knew at last that these schools were natural recruiting grounds for new Jesuits: eighteen-year-old graduates who wished to become priests often did so simply by staying on with the Jesuits rather than by entering a bishop's seminary. In any town but Mechelen, the archbishop might have gone along with a Jesuit school for boys or even the Jesuits' efforts to recruit to their order. But the cathedral city was different: should the Jesuits open one of their novel, free schools there, the old-fashioned, tuition-charging Latin School run by the city would be ruined—and the seminary along with it. Where would the archbishop then find already scarce rural priests?

Here was a monumental dilemma even for someone used to them. Before this dispute over the Latin School, Archbishop Hovius had for a long time had reason to admire and support the Jesuit order. When he needed teachers for the rural flock, they answered. When they consecrated their novice house in Mechelen, he was present among the invited and even hosted a celebratory dinner. When Jesuits of Brussels and Antwerp needed stone for their churches, he helped them gain access to quarries near Laken. When he needed a catechism for children, he adopted a Jesuit version. When he needed a substitute to make his *ad limina* journey to Rome, he sent a Jesuit. And when the archbishop's judge or vicar-general assigned confessors to penitents, they often assigned a Jesuit.

But the archbishop also had cause to be suspicious. More than other orders did the Jesuits stress loyalty to Rome and exemption from bishops. Further, they were accused often of accepting novices who entered against the wishes of parents. Moreover, they provoked arguments about schools in many towns around Catholic Europe, especially in France, the one nation where their influence was blunted. And, last, they had a reputation for acting first and asking permission later, as they had demonstrated so ably in the Holland Mission. How closely would these Jesuits cooperate with the archbishop if they opened a school in Mechelen?

Ultimately the archbishop's anxieties bore fruit. In 1613 the Jesuits bought a second building in Mechelen, just the right size for a new school. Then, in May 1615, while the archbishop was conveniently away in Den Bosch, magistrates and Jesuits struck a working agreement for a new Jesuit School. The city even promised one thousand florins a year to ensure that students could attend free. Many of the two hundred students at the Latin School of Mechelen heard the rumors about the new Jesuit School and its free tuition and talked of transferring.

When he returned from Den Bosch, the archbishop was livid. It was too late to block the Jesuit School altogether, for magistrates were enthusiastic and the Jesuits had already enlisted such powerful patrons as the archdukes. But the archbishop could insist that the magistrates subsidize the city's Latin School just as they had the Jesuit, to keep things even—after all, other towns of Europe were now providing free education as well. He could also ask the archdukes to mediate a compromise. He could in addition argue fiercely that the choir of St. Rombout's, "more venerable than opulent," depended on the Latin School and seminary to boost its numbers. He could further point out that if the seminary died then so would the ancient art of Gregorian chant, for though still the most universal form of church music it was now taught no-where else in the archdiocese, being deemed too old-fashioned by younger musicians and the new Jesuit curricula. And most tangibly of all the archbishop could at last threaten that if magistrates did not subsidize the Latin School then he would move his see from Mechelen to Brussels. Over no other dispute did the archbishop ever make such a drastic threat.

Eventually the city agreed to subsidize the old Latin School as well, but too late. Many boys remained firm about transferring to the Jesuit School, including Jan Berchmans, whose academic and spiritual gifts were glowing in Mechelen as brightly as they had in Diest. Both archbishop and Jesuits wanted this pupil for their own school. But in June 1615, just before the archbishop's visit to Pastor Timmermans in Diest, Jan finally transferred to the Jesuits. His transfer, more than any other, created a "deep chasm" between the two schools. One Jesuit even labeled it a "tempest."

Few could doubt that Jan was genuinely attracted to the Jesuit program. But some must have wondered whether he had acted alone. Was Cantor Froidmont as much behind Jan's transfer this time as Canon Groenendonk had been in Diest? One might have expected Jean de Froidmont, member of the cathedral chap-ter, to recommend that Jan attend the local Latin School and then the archbishop's seminary, for canons were secular priests and reli-gious orders such as the Jesuits their rivals. But probability and logic rarely explained Jean de Froidmont, certainly not in the sum-mer of 1615 when he was embroiled in lawsuits against archbishop and dean over his income as cantor. When Jan Berchmans chose in May 1615 to become part of the first class to enter the new Jesuit School, he therefore did so with the approval, even the encourage-ment, of Jean de Froidmont.

A friend of Jan's later said that given opposition in "high places" to his transfer, "divine providence" must have brought Jan to the Jesuit School. But archbishop and pastor, together in Diest, saw things otherwise. They had lost that boy by stealth. Tonight on the Feast of the Baptist, they could only wonder whether the recently transferred Jan, now sixteen, would become a Jesuit when his studies were completed two years hence. They could only wonder whether Jan would have stayed with Pastor Timmermans had the pastor not consented to a lay rector at the Latin School of Diest. And they could only wonder why Jan, in all apparent innocence, still regarded Canons Groenendonk and Froidmont as his "very best patrons."

PARTINGS

The two friends did not remain talking forever, for with rapid action they might salvage a portion of these predicaments, or at least punish the instigators.

First, the archbishop made sure before leaving Diest to issue his usual criticism of the chapter of St. Sulpitius', home of Frans van Groenendonk. In addition to a long list of condemnations of the chapter as a whole, Archbishop Hovius singled out for special condemnation Canon Groenendonk. This condemnation did not mention specifically the tragedy of Jan Berchmans: instead it merely noted the canon's failure to do accounts and say Masses. Yet the unusual act of this public rebuke over the rather pedestrian matter of untidy account books caused one to wonder whether there wasn't more to this embarrassment: was it not just as much about Jan Berchmans, Haymo Timmermans, and the Latin Schools of Diest and Mechelen? Perhaps wrongly added sums or long-neglected accounts might alone have been enough to provoke the archbishop to pressure the chapter into placing Canon Groenendonk under house arrest. But alone they could not explain why the archbishop was so angry at the chapter that he refused to deliver his decrees in person to them, or even to send his secretary to perform the task; instead he went to the trouble of searching out and dispatching in his place the "slow" Jan vanden Brule, whom everyone recognized was such a dismal failure as rector of the Latin School years before. It was the lowly Vanden Brule who delivered the decrees, then read them aloud to insulted canons.

Next, when the archbishop returned to Mechelen he made sure its Latin School stayed open. Over the following months compromises were struck, movement between the Latin School and Jesuit School was regulated, and the archbishop was designated the Latin School's official protector. In public he hid disappointment and played the good shepherd toward both Latin and Jesuit Schools, attending plays put on by the boys at each and even criticizing a production at the Latin School for its prolixity and dryness. But in private he still fumed. The rectors of the Latin School and seminary showed up more often as his dinner guests than did Jesuits. He wrote friends that he still feared the demise of the Latin School and thus the demise of the church in all the land. He told the secretary of the privy council that the Jesuits were soon ignoring all agreements about the Latin School of Mechelen. Most revealing, he warned colleagues and old teachers at the University of Leuven to be wary of Jesuits, who were highly skilled at obscuring their intentions. They once promised not to teach in Mechelen, recounted the archbishop, but as soon as they were in they set out to destroy the Latin School. He went further: all stated intentions of the Jesuits "were now suspicious to him."

Obviously Mathias Hovius was less than an unqualified supporter of this celebrated order. Especially two years later when all his fears came true. In September 1617, having scored first in his class at the Jesuit School, Jan Berchmans entered the Jesuit novice house in Mechelen with the intent of becoming a Jesuit missionary in China rather than a local pastor for the archbishop. Friends said that Jan cried for joy the entire first night inside.

The response of others to Jan's entry among the Jesuits was mixed. His father was initially reluctant but then surprisingly inspired. For when Mother Berchmans died within weeks of Jan's entry, Jan senior decided to become a priest himself. His first and only ecclesiastical post was not terribly surprising: canon in the chapter of St. Sulpitius' in Diest! But he died within a year. Jan's response upon hearing news of his father's death was typically stoic: now he could doubly say, he told others, "Our Father who art in Heaven."

The Jesuits of Mechelen offered the disappointed Archbishop Hovius an olive branch. As part of the jubilee for his fiftieth year as a priest, in October 1617, celebrated over several days with some two hundred friends who came for processions, excellent dining, and the inevitable bell ringing, students of the Jesuit School (probably not including the recently graduated Jan Berchmans) performed in the archbishop's honor a tragedy of Blessed Aloysius Gonzaga, a Jesuit martyr. But did the archbishop already know that Aloysius was the greatest hero of young Jan?

Of Cantor Froidmont it was said afterward that he could not speak of Jan "without shedding tears," a sentiment the boy unwittingly managed to evoke in most of his patrons. Indeed, during the few years of life that remained to Jan his reputation for piety grew only greater, so that at his premature death in Rome in 1621 the whispers urging his sainthood turned quickly into clamor. Those who trumpeted his virtues predictably embellished the already marvelous and true tales that could be told, yet even in the face of the silliest exaggeration it was difficult for anyone who became acquainted with Jan Berchmans to escape the impression that this unusual boy from Diest truly was oblivious to such trifles as school politics or scheming patrons, but, smiling all the while, simply wished to please God.

ELEVEN

Table Talk

Any year.

Whatever the season or year, a never-ending line of guests bellied up eagerly to the archbishop's well-appointed table. Not only pastors, monks, and nuns, but rulers, nobles, magistrates, family, members of the diocesan hierarchy, and simple parishioners could be found among the invited.

Though the invitation was surely attractive, it was just as sure that the archbishop's household was, given his stature, quite modest. He had no great library. His furniture was practical, featuring straight-backed Spanish chairs, plain beds and tables, and the predictable purples and greens of bishoply decor. His paintings were about devotion, not art, featuring typical saints in typical poses. And his alms went to assist exiled bishops, poor students, or broken priests, rather than to purchase yet another frilly robe for Our Dear Lady of the Sharp Hill.

Only for images of his office would the archbishop match the extravagance of brother bishops and indulge in unmitigated finery, for such images were about the position, not the man. A bishop simply had to display the trappings that in his world said, without words, here is authority. Thus he allowed himself a pair of red silken gloves and a white pair with two gold roses. Thus he insisted, like all bishops, that liturgical objects be made of genuine

preceding page: David Teniers, *Flemish Kermesse.* The kermis was a favorite time for feasting, and a prime occasion to break rules.
Private collection

silver or gold, not tin. And thus he created a striking reception hall in his residence in Mechelen, with a stark black pontifical throne, yards of draped velvet in violet and black, matching cushions, and giant tapestries and gilded leather on the walls.

Yet for all the archbishop's moderation, his very ability to grant alms and afford such symbols placed him undeniably among the materially great of his world. Thanks to the revived bounties of Affligem, by the time of peace he owned residences in Brussels and Mechelen and a country house on seventy-five acres in Hofstade, near Mechelen. He spent one thousand florins a year on a porter, chamberlain, maids, coachman, coachman's assistant, and stable boy, nine hundred on the staff of the diocesan hierarchy, four hundred on salaries for musicians of St. Rombout's, and far more on the seminary. Then of course he set before guests at his table a variety of desirable dishes, according to season: mutton, meat pies, poultry, Majorcan capers, Genoan pasta, and local eel and carp, prepared with such dear spices as pepper, cloves, or even saffron, adorned by such delights as marzipan, tarts, figs, plums, oranges, lemons, and olives, and fortified in abundance by such staples as heavy white bread, strong brown beer, and jugs of wine.

One reason the archbishop invited so many to his table was that it was expected of the great: thus did they avoid the sin of greed. But as important to the archbishop as the virtue or the food of the occasion was the talk. Some of it was idle, such as the medical doctor who astounded the archbishop with news that Archduchess Isabella was thirty-three when she first tasted wine, or the visiting priests from Holland who told of a diver able (thanks to a technique he had learned among the Turks) to stay underwater for fifteen minutes. But much of the conversation was on the state of religious life within the archbishop's flock.

Difficult as it was to deal with dozens of seminarians, scores of pastors, and hundreds of heretics, it was far more difficult still to shepherd tens of thousands of ordinary believers. Travels and audiences and letters connected him personally to an astonishing number, yielding a familiarity much deeper than that of Bishop Camus

of Grenoble, who upon first visiting his diocese thought himself
in China. But not even the horse-weary Archbishop Hovius could
hope to possess, in an absolute sense, more than a fleeting knowledge of so many. Most of what he knew still came secondhand,
such as during meetings with his staff—or the multitude of conversations at his table.

The tales were endless and varied: from frightening accounts
of blasphemers and witches to mundane reports on the progress
of a new catechism or the foundation of new confraternities. But
much of the talk had to do with holy times, objects, and places, for
these aspects of religion seemed to occupy the flock most. After
forty years as a priest, after his memorable experiences at the Sharp
Hill, little surprised him on this and other subjects, though much
still interested him.

THE MILLER'S SABBATH

Perhaps the most colorful storytellers at the archbishop's table were
the staff of his diocesan court, who to reach his residence walked
ten minutes across town from their new straw-roofed building just
outside the gates of Mechelen.

The judge, called the "Official," ate often with the archbishop. But more frequently still came the court's prosecuting lawyers, called "promotors," and the court's bailiffs. These men were
at the vanguard of the final front of religious life: enforcement.
Trouble was built more squarely into their jobs than even the archbishop's. With other guests Archbishop Hovius might speak of
wonders or pleasant diversions as well as of ill-doers within the
flock, but with promotors and bailiffs the talk was relentlessly of
trouble.

Sometimes the stories were of personal peril and even attacks, for who liked to see bailiffs coming, with their warrants
or their summons to appear in the archbishop's court? Every bailiff and promotor knew hot and cold weather, dirty hostels, old

horses, uncooperative family and friends, and of course resistance to arrest. Which bailiff—Sainctsaulne, Bullestraten, or Van Doornik, it didn't matter—had told the archbishop of Joris de Buel, a parishioner of Willebroek, who was "rebellious" against pastor, bailiff, and archbishop all at once? Who promised to "set fire to the church court, and the bishop, and all other long robes"? Who warned bailiffs that they would not get him to the prison in Vilvoorde "without some red necks being carried about," or in other words a few people being killed? Who struck a bailiff and said, "I'm sick of the bishop"? Who so intimidated villagers that no one would raise a hand to help when a cudgel-wielding De Buel chased the bailiff half a mile down the road?

The archbishop did not ignore these tales of peril to his bailiffs' health and well-being. But his ears perked even more sharply at tales of the sins that got laypeople in trouble to begin with, or of lay magistrates who failed to cooperate with the church in punishing those sins—or in other words when his sense of proper religion, especially the holy, was violated. One of a thousand such tales was of the Sabbath-breaking miller of Brussels, named Aert Goosens.

Early in his term of office, the archbishop grew concerned over the masses of people who thanks to ugly habits learned during war had forgotten proper and improper behavior on the Sabbath and other holy days. Thus in 1598 he persuaded the archdukes to issue a decree on the subject. None of the archbishop's men kept precise statistics on the numerous violators of that decree, but they did inevitably gather anecdotal evidence and they certainly knew the story of Aert.

Trouble began one December day when two of the archbishop's bailiffs handed Aert a summons to appear in the diocesan court, for someone had seen him milling on the previous Sabbath and reported it. Aert responded, "I won't go to Mechelen for that! The bishop can come to Brussels, I'm just as good as he is." Aert also threatened to drive the bailiffs from his mill with "big sticks," and called them scoundrels and other unflattering names. When the bailiffs cited him for resisting arrest as well, Aert grew even madder.

Several months later, on the feast of the Ascension, the bailiffs visited Aert again and caught him milling once more. Once more they ordered him to appear in court. Once more he refused: "The judge may come here but I won't come to him." Aert's wife, holding a cudgel, followed the bailiffs to the door, and with raised hand repeated her husband's insults, adding: "Come one more time, if you have the heart, and I'll break your head in two with this stick." Aert yelled as well, "Why do you always bother us, and interfere in this or that?"

On a third trip to the house, Aert's wife swung a broom at the bailiffs and muttered "filthy" words. A final run-in occurred fittingly on another feast day, the Visitation of Our Dear Lady, in July. Aert wished to cart some grain into Brussels, but because it was a holy day he had to go to St. Katheline's church to ask for special permission from the archbishop's dean of Brussels, Peter Vinckius. The dean, in the sacristy arranging his vestments, refused. Aert yelled that he would cart it inside anyway. The dean had five men block Aert's wagon. Aert tried bribing them, but to no avail. So he raged: "I'm sick of the bishop, and all of you, and the dean, and the judge. You're all just a pile of shitsweepers from Mechelen."

Aert's defiance disturbed the archbishop, but just as disturbing was how long Aert avoided punishment. The *amman,* or sheriff, of Brussels, responsible for enforcing that city's laws, refused to help arrest Aert, or to compel him to pay the fine imposed by the archbishop's diocesan court. Though the amman had on previous occasions arrested scandalous heretics himself, he obviously did not believe that Aert deserved such treatment. This was exactly why the archbishop during the Provincial Council of 1607 asked the archdukes to require officers of the state to assist officers of the church whenever asked—without being told why. If the church had to explain each case, the state's officers could too easily pick and choose discipline as they saw fit rather than as the church thought necessary. But the archdukes refused the archbishop's request. All they would do was issue their usual general decree urging magistrates to cooperate, leaving Brussels and every town and village to discipline according to its own interests and judgment. When those interests matched the church's, then everyone was happy. In fact, on one matter, the prosecution of witchcraft, magistrates may even have exceeded the vigilance desired by the archbishop. But in almost all other matters touching on religion, including the proper observance of holy days, the interests of the state led it to punish too laxly or inconsistently for the church. With so many feast days, implied magistrates, why should a city observe every one? More workdays meant a more productive, more taxable populace. Even solemn feast days required some work; why should burghers who provided it be fined?

Brussels and Aert were not alone. Various brewers and butchers of the archdiocese were also bold enough to give "sinister answers," sometimes using even the same unforgettable words, when bailiffs summoned them to the ecclesiastical court. To one summons, Willem den Brouwer and his servant yelled at bailiffs much as had Aert Goosens: "Look, there go the shitsweepers of Mechelen, I think they've got something!" To a fourth summons, Willem said: "I won't go to court in Mechelen, I don't want anything to do with the bishop; I do have a raging wife, can you help me do something about her?" The butcher Pieter Callae, summoned for working during High Mass, replied: "If I had another beast I'd slaughter it on the spot, even if the dean and the bailiff were sitting on top of it!" The state's bailiffs, called by the church to help, not only refused to do so at times but even went out of their way to inform the accused when the archbishop's bailiffs were in town.

In addition to battles over turf between church and state, there was another obstacle to the archbishop's type of feast day: each required numerous exceptions, as even the archbishop admitted. The official catechism for the archdiocese forbade bodily works but added the inevitable, "except as needed." And though the Sabbath decree of 1598 established a long list of do's and don'ts it added an even longer list of exceptions. Millers such as Aert, for instance, were allowed to work on holy days after five or six in the afternoon, bakers when there were three feast days in a row, brewers whenever there was more than one feast day in a week. Butchers could make sausages after Vespers on feast days, but not sell them—though "Sausage Women" could "quietly" sell perishable sausages until one o'clock. And so on, for cloth shearers, fishers, leatherworkers, transporters, glass sellers, even dance teachers, and of course anyone "fleeing from soldiers." If the archbishop thought his decree would halt confusion, instead it only reinforced the demands of need and custom.

And so there were plentiful reasons why the archbishop's decrees on the Sabbath were less than fully observed, by Aert Goosens or others. Aert's fate was never recorded: possibly the archbishop was able to pressure the amman, through the archdukes, into enforcing a token fine. But even if successful in this case, the archbishop could hardly intervene personally in all others. It was likely that the miller Aert Goosens returned to his old ways, at least now and again.

THE WOMEN OF LIMAL

Besides the theme of holy times, another favorite motif at the archbishop's table—related by any number of guests, lay or clerical, great or small—was that of holy powers.

Here was a subject that interested all. But often implicit in the telling of such stories at the archbishop's table was tension as well, in the form of a quiet or occasionally outright struggle between clergy and laity for control of those powers. In some cases believers resisted the archbishop outright, such as in their persistent use of dubious popular rituals at the Sharp Hill or at home. But just as common were instances when believers subtly appropriated the church's own powers for their own ends, and even in their own forms—such as the positively typical story that reached the archbishop from the village of Limal, in the French-speaking regions of the archdiocese.

In the early morning hours of one 14 June, Gislaine de Haultefenne prepared to give birth. The village midwife, sixty-seven-year-old Anne le Blan, and three other women saw that Gislaine's labor was becoming dangerously hard: as permitted in such cases Anne baptized the baby while he was still in the womb, to assure salvation and proper burial. When the wracked body finally emerged, it was, as feared, lifeless, but the act of baptism allowed him at least to be buried in consecrated ground near the church. Then came a surprise: the next night Gislaine felt a second child coming and called for Anne again. This child too was born dead, but this time Anne was too late with baptism, as five other women present saw. Without baptism, the sacrament that removed the taint of original sin, the child was, according to the church, damned forever, and unable to be buried in the consecrated ground of the churchyard. Hence he was buried in the family garden, in a hole dug by Gislaine's husband, Pierre Semalle.

Whether heartbroken more over the death or the ignoble burial of this second infant, Pierre lingered in the garden until three that afternoon, when the pastor of Limal stopped to chat. Pierre sadly told the pastor the fate of the second child. Suddenly inspired, the pastor urged Pierre to disinter the body and have three virgins carry it to the miracle-working image of Our Dear Lady in the monastery church of Lower Wavre, which had stood since the twelfth century but recently seemed especially potent in the ability to bring dead infants to life—just long enough for them to receive baptism and a proper burial. Such shrines, known for their effectiveness in temporarily restoring life to dead children, were hardly brand new or rare in Catholic Europe, but here was the closest one for Pierre. The pastor instructed Pierre to accompany the procession and to clothe himself only in white.

Emotionally and physically weary, Pierre asked his friend Pasquet Massaert to unearth the tiny body. It was carried inside the family's home, laid on a table, washed by an elderly woman still helping about the house during Gislaine's lying-in, and placed on a linen near the fire, where it was warmed. At about eight that evening a drop of bright red blood fell from the dead child's left eye. The next morning, 16 June, a small party set out for the few miles to Lower Wavre. Contrary to the pastor's instruction, Pierre did not go himself, but Pasquet went for him, along with a local chaplain named Lambert le Blan, plus Anne le Blan, three other women from Gislaine's bedside, and finally two young girls — one less than the three recommended, but sufficient for Pierre and Gislaine.

On arriving in Lower Wavre, the party made the customary circle of the church. They placed the infant on the altar in the chapel of Our Dear Lady, where Chaplain le Blan celebrated Mass. When he finished, the women and Pasquet took the boy off the altar, laid him on a bench, and commenced praying. After three hours the black body showed no life. The dejected chaplain went to find a shovel, so that he might bury the boy in the plot of unconsecrated ground near every churchyard, reserved for the unbaptized, the expelled, the excluded.

With the hole dug, the chaplain headed back to the chapel. On his way, he heard the excited voices of the women inside: the boy showed life! The chaplain ran ahead and then looked closely as the signs of life were pointed out. The body seemed whiter than before, said the women. Some tears fell from the left eye, which was shut, while the right eye, previously shut, was now open a bit. Most tellingly the child now had a lovely, rosy face, "gave off some sweat" on his forehead, and seemed to close his mouth. He even seemed to let out breath. Convinced, the chaplain ran to fetch some holy water and baptized the child. All praised God. Soon the body turned black again. But now that it was baptized, it could at least be buried in consecrated ground. Within days the story made the rounds. Because of its miraculous nature, the lay rulers of Lower Wavre and Limal called all present to testify, then sent a report to Archbishop Hovius, for the monastery of Lower Wavre was a priory of the archbishop's abbey in Affligem, and thus the shrine in the church lay under his jurisdiction.

It was a story the archbishop, and bishops all over Catholic Europe, had heard many times before and would hear often again, for parents cared about proper burial of their children. A month earlier another couple had reported almost exactly the same events in the same church in Lower Wavre: a village priest had advised the couple to carry their dead baby there; after arriving the inevitable group accompanying the couple and child had prayed without effect; the pastor then walked off to prepare the miserable burial; while he was gone others suddenly saw signs of life; when the pastor returned he was convinced as well that the child seemed alive and therefore performed baptism; almost immediately the signs of life departed, but the body now could be buried in consecrated ground.

That such stories were common did not make them all true to Mathias Hovius, when he was asked to investigate yet another. Like most bishops, he was slow to proclaim miracles, in this and other cases, partly for fear of ridicule from Protestants at dubious stories, partly because it truly was difficult to discern natural from supernatural cures (the test of a miracle), and partly because even believers were not beyond deliberate fraud in trying to achieve their purposes. The Council of Brabant, for instance, had not long before condemned a certain Marie de l'Hospital for lying about a miracle in regard to the baptism of her deceased baby.

In the case of Gislaine's infant, the archbishop could consider that the child had been warmed near a fire at home, and then while on the altar in Lower Wavre had a candle placed in his hand for forty-five minutes. Did these cause the sweat, movements, and lightening of color? Was it possible that the friends of Gislaine, most of whom had suffered much childbirth and child-death themselves, were so determined to have the infant buried in socially and religiously desirable fashion that they either willfully contrived what they saw, as Marie de l'Hospital had, or unwillfully been deluded, and led the chaplain to delusion as well?

In the end the archbishop followed his usual thriftiness with miracles: he would not proclaim the event officially wondrous. Perhaps like an ambivalent Council of Cambrai some years later did he settle in his mind on a compromise solution: namely, that the child must never have been quite dead and therefore of course it could be baptized—but there could then be no talk of miracle either. Still, family and friends were free to believe what they pleased, and that their child had been favored from on high. Moreover, since a priest—persuaded by evidence or by others—had been the chief witness of the awakening, the archbishop could hardly call the child's baptism and burial invalid. Which, short of the child's life, was all the women of Limal really wanted.

BONES OF A SAINT

The autumn of 1617.

Since the time of the Troubles, there had been no proper reliquary in Mechelen for the remains of Rombout, patron saint of the city. Instead the bones now rested in a simple wooden box covered by a cloth of gold. But with the improved fortunes that accompanied peace, both archbishop and city began drawing up plans for a more dignified replacement.

On several occasions magistrates and archbishop had recently come together to discuss details of design and expense. Once the archbishop even invited magistrates to his home. All decided that local coffers, though fuller, still did not permit duplication of the old, massive vessel, with its 650 pounds of silver and gold. But something about two-thirds the size, and much less the cost, might be managed—if the archdukes would allow a debasement of silver used in the reliquary, which in fact they were willing to do.

Thus continued the talks and details, all of which surely gave the archbishop occasion to recount to others at table his own involvement so long ago with the remains of Rombout, the saint from Scotland.

In the story of the relics of St. Rombout was yet another variation on the motif of the holy, and its twin motif of who ought to control it.

Rombout was credited with bringing Christianity to Mechelen around 770, and beginning its first church. He found his martyrdom there as well, when an angry workman on the growing structure hit Rombout in the head with an ax. Locals preserved Rombout's corpse and then his skeleton, for they knew his piety and anticipated his sainthood. Just as other villages had their special link with heaven, Rombout would be Mechelen's. His canonization by Rome was made official in 930, thus making official his specific patronage of Mechelen. A gilded reliquary built to hold his remains with the utmost dignity was finished in 1369. That reliquary lasted until 1578, when it was sold to pay for the city's defenses. The skeleton itself stayed intact until 1580, when it was scattered and broken on the first night of the English Fury.

When the clergy trickled back to a Catholic Mechelen in 1585, word spread quickly that brave townspeople had preserved at least part of the saint's jumbled remains. Archbishop Hauchinus assigned to Canon Mathias Hovius the task of gathering and inspecting those remains, so that they might be returned to their rightful place behind the high altar of the cathedral. On the day prescribed for the inspection, more than sixty Mechelaars, almost all laypeople and including even children, appeared in the chapel of St. Martin to present to Canon Hovius the pieces of Rombout they had kept hidden during the entire five years of the Calvinist regime.

Almost every story was the same. When the invasion began, each relic-saver had been struck by the thought that rebel soldiers might desecrate the bones of Rombout and so ran to the cathedral to save something. At different times, each one climbed the platform on which the reliquary rested, saw the scattered bones, grabbed a few, fled, and then hid or shared relics with friends and family.

A critical witness was the gravedigger Rombout Vercammen, for he was the first to arrive in the cathedral on that awful morning. In the darkness he could see enough to conclude that soldiers had already scattered the saint's bones. Upon reaching inside the wooden reliquary to see whether any might remain, he pulled out what he thought was a hand bone, then ran for his life. At home later, he broke the bone into pieces, which made it easier to hide from Calvinists and share with Catholic friends. But the champion relic-gatherer proved to be Anna van Roye, a thirty-seven-year-old beguine, who ran to the cathedral dressed as a laywoman. On the way she met a singer in the choir of Rombout's, nineteen-year-old Guilliam de Lannoy, and brought him along to help. Inside, Anna instructed Guilliam first to remove a "lovely" golden mantle from a statue of Our Dear Lady, which she hid in her apron. Then she dashed to the choir to have a look at the relics. There she ordered Guilliam up the platform where the relics were displayed, to tell what he saw. He yelled back down that there was a torn silken cloth inside the chest, containing several human bones. At her instruction, and with great haste, he removed the skull, the most whole and important piece, which Anna hid inside her dress. There was no time to take more. In fact, as she left the church soldiers confronted her and demanded her valuables. She handed them the golden mantle of Our Dear Lady, with which they were content. Thankfully they did not press further, and the skull was safe. She ran to her room and hid it.

When the Fury ended, Anna remained in Calvinist Mechelen and secretly told her friend, the pious silk merchant Hendrik Deens, about her treasure. Others heard of her good deed as well: because demand for relics was great on the Catholic underground inside the city, people were soon quietly asking to borrow the skull for this secret Mass or that. Once it came back to Anna with a piece missing; someone had broken it off on purpose, in the knowledge that the smallest piece of a relic was as powerful as the whole. That was when Anna decided to place the skull in a specially built case, enclosed in glass on three sides, so that people might see but not touch.

These and other tales, along with the soberness of those who swore "on their small piece of heaven" that their relics were genuine, must have given Mathias Hovius a strong sense of unity with one and all as he listened to them. But perhaps they produced twinges of shame as well. For at the very moment when these beguines, glassmakers, shippers, hosiers, dyers, masons, plumbers, orphans, girls and boys, and even a few clergymen were scurrying into the church to see what soldiers had left behind of St. Rombout, Mathias Hovius was hiding in a wardrobe across town. But if witnesses resented this, they did not show it. And how could the stories not have produced a measure of frustration inside him as well, given the typical overexuberance of laypeople for the material rather than spiritual benefits of relics? One shipper expressed the belief that his piece of Rombout had preserved his boat from harm these past several years. Some holders of relics, eager to continue under the saint's protection, had obviously kept bones to themselves and not come forward. Still others were disturbingly willing to share their good fortune and thus broke their pieces of Rombout into still tinier pieces for friends. The small hand bone in the possession of Rombout Vercammen, for instance, was divided among no fewer than ten people! Indeed enough witnesses had gained their pieces this way that it was easy to imagine believers all around Mechelen secretly breaking off tinier and tinier splinters of the saint. The only solace Mathias Hovius might have taken in this enthusiasm was that in the end most preservers of Rombout appeared to have come forward after all, acknowledging that the church was solely in charge of the supernatural, however things might seem to outsiders.

In the end here was what lay before him: a skull, two femurs, dozens of ribs, two shinbones, the "bone that connects the hip to the backbone," the smallest bone of the hand, the neck bone, a bone from the thumb, a knuckle, an arm bone, the paternoster bone, the tailbone, and various unidentifiable tiny bones. At least a recognizable skeleton.

To distinguish genuine relics from the spurious, Archdeacon Hovius was guided by the rules of his day. The favorite proofs of authenticity were documents and seals that declared the provenance of relics. But relic-shattering, paper-burning iconoclastic furies made the preservation of neat documents almost impossible, including for St. Rombout. And so other methods would have to suffice.

There was first of all reason: what made Anna's story so convincing and critical, for instance, was the corroborating evidence of other witnesses. One brought forward a small piece that fit perfectly into the missing space on Rombout's skull: the witness had not taken it herself but received it from a friend, and now the witness was returning it. A second witness had seen the skull of Rombout back in 1572, during the Spanish Fury, when the reliquary was broken open for the first time: on that occasion he saw the scar from the blow that legend said struck the saint dead. That scar was still perfectly visible on the skull displayed by Anna van Roye. Another witness had seen the bones when the reliquary was opened for repairs in 1561; Anna's skull looked the same as the skull he remembered seeing.

There was also reputation: what was the position and character of the individual who brought a bone forward? Most were respectable artisans, whose tales were taken seriously.

Last of all was the tried and proven method of smell: genuine relics simply had the pleasant odor of saintliness about them. Several witnesses mentioned this, but the archbishop himself, many years later, told Vicar-General van der Burch that this was how he finally confirmed which bones of Rombout were authentic and which were not.

After this inspection, Mathias Hovius and another canon of

St. Rombout's, Melchior Huys, spent the next several weeks dividing bones between two chests: in one they placed bones that were certainly authentic, and in the second bones that were possibly authentic. The second was taken to the archives for storage. But the first was marched processionally back to Rombout's in November 1585, by all the clergy, all the magistrates, all the members of the Grand Council, and innumerable citizens, confirming that they were again under the protection of their patron saint and the umbrella of the Roman faith. Eventually the plain chest of authentic bones made its way to the altar in the personal chapel of the new Archbishop Hovius, in 1596. The lay confraternity of the church of St. Rombout agreed to burn a lamp before the chest. Two pious daughters, one of them the archbishop's niece, stood watch to keep the flame in the lamp alive.

Surely this personal and emotional connection to the saint sparked the archbishop in 1617, and the city with him, to make the necessary sacrifices and arrangements for a proper reliquary for Rombout, to replace the wooden chest now in his chapel.

Despite the archdukes' permission to debase the silver used in a new reliquary, costs still would run to a burdensome ten thousand florins, to be divided among city, archbishop, chapter, and all who wished to contribute. Craftsmen were found but caused more headaches than bargained for, so although the reliquary was finally begun it was not finished in the archbishop's lifetime. Still, that it was begun at all helped to soothe a heartbreaking episode from his troubled past.

There was one other matter the archbishop wished to clarify about the reliquary, though it wasn't yet finished: the old question of who had ultimate charge over it and its relics. Hence, while the reliquary was still being built, the archbishop made his bid for control by means of a specific request to the archdukes: would they decree that only clergy be allowed to carry the new reliquary, once completed? For guarding the holy was primarily the clergy's responsibility, thought the archbishop, and laypeople were always a bit overeager to approach it. The request was granted, and the archbishop won that round.

Or at least until the next feast day of St. Rombout, when during Mass several magistrates and other prominent laypeople crowded between the archbishop and the wooden chest still holding the relics. Magistrates and burghers considered this their saint-given right, but the archbishop considered it a most serious breach of decorum. It was serious enough that he bothered to note it disapprovingly in his journal, and no doubt to speak of it in the same tone that evening at table.

All his days the archbishop heard and told such stories, of Sabbath breakers, of wonders, of the battle for the holy. Occasionally he imposed his will outright, as when he happened to be in town and overwhelmed offenders with his grandeur, or when he enlisted the aid of the archdukes. But most of the time bishop and flock negotiated, implicitly and otherwise, on these subjects and so much else. He could not shut down every unruly miller, he could not do violence to the faith of mourning mothers holding dead children, and he could not keep believers great and small from laying claim to their favorite saints. It was that very negotiation, that unfixed state of belief, that very need to approve and complain and hatch plans around the deeds of his flock, that contributed so greatly to the archbishop's habit of talking eagerly with guests of all kinds.

✝ TWELVE ✝

Ladies of the Garden

WALLS OF JERICHO

The thirtieth of November, 1617, on the road from Brussels.

S ince his earliest days in office, the archbishop had labored to get all the nuns of the diocese behind walls. Where there were none around a convent or where there were gaps he wanted walls built. Where they had been ruined by war he wanted them built again. Where there were such unconvincing barriers as hedges he wanted bricks and stone. And where walls were up he wanted them respected: no nuns outside, no visitors inside. To encourage building, he offered convents loans and even gifts. To encourage respect, he usually prodded—which was his purpose today.

Some religious women, he had learned, did not wish to be cloistered at all. Here he had in mind not the "active" religious, the Marthas who engaged in hospital or poor care, for they obviously had to move in and out of the convent and the world. Rather he had in mind the contemplatives, the Marys who had chosen the "better part" of divine contemplation yet still wished to come and go as they pleased, walls or no. To Archbishop Hovius such freedom endangered salvation, for it prevented these women from fulfilling a religious vocation born more than a millennium before, during the fourth century A.D., in the deserts of Roman Egypt: spiritual union with God through physical separation from the world.

Walls were only a starting point, of course, for true separation from this world was ultimately spiritual. But in the days of Mathias

preceding page: Follower of Aertsen, *Friars in a Nunnery,* ca. 1600
The Royal Collection © HM Queen Elizabeth II

Hovius and in the decrees of the Council of Trent, walls were the essential starting point, even the sine qua non, for professional female religious. Walls around convents were meant to slow down soldiers who pillaged, men who lusted, and friends who socialized. Walls were meant as well, said men, to protect women from their own lusts, which, said men again, were greater than those of men. Last of all walls were meant to protect society's notion that a chaste, truly pious woman did not wander—on streets or in the countryside. The archbishop was altogether typical among churchmen in believing that if cloister was merely desirable for male contemplatives, it was essential for female.

Some of the forty or so houses of female contemplatives within the archdiocese eagerly complied with the archbishop's wishes, becoming as passionate about cloister as nuns in Marcigny, France, who refused to leave their convent even while it was burning to the ground. But others presented him problems. Some (about one-fourth of the forty) were exempt from his jurisdiction, and in these he had no say. Among those under his jurisdiction, some refused his loans for the building of walls, or insisted that because they had no walls before the Council of Trent they were under no obligation to build any now. Still others dusted off ancient parchments that guaranteed their right to come and go, whether they had walls or not. And most argued, by their deeds, that their vows of poverty, chastity, and obedience were hardly incompatible with the occasional trip outside, or the odd conversation among worldly friends inside.

Scores of visitations to female convents of all sorts by this, his seventy-fifth and ailing year, had taught the archbishop that he would not achieve every reform he wished to see in conventual life: more kindness among sisters, more reverence in choir, more suitable clothing, or stricter silence, were impossible to enforce always. He might not even win his most constant debate with convents, over the *spirit* of cloister: once walls were up, how often, and in what manner, should nuns greet visitors at the grille, that small, barred space in convents reserved for "necessary" communications with the world? But if he could not win such messy problems always and absolutely, this basic, measurable ideal of physical walls was truly within reach. There remained only a couple of holdovers in the archdiocese by now and his destination today was one of them. He was determined to conquer it before going to the grave.

The female Benedictine abbey of Grand Bigard, begun in 1130 on land granted, coincidentally, by the abbey of Affligem, lay at the base of a hill in the farmlands west of Brussels. Ruined and deserted during the Troubles, the abbey was once again beginning to resemble the part. Dormitory, church, guestrooms, and barns were already rebuilt, north of two placid lakes. But the nuns showed no signs of completing a surrounding wall or respecting what was left of it. To the archbishop the convent was more a Beehive, one connotation of its old Dutch name, *Bigaerd,* than it was an Enclosed Garden, the connotation intended.

In fact the Ladies of the Garden were, despite their new buildings, quite the model of an old-style female convent: full of titled women who boasted four generations of nobility on both sides, who called one another "Madam" rather than "Sister," and who cared little for the walls or the discipline of cloister but very much about the privileges of noble rank—especially the privilege of maintaining close ties with their distinguished family and friends outside. The archbishop did not oppose such ties outright, for outside benefactors were vital to the temporal well-being of convents. But the women of Grand Bigard were after all religious, and so Archbishop Hovius sought to eliminate the most indecent forms of worldly contact. Worst at Grand Bigard was the timeless tradition that not only allowed family and friends to come visit nuns excessively, even outside the convent's front gate, but also allowed nuns themselves to travel home every three years, plus in "emergencies."

Look what the custom had yielded, marveled the archbishop, who knew the reports. Traveling nuns stayed out months at a time and went places they should not. One nun outside was seen riding behind a monk on horseback. The archbishop had acted before against such abuses. In 1601 he installed a new abbess. In 1614 he began requiring new nuns to promise they would accept full cloister when all the old nuns died off. In December 1616 he even restricted the precious outside trips of the nuns to ten days at a time and insisted that at other times only laysisters, who were religious of a lesser status and whose task was to run errands outside for the nuns, should ever leave the convent. But the battle was far from over.

For the next year, the nuns of Grand Bigard showed their determination to ignore the archbishop's restrictions. They continued to take their extended trips outside, and to stroll with friends on the worldly side of the convent's front gate. In response, the archbishop suspended outside trips altogether, and instructed the house confessor to cease granting any absolutions from sin until each nun admitted her wrongdoing in writing. So serious was this punishment, which effectively prevented the nuns from partaking of the Eucharist as well, that the nuns of Bigard turned to their powerful families, in the hopes that they would intercede with the Archdukes Albert and Isabella, official patrons of Grand Bigard. But the archbishop had anticipated such a move, and took care in advance to get the archdukes, and nuncio, on his side: like most southern Europeans, all three of these great nobles apparently held even stricter notions about the cloistering of female religious than did Mathias Hovius, and hence it was little trouble to persuade them to his cause. With archduke and nuncio against them, the nuns' only recourse for months was to "cry and shout" about the wrongs heaped upon them by their archbishop. In fact their resentment ran so deep that the confessor gently urged the archbishop to compromise, lest relations with the nuns become irreversibly damaged.

Only by this past month was Archbishop Hovius finally in the mood to do so, after the nuns began to hint that they were willing to compromise. First, he instructed the confessor, in October 1617, to again grant absolution to penitent nuns. And second, he drafted an agreement that required both him and the nuns to make concessions on the matter of outside trips, which he was sure would placate both sides. This was what he carried to the convent today, determined to see it signed.

The road was all dirt and mainly uphill. Just before the convent it turned sharply downward until reaching the main gate, on the north. Soon after arriving and no doubt after refreshment, Archbishop Hovius convened the sixteen noble nuns of Grand Bigard. Like any experienced negotiator he did not immediately reveal how far he was willing to compromise, instead presenting first a plan harder than the one in his pocket: he would allow the nuns to travel every three years, but for a fixed period of fourteen days only. The nuns knew this game of negotiation nearly as well as the archbishop, and hence they too asked for more than they hoped to receive: an annual trip of fourteen days was their stated wish now. Though he had just arrived, the elderly archbishop theatrically stood and called for his horses to be reharnessed, for he was offended by the stubborness of the nuns and intended to ride straight back to Brussels and say so to Archduke Albert himself. On his way out he added, "If you wish to do what I say then you may call me back, but if you wish to tell me something else, it will be in vain." The threat of departure and of entrusting the matter to the possibly heavier hand of their patron Albert had its effect, for the nuns relented.

Now the archbishop revealed his real compromise. The nuns were to complete the wall around their convent, and more important they were to respect it. And though the archbishop now allowed the nuns to travel outside once every two years for fourteen days, they were not to travel during the wild celebrations of kermis and they were not to attend weddings. At other times, they might visit deathly ill friends, but only with the archbishop's express consent. Last, they might walk outside the front gate with friends, but in pairs, not alone. It was not all the nuns wanted, but it was better than the archbishop's first proposal. Hence all came forward to sign, even the travel-loving Joanna Boisot, whose signature was largest.

It was not all the archbishop wanted either, but the realities of the situation required him to settle for one small victory at a time. As he explained later to the nuncio, it was difficult to go "from one extreme to another" when dealing with such strong-minded, well-connected women. It was also imprudent, because unlike in Italy the nearness of heretics in the Dutch Republic made apostasy—a worse alternative than compromise—attractive to disgruntled nuns. Finally, it was not at all clear that local courts would uphold the nuncio's view that cloister was implicit in a nun's vow of chastity. For these many reasons the archbishop compromised. He was content enough with the agreement that rather than rush off, as he had threatened to do earlier in the afternoon of this 30 November, he stayed the night in a guestroom of the convent and dined with the abbess before reciting his evening prayers and retiring.

MADAM BOISOT

Before riding back to Brussels the next morning, where he would soon report his triumph to a delighted Archduke Albert, the archbishop took care to have a chat with Madam Joanna Boisot. He let her know that her frequent and long trips outside the convent did not fool him: she was out partly on pleasure and partly to collect moneys owed her family's estate—both of which she was supposed to have left behind when she entered the religious life. After this rebuke, Madam Boisot promised improvement, while the archbishop promised to keep watch.

But of course one problem was that the archbishop could watch only so closely. Another problem was this: even when walls were up it was difficult not only to keep nuns out of the world, but to keep the world out of the convent. Especially in the countryside, where there were few other places for visitors to stay. Especially in the Low Countries, where traditions of liberty were difficult to quench. And especially in noble convents, where lay servants, lay lodgers, lay goods, and lay visitors outnumbered nuns by far.

In the convent of Grand Bigard, when nuns engaged in the usual monastic rituals of prayer, song, confession, Mass, and labor (usually handicrafts), they hardly did so alone. Besides the dozen or so laysisters who lived alongside the nuns and ran to market for delicacies that could not be raised within, such as herring, sugar, and artichokes, there was a steward, who purchased the convent's livestock and guard dogs in consultation with nuns. Doctors and expert women came and set plasters upon the sore bodies of nuns. Swineherds, stable boys, and milkmaids cared for the convent's animals, while gardeners tended trees and flowers. Carpenters and craftsmen reconstructed the convent's buildings, fishermen harvested the convent's lakes, seasonal workers picked its hops, chopped its wood, trapped its wolves and otters, lawyers guarded its rights, priests provided its sacraments. In fact anyone observing all the bustle in the convent would have wondered how the ladies of Grand Bigard could possibly have considered themselves shut off from the world at all.

Of no one was this more true than Joanna Boisot. Despite the size of her signature on the convent's new compromise with the archbishop, Madam Boisot's tastes ran decidedly contrary to it. Not only did she mingle readily with guests, but only weeks after promising improvement she began asking again whether she might exit the convent to again collect moneys owed her estate.

Mathias Hovius responded in writing as he had previously in person. It was time for Joanna "to act according to her vocation" and to be grateful that he had been patient with her thus far. But this did not deter Madam Boisot. In February 1618 she asked leave again to go out, this time to care for an ill relative. The archbishop sent a medical doctor to investigate that relative. The doctor confirmed the archbishop's suspicions: the relative wasn't ill at all. In fact the doctor even went beyond his proper field of inquiry to investigate further, and he arrived at a most unmedical conclusion: Joanna wished to go out only because it was carnival and because she wished to visit her paternal aunt, widow of the lord of Gooik, who enjoyed the company of young men. Hearing this, the archbishop denied Joanna's request.

But Joanna went anyway. Weeks later she was excommunicated, probably by Archbishop Hovius. This was when Joanna decided that despite two decades as a nun in the convent of Grand Bigard she had never really been a nun at all. Her vows, she suddenly claimed, were invalid—for two reasons. First, soon after her parents died, she had been forced inside the convent by her guardian, a maternal aunt, who merely wanted Joanna's inheritance. And second, she had professed before the age of sixteen, the minimum age required by the Council of Trent.

The archbishop had heard such claims before, and he sometimes believed them. But Joanna's were suspicious. Why didn't she speak sooner, within the first five years of her profession, the usual limit in such matters? Moreover, if it was true that the maternal aunt had such a stranglehold on Joanna's inheritance, then why was Joanna still running around collecting money from it? Yet it was also possible that Joanna told the truth: maybe she was never a nun at all. She obviously longed for adventure and had never shown much sign of possessing a true vocation inside the convent. Still, Archbishop Hovius ordered her to return, and Joanna finally complied.

No doubt thanks to her prominent family, the pope lifted Joanna's excommunication in June of 1618. He also declared that if Joanna had truly entered the convent against her will, then she could hardly be held to her original vows—however much time had passed. Heartened, Joanna left the convent again, again without permission, to discuss her future life with friends and Jesuits. But then the archbishop's secretaries, sent to dig in his archives for evidence, found the critical document: during her interview for profession, some two decades before, Joanna had claimed to be seventeen, a full year beyond the minimum required. With no other proof to the contrary, Rome and Joanna could do nothing.

The archbishop ordered her to return at once to Grand Bigard and had his diocesan court charge her with contempt. But Joanna, determined as ever, initiated a countersuit of her own.

And so it went. This personal struggle between Madam Boisot and Archbishop Hovius lasted the remainder of his days, back and forth. In the midst of it there was one respite: a cordial luncheon at the archbishop's residence in Brussels, on 3 November 1618, just after another long audience between the two of them. Perhaps this luncheon had no extra significance and instead was mere politeness after a morning of talk. But perhaps the archbishop meant more by the invitation. For also invited to table that afternoon was someone Joanna did not know, Judoca van Belle, Mother Superior of a humble convent in Leuven, plus someone Joanna knew very well, Jan Kerremans, the beloved confessor of Grand Bigard. Although Madam Boisot, Mother Judoca, and Father Kerremans were all there on different business, the archbishop at least knew they had something in common. Just days before, Archbishop Hovius had suspended the confessor of Mother Judoca's convent for being too familiar with nuns; Judoca was here in Brussels so that the archbishop could explain the full details.* At almost the same time, the archbishop likewise suspended Jan Kerremans, confessor of Grand Bigard, for the same sin; it was a sin in which Madam Joanna Boisot, here present, had played no small role.

FATHER KERREMANS

Jan Kerremans was in the first place a monk and longtime prior of the Celestine monastery of Heverlee, near Leuven. But it was

---

* The full story of Mater Judoca and her convent of Gray Sisters in Leuven is told in Craig Harline, *The Burdens of Sister Margaret* (New York, 1994; reissued in an abridged version by Yale University Press, 2000).

as confessor of Grand Bigard that he made his biggest mark in the life of Mathias Hovius.

Father Kerremans began his services in Bigard and his prior-ship in Heverlee at about the same time, around 1606. Though it was not uncommon for monks to serve as confessors for female religious, this particular arrangement was unusual for its distance: Grand Bigard lay at least several hours by coach from Heverlee. Partly because his monastery in Heverlee was in the midst of tem-poral and spiritual decline, partly because the nuns (unlike his monks) were unspeakably delighted with him, and partly because the two houses were so far apart, Prior Kerremans soon decided to spend most of his time in Grand Bigard. Soon the pleased nuns provided him, as did many female religious, with private rooms at their convent. Soon, quite against decorum, he joined in the con-vent's recreation days, and ate at the nuns' table. And soon there came a report that one of the nuns had, just for fun, worn the confessor's vestments into church. The nuns were so happy with Jan Kerremans that after several years they made him their stew-ard as well, in charge of the convent's temporal affairs, which he managed in tandem with his brother Michel, who was likewise so familiar with the nuns that they called him "cousin." This perfect little world, this happy arrangement, lasted more than a decade, with few interruptions from outside. Then in the summer of 1618 it began to fall ungracefully apart.

The trouble began in August, when a new nuncio in Brus-sels, Lucio Morra, first heard tales of disorder among the Celestine monks of Heverlee. An investigation only confirmed these unfor-tunate tales. Once consulted by theologians at the University of Paris, now the monks were known more for drinking than think-ing. This ill-discipline was partly because the monastery, like so many, had no close supervision from outside: since it was exempt (again like most male monasteries) from the local bishop, and since monastic superiors it did recognize were far away, in France and Rome, there was no power nearby to keep watch. The state of disci-pline lay entirely in the hands of the prior, Jan Kerremans—who by now of course could almost always be found hours away in the convent of Grand Bigard. To the nuncio the solution was easy: dismiss Father Kerremans as confessor of Bigard and get him back to Heverlee.

This was where Archbishop Hovius came in: though he had no authority over Jan Kerremans as a monk, the archbishop did have authority to appoint and remove all confessors in female convents under his jurisdiction, including Grand Bigard. Hence, to get Father Kerremans out, the nuncio would have to go through Mechelen. In fact the nuncio Morra soon made a trip to Mechelen and pushed the archbishop to remove Jan Kerremans as confessor. But it was all very delicate, said the archbishop. Although he had every legal right to dismiss the man, it always went more smoothly when the nuns consented and in this case they would not. They liked the confessor, there was at the moment no obvious scandal, and the ladies of Bigard would only have cause to resent the archbishop and resist his more important reforms issued in the past and those still to come.

But the nuncio was determined. No other matter seemed to absorb so much of Lucio Morra's energy during his entire short stay in the Low Countries. For weeks he attacked Jan Kerremans — in Rome among the papal curia, in Paris among leaders of the Celestine Order, and in Brussels among the archdukes, trying to embarrass the archbishop into action. For weeks Mathias Hovius resisted the nuncio's pressure, not because of any merit in the confessor, whom the archbishop as yet hardly knew, but because of complexities in Grand Bigard, because he thought the matter the business of the local church, and because he doubted that a nuncio had any authority over a Netherlandish monk whose superiors resided in France. Surely this new nuncio caused Mathias Hovius to look back with nostalgia on the days of Guido Bentivoglio, now nuncio in Paris, who understood and respected local ways so greatly that upon departing Brussels he declared himself "more Netherlander than Italian." Lucio Morra, on the other hand, showed little regard for tact or custom — or perhaps, as the archbishop feared, he was offended after all at having been uninvited to the archbishop's jubilee the year before.

No doubt because of the archbishop's refusal to dismiss Jan Kerremans as confessor did Lucio Morra decide that the seventy-six-year-old Mathias Hovius was a phlegmatic old man: too soft, too tired to fight, interested only in avoiding troubles. All the arch-bishop did, the nuncio told Rome, was consecrate churches and altars and confer orders. A week later, the nuncio went further: the archbishop was "losing his memory" and was incapable of "han-dling important affairs."

The nuncio was angry with Jan Kerremans as well, who kept traveling to France to receive assurances and letters from Celestine brothers that he was indeed exempt from any nuncio. Angering the nuncio even more was the prior's maddening solution to the crisis in Grand Bigard and the disorder in Heverlee: rather than resign as confessor of the nuns, Jan Kerremans offered to resign as prior of the monks instead. The nuncio exploded and informed Archbishop Hovius that Jan Kerremans, whatever his position in Heverlee, was by no means to remain confessor of Bigard. Still the archbishop hesitated. Finally, on 4 October 1618 Lucio Morra virtually ordered Archbishop Hovius to dismiss Jan Kerremans as confessor.

Had he looked hard enough or thought it worth his energy, the archbishop could have found grounds and protectors to resist the nuncio's order. But perhaps he was as weary as Lucio Morra supposed, because he immediately complied. The archbishop's let-ters of dismissal went out the next day, with copies to the nuns of Bigard.

There was surely a better reason why the archbishop complied with the nuncio: a growing sense that Jan Kerremans was not worth the trouble.

For a long time the archbishop gave no hint of this. But that began to change when Jan Kerremans, despite having been re-leased in October 1618 as confessor, continued in the next weeks and months to visit Grand Bigard as enthusiastically as ever, and when the nuncio subsequently decided that the archbishop was to blame for it. In fact, thanks to Father Kerremans the archbishop now felt "odious" to nuncio and archduke alike. By December the archbishop finally concluded that he had suffered enough for an obscure and shiftless Celestine monk: despite the lunchtime pleasantries of the month before, Jan Kerremans had to be removed from Grand Bigard for good—not only as confessor, but even as visitor. Hence in January 1619 he issued the order: Father Kerremans was never to set foot in the convent again.

Within weeks the new confessor of Bigard, the archbishop's trusted dean Hendrik Calenus, began to uncover the full extent of the damage caused by his predecessor. To the archbishop's utter embarrassment, the nuncio had been right about the man after all. Jan Kerremans and his brother Michel, learned the dean, had long treated the convent's property as a private fiefdom. Jan Kerremans was still hiding accounts from the convent's new steward and still conducting business through Michel, who still lived in one of the convent's guestrooms. Worse, Jan Kerremans had been more than a loyal confessor: he had also been intimate with a certain nun, perhaps for years.

Rumors of unchastity between priests and nuns were more unbearable to the archbishop than even criticism from the nuncio. Long before Boccaccio's *Decameron* or Chaucer's *Canterbury Tales,* satirists and critics understood that sexual indiscretions among the religious made for lively stories, not to mention more embarrassment to the church than anything else. Only some rumors of indiscretion were true, and most were unfounded, but every one meant trouble. In the days of Mathias Hovius, rumors kept tongues wagging on Catholic and Protestant sides of the border. No one recorded how many cases there actually were: for there were plenty of convents and individual nuns who likewise became famous for their heroic deeds of chastity. But statistical precision mattered little: a few genuine scandals were enough to produce a stereotype among enemies.

Mathias Hovius had long tried to combat such scandals—
just recently at the convent of Mater Judoca in Leuven, or in
Zichem, where nuns and confessor drank cinnamon-flavored beer
they called "brothel soup" and played frivolous games into the
night. In Grand Bigard, a chaplain years before had fathered three
children by a laywoman and one nun had run off to Holland with
a male servant. There had been the reports, two decades before,
of Livinus Mulder's familiarity in Grand Bigard. And there had
been whispers during the archbishop's visitation of 1616 about Jan
Kerremans and Joanna Boisot. When the abbess of Grand Bigard
denied everything, the archbishop left it alone.

But the archbishop's suspicions must have revived when Jan
Kerremans decided that he would resign as prior of Heverlee rather
than give up his position as confessor of Grand Bigard. Or when,
after the archbishop banned Kerremans from Grand Bigard, several nuns, including Joanna Boisot, decided they would go instead
to Heverlee and visit their favorite confessor there. Or when the
former confessor, despite the ban, continued to visit the nuns in
return, even hiding in the convent while the archbishop was there
on one visit. Or when the nuncio Morra at last told the archbishop,
during a farewell audience before returning to Italy, that the confessor had once admitted to a romance with a nun of Bigard named
"Elcken." Or when Hendrik Calenus told the archbishop in person what he would report in writing several years later: that Jan
Kerremans had a lover among the nuns.

The name of this lover the archbishop knew, but he never
recorded it. To his chagrin, however, he would have admitted that
there was no shortage of candidates for outsiders to guess at. There
was the "Elcken" mentioned by the nuncio; closest to this nickname was Helena Maes, the youngest nun. There was also Joanna
Boisot, often seen gossiping with the prior as well as the prior's
niece and intermediary, Margaret Kerremans, who once said that
she would "rather a thousand demons carry her uncle away than
that he fall into the hands of the demons in Brussels." There was
Maria Boiselli, disciplined by the archbishop for unnamed of-

fenses, who later entertained another confessor in her locked room while still in her bed, who was seen taking asparagus into her mouth from the hand of that confessor, and who one night was seen bouncing in front of the fireplace on the confessor's knee. On that confessor's other knee was seen Wivina Tserclaes, daughter of a prominent Brusselaar. There was Johanna Heresim, who loved to go out, who spent nights in Heverlee, and who criticized Archbishop Hovius. There was at last Maria D'Ombre, restricted by the archbishop for vague "reasons seen fit."

Despite these possibilities, Jan Kerremans always insisted he was innocent. A later observer would declare it impossible to know whether there was anything "reprehensible" between prior and nuns. But the archbishop had no doubts at all and much remorse about his lateness in removing him.

A NEW ABBESS FOR THE GARDEN

The most effective way for the archbishop to combat the influence of Jan Kerremans was to get not only the right confessor in place but the right abbess as well. The longtime abbess, Anna D'Ittre, had for years resisted the reforms of the archbishop, in the name of the convent's independence and privileges and befitting the lion on her coat of arms, but she was now bedridden and seventy-nine years old. The second-in-command, the prioress, was seventy-seven, nearly blind, and suffering from gout. Most other nuns, however, were in their twenties and thirties, and decidedly energetic.

The problem was that abbesses of noble convents were ordinarily removed only by death or voluntary resignation. Any other type of removal, even one brought about by obvious incapacitation, was easily seen as an affront to the abbess. And so the nuns were likely to resist such a move. But the archbishop proposed a plan designed to mollify them, a plan not uncommon in such circumstances: let the nuns elect a coadjutrice, or vice-abbess, who would govern in Anna's name and have the right of succession upon Anna's death. He mentioned this plan first in April 1619 to the archdukes, who in addition to being the special patrons of Grand Bigard also possessed the right to oversee elections in all the abbeys of Brabant. But not until June, when Jan Kerremans was once again seen illicitly visiting the convent, did the archdukes finally get around to approving this plan. The archbishop set off for Grand Bigard in early July.

Along to help conduct this election was, as usual for the abbeys of Brabant, the chancellor Peter Peckius, the *sage flamand* who had helped to assuage Henri IV of France during the king's final infatuation in 1610. Surely here was someone who could win over the nuns of Grand Bigard as well. When the two men arrived, Abbess Anna lay sick in bed, but they read aloud their charge from Albert anyway. Though the nuns resisted, by the end of the day archbishop and chancellor had persuaded them to agree to an election, to be held the following week. When the time arrived, each nun came forward to tell the visitors her preference. Some declared they would have voted for Joanna Boisot, but she had "pretensions of leaving the convent." Most therefore chose Catherina Martigny, of whom there had been little complaint in the past. The archbishop enthroned Catherina in August 1619, then in February 1620 (though Anna D'Ittre still lived) elevated Catherina to abbess. As Catherina knelt before him, the archbishop handed her the keys and book of the monastery, then watched as the nuns came forward one by one to swear loyalty to her. Afterward, Catherina's parents received the archbishop lavishly—too lavishly, he said. He declined their first gift, a gilded drinking cup, but accepted the second: an image of the "savior" and "the Virgin," along with "six beautiful fish."

The archbishop was proud of his triumph and wrote to the great to say so, surely in hopes of restoring his good name after the travesty caused by Jan Kerremans. But it remained to be seen whether the election and the congratulations from all sides would indeed do much to change the nature of life in the Garden, or polish his name as brightly as he hoped. After all, Joanna Boisot was still asking to go on trips and to leave the religious life altogether. Sealed letters, unread by superiors, kept moving back and forth between nuns and outsiders. Several Dominicans who visited Grand Bigard told the nuns that the archbishop had no right to punish transgression of his statutes but only to admonish. Worst of all, a defiant Jan Kerremans continued to visit, prompting yet another new nuncio in Brussels to blame Archbishop Hovius for the mess and to wonder aloud, what could be so difficult about imposing cloister on a convent of mere nuns?

For his part the archbishop continued his warnings. He continued to fight with Joanna Boisot, once even locking her up in the convent's jail where she could "better ponder" things. And on another occasion he instructed Dean Calenus to take away the Eucharist from the convent. Though walls were up at last in Grand Bigard, surely the archbishop's days there could not have been his happiest. In the end the tone of life in the convent was, as in so many others, determined ultimately not only by archbishop or nuncio or even confessor, but by the nuns themselves.

Sisters of the World

THE TAVERNKEEPER'S GOLD

The twenty-fourth of August, 1618, Leuven.

Thue lonely old widower who had survived war and plague was faring less well against the more subtle adversary of age. As death neared, he entrusted the keys of his household to his sister and heir, Gertrude. When death finally came, Gertrude, keys in hand, went looking for brother's gold.

Though this newly deceased, Hendrik van Bierbeek, had already provided generously for Gertrude in his will, in times past he had also whispered to her about two additional stashes of money in the house: a thousand florins in a kitchen cabinet, plus a "remarkable sum" in coin collected over thirty-six years—the location of which he neglected to reveal before dying. Surely these stashes were for Gertrude as well. While Hendrik lived, she had refrained from searching for them, out of decency, but now she went in earnest.

She unlocked the cabinet in the kitchen first. To her surprise, there was no thousand florins but only pennies. She had more luck in Hendrik's bedroom, where she found a pile of eight hundred florins in one cabinet and eighteen hundred in another. These must have been the treasures. But over the next several days Gertrude started thinking. Hendrik had been clear that the one stash was exactly one thousand florins. And the second "remarkable" stash, he emphasized, consisted of old coins only. Yet the coins Gertrude

preceding page: J. Stevens, *The Hospital Sisters of Lier as the Wise Virgins,* 1668
Lier, collectie OCMW, inv. nr. OCMW S 1, hal Heilig-Hartziekenhuis

found in the bedroom were all of new varieties, such as *Albertussen* and *patacons*. She told her worries to her landlord and lawyer, Raphael Lintermans. After examining the coins, he concluded that they had come from sales of property made by Hendrik just before his death, and then were placed temporarily in cabinets in the bedroom. The coins found by Gertrude were not, therefore, the old stashes spoken of. Then where could they have gone to? Come to think of it, wondered Gertrude, where were the silver serving tray, the golden chain, the fine linens, and precious jewels she had seen around the house for many years?

It did not take Gertrude long to decide that the thief was Hendrik's last nurse, a woman named Sister Cornelia. During most of the time Hendrik lay ill in bed, it was Cornelia who held the keys and thus the secrets of the household: Gertrude took the keys only at the end. Though she had no proof as yet, Gertrude felt sure enough of her conclusion to issue a warning: when the last piece of furniture in Hendrik's household was sold and Cornelia walked out the door for the last time, Gertrude said, "Sister Nelia, if you took something we'll find out about it, even if the crows have to tell us." True to her word, Gertrude and the lawyer Lintermans compiled over the next months a stack of evidence against Cornelia, then sent it to Mechelen and the crowded worktable of Mathias Hovius. For Sister Cornelia was, after all, one of his.

The archbishop learned the disconcerting story of Sister Cornelia vande Vinne in January 1619, precisely the time he was struggling to keep Jan Kerremans out of Grand Bigard. Cornelia's troubles would never receive the same attention from the great, or produce the same intense pressure on the archbishop, as did the affairs of prestigious Grand Bigard, but they were nonetheless not to be ignored. For aside from sexual sins real or imagined, financial misdeeds always caused the biggest scandal for the church. Gertrude's evidence against Cornelia was serious enough that the archbishop sent his men to Leuven to investigate.

Here was what they uncovered. Hendrik van Bierbeek and

his wife, Maria Luenis, ran for decades a tavern called The Wild-
man, located behind St. Peter's church. Despite the name of the
tavern, Hendrik and Maria lived soberly. This, along with the fact
that they had no children, caused neighbors and friends to assume
that they were "mighty of cash." In 1617 Maria died, leaving Hendrik alone and despondent. By Easter of 1618 he began to wither
for good. In the early stages of illness he was cared for by his maid
Margaret and his sister Gertrude. But as his condition worsened
Hendrik came to require full-time attention. This was when he
and Gertrude called upon the Black Sisters, religious women of
the Augustinian order who specialized in at-home sick care. And
this was how, of the twenty or so Black Sisters in the convent of
Leuven, Sister Cornelia came into the Bierbeek home.

Indeed, Cornelia was soon a fixture there, arriving early in
the day and leaving late. She, not Gertrude, prepared medicines,
helped with meals, and stayed by her patient's side. And she was
present in June, when the declining Hendrik drew up his last testament.

Neighbors were right: it was a most respectable testament.
Besides the usual Masses for his soul, an honorable sepulcher, and
assorted alms, Hendrik left some eight hundred florins in cash and
canceled debts to friends and relatives of his beloved deceased wife.
But his universal heir (and thus the implicit heir of any stashes
of money) was Gertrude. All seemed in good order, everything
seemed settled, when Hendrik died on 24 August 1618, surrounded
by kin, his small household (including Cornelia), burning candles,
and prayer-chanting priests. But then Gertrude could not find all
the money.

After her suspicions fell on Sister Cornelia, Gertrude sent
her lawyer to interview Hendrik's former maid Margaret, who had
worked even longer in the home. Surely Margaret would expose
Cornelia, if only to protect herself. As Gertrude had hoped, this
opened the floodgates. Maid Margaret admitted that she had seen
Cornelia carry away from the house a total of one thousand florins.
The lawyer Lintermans passed along this evidence to the confes-

sor of the Black Sisters, so that he might confront Cornelia. This tactic worked, too, for at last Cornelia admitted to him that she had indeed taken away a thousand florins, and that it had come from a stash in the kitchen. But there was a problem: Cornelia also claimed that her carrying away of the secret money was the idea of Hendrik van Bierbeek himself, who had instructed her to distribute it among various of his poor friends! When the lawyer relayed this information, Gertrude could hardly believe her ears. One autumn day in 1618 she therefore went to see Cornelia in person, bumping into her purposely on the street. But Cornelia stood by her story. This only made Gertrude more livid. No doubt it was thanks to Gertrude that people in Leuven were soon gossiping that a Black Sister had stolen money from the home of a patient: let all beware.

This was not how Archbishop Hovius wanted people to think of his female religious, but he knew the risk, especially among the "active" religious, who went out of their convents to work in the world.

Since the twelfth and thirteenth centuries, active religious women dominated nursing in the Low Countries, especially in cities. Some male religious cared for the sick and of course laypeople mixed favorite home remedies, but by now professional day-to-day care in urban, Catholic Europe meant the presence of a sister from one active religious order or another. In the Low Countries there were Augustinian Hospital Sisters, who tended to the sick in a single building; Franciscan Gray Sisters, who ran hospitals and provided some at-home care; and Augustinian Black Sisters, who worked exclusively in people's homes. By the time of Cornelia vande Vinne, around fifty houses of active women dotted the archdiocese, even more than for contemplative women.

Despite their majority, active religious women made churchmen uncomfortable. Active women were not only of lower social standing than most contemplatives, but they engaged in physical works that left them little time to pursue the monastic ideals of prayer, meditation, and calm living. Worst of all they ventured into the midst of a messy world. Though the internal troubles of a Grand Bigard might reach the ears of outsiders, the troubles of active women might happen before the world's eyes, with no hope of concealment, thus wounding faith and the church's reputation even more deeply. This was why the latest papal nuncio in Brussels, Lucio Sanseverino, quite predictably told the archbishop that the solution to all troubles of all Black Sisters was the same as for Grand Bigard: strict cloister. If implemented, this would of course make impossible the active ministry of the Black Sisters, but to the nuncio that seemed a secondary concern. Of greater importance to him was the potential for harm that accompanied female immersion in the world: too much talk with outsiders, too much eating and drinking, too little discipline and obedience, and of course too many complications such as those swirling currently around Sister Cornelia — even if she were innocent.

Archbishop Hovius was more optimistic than the nuncio about active sisters and therefore preferred vigilance to elimination. He was among the many who understood that these women survived in the Low Countries because they were indispensable. Society demanded their organized physical care and their famous plastering, cupping, and pharmaceutical concoctions, whatever Rome's concerns about cloister. Even in newly Protestant towns around Europe were magistrates reluctant to give up the services of active Catholic sisters, so that in some such places they were quietly tolerated. And in Catholic towns sisters were important not only for their medicines but their spiritual care, which prepared patients for a good and faithful death.

And so if Mathias Hovius made in his lifetime more official visitations to prestigious contemplative houses than he did to active houses, he nevertheless cared deeply about how women in the latter lived. This was not only because proper attention to patients and proper discipline among sisters were desirable for their own sakes, but because active women lived in the world, where their actions were more visible to a curious and judgmental public.

Hence, those sent among the sick must be of the highest character, insisted the archbishop. They must suffer in silence the ingratitude and demands of patients. They must conduct themselves honorably, avoid idleness, coarse manners, and "remarkable abundances" of drink and food, for ravenous sisters were the object of much "ridicule and scandal" among the laity. They must shun drink not only to avoid gluttony but to escape "perils to chastity." They must arm themselves against temptation with good thoughts and the fear of God. They must refrain from becoming attached to members of the opposite sex. When attending men they must "watch, as befitting virgins of Christ, all your senses, especially your eyes." Mother Superiors must consider well whom they assigned to go out, "lest you perchance send a young and spotless lamb into the teeth of wolves." And of course it went without saying that sisters must not steal. Which brought the archbishop to Sister Cornelia.

Her explanation of events was as follows. On a Sunday in early July 1618, an ailing Hendrik van Bierbeek had sent her to two different coffers in the house and asked her to bring him the money inside. She did so. He then placed the money in five bound handkerchiefs of two hundred florins each, and asked Cornelia to take them to five poor, humble friends and relatives of his deceased wife: a married woman, a grown single woman, and three adolescent sisters. So reluctant was Cornelia to perform this task, because of the appearance of theft, that she delayed for long. But shortly before dying, Hendrik van Bierbeek chastised her for failing to do as he had asked. And so finally Cornelia complied and distributed the bundles. She also admitted having given away three hundred florins on other occasions, again at her patient's instruction, to still other poor family and friends. In all this she believed herself on solid ground. In fact, when accusations began to fly about her, Cornelia sought reassurance from the pastor of St. Peter's in Leuven, Johannes Paludanus, that she had acted properly. He told her, "It's a good work you've done, for I doubt not that the deceased did this with the intent of clearing his conscience, and the sick are free to do as they please in this regard."

Needless to say, Gertrude van Bierbeek's version of events was much different from Cornelia's. Gertrude wrote the archbishop to say that "It is not the way these things are done." She believed Cornelia had simply learned the secrets of the house, taken advantage of the feeble Hendrik, stolen his money, then redistributed it among those Cornelia deemed most needy. Cornelia may even have taken, suspected Gertrude, more than the thirteen hundred she admitted to, but this could not be proven.

Gertrude could, however, try to prove much else to Archbishop Hovius, and so her letters to him continued. There was first of all the evidence of logic. Why would Hendrik, who told Gertrude all the secrets of his heart, not have revealed to her his wish to give away a thousand florins? And why did the five recipients of the money need it at all, since none were poor but belonged to the families of respectable craftsmen, and were already provided for anyway in Hendrik's will? Gertrude's implication was clear: Cornelia had taken the money at her own initiative and used it as she saw fit. If the laws of inheritance were not enforced in this case and others, then every estate in the land "would stand at the mercy of the Black Sisters," warned Gertrude.

There was also the evidence of Cornelia's strange actions. She had not delivered the thousand florins straightaway to the supposedly designated recipients, but instead stopped to visit an aimless young nobleman, the lord of Attenhoven, with whom she had counted the money. Cornelia explained that there was nothing sinister about this action: she simply wanted to get the amounts right. But why was that necessary, wondered Gertrude, since Hendrik had already counted it? Why was it necessary for Cornelia and the nobleman playfully to throw the money around on his bed? And why did a second nobleman in the room yell out in delight, "Jesus, aren't we overflowing in money here!" How pious a work could this have been?

There was in addition a most disturbing piece of indirect evidence against Cornelia. Though Gertrude could not prove the existence of the "remarkable sum," she could invite the archbishop to pay a visit to the convent of the Black Sisters and see for himself the impressive remodeling undertaken very recently there—especially for the benefit of Sister Cornelia! A brand new cell had been built just for her, which included leaden windows emblazoned with her motto and framed in curtains of silk, not to mention other "expensive" items. Who had paid for this, wondered Gertrude? Other sisters assumed that it was not the convent, but some outside donor. So great and conspicuous was the expense for Cornelia's room that other sisters in the convent marveled, for though they too had brought home gifts in cash and kind from "respectable" patients, never were they so grand and never had Mother Superior allowed them to keep so much for their own use.

Last of all, Gertrude and her lawyer found evidence that when it came to other people's property Cornelia simply felt that she knew best. When she learned about the coins found by Gertrude in Hendrik's bedroom, for instance, Cornelia was heard to say that had she known there was still so much lying around the house then she would have used it to help the children of yet another poor family. On other occasions Cornelia pressured Hendrik to absolve various persons of their debts, including four hundred florins owed by a Jerome van Zoetem, "burdened with many children." When Hendrik refused, explaining that he had already absolved Jerome of half that debt, Cornelia went and gave Jerome two hundred florins anyway, to cover the rest.

With these conflicting stories on his mind, Archbishop Hovius decided in February and March 1619 to send still more investigators to interview witnesses around Leuven.

These interviews did not bode well for Cornelia. In the first place, the dean of Leuven entitled the notes for his interviews not "Alleged Misdeeds of Sister Cornelia" but simply "Misdeeds." Second, the archbishop enlisted not only the dean and various lawyers of the diocesan court to conduct interviews but his reliable friend, Jacob Jansonius, whom he called in only when any matter had become terribly serious. Third, the pastor of St. Peter's, who

according to Cornelia had quite approved of her deeds, now ada-
mantly denied to interviewers that he had ever done as she claimed.
Cornelia was "embellishing," said the pastor: though he had said
it was good to help the poor, he had assumed that she had proper
permission and that only modest sums of money were involved.
The pastor, eager to distance himself from Cornelia, went even
further than interviewers requested and volunteered stories meant
to highlight defects in Cornelia's character: she had aspired shamelessly to be Mother Superior in Mechelen, where she had begun
her vocation, and ended up in Leuven only after failing miserably.
It wasn't long before the pastor was also saying on the street that
Cornelia had committed similar misdeeds with money in other
households in Leuven.

  During this new round of interviews, Gertrude Bierbeek and
the lawyer Lintermans stayed tenacious as ever, poring over written testimonies new and old to find, as only lawyers can find so
well, every shocking inconsistency in Cornelia's story. All these in-
consistencies confirmed Gertrude in her belief that Cornelia was
lying. Gertrude therefore urged the archbishop, when the interviews were over, to lock Cornelia up and compel the Black Sisters
to repay at least the thirteen hundred florins Cornelia admitted
taking.

  By his next trip to Leuven, on 21 May 1619, the archbishop
was prepared with a decision. He remained in town an entire week,
installing a new Mother Superior of the Gray Sisters, ordaining
dozens of priests, confirming hundreds of children, dining with
Dr. Jansonius, and catching a chill. But in the midst of all this
he also received a visit from the lawyer Lintermans, and of course
made sure to visit himself the convent of the Black Sisters.

  Unlike in the case of noble Grand Bigard the archbishop did
not bother to record his final decision, only that he made one. After
all, there was little need in this case for paperwork or complicated
responses to nuncio or archdukes. From the archbishop's point of
view it was better this way. But surely his possibilities were few.

  It was possible that Hendrik van Bierbeek, sick in bed, truly wanted Cornelia to distribute the money, as she claimed. It was possible that the many contradictions in Cornelia's testimony were the result of human frailty rather than a sinister attempt to conceal. It was possible that even if Cornelia were lying, the archbishop admired her concern for the poor: the sum of two hundred florins, over half the annual income of most craftsmen, would pay many debts of struggling women or provide fine dowries for teenaged girls. The archbishop understood all this, for he himself was a conscientious defender of the poor and a reliable giver of alms.

But too much other evidence worked against Cornelia. Her new cell and window, drops in an ocean of finery at Grand Bigard, screamed suspicion in the poorer convent of the Black Sisters. The sentiments against her in town, including among the dean of Leuven, the pastor of St. Peter's, and even Dr. Jansonius, were too strong to ignore. And much as he wished to defend the poor, the archbishop could hardly condone Cornelia's forcible redistribution of wealth, however subtle it may have seemed to her. It robbed the giver of initiative and thus virtue, and the receiver of genuine gratitude. Almsgiving was not about material life and certainly not about eliminating poverty altogether: like most of the great, Archbishop Hovius believed that the poor would always be with them, for Our Dear Lord had said so himself. Rich and poor needed each other for salvation—the one providing alms, the other prayers. Cornelia vande Vinne's spiritual sin was to upset immaterial benefits to both parties. Her earthly sins were to steal and to put a blemish on the reputation of the active religious—and their superior.

The most likely action, therefore, was for Archbishop Hovius to require the Black Sisters to reimburse Gertrude van Bierbeek at least part of the thirteen hundred florins Cornelia admitted taking. But he probably did not punish her in open court—private punishment was enough to satisfy those concerned and to get out word in town that the archbishop had acted. And certainly he did not punish harshly, for many years later Cornelia vande Vinne appeared in the *obituarium* of the Black Sisters of Leuven, where it was noted that she died at eighty-four years of age and was known for her vast knowledge of herbs and remedies. It said nothing about her largess with coins or her gift to the convent of lovely new windows and curtains.

A GODLY HOSPITAL

The twenty-third of September, 1619, between Tienen and Diest.

When more muscled, better balanced, and much younger, Archbishop Hovius used to make some visitations by horseback, but these days he went solely by coach. This hardly diminished the jarring: deep-rutted roads forsaken by God, nature, and work crews did little to relieve his most recent fevers, headaches, and dizziness. They also had ruined his last coach, which broke down the year before with him inside it.

Yet even more distressing than the ride itself were the inevitable unpleasant reports awaiting him at the end. In his old age the archbishop certainly had reason to restrict his energies (as the nuncio Morra once accused) to a simple regime of consecrating altars, confirming the young, and ordaining priests. But the nuncio was wrong that the archbishop had somehow become incapable of anything more demanding, or sought to avoid confrontation, or had lost his zeal. Mathias Hovius understood as well as ever that his visits were more about trouble than calm, and he did not shy from correcting as he saw necessary, even to his last days.

On the way from his last destination, Tienen, to his next, Diest, there was time to review the plenitude of tasks that awaited him. Much had changed in Diest since his last visit. The family Berchmans was gone. So was Haymo Timmermans, who had died of the plague the previous April. But some things remained the same. The canons of St. Sulpitius' were still making trouble, and the local hospital was still so badly in need of reform that the archbishop declared it more a "filthy barnyard" than a place for the sick.

Unlike houses of Black Sisters, subject only to bishops, hospitals were for long run by clergy and laity together—bishop and local magistrates in charge, hospital sisters giving care. But thanks to the wars of the 1580s and '90s the old order was confused: lay rulers in many towns tried to assume total control. By 1619, the archbishop still had not gotten around to sorting things out everywhere. As he once told the Baron of Boelare on the subject: "I'm willing to admit that in such a great diocese, comprised of so many parishes and hospitals and pious foundations, not everything has been put into place as it ought and indeed many years are still necessary, given the unbearable multitude of affairs which bishops must see to and that in these evil times so many things have fallen into ruin."

The most common argument between church and magistrates over hospitals was the matter of who should control accounts: clergy or laity? The mayor of Asse not only refused to let any clergy see the accounts of the local hospital but appointed illiterate laypeople to oversee those accounts, so that he might enjoy total control. At the annual accounting of the hospital in Landen, magistrates hosted an expensive dinner paid for by the hospital, to which they invited their wives but no clergy. Magistrates of Geraardsbergen began allowing clergy to attend accountings only because they needed a favor from the archbishop and he insisted in return for that favor on having a priest present at accountings. Such victories, however, even with a helpful decree from the archdukes in 1606 that supported the clergy's right to supervise hospitals, came slowly—especially in Diest.

Like most hospitals, that in Diest functioned partly as hostel, partly as isolation ward. But in other ways it was a species all its own. First, it took in only travelers rather than natives of Diest. Second, it treated those from Diest in their own homes—a practice better left to Black Sisters, thought the archbishop. Third, there was no local rector over the hospital's staff: the only day-to-day manager of the place was the hospital's tenant farmer. Fourth, that staff consisted solely of "dissolute" and "sumptuous" laypeople hired by the city, rather than religious sisters supervised by the archbishop: only if someone fell ill were religious called in, including Cell brothers, of whom the archbishop had heard "little good," or Cell sisters, who complained that the hospital was "inconvenient" and "filthy" and the "air too corrupt" to ensure good care. Fifth, travelers who stayed in the hospital were often troublemakers who lingered longer than necessary. Sixth, the hospital's assets were not held separately, as in most towns, but pooled together with those of the three parish Poor Tables in Diest. And last, accounts for hospital and Poor Tables, when rendered at all, were done without any representative of the archbishop or clergy present. All these undesirable innovations the archbishop wished to change.

He had taken his first action in the spring of 1619, sending to the nine magistrates of Diest a letter that outlined his concerns and a list of desired reforms. But they had responded that, with respect, they liked their unorthodox arrangement just fine. Few travelers fell ill, thus they needed no permanent sisters. There was little need to take in the sick of Diest, for they preferred treatment in their own homes (thus avoiding the stigma of going to a hospital). Most of all, though this went unsaid, the arrangement also allowed magistrates absolute control over (and abuse of) the combined income of hospital and Poor Tables, estimated together at four thousand florins per year.

Since magistrates paid no heed to his suggestions, the archbishop called in the archdukes, whose singular assistance he reserved for precisely such pressing matters as this. He explained to Albert more than once that the hospital of Diest served as a place for getting sick rather than well. That it offered little help to the soul or salvation but instead much opportunity for sin. That his conscience had moved him to fix it. That he could not fix it without the help of magistrates. And that magistrates would not move without Albert.

Albert promised to send a letter to the magistrates of Diest, but as usual he grew busy with other matters he considered more pressing still. In fact it took Albert so long to write the letter that the impatient archbishop, as he had done more than once in such situations, wrote the letter for him and sent it along for his signature. Princely movement was slow enough that the archbishop decided, in May 1619, to make a trip to Diest in person—not coincidentally, when the archdukes would be there as well. Because of the presence of the archdukes, the nine magistrates of Diest made a show of negotiating on the hospital by coming to talk with the archbishop in his quarters, but in truth they had no intention of allowing something tangible to result from these talks. All magistrates were privately against the archbishop's proposals— even a magistrate whose son was attending the archbishop's seminary "at no cost." Hence, as soon as the archdukes left, so did the magistrates' desire to talk with Archbishop Hovius.

But this May trip to Diest was not in vain, for it also brought two strokes of luck. First, one of the magistrates, Anthony de Jonge, decided for reasons unknown to support the archbishop's reforms. He therefore came forward secretly, like Nicodemus, and offered to Archbishop Hovius intelligence that would aid the cause: Magistrate Thomas Cogen, revealed the informant, had borrowed (and still owed) three hundred florins from the hospital—and the hospital was not a lending institution! Here was firm evidence of financial abuse. And second, during the summer the Council of State in Brussels (on which the archbishop sat) approved the archbishop's draft of revised statutes for the hospital of Diest. Now victory, felt the archbishop, was a matter of time. He even wrote magistrates in Diest a letter, saying that he was quite frankly weary of arguing: from now on they would do well simply to accept his reforms, as instructed by the Council of State. At the first opportunity he planned to travel to Diest, examine accounts, separate the goods of the Poor Tables from the goods of the hospital, forbid magistrates from "supporting all those worldly and expensive servants and maids" who populated the hospital, and install religious sisters, all "as in other cities, to the solace of the poor sick believers of Christ."

Thus here in September 1619 he now rode to Diest, armed

with moral and tangible support from the archdukes and intent on getting magistrates to sign his statutes.

To his happy surprise, the archbishop found almost immediately upon arrival yet another local supporter of reform among the rulers of Diest: the sheriff. This man even promised the archbishop that he could persuade a majority of magistrates to accept reform. If the archbishop was skeptical, he was grateful as well, for within a week the sheriff seemed to deliver: on 1 October 1619, the nine magistrates plus the two current lay supervisors of the hospital visited Archbishop Hovius at his lodgings in the convent of Mariendal. They declared themselves content with the reform of the hospital and no longer wished to oppose him or the archdukes. The archbishop expressed gratitude "in the name of the city's poor."

Yet as the archbishop surely suspected, it was all too easy. For it emerged that the magistrates cooperated not because of some smooth-talking sheriff but because they wanted their terms of office renewed: the ceremony of renewal was to take place that afternoon, immediately after their meeting with Archbishop Hovius! The magistrates did not wish to threaten their chances of renewal by opposing the archbishop in public, especially not when the man performing the ceremony, Councilor Fourneau of the Council of Brabant, was an agent of the archdukes and a good friend of Mathias Hovius.

That the magistrates were less than genuine about reforming the hospital emerged that same evening, only hours after the renewal of offices had occurred. Councilor Fourneau, learning that the archbishop was in town, expressed a wish to go pay his respects. The sheriff volunteered to show the councilor the way. As they walked, the sheriff dared to express the opinion that the archbishop had been sadly misinformed regarding the state of the hospital: his reforms hadn't really been necessary after all. Naturally the councilor soon reported this conversation to the archbishop and his men, who grew furious: never again would they trust the sheriff, who had claimed to be displeased about the hospital and to have persuaded magistrates to the archbishop's plan. Now it was clear that magistrates had accepted the reforms on paper only, and that to ensure their hold on power.

To this disturbing revelation Councilor Fourneau added another, the significance of which he did not immediately grasp. Offhandedly he told how at the ceremony of renewal earlier that day many magistrates had persuaded him that one officer, a certain Anthony de Jonge, should not have his term renewed, on grounds that he had recently used his walking stick to hit a citizen of Diest named Hendricx. Under the circumstances, said the councilor, there was little he could do but swear in another man in De Jonge's place. This too must have dismayed the archbishop, for Anthony de Jonge had of course been the major supporter of the archbishop's reforms for the hospital.

In the end, by October 1619, the archbishop won the official, legal battle over the hospital. All the reforms he had desired were promulgated later that month with the usual red waxen seal and green silk bow. Two hospital sisters from Tienen, under the jurisdiction of Archbishop Hovius, soon moved to Diest to serve the sick. The archbishop even helped salvage the career of Anthony de Jonge by recommending him to Peter Peckius of the Council of Brabant, and by appointing De Jonge as one of the first two lay supervisors of the hospital. But the magistrates of Diest, more skilled in the finer points of local politics, knew how to tweak: they mitigated the archbishop's victory and they had revenge on Anthony de Jonge, whose real crime in their eyes was not about any walking stick but betrayal of local ways. It wasn't long before the magistrates were causing trouble again, by attacking the tax-exempt status of their newly reorganized hospital and its newly appointed sisters. Surely this world and its ways was, as Jesus said himself, for serpents, not religious.

✝ FOURTEEN ✝
The Sportsman's Mass

The third of October, 1619, in Diest.

While the dust from the reform of the hospital in Diest still settled, the tiring archbishop undertook what would prove to be his final colossal endeavor in that oft-visited town: reform of the canons of St. Sulpitius', whose patron saint may as well have been Our Lady of Perpetual Trouble.

Those who gazed later upon the lustrous, dignified portraits of canons in this age could scarcely imagine that in the flesh many were exceedingly fallible human beings. But the archbishop had no such want of imagination, for he knew them up close. Among the canons of St. Sulpitius', his old nemesis in the Berchmans affair, Frans van Groenendonk, was unfortunately not even the worst of the bunch. Though still wonderfully indifferent to his accounts, though the archbishop did nothing for eighteen months to ease the house arrest that had been arranged for the canon back in 1615, on the whole Frans Groenendonk was, astoundingly, guilty of lesser sins than his confreres.

The archbishop could name, for instance, the chapter's former provost, Jan Coen, who for years was accused of drunkenness and all its attendant vices. Drinking himself into a stupor at the Archer's Guild. Dancing himself into torrential sweats. Kissing women and men. Gorging himself at feasts. Kicking a magistrate

opposite: Attributed to Rubens, *Licentiate Hendrik van Thulden,* first half of the seventeenth century
Private collection

in the shins. Head-butting one man to the ground. Falling half-conscious from his horse. Giggling with servant girls. Trying to sleep with the wife of the king of the Archer's Guild. Undressing servant boys. Consecrating an empty chalice during Mass. And locking up guests in his house to drink with him. When sober, he heard in secluded rooms uncommonly lengthy confessions from women. Or he devoted his sermons to that well-known biblical text: the vices of his brother canons in St. Sulpitius'. The provost's two vicars, who served in his name the parishioners of Sulpitius', often refused to arise at night when summoned by the sick: one said it wasn't his week, the other that he spoke no French, the language of a sick woman who asked for him. Fortunately the provost quit the chapter after the archbishop's last visit, surely under pressure.

Unfortunately two other canons had filled most ably the iniquity vacuum left in the chapter by the departure of Provost Coen: Henri Wiggers, dean of the chapter no less, and Arnold Cryters, the treasurer. Resting in his quarters after his triumph over the nearby hospital, it was not hard for the archbishop, after so many unseemly reports, to imagine a typical day in the lives of these two friends.

SOULMATES

The day began, of course, on the river. Winding through the hills of the Brabantine countryside, the Demer flowed up alongside the walls of Diest, bent slightly, then continued west, leisurely as it had come. Through the long, dewy grasses that lined the banks stepped the middle-aged Henri Wiggers, no doubt dressed far too elegantly for his purpose, which was to catch fish.

Everyone in this town of forty-two hundred knew that Dean Wiggers liked to be on the river early. A pair of tall boots defended the lowest realms of his costly attire from the perils of mud and water. Even more perilous, however, was the possibility of arrest, for the dean's favorite fishing holes lay invariably on property belonging to someone else and he had no permission to be there.

But so good was the sport and even the profit, and so sure Henri Wiggers of his status, that he treated all impediments with equal indifference. For long he preferred to cast his nets from a secluded riverbank located on property belonging to the local Carthusians. When encounters with guards grew tiresome, Dean Wiggers testily informed the prior of the Carthusians that he refused to fish on that riverbank any longer, as if the prior should count this a great loss. Or perhaps it was a ruse: for soon after this declaration, the dean was seen sneaking to his beloved spot anyway.

Wherever he muddied his boots, Henri Wiggers never fished past the opening of market. In fact it was possible that he preferred buying and selling even to fishing. Every type of cattle he knew. No estate auction was complete without him. No opportune purchase of land escaped his notice, such as the meadow he had recently bought at a widow-robbing price from the cash-hungry Poor Table of St. Sulpitius'. Like most shrewd bargainers he was more envied than respected, but because he was a priest envy ran deeper than usual.

Priests should not have fished so ardently nor bartered so cunningly, for these diminished dignity and respect. Such activities might also result in affronts to fair trade, for priests were exempt from most taxes and the unscrupulous among them could easily undercut lay competitors. If cupidity caused resentment against such ordinary pastors as Hendrik Heynot of Opwijk, it caused even greater against elite canons—especially when that canon was the chapter's dean, the town's brightest, most fixed clerical star. Yet if Henri Wiggers chose to frequent markets and to justify it by claiming that he was merely following the example of Christ going among sinners, then locals could only complain, not punish. As a member of the chapter he was subject to no one else in town, only to the archbishop in faraway Mechelen—and if the dean would have his way, not even to him.

Going to or from market, Dean Wiggers regularly met his "best friend next to God," Arnold Cryters. While the dean's tastes ran to sport and trade, Canon Cryters favored style and good company. Contrary to the archbishop's statutes, the canon wore his collars long, well down his robes, in French style, and his tunic short, above his knees, in noble style. He also enjoyed from his thirties onward a promising relationship with a young widow named Maria Vyvens. Just recently the two had taken a short trip to Leuven, where they shared a room in a respectable hospice. But this was no temporary fling: the canon was also rumored to be the father of Maria's lovely teenaged daughter, Petronilla.

Though their daytime interests varied, the two canons were united perfectly in their loyalty to each other. Once when parishioners, offended by Henri Wiggers' fervor for fishing and hunting, irreverently referred to the weekly "Dean's Mass" as "The Sportsman's Mass," Canon Cryters rebuked them. And when the lay guard of the Carthusians once dared to banish Dean Wiggers from the monastery's fishing grounds, the canon threatened the guard so viciously that the guard's wife feared for her husband's life. Dean Wiggers was in turn most loyal to Arnold Cryters, never bothering to discipline him for shortcomings—no doubt, claimed other canons, because Canon Cryters knew the dean's shortcomings as well. In short, Dean Wiggers and Canon Cryters made real a motto devised in the previous century for a merely fictional and farcical religious community imagined by the French author Rabelais: that motto was "Do What You Will."

After marketing, fishing, and visiting, the day was far from over for the friends. As priests, both Dean Wiggers and Canon Cryters were obligated to say Mass for the living and the dead. It was from performing these services that they, like most canons, received the largest portion of their income, drawn from pious bequests left by the faithful. But the accounts of bequests to St. Sulpitius' were in such disarray, thanks to the neglect of the archbishop's old nemesis Frans van Groenendonk, that it was quite easy for any canon to skip a Mass or two and still receive the full income attached to it. It was also easy to justify this neglect in the sure knowledge that most Masses were inadequately funded anyway. During one heavily attended public Mass years before, for instance, all canons of Sulpitius' but one stopped singing, right in the middle, in protest of the meager income: half a Mass was all this bequest was worth. The audience was scandalized.

As members of the chapter, canon and dean had one other daily obligation: singing the divine office, especially Matins in the morning and Vespers in the late afternoon. It should have been a pleasant duty: the music was lovely, the stone Sacrament Tower or the carving of Job sitting on the dunghill magnificent to look at, and the twenty-four choir stalls glorious to behold, with armrests carved in the shape of animals and seats carved with humorous allegorical figures. But Canon Cryters and Dean Wiggers did not much enjoy divine office. In fact they were "rare birds" in choir. And when they did attend, their behavior left much to be desired. They often laughed aloud about the dean's latest exploits at market. They often grew bored and after the first verse stood up to walk around the church. And they especially loved to argue, right in choir, over how services should be performed. They argued with the boys from the Latin School over who should sing first. They argued with Frans van Groenendonk and Adrian Claes over who should set the pace in singing, often skipping verses, mumbling through as fast as they could, and starting a new verse before the other side of the choir had finished the last. Canon Cryters even tapped his foot at an impossible rate to keep everyone moving as he pleased, while Dean Wiggers boasted that he could say an entire Mass in fifteen minutes. And they argued against the ridiculous notion that the chapter should sing the entire divine office: this would only introduce new customs.

Of course these arguments in choir did not go on long, for dean and canon had much better things to do when the office was over. Here was a final interest they had in common: night games. Regularly in Diest they gambled and drank at various taverns, such as the Golden Head, the Shooters' Room, or the Wandering Man.

The dean's favorite was the Emperor Tavern, home of the Archer's Guild, which sponsored plenty of shooting but was even more enthusiastic about parties. There on the eve of Annunciation Day the dean lost thirty florins playing dice and cards, about one-tenth of a pastor's annual salary. To compound his sins the dean was a notorious cheater, once angering opponents so that they chased him with sticks and told their friends that had he not been a priest they would have hurt him more. But the dean gave as well as he got: one night at the Corona Tavern he brawled with another opponent, cheered on by Canon Cryters who urged the dean to "run him through, everyone will thank you." The dean also enjoyed dancing with various women, as he demonstrated most convincingly at a dinner celebrating the entry into the chapter of the late Jan Berchmans senior.

Whether dancing, dicing, brawling, or drinking, the two men played late. The dean gambled some nights until five in the morning, which gave him just enough time to reach the church for Matins. More than once did he head straight from the tavern to his stall in the choir of St. Sulpitius' and begin chanting the Gloria.

And thus ended another deplorable day in the life of the chapter's leading spirits. Like Franciscus Pussius, they were quite the old style of canons, supposedly outlawed by the church's most recent reforms at Trent. Even discipline-shirking brother canons in Sulpitius' concluded that Henri Wiggers had gone too far, that he had "no morals, no piety, no dignity, no doctrine." One brother canon revealed a more tangible consequence: during the dean's years in office the people of Diest had not offered "one florin" for new pious foundations in St. Sulpitius', the lifeblood of clerical income.

CHANGING HENRI

Here was a regime Archbishop Hovius wanted to end.

He had reason to hope for better—at least in theory. Elite

chapters of canons originated in tenth-century Europe to promote education, clerical discipline, and lustrous singing in the major churches of towns. They were even meant to help bishops in pastoral work. By the days of Mathias Hovius there were seventy-five such chapters in the Spanish Netherlands as a whole, and thirteen in the archdiocese of Mechelen; had they fulfilled their tasks as once envisioned they would have been a formidable help indeed. Yet by now few of these chapters still ran schools. Few canons of chapters even lived in town, much less together. Few canons were accused of singing on pitch. Most canons cared more about their incomes and social lives than the clerical state. Most spent more energy resisting bishops than helping them. And most cared not at all about actually performing pastoral work but merely about controlling appointments of pastors, to maintain and strengthen their patronage. Though it was true that many in the cathedral chapter of Mechelen labored diligently alongside the archbishop in the task of reform, there was no question he could have used far more of the 150 or so canons in the twelve "collegiate" chapters of the archdiocese to promote his vision of religious life—either directly, through their engaging in pastoral work, or at least indirectly, through providing examples of piety to the faithful. Every other bishop in the land could have said the same.

The archbishop's first step in disciplining unruly chapters was quite basic: submit them to his jurisdiction. Though the Council of Trent had subjected all chapters to bishops, it was a long, arduous process, not at all expedited by the chapters' long traditions of independence, nor by the foot-dragging that occurred when Rome weighed a chapter's inevitable appeal for papal protection. Still, by the time of his visit to Diest in 1619, Archbishop Hovius had succeeded in compelling all but one chapter in the archdiocese to recognize his authority (Rome eventually upheld the appeals for independence of St. Peter's in Leuven).

What proved even tricker for the archbishop, however, than asserting jurisdiction over chapters was the implementation of discipline within them. After several visits each to every chapter, from the beginning of his days to the end, the archbishop found too many canons who actually hindered his pastoral work—including the twins of Diest. Their chief contribution, like that of a Pussius, Costerius, or Froidmont, was to adorn the unflattering description of the bad canon: Latin for the occasional Vespers and Mass. Great diligence in defending rights real and perceived. Canon law desirable, means to afford lawyers a must. Taste in dining and wines. Four generations of nobility preferable. Opportunity for discreet recreation during one's plentiful free time, plus tax-free income and drink. In sum, for younger noble sons in search of an "easy life" that suited their station, and possessed of "average ability, little initiative," and no inclination to be a soldier or monk, a canonry was just the thing. It was an image Mathias Hovius wished to change, beginning with such characters as Arnold Cryters and Henri Wiggers.

Fully aware of what awaited him in the chapter of St. Sulpitius', Archbishop Hovius bided his time patiently during his visit to Diest, occupying himself with other affairs and letting the canons sweat. For more than a week he labored over the hospital and received the usual stream of visitors and gifts, including a ram from the abbot of nearby Tongerlo and two rams from the abbot of Averbode. There was also much opportunity to dine. But not once did he send a dinner invitation, or receive one, from any canon of St. Sulpitius'.

His only contact with the chapter before his formal visitation on 3 October was a brief visit from a nervous Henri Wiggers, who sensed that an attack was imminent and wished to preempt it. To this end he reported to the archbishop the troubling news that Frans van Groenendonk was again neglecting accounts and failing to say Mass. But the archbishop was not as distracted as the dean had hoped, asking straight out whether the dean was still gambling. The dean said he was not. And that was all for today.

Only on his tenth day in Diest did Archbishop Hovius move the few streets required to reach St. Sulpitius' in order to interview the canons of the chapter. One by one the six resident canons (six others lived elsewhere) appeared before the archbishop and the vicar-general, Peter van der Wiel, and promised on their oaths as priests to tell the truth about the state of things in their chapter.

The results were predictable to someone as experienced as Mathias Hovius. Arnold Cryters and Henri Wiggers believed that conditions in the chapter were quite good, in regard to both discipline and morale. More specifically, the divine office was performed quite well, and they knew of no scandals, no drunkenness, no sexual incontinence, or anything like it, except perhaps for some disturbing behavior by the new provost, who enjoyed a late-night game of cards.

But all other canons told a far more unsettling story, and it featured Henri Wiggers and Arnold Cryters. All wanted Dean Wiggers, who was of late called "The Merchant" rather than "The Sportsman," to resign, repeating the words of St. Jerome: "flee the banker-cleric as the plague!" All told how Canon Cryters, in addition to his usual unsavory exploits, had recently flung a precious drinking glass at the head of the provost. Yet all had to admit as well that in recent weeks the two notorious transgressors had improved themselves. Dean Wiggers just days before had prostrated himself at the feet of the chapter and begged forgiveness for past misdeeds. And Canon Cryters shortened his French collars and lengthened his robes. He may even have cooled things with his long-suspected lover Maria Vyvens—but this conclusion was unhappily based on the fact that he had been seen with another woman recently instead: one Anna Gelders, of suspect morals.

With due respect to the complexities of visitation, including the possibility of human error and selfish motives among witnesses, the archbishop concluded in the end that other canons told more truth than did Dean Wiggers and Arnold Cryters. The history of their misdeeds was simply too long and substantial to ignore. As for their recent improvement, the archbishop knew they had on previous visitations shown similar fits of penance, then laughed about it once the archbishop left town. Mathias Hovius was willing to allow for human frailty and give second and third chances to his priests, but he would not be mocked by them. This alone put him in a mood to discipline.

The problem, of course, was achieving it. The usual obstacles to discipline were even greater in chapters than elsewhere. Socially, many canons were noblemen, with especially powerful patrons. Legally, all chapters possessed ancient privileges, dressed up with big papal seals. Some of these were formally undone by the Council of Trent, but some were not. One of these was the right of chapters to discipline their own, including their dean. The archbishop could cite any of his pastors in the diocesan court, but it was debatable whether he could, on his own, go beyond chastisement and actually prosecute a canon or remove a dean, except in the most extreme, Costerius-like cases. Custom required that he work through the canons themselves or through their patrons, or that he bring still other indirect pressure to bear—but such measures took time, of which he had little. Custom also compromised the archbishop's real authority, however official his jurisdiction. And so when the archbishop battled chapters he fought uphill—against tradition, against chestfuls of sprawling noble genealogies and papal bulls, against stubborn, prominent individuals, and against a mountain of other cares on his agenda.

These impediments were precisely how such people as Henri Wiggers and Arnold Cryters went on for years and weathered the force of the archbishop's strict decrees. They could not blatantly rebel, but if they were discreet enough and were careful when the archbishop was in town, they stood a good chance of survival. This was how Arnold Cortenbosch survived so long in the chapter of Aarschot, despite being condemned by Archbishop Hovius for addiction to drink, for swearing obscenities, for hitting the dean in the face, for drawing his noble sword against people of all stations, for reading the Mass while drunk, and for being called the "greatest whore chaser in Aarschot." This was how five other canons in that chapter, suspected of unchastity, seemed almost forgettable in comparison. This was how Willem Lindanus endured in Zoutleeuw, despite notorious drinking, despite being chased by ridiculing boys, despite openly entering houses of ill repute, despite sleeping through Masses he was supposed to celebrate, and despite a short imprisonment. This was how various canons of Ronse were so long notorious for their "pouring and whoring," for their improper exorcisms (including the habit of shamelessly stripping the female possessed), for relationships with women, for fathering children, and for their regular gathering at a drinking house dubbed by locals as "the little chapter." This was why Otto Hartius, grand councilor of the Grand Council of Mechelen, asked Archbishop Hovius in a heart-wrenching letter to lock up his son Jacob, a scandalous canon in the chapter of Anderlecht who spent himself into debt more than once, who used his father's connections to procure favors and even a university degree, who flashed his undeserved but striking protonotarial robes all around town while carrying on illicit business, who contracted great sores on his groin from prostitutes, and whose distressed father and mother finally called their son a "monster" of a man and wished him removed from society. Not all canons were like these, of course, but enough were and the obstacles to discipline so formidable that reform was slow and sporadic, even in scandalous cases.

To achieve correction, the archbishop tried first the word: decrees and statutes. While still in Diest, for instance, he carried out his usual intimidating interviews with canons, prepared for them the usual set of condemning decrees, then gathered the canons to hear them: they were to perform the entire office, sing more slowly, name a new steward, do all their Masses, hold a weekly meeting for business and discipline, stop buying and selling, stop entering taverns, and stop getting drunk. Surely he tried here as elsewhere—or were they beyond feeling?—to sear their consciences with a barrage of his favorite passages on priests, drawn from the Bible especially. If the priest that is anointed do sin then let him bring a sin offering. Let the priests, the ministers of the Lord, weep between the porch and the altar, and let them say, "Spare thy people, O Lord," then will the Lord pity his people. O ye priests this commandment is for you, and if ye will not hear I will send a curse upon

you, and I will curse your blessings, for the priest's lips should keep
knowledge, and they should seek the law at his mouth, for he is
the messenger of the Lord of hosts, but ye are departed out of the
way, ye have caused many to stumble at the law, ye have corrupted
the covenant. Give no offense in any thing, that the ministry be
not blamed, but in all things approving ourselves as the ministers
of God, by pureness, by knowledge, by longsuffering, by kindness,
by the Holy Ghost, by love unfeigned, by the word of truth, by
the power of God, by the armor of righteousness on the right hand
and on the left.

But after these exhortations, the archbishop was experienced
enough to know that especially in chapters discipline could not be
left to texts and words alone: more tangible tactics were required
as well. And so after a brief, restorative visit to the Sharp Hill on
6 October 1619, Archbishop Hovius called certain canons of Sulpitius' to him for a rare second interview. As usual he told Frans van
Groenendonk to start doing his accounts. But this time around
the archbishop was concerned more about Henri Wiggers, and so
spoke with him at much greater length and in a much less pleasant tone. After reciting the dean's offenses, the archbishop ended
the interview as follows: "Everyone is against you, I want you to
resign, and if you don't I will tell all to the nuncio."

Here was just the type of outside pressure the archbishop
needed. For in defending themselves canons often depended on
the support of nuncios; but if the nuncio decided to work in tandem with the archbishop against the canons of Diest, then who
would be for them? The nuncio Morra, despite other disagree-
ments with Archbishop Hovius, had even hinted that he might
be willing to visit Sulpitius' himself. He had also praised the archbishop for always bringing the chapter's troubles to his attention,
since this was an implicit recognition of Rome's authority over the
local church. But the archbishop's intent was otherwise: he simply
wanted help. That he was willing to rely upon nuncios to cooperate
against chapters, and indeed allow Rome to exercise authority over

the matter, revealed how determined he was to reform chapters and how enormous the obstacles to reform were.

The threat of going to the nuncio only made Henri Wiggers irate. He refused to resign — quite unlike recent occasions when he had penitently informed the chapter that he intended to quit his post, held since 1605, out of sorrow for his misdeeds, but then never actually followed through. To the archbishop the dean showed not even feigned penance, but instead stood up from his seat, shook his head, and yelled that he was going to Leuven, the meaning of which the archbishop understood well enough: the dean's cousin was the famous theologian Joannes Wiggers, who was yet another confidant of Mathias Hovius. The cousin would protect him.

In this instance, as in most, kinship proved indeed the strongest bond of all, even stronger than that between such zealous churchmen as the archbishop and the theologian. Joannes Wiggers proved very willing to come to Diest, the next day, and carefully plead his cousin Henri's case. An audience with the archbishop was easily arranged. Negotiations began. Would the archbishop, wondered Dr. Wiggers, consider softening the decrees against the dean that he was preparing to issue at the conclusion of the visitation? This would help preserve the dean's dignity and office. The archbishop did not commit himself one way or the other, but he would not ignore the request of such a distinguished man as Joannes Wiggers.

In keeping with his usual flight between penance and excess, Henri Wiggers visited the archbishop once more, on bended knee, pleading forgiveness for his recent outburst and promising that the archbishop would never hear ill of him again. Two days later, archbishop and dean met for a fourth time during this trip and the archbishop delivered his verdict. He would not push for Henri Wiggers' removal as dean, provided the dean sign a statement acknowledging that he had sinned against the eighteenth chapter of the Provincial Council, and promising that if he ever sold goods or got drunk or violated any of the other standards of canonly behavior, then he would quit not only his office but the chapter itself. Such a promise would satisfy the archbishop. It would satisfy the dean's cousin, the theologian. And it satisfied the dean himself, who signed after all and no doubt left the interview with a smile on his face, before heading to the Archer's Guild.

After his success with the hospital and his encounters with the chapter of Sulpitius', Mathias Hovius left Diest for the last time, with no false illusions about the permanence of Henri Wiggers' penance nor the likelihood of reforming chapters overnight. The archbishop coerced chapters as he could. He helped other bishops as he could in their dealings with chapters. But always he came face to face with the one thing that chapters—especially collegiate chapters, kings of their provincial towns—had perfected more than most: the "policy of inertia." If chapters waited long enough, bishops and their decrees eventually went away. The archbishop's visitations raised awareness of standards for canons, but in essence such visits were a temporary interruption from an existence that was nearly free as a bird's, and far more privileged.

✝ F I F T E E N ✝

Almost Eternity

A s it was in the beginning, so in the end: the archbishop's waning years continued to be filled with one ritual after
the next, lending the illusion of wholeness and timelessness to this
otherwise fragmented life.

True, rituals of the mundane—visitations, audiences, and
dinners—were familiar enough, sometimes even maddeningly the
same, that they brought to mind and spirit a less comforting sort
of eternity than the one the archbishop might envision. Too often
did he hear over and over the problems of years or decades before,
with only names and faces changed, confirming repeatedly that
Hell was every bit as lasting as Heaven.

Yet in the seemingly immutable rituals of sacraments, of processions, of divine office, did Mathias Hovius find himself standing
at the brink of a joyous eternity. For though his voice now quiv-
ered and his hands and legs now trembled, at the moment of per-
formance the words and gestures and robes and aromas and even
emotions of the elderly archbishop were much the same as those
of the young pastor: all time and scars and pain and enemies confronted in the meanwhile ceased to be, only a happy eternity and
the things of God remained. Surely, as with mundane rituals, he
had been here a thousand times before, but now gladly—or better
yet he had never left. Everything in between was an illusion.

preceding page: Adriaan De Bie, *St. Eloi Preaching,* 1626
© Kerkfabriek, St. Gummarus Church, Lier

13 FEBRUARY

Jan Coucke sat with his wife, son, and daughter-in-law on one side of the archbishop's work table. On the other sat the archbishop himself, who made no attempt to hide his displeasure.

It was the season for accounting and the archbishop was hunting for answers. On any given day his table was crowded with rent contracts, receipts, and household ledgers, but it was especially crowded in January and February, when for days at a time the archbishop no longer fished for souls but florins. What had his three stewards done with the talents entrusted to them, namely the fifteen to twenty thousand worth of rents and grain owed him every year as abbot of Affligem and Councilor of State and as holder of recently acquired income-producing assets? Unlike the noble French bishop Francis de Sales, who handed all temporal responsibilities over to a steward, the archbishop insisted on auditing the stewards himself, not out of simple greed but surely out of that abhorrence of debt so typical in those who grew up common or those who inherited an impoverished bishopric and then sweat blood to fund it.

During days of earnest adding and subtracting, the archbishop approved without incident the accounts of his first two stewards. But several more days alone with the books of the third, Jan Coucke, had strained the archbishop's patience, especially because the man had caused trouble before, thanks to his shortfalls (which he blamed on his wife) and his outstanding loans (to be repaid "soon" was the usual promise, no doubt hoping the aging archbishop would die and take his debts with him).

But today was the day of reckoning. The archbishop began: Why had the steward recently submitted accounts that were nothing more than copies of accounts submitted two years before? Did the family really think the archbishop was so simple not to notice? This was the cue for Madam Coucke to play her accustomed role of blametaker in the family business: they had submitted an old account because she was short a thousand florins and afraid to admit it. But the archbishop was unmoved: to avoid such problems in the future the family was to deposit eight thousand florins with him, before Easter, from which he could draw in the event of discrepancies.

With that agreed, Jan Coucke then had the nerve to ask whether the archbishop might have a position for his son, here present. Taken aback, the archbishop refused to discuss the matter until the current accounts were balanced. He invited the family to stay for lunch, but how pleasant an occasion could that have been? Afterward, the chastened family of accountants escaped the residence of the frugal archbishop.

Surely Jan Coucke would have gladly traded places with the undisturbed stewards of Bishop Francis de Sales. Indeed it wasn't long before the task proved too much for him: several months later, Jan Coucke gave up his position in favor of his son. It also wasn't long before the archbishop was singing to the son the same song sung to the father: no more late and vague accounts, pay a deposit, and so forth. Here was a tiresome ritual for one and all.

LATE MARCH

Every year the archbishop, as required of all bishops, celebrated the everlasting events of Easter in his own cathedral.

This richest ritual season of the year began a week before, on Palm Sunday, which commemorated the Joyous Entry of Christ into Jerusalem. The archbishop did the usual blessing of palm branches (for want of genuine palms, Netherlanders used boxwood trimmings), which the faithful took home to place behind their crosses and in the dirt of their fields, to ensure good fortune.

During the vigils of Rope Wednesday, commemorating the betrayal of Our Dear Lord, the ropes of bells were tied up, silencing the heavens. On White Thursday, commemorating the Last Supper, the archbishop, assisted by twelve priests, seven deacons, and seven subdeacons (all holy numbers), blessed the holy oils to be used in the archdiocese for the next year: oil to anoint the dying, oil for the sacraments of confirmation, baptism, and ordination. No doubt as well did the archbishop perform the washing of feet, in imitation of Christ and his disciples. Archduke Albert also performed this ritual, in Brussels, for twelve poor men, while the male nobles of the court walked barefoot in procession and disciplined themselves. Isabella and her ladies prayed in every church of the city.

On Good Friday, the day of death, and Silent Saturday, the day of waiting, the archbishop ordained several young men to the priesthood. And now today, on Easter, the day of Resurrection, the day of rejoicing and renewal, the end of the somber season of fasting, he prepared to celebrate a solemn Mass and administer the Eucharist to the faithful. All parishioners were obligated to commune during Easter week or risk having their names sent to the archbishop, who in turn would send them along to his diocesan court for prosecution.

At the high altar, with his back to the standing multitude, Mathias Hovius performed yet again the miracle of transubstantiation, uttering the words he was sure Christ had uttered himself, and certain that the wafer and wine before him were now His flesh and blood. For a priest there was perhaps no more important moment. Inasmuch as his steadily failing health permitted it, the archbishop usually performed Mass in private, in his own chapel. But on great feast days, especially today, he stood at the center of attention in a sung and incensed Mass in his cathedral. The end of Mass marked the end of another week of hopeful Easter rituals.

Or at least almost. One last ritual remained that evening: priests from around the archdiocese began knocking on the archbishop's door to fetch their particular institution's allotment of holy oils. On this particular Sunday there was a small incident caused by a Pater Zoes, a local Jesuit. In violation of the archbishop's decrees, the good pater was not wearing a surplice, nor did he come with two torches to light the way—both signs of respect for the sacraments. And so he was refused his oils.

After discussing the matter with fellow Jesuits, Pater Zoes returned again to the archbishop's residence, this time to speak with Mathias Hovius himself. Jesuits, explained the pater, were ordinarily not allowed to wear a surplice outside their establishments. The archbishop responded that if the Jesuits wanted their oils, then they had best conform to local custom. He was scandalized that the fathers were prepared to carry the holy oils through the streets in such an irreverent manner. Finally, days later, Pater Zoes arrived once more, this time in his Easter best: a proper surplice, with two bright torches. Here was a battle not worth fighting, concluded the Jesuits, especially since they had won several others more important. And here was a battle, knew the archbishop, that he could at last win easily.

15 APRIL

The archbishop's shaking but experienced fingers carefully examined one complete skull, various fragments of skulls, and a few long bones. The men who brought the bones, Jacob Nesseus and Arnold de Witte, two Franciscans just returned from a journey to Holland, sat before him awaiting his verdict. These men were convinced that on their journey they had found remains of the martyrs of Gorcum and they wanted the archbishop to confirm it.

In 1572 in the town of Gorcum, near Den Briel in the Dutch Republic, a band of drunken soldiers in the service of the Dutch, and let loose by the infamous lord of Lumey, had brutally murdered nineteen Catholic clergymen, mostly Franciscan friars. The deaths took on immense symbolic importance in the struggle between north and south in the Netherlands, between old faith and new: indeed many Catholics regarded the victims as martyrs. In 1603 came the first printed account of their execution, followed during the Truce by various expeditions, organized by Franciscans, to find physical remains in the field of blood.

In 1616 Archbishop Hovius declared that several of the bones from the first of those expeditions were authentic and thus ordered public processions to honor them. These attracted the archdukes, the nuncio, the governing councils, the magistrates of Brussels, all the guilds of Brussels, and more than five thousand other believers who walked before or behind the relics, candles in hand.

Driven on by their confrere, Andreas de Soto, Isabella's own confessor, the Franciscans made still more trips to Gorcum to find still more remains. It was from the latest expedition that the bones on the table before Mathias Hovius had come. The two friars declared that they had dug up these bones in person. They also displayed a notarial act, so critical to the bureaucratic mind, in which two residents of Gorcum testified that where the friars had unearthed the bones was precisely where the martyrs had been condemned and executed.

After his usual tests and consideration, the archbishop was convinced. He therefore drew up yet another authenticity-lending document and ordered further celebrations for the martyrs of Gorcum. But some remained skeptical. The diocese of Ieper forbade public celebrations within its boundaries. And the nuncio Sanseverino counseled the archbishop that it would be wise to await a response from Rome before proceeding with celebrations. The archbishop tried to persuade the nuncio otherwise, reasoning that delay would, in a case as well publicized as this, only cultivate doubt among the faithful, for it would seem the church was uncertain. But the nuncio did not budge.

Cardinal Borghese in Rome agreed with the nuncio. He insisted that, despite the archbishop's plans, the veneration of the martyrs of Gorcum was to be delayed until the Congregation of Sacred Rites determined the authenticity of the bones. The archbishop would do well, said the cardinal, to show more patience. For though Mathias Hovius insisted that Trent had empowered bishops to make such decisions, Rome maintained that the declaration of relics and celebrations belonged to it and required an act of canonization.

When the archbishop therefore pushed for a Roman inquest into the martyrdom, he was politely ignored and the case was left dormant. Perhaps the archbishop could have learned something from the Jesuits, who in such matters acted first and sought approval later: Peter Paul Rubens, for instance, painted two altarpieces of Ignatius Loyola and Francis Xavier for the Jesuit church of Antwerp years before the two men were canonized. By the end of the life of Mathias Hovius the inquest into the relics from Gorcum had gone nowhere: it would come to fruition only centuries later, when the archbishop was less than dust. If his ritual of relic-inspecting itself often proved salutary and inspiring, the ritual of arguing with Rome was neither. After Gorcum, after tithes, after Henri Costerius, after much else, it was no wonder the archbishop never traveled to the seat of St. Peter.

14 JUNE

In the episcopal reception hall, twenty-two-year-old Jenne vande Slype was pleading for an annulment of her "marriage." It was the ritual of the audience.

Jenne told the archbishop that two years before she had, like many Netherlandish girls of the time, married a Spanish soldier stationed in Flanders. But a year after the wedding, her husband, Rodrigo, wailed that he was a lost soul and wanted to go far away. When she pressed him to explain, he replied that he would do so only outside the gates of the city, because women could not keep secrets and Jenne would immediately tell his to everyone in town. When she refused to go with him, Rodrigo went alone, saying she would never see him again and begging forgiveness that he had deceived her, "for you are young."

Jenne and the church's lawyers soon discovered Rodrigo's secret. Before coming to Flanders, he had married a woman in Spain and even fathered two children by her. He left Spain because he had killed his wife's brother in a fight and feared the wrath of the king. Thus he came to Flanders and married Jenne. Against all expectations, there came a recent letter from Spain informing Rodrigo that his wife had made peace with her other brothers and the king and that it was safe for him to return. This explained Rodrigo's turmoil and departure. And it explained why Jenne believed her marriage had never occurred, and why she sought from the archbishop an annulment.

In all the audiences he hosted, in all the meetings with his staff, among all the entries in his journal, the single most common subject was love. It was also the messiest and the worst recorded, surviving the centuries in fragments only. Almost no whole story was preserved. Still, reports of adultery, children born out of wedlock, requests for financial support by abandoned spouses and children, the return of a husband presumed dead, dispensations to marry relatives, dispensations from the three banns (official proclamations of intent to marry), abuse of spouses, incest, wandering harlots, clandestine marriages, bigamy with Spanish soldiers, and most especially alleged engagements and broken engagements, gave the archbishop and his celibate men more detailed knowledge of the intimate lives of the flock than they had ever dreamed. He did not hear all such cases himself, of course, but during the most serious, such as Jenne and Rodrigo's, he often intervened at the critical moment.

If Jenne's evidence was as she claimed, or close to it—for the archbishop knew well that she and her lawyers would have presented her story in a light most favorable to her—then she could count on the archbishop's consistent sympathy for the many scorned women who appeared before him and his ecclesiastical court: pregnant women abandoned after promises of marriage from a lover, wives abused by husbands, or brides lied to by grooms. There were thousands of Jennes in the archdiocese and surely this one was freed to marry again, helped in no small measure by her personal appearance before Archbishop Hovius.

26 JULY

When he was in Leuven, the archbishop almost always invited
Dr. Jacob Jansonius to dine and counsel. Rarely was the invitation
the other way around, for the theologian was famously frugal. But
the archbishop seemed not to mind, for it was the theologian's
company that mattered most.

Both men had studied theology under the same master in
Leuven at nearly the same time. Though the archbishop had chosen
the pastoral life while the theologian continued in the world of
learning, the two were quite kindred spirits: acquainted with grief,
more sober than jovial, and intensely serious about proper religious
living. That was why the theologian was present when Mathias
Hovius was consecrated archbishop. That was why the archbishop
visited the theologian when he lay sick. That was why the archbishop called so often upon the theologian for advice and assistance.

Yet the surest measure of the strength of their attachment
was not in agreement but in disputes. Their mutual respect never
waned, even during these. They battled for months over whether
the chapter of St. Peter's, where Dr. Jansonius was dean, was independent from the jurisdiction of the archbishop and subject only
to Rome. Dean and chapter won that battle, claiming their independence as stubbornly as the most dissolute chapters in the land,
although the men of St. Peter's were hardly dissolute at all. Archbishop and theologian also argued for years over whether the new
Mountains of Charity (pawnshops offering low-interest loans to
the poor, and favored by the archbishop) ran contrary to scriptural
prohibitions on usury. This round was won by the archbishop, due
as usual to the support of the archdukes.

They even disagreed over the finer points of material life.
Modest as the archbishop was in this regard, he still did not go far
enough for his conscience-pricking friend. The latter, born poor in
Amsterdam, robbed of his father, sent as a child by his blind, devout mother to Leuven to learn "true religion," had suffered even

more for the faith than Mathias Hovius—and was thus an even stronger believer in the virtues of hardship. Not for nothing did the students of Jacob Jansonius call him behind his back "pater severus."

And so at one meeting, when the archbishop asked whether there was anything in his episcopal lifestyle that displeased his friend, the doctor replied that there was: the archbishop's silk robe, for silk was the material of status. The archbishop defended himself: the robe was given to him two decades ago by the States of Brabant in order to take properly the oath of the new archdukes. Surely, observed the theologian, that ceremony is long since finished, and thus it is time to finish wearing the robe as well. The archbishop put his robe away.

On another occasion the subject arose again. My robe is gone, began the archbishop: is there anything else which displeases you? Again the reply was affirmative. Again the archbishop wondered to what his friend could possibly object. The answer came quickly: your silver water jug, when tin was perfectly adequate. Here, responded the archbishop, the theologian was overly scrupulous, for lawyers and other distinguished people of his rank also used such items. But that was precisely the doctor's point: should priests imitate the luxury of the laity, or should laypeople learn modesty from priests?

This time the archbishop decided against the counsel and kept his water jug. He also kept a sapphire, diamond, and ruby—probably given him by the archdukes—and a nightgown worth sixty florins. Still, Jacob Jansonius was one of the very few who might compel the archbishop to examine his conscience. In fact it could hardly have been lost on Mathias Hovius that during ritual luncheons with his friend in Leuven the tables might be briefly turned, so that the archbishop became the visited rather than the visitor.

18 AUGUST

In the small city of Aalst, there stood this morning hundreds of children, ready to receive the sacrament of confirmation from the hand of Archbishop Hovius.

By way of preparation they had first confessed and, if necessary, cut back stray hairs on their foreheads. Accompanied by a godmother or godfather, they came one by one to the archbishop, adorned in full ecclesiastical raiment, who laid his hands upon them and anointed their foreheads with the holy chrism while uttering the ancient formula incomprehensible to most who received it, "Signo te signo crucis et confirmo te chrismate salutis, in nomine Patris, et Filii et Spiritus Sancti." Then an assistant wrapped a cloth, worn for three days, around each child's head. The archbishop repeated this hundreds of times until all candidates were anointed.

For inhabitants of the countryside, a visit by the archbishop was always an event of great moment, even if some still doubted the value of confirmation. Martin Luther had denied its sacramental character, causing the Council of Trent to affirm it: confirmation sealed baptism, and anointing strengthened the young faith of the recipient. But for long even some Catholics considered it a second-rate sacrament, even an unnecessary one in comparison, for instance, with baptism. That was why the archbishop sometimes had to use threats, promising that those who had not received confirmation would not be allowed to proceed to the sacrament of marriage.

Nowhere did the archbishop or his secretary record how many he confirmed during his episcopacy. Occasionally he noted confirming "several hundred" or "a multitude" on a given day. Surely by the end of his life the total ran into the tens of thousands. And surely he was busiest during the peace, when bishops made up for lost time and confirmed many adults who had missed the sacrament during war, especially those come from the Dutch Republic. In 1618 the archbishop performed the sacrament on no fewer than thirty-one days, focusing on Brussels and Mechelen during the great feast days and on the countryside during the summer. If the local church was too small to fit everyone, then he confirmed in the open air.

Today in Aalst he anointed his usual hundreds, then attended the usual luncheon in his honor, this one sponsored by magistrates and held in the home of the dean. The reception pleased the archbishop greatly, despite warnings from doctors and well-meaning friends that he would do best to avoid large meals and strong beer. At times, when the task of confirming proved tiresome, he would compliantly skip the meal and go rest in the home of the pastor or another local notable. But most of the time he was at least healthy enough to join his fellow Flemings and Brabanders and indulge in the finer things of life, before moving on to the next village for the next round.

21 SEPTEMBER

In the St. Germanus church of Tienen, thirty-six young men waited to be ordained priests. Forty-nine others were to be made deacons or subdeacons.

They had already been interviewed, by the archbishop, a local pastor, and a monk, to determine their worthiness. At times these interviews produced the most unexpected responses: one unsuccessful candidate had recently offered the archbishop's secretary five or six gold pieces in return for a second chance at answering the questions, but was denied. Perhaps such "arrangements" were possible in the past, but with the current archbishop times had changed.

Ordination was the culmination of a series of rituals that led to the priesthood. First came the shaving of the crown (or tonsure). Then the bestowal of the four minor orders of the priesthood all at once (porter, exorcist, lector, acolyte), often during the student's first year of theology. Finally came the three greater orders (subdeacon, deacon, and priest). The conditions for the last were, among others, legitimate birth of Catholic parents, and a minimum of twenty-five years of age. Dispensations were always possible, but they were reserved by Rome and thus slow. The archbishop therefore sought only thirty-eight such dispensations during his episcopacy, though he likely would have preferred to ask for more and thus expand the pool of available priests.

The archbishop laid his hands on the candidates and uttered the appropriate words, as he did many times a year. His dutiful secretaries proudly recorded that during his life he would ordain 2,500 priests, 2,777 deacons and 2,790 subdeacons. But the archbishop himself brooded that only 200 of these priests came from his seminary and ended up as pastors in rural parishes.

For these young men—and sometimes the less young—the ceremony of ordination was a critical rite of passage. Like marriage, the priesthood was for life. So memorable was it that anniversaries of one's ordination were celebrated more vigorously than one's day of birth. Surely the archbishop recalled his anniversary often, most dramatically at his fiftieth jubilee in 1617. Indeed if ordination was after all these years a rather routine ritual for the archbishop, it was surely as well a moment to recall his own ordination, which occurred in the wake of the Iconoclastic Fury. Tonight, with some sense of relief, the archbishop wrote in his journal that the day's ceremonies had not made him as tired as he had feared they would.

NOVEMBER

The archbishop could not begin to count the letters that landed on his desk or name the messengers who brought them from all corners of the land. Usually there was a seal to be broken and sand (used to help dry the ink) to be brushed off. And inside, more than not, was a petition or tale of woe, and of course a request for his expertise in solving the petitioner's highly complicated problem.

Did the archbishop read them all himself or did he have a

secretary read them aloud first? Whatever the case, today came another, this time from a female religious—or was she? After all, Genoveva Schafts had been out of the convent for thirty years and did not want to go back, as she now told in writing.

In 1580 Genoveva had entered a convent in the city of St. Truiden—but against her will. She explained: her guardian, one Uncle Nicholas with many children of his own, forced her inside in order to lighten his burden and to have Genoveva's modest inheritance, left by her parents when they died. And so when she turned fourteen, he arranged a place for her in the convent, paying her entry fee, the "dowry," from part of her inheritance, but keeping the rest himself—for upon entering the convent Genoveva, like all nuns, was legally dead to the world.

Genoveva made her final profession two years later, but the entire time inside the convent she was profoundly unhappy, without a true vocation. Soon she allowed herself to be seduced by the convent's "chief servant." When her pregnancy became impossible to hide, the lovers ran away together and were married by an unsuspecting, rule-bending priest in a nearby village. Whatever joy they had was burdened by the tension that they might be discovered and by the repeated efforts of intermediaries to persuade Genoveva to return. In fact she was found and returned two or three times, but she left as often, escaping at night through a window and then over the convent's walls. During one escape she suffered a fall that ended her pregnancy in a miscarriage. Distraught, she never returned to the convent again. Her distress deepened when after two years her husband was murdered by freebooters, and she was left alone.

To support herself, Genoveva moved to Brussels, where she "spun, washed, and performed other services" for "good people." Surely such language was meant in part to erase suspicions in the archbishop's mind that Genoveva, like many poor single girls faced with the formidable task of making a living in Brussels, might have tried prostitution as well. Eventually she married again and bore several children, with never a word of trouble from pastor or magistrate for these past thirty years.

Then just weeks before, the archbishop's dean in Brussels came to her doorstep and declared—were any of her children witnesses to the scene?—that he knew about her past as a nun. She was to separate immediately from her husband, for she was possibly not married at all, her vows of profession were probably still valid, and she ought to prepare to return to her convent. The dean had even contacted the nuns there and they wanted her back, "for her salvation." It was as if the last three decades of her life now counted for nothing. Genoveva must have wondered how the dean had learned her secret: a careless word to a disloyal neighbor, who had passed it along?

Genoveva obeyed the dean and moved from under her husband's roof, but she was determined to save her chosen life. She sought out her childhood pastor, now an aging priest, who sent an urgent note to the archbishop pleading Genoveva's cause. This priest had long ago heard Uncle Nicholas admit that he sent Genoveva to the convent to have her money, and by now everyone in the village knew it too. Many villagers, assured the priest, were prepared to testify that Uncle Nicholas was a "nasty man."

Here was a difficult issue. Mathias Hovius was not one to take religious vows lightly, as he proved in the case of Joanna Boisot. And he surely appreciated the zeal of his dean. But in the end his dean proved overly zealous. The archbishop let Genoveva be. Still, like any good bureaucrat he was wary of setting undesirable precedents: because he did not wish to encourage disgruntled nuns who had been legally vowed, he decided Genoveva's case not on the perpetually murky question of forced entry but on the more black and white issue of her age at profession. Enough witnesses could testify that Genoveva was under sixteen when she professed, automatically nullifying her vows and rendering irrelevant any debate over the question of compulsion. Whatever the reason for her release, however, most important to Genoveva was that she could now go back to her husband and children, and no doubt, by now, even grandchildren.

5 DECEMBER

It was enough to make anyone blush.

There in an audience in the archbishop's own residence, a bookseller from Antwerp named Alexander Trognesius was busy displaying several examples of pornographic works, which he claimed various unscrupulous printers and booksellers of his fair city were selling, quite literally, under their counters. These particular copies featured the highly indecent engravings of the Italian Giulio Romano, with accompanying verse by Pietro Aretino. The unsettled archbishop wondered whether he should show these works to the archdukes, but decided against it. Just in case, he kept one copy as evidence, then let the bookseller take the rest.

When Archbishop Hovius subsequently confronted the accused booksellers of Antwerp with these charges, they grew furious, and even launched an investigation of their own into the origins of the suspect works. And what they discovered they made sure to pass along: it was not they who traded in unsavory works, said the booksellers, but Alexander Trognesius himself, who was seen buying such works in Brussels. Trognesius had concocted his lies about the booksellers of Antwerp, and taken them to Archbishop Hovius, in order to deflect attention from charges that the booksellers were about to make against Trognesius himself, on other grounds: namely, that he was printing pirated editions of religious works for which they had been granted monopolies.

Although the pornographic books shocked the archbishop, he realized that there was more to this drama than lewdness: in the highly competitive world of the book trade, dealers did not hesitate to attack one another when it suited their interests. It was a lesson the archbishop learned well in dealing with these men himself: booksellers could be played off against one another rather easily.

This realization proved especially useful in the archbishop's efforts to have a say in what came from the press, for most publications of the day were still of a religious nature, and the archbishop felt he deserved to play a role in determining both content and price. If he played the game right, the archbishop might assure himself, his pastors, and his flock of high-quality, inexpensive products.

At the moment it happened that although the archbishop was displeased with Alexander Trognesius, both for his pornographic works and for his violation of monopolies on religious works, he was also displeased with the most reputable of Trognesius' rivals in Antwerp, Balthazar Moretus, grandson of the world-famous Christopher Plantin. Moretus printed each year more than 450,000 copies of liturgical works, including many sponsored by the archbishop. But of late he showed himself reluctant to publish an oversized and thus expensive version of the archbishop's beloved provincial and diocesan decrees: it was too financially risky. The archbishop felt that in light of the Moretus firm's possessing a monopoly on so many of the church's big-selling publications, it had an obligation to print less profitable but necessary books as well. And so the archbishop conceived a plan.

The next time Balthazar Moretus dined at the archbishop's table, and made his usual complaints about violations of his monopolies on church books by such unprincipled characters as Alexander Trognesius, the archbishop acted bored. Why should he involve himself in this matter, he wondered aloud? In fact, why should not any printer who produced good religious books and sold them at reasonable prices be allowed to print any of the church's books? These words were meant to strike horror in the heart of the printer Moretus, but in case they weren't enough the archbishop became explicit: should the Moretus firm remain unwilling to print the decrees of his provincial council, then he would do all in his power to allow other printers to publish official religious works as well.

The trick worked: Balthazar Moretus proved henceforth amazingly compliant. He not only finally printed the decrees of the archbishop's councils, but at a reception hosted by the bishop of Antwerp, in the last year of Mathias Hovius' life, he happily informed the archbishop that his recent statutes for ecclesiastical courts, another sure worst-seller, were now at press. It was a fact the archbishop noted in his journal with unmistakable satisfaction. Even an earthly ritual, such as a luncheon or an audience or old-fashioned economic pressure, might, like sacramental rituals of the next life, result in miracles.

Mathias at Rest

The thirty-first of May, 1620, Mechelen.

A t four in the early morning the three new great bells of St. Rombout's broke the silence of night. For an entire hour the air above the sleeping city on the Dijle pulsated with heavy, mournful ringing. It was not an alarm this time, as it had been forty years before, when Mechelen's bells announced the travesty of invasion. Rather the deep tones declared to all Mechelaars that their archbishop was dead. The day before, in the abbey of Affligem, he had taken the last breath of his seventy-eight years. His bodily remains arrived in Mechelen that evening, around ten, in stillness. But now his death was sounded for all the sleeping world to hear.

The end was not unexpected. Papal nuncios had predicted it for years. The archbishop himself had long considered requesting a coadjutor, to help him in his old age and then to succeed him, for his health had been in decline for more than a decade. Coughs, fevers, dizziness, difficulty urinating, chills, pains in his left foot, aches in his gums and teeth, all caused him to lose sleep, to cut short audiences, to celebrate Mass with difficulty, to miss Mass altogether, and surely to ponder that Isaiah had been right: instead of a sweet smell there was indeed stink, instead of well-set hair there was baldness, and instead of beauty there was burn-

opposite: Lucas Fayd'herbe, funerary monument of Mathias Hovius, ca. 1665
St. Rombout's Cathedral, Mechelen

ing. Once while celebrating he fell down the steps before the altar, but "thank God" did not hit his head. Nuns of the local hospital, medical doctors, surgeons, and pharmacists all came calling with assorted potions and remedies, all of which he endured, including a "violent purge." He even tried cupping, which involved attaching five special glass cups to his buttocks, meant to create a vacuum and thus draw out the impurities that coursed through his body. At last, as if admitting defeat, he spent three days in January 1619 putting together his will and going through his papers, deciding what to keep and what to throw out.

Death came finally in May 1620. Fittingly, it came while he was on visitation, in the western part of his diocese, and thus lodging as usual in Affligem. One of his last official acts was an unpleasant audience with Godfried Pontanus, a monk from Old Affligem, who now served as prior of Affligem's daughter house in Lower Wavre, where stillborn babies were brought to life. In that audience the archbishop rebuked Prior Pontanus for his sloppy accounts and unexemplary leadership. Just a few days after delivering this tongue-lashing, Archbishop Hovius felt faint and took to his bed, never to rise again. Prior Pontanus, seizing the moment, returned to Lower Wavre and immediately began embezzling the archbishop's assets there.

While the archbishop lay in agony, a doctor from nearby Aalst was put on constant alert to administer physical care. Other surgeons and doctors tried their luck as well. A notary came on 27 May, so that the fading archbishop might amend his will. Concerned friends and dignitaries arrived, including a delegate sent by the magistrates of Mechelen. The archbishop, reported the delegate, possessed full understanding until the end but spoke with much difficulty. On the afternoon of 29 May he fell into such a deep sleep that everyone imagined it was finished: but around six that evening he awoke.

The crowd around him that evening, during his final moments, consisted especially of his brother clergy, there to administer spiritual care: a dean, a pastor, a canon, a bishop, all fortified him, for there was no time "wherein the devil strained more vehe-mently all the powers of his craft to ruin us utterly, and, if he can possibly, make us fall even from trust in the mercy of God, than when he perceives the end of our life is at hand." Jacob Boonen, who years before had begun his career in the chapter of St. Rom-bout's as the archbishop's loyal protégé and who now was bishop of Gent, was most prominent among the small crowd. It was he who administered last rites on this difficult night, and extended the cross for the archbishop to kiss one last time. After making that kiss, the archbishop embraced the cross in his exhausted arms, then lay for hours until expiring at five the next morning, 30 May 1620.

It was a measure of the archbishop's popular appeal, or lack of it, that no crowds swarmed around to take pieces of the corpse or articles of his clothing, as often occurred when someone believed to be a potential saint passed on. Mathias Hovius was not beloved, but rather respected, and the quite routine ceremonies that fol-lowed his death reflected that. The cathedral chapter, as was its right, gathered the day after the archbishop's demise to open his will and to make preparations for his burial and a Memorial Mass. Without delay, various churches in Brussels, Mechelen, Leuven, and the Sharp Hill began chanting the thousand or so Requiem Masses already provided by the deceased for the salvation of his soul. It was a modest figure for the time, far less than the twenty-five thousand funded by Archduke Albert at his death, but still reflecting the inflation of Requiem Masses begun in the Middle Ages by a status-conscious world. Likewise with the archbishop's provision of three thousand booklets containing prayers for his soul, distributed among the flock.

A surgeon, two sisters from the hospital, and several priests laid out and embalmed the corpse. The heart was placed in a leaden chest, which later, at the request of the monks, was kept in the abbey of Affligem. The corpse, clothed in pontifical habit, lay in state in the chapel of the archbishop's residence, where Mechelaars could come pay their last respects. Day and night two Franciscan friars stayed near the body and offered up continuous prayers. As usual, burial occurred before any special Memorial Mass: on 2 June members of the magistracy, the five guilds, and all the clergy bore the corpse from the chapel to the cathedral and laid it to rest in the choir, near the high altar.

The first Memorial Mass took place only two weeks later, on 16 June, which allowed time to make arrangements and embellish the cathedral properly. It began with a short procession, from the archbishop's residence on the Wool Market to the cathedral a few hundred yards away, a path the archbishop had walked thousands of times during his life, including thirteen years before at the opening session of his precious Provincial Council.

At the head of this final procession marched forty-eight seminarians, torches in hand, many of whom received their training at the seminary for free, thanks to Mathias Hovius. Then came servants of the deceased, the first of whom carried the dead archbishop's weapon and motto, and all of whom were arrayed for the occasion in brand new clothing, perhaps a bit stiff, paid for by the estate so that everyone would look their best. Margaret van Eertrijk, the kitchen maid, was there, as were Mayke Paterson and Anna Boels, who had served so many meals and guests. Also the manservants Bartholomew de Laterre and Paschier Veersen, and the coachman Hendrik Pauwels, and the chamberlain Peter Steps, and the archbishop's last chaplain Adrian Zoes, and even stewards and woodsmasters.

Next came the standard-bearer of the cathedral chapter and assorted clergymen who solemnly bore the deceased's symbols of office, from his miter to his ring. Bishops in the procession were led by the bishop of Antwerp and his servant, but none of them had participated in the Provincial Council of 1607: Mathias Hovius had outlived all those. There followed the three executors of the archbishop's estate, one of whom was Robert Meynaerts, now canon of St. Donatus in Brugge but long the personal secretary and chaplain of Mathias Hovius. Then members of the clergy, including the prior and subprior of Affligem and the rural deans. Then councilors and dignitaries of the Grand Council, the magistrates of Mechelen, and assorted noblemen.

Next came the family. Several members had of course preceded him in death. His brother Jan, killed in the invasion of 1580. His sister Clara. His sister Catharina, who for so long had run his household and who had died just years before. But surely present were his sister Anna, her husband Cornelius Estrix, and their two sons, Mathias and Joos, whose studies at the University of Douai were funded by uncle archbishop, as well as the daughter of the deceased Jan, named Clara, who dined with Archbishop Hovius so often at the end. The five guilds of Mechelen added color to the occasion with their bright banners.

The cathedral was fully trimmed. The high altar and the walls of the choir were hung with yards and yards of black cloth, dark as mortal sin. They were provided by the cloth merchant Jan Vlemincx at a cost of five hundred florins to the estate, surely making this a highlight of the merchant's career. Hundreds of painted shields bearing the symbols and motto of the deceased hung on the church doors, on the rood screen, on the torches and candles, and on the black cloth draped in the choir. Patience Conquers the Mighty was everywhere: even if he did not always conquer stubborn and influential canons or unruly pastors or unbreakable nuns, it was an apt choice of motto for a man who never ceased trying.

In the middle of the choir was the fortress-like catafalque, constructed especially for the occasion and adorned with thirty-two torches and shields of the deceased. Here was a truly baroque monument of death. Countless candles and torches penetrated the air with their smoky aroma. The organist at the great new instrument in the choir surely opened every register to the fullest. At the rear of the church, servants of the sheriff ensured proper order. No doubt they had a quieter day than that Sunday almost exactly ten years before when the archbishop asked them to chase down Dutch sailors who so brazenly ridiculed the Holy Sacrament.

All the bishop's symbols of office were set next to the catafalque. There was the pectoral cross, received twenty-five years earlier from the hands of the bishop of Ieper. Most prominent was the miter, every bishop's most basic article of dress, worn at every ceremony and seen in a false dream by Franciscus Pussius. The green bishop's cap and black notarial cap were carried on a pole, as was his favorite chasuble. A paten covered a chalice, lifted so many times during Mass. Next to it lay a cruet of holy oil, used to anoint multitudes of children and priests. The episcopal cross, present at every procession, was draped now in black cloth. And finally the audience saw the bishop's ring, impressed upon endless letters, and kissed by hundreds and thousands received in audience: priests in search of a prebend, deceived spouses, dissatisfied parishioners, sinners, intriguers, princes, and beggars.

The peasant's smock in which he had escaped from a falling Mechelen forty years before was nowhere to be seen. But it should have been there, to complete the story. So should have his high traveling boots, rather than his elegant ceremonial dress boots, for he wore the first more than the second. And his daybook, always near his side, should have lain there as well, open, where one could see, year after year, the promises and threats he had made, which people he had met, what he needed to do.

With the music and chanting now still, all senses turned to the pulpit, from where the seventy-three-year-old theologian Jacob Jansonius delivered the eulogy. He was obviously so suited to the task that the executors had arranged for a special coach to fetch him from Leuven and, when everything was over, to take him back to his doorstep. In print Dr. Jansonius' address ran to thirty baroque pages, full of citations from the Bible and brimming with judgment of the deceased. In duration it must have run forty-five minutes. As usual the professor spoke the plain truth as he saw it. Mathias Hovius, he declared, was a careful but energetic and determined man, who even in old age was constantly on the road, confirming and visiting his flock. With typical clerical bias, the theologian reckoned that the archbishop's greatest achievements were the establishment of the seminary and the gathering of the Provincial Council in 1607. Also worthy of note to the eulogist were the total numbers of priests, deacons, and subdeacons ordained, and the number of bishops consecrated, numbers now repeated for all to hear. Mathias Hovius was, concluded Dr. Jansonius, "the father of bishops" in the land. Surely these all mattered greatly to the archbishop, but passed over for consideration during the theologian's speech were other such crucial matters as the deceased's heroic struggles with disgruntled canons and monks and protonotaries and nuns, his settlement of marital disputes, his establishment of sacred shrines, and his gathering of wildly popular relics.

After the service, executors made the usual distribution of alms to the poor, in this case two hundred florins, and hosted, against the express wishes of the deceased, a modest luncheon for invited guests. Executors also saw to it that for six weeks black cloth should hang in the archbishop's private chapel in St. Rombout's, the same chapel where years before he had discovered the pasquil of Franciscus Pussius.

A second Memorial Mass took place three weeks later, on 7 July, in the abbey of Affligem, where the archbishop had known so much annoyance over the years but where he had also received the income that allowed him to run the archdiocese at all. Jacob Boonen celebrated Mass this time. And another of the archbishop's clerical friends, the archpriest of Antwerp, Laurentius Beyerlinck, delivered the eulogy. Like Dr. Jansonius, he offered an assessment, in elegant Latin, of the great accomplishments of Mathias Hovius, plus a sketch of his personality. And like Dr. Jansonius, the archpriest was silent in every language about any troubles, including the archbishop's past and unsteady relationship with Affligem.

A final pronouncement on the end of the archbishop's life was made more privately, by a secretary in a note at the end of the archbishop's register of ecclesiastical appointments. It read: After today the most illustrious and reverend lord, Mathias Hovius, Archbishop of Mechelen, made no other appointments, because on his last day he died in his monastery of Affligem on 30 May

1620, 78 years old, 53 years a priest, 25 years, 3 months, and 12 days a bishop. May he rest in holy peace.

It took executors a rather typical six years to settle the archbishop's estate. Gradually they paid all bills outstanding. More quickly they granted several months' wages to the archbishop's former servants. Willingly they awarded an extra week's pay to the bell ringers Hendrik van der Veken of St. Rombout's church and Rombout Oliviers of St. Peter's and Paul's for the twisted backs they suffered as a result of sounding the archbishop's death knell so long. Eventually the executors provided all heirs with their designated portions, whether books, income, or shoes. And efficiently the executors auctioned off, in Brussels and Mechelen, whatever else remained: from chests, beds, paintings, and crosses to the last mousetrap and "pisspot," as the author of the inventory called it.

This time there was no seven-year gap between archbishops of Mechelen, for, thanks largely to Mathias Hovius, the position was now an attractive one. When Archduke Albert, after consulting with other bishops, named Jacob Boonen to the post, the nominee required no persuasion at all. There followed quickly a new Scrutiny of the candidate. A new meeting of cardinals in Rome. And a new consecration of the next archbishop. Jacob Boonen purchased from his predecessor's estate not only a ceremonial stole, and the tapestries and gilded leather in the reception hall, but an image of the famous Italian bishop Carlo Borromeo, defender of the local church above the universal. It was a model Jacob Boonen would follow with even more nerve than Mathias Hovius, and with more tragic results.

The monks of Affligem used the brief interval between archbishops just as they had the last: sending petitions to Rome for the right to elect their own abbot and even to be granted independence. This despite the abbey's sentimental Memorial Mass for Mathias Hovius. This despite the thousand florins Mathias Hovius left the abbey for the purchase of church ornaments. And this despite his most personal gift of all, left in gratitude for services rendered by the abbey at his deathbed: his silver water jug, the same jug denounced by Jacob Jansonius. But the monks once again lost their attempt at independence and remained under the archbishops of Mechelen until the French Revolution, when the abbey was ruined. Some fled to new quarters in Dendermonde. Others rebuilt the abbey in the nineteenth century. Monks still live on the original site today, in buildings from various ages and surrounded by old ruins.

Archduke Albert died in 1621, after years of suffering from gout and after a final trip to the Sharp Hill. With Albert's death went any hope for continuing peace, as war with the Dutch resumed within months. Priests were again soon writing bishops to complain about sacrileges committed by soldiers from both sides and about the ruin of churches just rebuilt. With Albert went as well the short-lived dream of an independent southern Netherlands, for as stipulated in Isabella's dowry the land reverted to the king of Spain.

Isabella was at Albert's side until the end, just as she had been at her father's. When he died, she said simply, "My cousin is dead," then rose from her knees and left the room. For the rest of her life she wore the habit of the Poor Clares. Yet she stayed in her adopted land, acting as governor-general in the name of the king and involving herself in its affairs until her own death in 1633.

The domed church of the Sharp Hill was completed in 1627, thanks to Isabella's near extortion of "donations" from every province. Miracles continued over the centuries, if in lesser number than during the first years. Still today, on feast days and Sundays, the church is full of people who sit quietly staring at the famous image or who sing hopeful songs. They, along with walls full of plaques commemorating healings and favors, along with priests who under the shade of large trees bless long lines of cars rather than the coaches or horses of ages past, along with the large crowds roaming easily about the sloping grounds, along with the vendors who surround the whole, along with the divinely named cafes just beyond them—including the Our Dear Lady Coffee House, the

Angelus, and the Eye of Christ, with their piped-in piano arrangements of "As Time Goes By," "My Love Is Blue," "Bridge Over
Troubled Waters," and "Claire de la Lune"—are the heirs of the
guiding shepherd of the shrine, Mathias Hovius.

Henri Costerius died in prison in Vilvoorde in 1618, even before Archbishop Hovius. Out of sight and mind, he proved much
less troublesome than the archbishop had once feared. Only at
the end did he cause anxiety, when he began a fast in protest, determined to prove at last that he was right and Mathias Hovius
wrong. Wenzel Coeberger told the archbishop not to worry: the
man had done this before in Rome to get attention, but soon quit.
This time, however, the protonotary fasted himself to death. On
18 March the archbishop recorded in his journal the laconic entry:
"Today Costerius died." After years of silence, that the archbishop
thought to record the event at all hinted at how the protonotary
had burdened him. If Henri Costerius' fast to the death was regarded as suicide, then he would have earned a final indignity by
being buried in unconsecrated ground.

The village of Opwijk is now dotted with factories, defiling
many of the fields where parishioners once struggled over sheaves
of grain with Hendrik Heynot. The church itself, however, is love-
lier than most and its surrounding lawn well tended. Inside, one
might see young adults singing and playing guitar in preparation
for an upcoming Mass, unaware of the turmoil that once filled the
place. Three hundred yards away, in a surviving peaceful field and
alongside a brook, is the most telling remain of all: an old rectory,
erected in 1618, in gratitude to the respected pastor who replaced
Hendrik Heynot.

Laar finally built a rectory as well, but only in 1736, long after
the death of Gendulphus van Schagen. Until that rectory was built,
the pastors of Laar continued, despite prohibitions by Mathias
Hovius, to live inside the church, in the portal of the tower. Ironi-
cally, given all the trouble it took to build, the rectory is now in
private hands, for the parish's pastor no longer lives there but dwells
in a neighboring village instead. The church stands as small as ever,

while across the street in a field dozens of wandering chickens recall the legacy of Pastor van Schagen.

The able nuncio with whom Mathias Hovius got on best, Guido Bentivoglio, finished his tours as nuncio of Brussels and Paris and in 1621 became a cardinal. In Rome he wrote well-known descriptions of elaborate pageantry, sat on one of the commissions that condemned the heretical Florentine scientist Galileo Galilei, and was almost elected pope. Despite his high office and the decrees of the Council of Trent, and like many churchmen in his position with an eye on retirement, he also accepted a bishopric (in France), which he never visited and from which he arranged a pension for his old age.

Jan Berchmans, like so many of his Jesuit friends, died young, at age twenty-two, in 1621 in Rome, where he had gone to study philosophy. Since his reputation for piety had already spread far and wide, Jesuit confreres, smelling a future saint, pillaged his room in search of relics. After an autopsy, the bodily remains of Jan Berchmans were broken up and spread all around Europe. His heart was taken to the Jesuit church of Leuven, which angered the Jesuits of Mechelen, who had expected it, and Jean de Froidmont as well, who demanded some other relic in compensation. The next year, the usual claims of miracles began, including from one of Jan's elderly aunts in the beguinage of Diest, who alleged she had been cured of an illness after praying for Jan's intercession. The usual canonization inquests soon followed. Walter van Stiphout, his former rector, Jean de Froidmont, and many others were summoned to testify to the boy's unusual spiritual gifts. But the proceedings were interrupted in 1625, then several other times over the centuries, so that only in 1888 was Jan Berchmans finally declared a saint—which probably never would have occurred had he toiled away as a pastor for Mathias Hovius. His modest birthplace still stands today in Diest, open to visitors. Jan's friend the convert Frans Boels also died young, at twenty-nine, in 1625 while at the Jesuit residence in Antwerp, still studying theology, still apparently unreconciled with his Dutch mother.

In 1630 Archbishop Jacob Boonen, the successor of Mathias Hovius, appointed the Congregation of the Oratorians, a new order that rivaled the Jesuits in education and theology, to take charge of instruction in the Latin School of Mechelen. This helped revive the school, even as the seminary showed some signs of decline: by 1640 its buildings were in disrepair, and most prospective priests were, as before, sent to the University of Leuven. But the seminary founded by Mathias Hovius, and whose guiding principles were still taken from his statutes of 1604, revived with a fury in the eighteenth century. In the nineteenth century it was even rebuilt with room for three hundred. The cycle repeated itself in the 1960s, as budding priests were once more sent to Leuven and the seminary was put to other uses, including as the repository of the archives of the archdiocese, and thus of the papers of Mathias Hovius. Those uses continue, but now some seminarians have returned once more.

The stunningly tall church of tiny Limal, in the middle of a green, narrow valley, is surrounded by an unkempt churchyard where the tall grass blows wildly in the wind and where only a gravestone or two still remain. Yet unless removed or decomposed, the bones of one, and likely two, of the children of Gislaine de Haultefenne and Pierre Semalle are buried there. The pilgrimage church of the priory of Lower Wavre still boasts a chapel with an altar dedicated to the Virgin, and across the street a quiet park in her honor.

The archbishop's long-awaited reliquary of St. Rombout was finally completed in 1624 but was very quickly deemed unsuitable. Another, more satisfactory model was fashioned, under the guidance of the well-heeled Jacob Boonen, in 1631.

In Grand Bigard, the ailing deposed abbess Anna D'Ittre had the last laugh on Mathias Hovius, for she outlived the archbishop by a full year. At her death conditions in the convent remained distressingly familiar. It was true that Catharina Martigny was said to be a much stricter abbess, and she even requested "more chaste habits" for the young sisters, but some nuns still visited too intimately with confessors, and Jan and Michel Kerremans continued to call. It was also true that the nuncio Sanseverino finally was able to lock up Jan Kerremans for indiscretions in Grand Bigard, but the ex-confessor's shadow still loomed large. Anyone holding doubts that Jan was involved intimately with one or more nuns in the place had them erased in 1622: this was the year he escaped from prison and fled to Holland, but not before the nuns of Grand Bigard worried that he would come fetch his lover on the way. In Holland, Jan Kerremans did not become apostate, but he spent his energies on a lawsuit to prove that he was still the rightful confessor of Grand Bigard and that they therefore owed him money. He also found himself denying accusations, from other Catholics no less, that he had fathered a child with one of the nuns and had it murdered. Both controversies eroded all good relations with his once-admiring nuns in Bigard. Eventually he returned to the Spanish Netherlands and lived out the rest of his days, into the 1650s, as a monk of Heverlee. Apparently he visited Grand Bigard no more, but his brother Michel was said to be visiting Joanna Boisot as late as the 1630s. Joanna herself died in 1645, still a nun.

The convent of Grand Bigard stood proudly until the French Revolution, when soldiers wasted it and peasants took away gravestones as flooring for animal stalls. In the twentieth century, the brothers of La Salle purchased the grounds and built a School of Christian Doctrine. Today the complex is primarily a retirement home for brothers of the order, with the buildings much changed, but the many fishponds and lakes still giving it seclusion and quiet. One of the kindest of the brothers, all stooped over from age, gladly takes visitors to see the ruins of the old nunnery and the unearthed bones of six abbesses, including Anna D'Ittre and Catharina Martigny, whose gravestones were eventually returned, with the writing on them still legible.

The Black Sisters' convent in Leuven was rebuilt in the 1660s, so that the windows of Cornelia vande Vinne are no more.

In St. Sulpitius', Henri Wiggers was for years still telling visitors that Arnold Cryters had stopped seeing Maria Vyvens, while

Arnold Cryters was still assuring one and all that Henri Wiggers fulfilled his obligations as dean. But by 1627 there were ten resident canons in Sulpitius' and thus even more witnesses to testify that Arnold Cryters had joined the dean as an expert at the Cattle Market, and sometimes wore his choir robes to the slaughterhouse, where he acted as if he were the Censor of Beef, spewing out, "I'd rather have my cows pillaged by enemy soldiers than sell them at that price." Canon Cryters' alleged daughter, Petronilla, was said to visit him at his home, jump into his lap, and sing bawdy songs, causing the canon to roar with delight. The loyal Maria Vyvens still visited Arnold Cryters two or three times a day, going in and out of his home as if she lived there. As for Henri Wiggers: he cheated at gambling as much as ever, still fished illegally, and remained fixed as dean. Archbishop Boonen could not remove him from office either, despite the dean's undisputed sins. Today the church still boasts charming works of art, while all around the square outside are the heirs of establishments that used to host Arnold Cryters and Henri Wiggers: the Chapter Restaurant, the Hunter's Horn, the Hare, the Do-Drop In, and the Emperor Tavern.

Jacob Jansonius died in 1625, the same age at death as Mathias Hovius but suffering even more, with gout in his hands and his arms almost useless, wrapped completely up around him like a baby, in his last years. But surely gout had not come, as it often did, from too much fine food.

Of Mathias Hovius himself much was lost. The chest containing his heart disappeared from Affligem during the French Revolution. His residence was razed in 1717 by a successor, who in its place built a genuine palace—paid for in a predictable way: five thousand florins from the abbey of Affligem, granted in exchange for the right of monks to elect their own abbot. This new palace, not the residence of Mathias Hovius, is what still stands on the Wool Market today.

Other aspects of the archbishop's legacy lasted far longer. Stacks of his papers, including the decrees of his Provincial Council, or scribbles about trivial matters, abound: if he did not always get his way, he at least burdened the consciences of his flock and those of future generations with clear and multitudinous declarations of what he thought were proper religious standards. These would stand for decades, even centuries. His bones, and the relics of St. Rombout, are also still present, in the cathedral. A house he ordered built with funds from his estate for ten beguines of Mechelen—hence its name "The Ten Commandments"—is arguably the most beautiful building on one of the most beautiful and quiet streets of Mechelen: Hovius Street. His portrait adorns the church of the beguinage, the walls of the seminary, and the hall of the archdiocesan palace. Most tangibly of all there stands the full-sized monument to him inside St. Rombout's, next to the high altar. Completed decades after his death, it portrays the archbishop in stone, lying on his side, draped in a habit of a hundred folds, the wrinkled right hand supporting his mitered head, his eyes closed, his mouth almost smiling. There is no trace of the nervous shepherd moving about his flock in wide, anxious circles, but instead only the unbreakable faith that kept him going during his most difficult struggles, reflected now in the calm of repose. The years of trouble were no more.

✝ A WORD AFTER ✝
How We Found Mathias

August 1987, Mechelen, Belgium.

T he archive we wanted had moved from the drafty, leaky sixteenth-century building where it was housed for so long to the more "modern" confines of the seminary. But the seminary didn't look terribly modern either. It was three massive stories of peeling paint, oppressively high ceilings, weedy courtyards, inefficient heaters, damaged paintings, unhinged doors, musty odors, and long, empty hallways, with not a seminarian in sight, for it was no seminary anymore at all.

The entry to the archive was at the end of the south wing, under a coat of arms proclaiming "In nomine domini." Surplus boxes, books, magazines, medallions, statuary, and papers lined the tiled, rounded staircase, which took us up two flights to the reading room. In good Belgian fashion, we knocked and entered, without waiting for an answer. There was a row of bare fluorescent lights. Two large, rectangular wooden tables, four chairs around each. A couple of patrons. An assistant archivist slapping documents into boxes. And in a windowed office to our right the archivist himself, a gray-haired man in his sixties, dominating the scene by his mere presence. He finished what he was doing, slowly rose, stood at the threshold of his office, peered over his glasses at us, and wondered aloud what we could possibly want.

opposite: Unknown artist, Mathias Hovius in his later years
© IRPA-KIK, Brussels

This, we knew already, was Constant Van de Wiel, a priest by vocation, a canon lawyer by training, and for more than two decades an archivist by assignment. Every Monday, Tuesday, and Thursday from 9 to 5:15, and in between teaching courses on canon law and writing opinions on marriage cases before the diocesan court, he sat at a desk in the archive and organized the voluminous papers and registers of more than four hundred years of history in the archdiocese of Mechelen. He obviously did not like interruptions.

Eddy Put, the native Belgian, who had braved working here before, explained that he was there to introduce Craig Harline, an American, who had heard of the archive's riches and was interested in organizing a study around one of Mechelen's early bishops. That provoked a question, not meant to be answered, about why in the world an American needed to come and study Belgian bishops. Not a terribly promising start, but not a surprising one either, for both of us knew the stories of the place and its legendary archivist, and they included the word "difficult."

All historians have tales of archives, but they usually tell them only to one another, not imagining that outsiders might ever be interested. To historians these tales are the closest thing to adventure in what is usually painstaking work. Moreover, the tales also serve a useful function: they provide intelligence—about the alleged secrets of the collection, how to gain access, and so forth. In fact much archival research is quite like war: it begins with reconnaissance missions, cool calculation, and foolproof planning, then never turns out quite as planned. It also frequently involves far more diplomacy than most people ever imagine. One might have to work as hard at getting documents as at actually studying them.

This is especially true in private archives. Public archives in much of Europe are, in the main, accessible and unmysterious. Virtually anyone can walk into the magnificently organized State Archives in Brussels, for instance, or a variety of provincial and municipal archives, and leisurely consult inventories describing kilometers of documents just waiting to be examined. But private archives (even some public archives) can be much more arbitrary, and therefore much more exciting. It is precisely the uncertainty of such archives, the gossip about what might be hidden there, the tact that might be necessary to get the archivist on one's side, that attract some historians. Ultimately, the documents resting there may be of no greater importance than those in well-ordered archives, but the sense of adventure is immeasurably greater.

That, in no small way, was why we ended up here, even if we would not admit it aloud. In previous weeks of that summer we had seen rich collections in other archives and were suitably impressed, but we saved Mechelen for last because it had been used less and the mystery was greater. We knew the rumors of its gatekeeper and its alleged disorder, which caused us anxiety, but also the stories of its vast treasures, which intrigued. Some told of an earlier archivist who so despaired of ever organizing the massive collections that when he needed a particular document he simply resorted to walking around the stacks with an image of St. Anthony, finder of lost objects. But others said that Constant had done much better, and had even gone far toward completing a detailed inventory.

With all this on our minds, Eddy explained further our purpose: we wished specifically to get a sense of the documentation available on Mathias Hovius, third archbishop of Mechelen, as well as his successor, Jacob Boonen. Constant disappeared behind a door. We took a seat and looked around the room. A large portrait of a former archivist hung on one wall. On another was an image of a saintly nun with a knife through her heart. Everywhere were yellowing photographs of diocesan life in the nineteenth and twentieth centuries. In the corners were a copy machine and several locked metal cabinets. Eddy guessed that the inventory was in there.

The assistant archivist, a retired "Pater," stayed in the reading room and entertained us while we waited. Unlike Constant, this man was an extrovert, but with more good will than skill. We watched in horror as he manhandled documents, jabbering good-naturedly in impossible dialect while he worked. His presence was a relief, but there was no question who was in charge, and it was Constant.

   After several minutes, he walked back into the reading room with a stack of documents brought from who knew where, then set them on the table before us. Unlike public archives, we had filled out no forms, and consulted no inventory. What we got depended largely on what the archivist chose to bring us, and thus on our good will with him. How did he know we were not enemies of the church, intent on seizing scandal-ridden documents? Or even thieves, with an eye to stealing the archive's treasures? He was the only security force, after all. Given our cool start, good will between us was something that would have to be developed over time. We could hardly have guessed at the moment that our relationship with Constant would eventually prove far more fruitful—both professionally and personally—than most of our relationships in more open institutions.

   The documents piled high before us were as fascinating as we had hoped, for both bishops. In addition to the usual and often impersonal administrative documents, there were pieces that revealed the personal as well. One of the best was a journal, or daybook, kept by Mathias Hovius between 1617 and his death in 1620. At first glance we imagined it was to aid his memory, for by then he was well over seventy. But eventually it became clear that the keeping of a daybook was an old habit of Mathias Hovius, for there was something more self-conscious about the daybook than merely memory.

   More than anything else it was this journal that decided our topic, for it helped better than other documents to reveal a personality. It did not tell many whole stories and the whole was too detailed to use in its entirety, but it provided important glimpses all along the way. We thumbed through it and the other papers, and in the process we perceived that each of us was as interested as the other in what we were seeing. On that afternoon, after those early moments, in the midst of crackling old parchment and disintegrating papers, and under the watchful gaze of our archivist, the idea struck us at once that here was a subject we might like to study together, for that was how we had found it.

We left late that afternoon, just before the archive closed at five, then walked through a fresh drizzle to the Grand Market, where we sat in one of the many outdoor cafés covered by canopies—perfect expressions of the typically Belgian mix of optimism and realism: outdoors in the hope of sun, and canopies in the likely event of rain. There, on the site of so many dramatic moments in the life of Mathias Hovius, we waited for the next train back to Leuven and made plans for our book.

Constant was right to wonder about one thing. Why would an American, or even a native Belgian, want to study a crusty old bishop from more than three centuries before? It was a question we wondered about as well, because it was the last thing we expected of ourselves.

One thing we knew from the start was that we preferred to study a topic related to the religious Reformations of the sixteenth and seventeenth centuries. Ancient Christianity and Modern seem to attract the most attention nowadays, but appealing to us about the Age of Reformation was its massive rupturing of a seemingly eternal premise of Christianity: that it was one. The emergence of large rival movements produced unprecedented tension and zeal in European Christianity, as Protestants and Catholics fought to make converts and to keep the believers they had. Never before had there been such widespread teaching, preaching, and fighting over souls, or such excellent preservation on paper of these efforts. Rich documents are often the fruit of zeal.

We knew as well that we wanted to study some aspect of religious life in Belgium, or what then was called the Spanish Netherlands. This place in this time lay right at the front of the debate over religion and of the new religious boundaries that divided Catholic south from Protestant north. Would this land be Protestant or Catholic? Would it stay loyal to Spain or become independent? If it stayed Catholic, how Catholic would it be?

All this we knew. What we did not know was that we wanted to study a bishop. Biographies of bishops used to be a staple in bookstores and libraries, but few historians write them anymore. They want to know now instead about the impact of big, impersonal forces, such as social or economic life, on Reformation: was religious conversion more the result of grace or price inflation? And they want to know especially about "ordinary" religion: what did religion mean to a miller, seamstress, peasant woman, or parish priest? As creatures of our own time, these questions interested us most as well. Thus our surprise as we slowly became convinced that to better understand "ordinary" Catholicism we needed to learn more about bishops.

Such a conviction seemed downright silly, given all the books already written about bishops. But most of these books were written by previous generations with different purposes in mind. They tended to regard history as theology, so bishops were either good guys or bad. They tended to label bishops as "major" or "minor," based usually on a judgment of a bishop's political influence rather than his work among the flock. They tended to assume that in understanding the great, they understood by extension everyone else. More recent books rejected these old biases, but introduced in many cases new biases by often stereotyping, confining, and marginalizing bishops: in the currently relentless and sometimes ingenious searches for the religion of the masses, bishops are too often relegated to predictable, incidental roles, or portrayed as flat and lifeless—just as the masses once were.

Yet if, as we now believe, the "religion of the people" was eclectic and colorful, so was the religion of bishops. If, as we also believe, Catholicism continued to vary all around Europe even after the famous reforms of the Council of Trent, then so must bishops have come in many ecclesiastical shapes and sizes. If, as charged, bishops strived to implement the decrees of Trent, then along the eventful way they should have regularly interacted with every group in Catholic society and thus offer arguably the single best vantage point from which to view the wider process of reli-

gion at work. And if, as we most of all believe, religious life was a
constant negotiation among all parties rather than a simple matter
of the hierarchy proclaiming and the flock obeying, then being a
bishop was hardly the mundane, absolutist task it has been made
out to be. Almost always were bishops negotiating, not merely
imposing.

In theory any bishop should therefore be suitable for study.
But long days in archives made us realize that some simply were
more interesting than others, at least according to what our generation of historians considers interesting: lots of documents giving
evidence of interaction with the flock, great and small. Such was
the case with a number of bishops we encountered in the archives,
but few could answer better the simple question—what was it like
to be a bishop at this time of religious reform?—than the unusually well-documented, highly praised, obviously zealous, and
little-studied Mathias Hovius.

As head of the archdiocese of Mechelen from 1589 to 1620,
he was not only primate of all the Low Countries, not only abbot,
adviser to the prince, chaplain to thousands of soldiers, superior to
hundreds of nuns, monks, and other religious, and a regular cor-
respondent of the mighty, but also a reformer of public health, a
frequent dinner companion of small and great, diligent shepherd
of more than 450 parishes, consecrator of hundreds of altars, con-
firmer of thousands of youthful Catholics, and gracious host of
exhausting audiences with people from the entire social spectrum,
who crossed his tiled floor to tell the deepest secrets or recount
the simplest troubles, most of which he dutifully recorded in his
overflowing book of days.

More than any other source did this one reflect that Mathias
Hovius was a regular shoulder rubber with all of society. He was
neither so holy that we must call him exceptional among the many
bishops of his time, nor so typical that we can easily stereotype
him. He was simply a flesh-and-blood prelate who descended his
throne and "muddied his boots" in the filthy streets, hopeless
roads, and eternally damp fields of the archdiocese, whose tri-

umphs moved him to expressions of self-satisfaction, whose defeats aggravated illnesses that made him even more dependent on the medications that prospering apothecaries so willingly mixed for him, and whose life as a whole confirms Professor Erik Midelfort's suggestion that "the *culture des élites*" may turn out to be every bit as interesting and mysterious as the "recently discovered *culture populaire.*"

Hence our purpose, we decided, was to set Mathias Hovius in the whirling midst of his busy world. However valuable his soul may have been to God, Mathias Hovius was to us primarily a useful starting point to begin to understand the religious life of his day. We intended the book less as a biography and more as an opportunity to immerse ourselves and readers as much as possible in his world. That is why we focused on him, and that is why we refer to Protestants as "heretics"—not because we think they are but because he considered them such. In an absolute sense his perspective is obviously limited, restricted to a small area, but in a relative sense it is huge: it puts him in the middle of a myriad of other people and impersonal forces and shows how these too contributed to the shaping of religious life—a task he presumed was primarily his.

After our initial discoveries, our work on Archbishop Hovius was interrupted often over the years—by other obligations, and by the growing realization of just how large this project was, with documents spread around much of Europe. But we continued to chip away at it and always returned to Mechelen, where the bulk of documents lay.

Constant seemed not so constant at all. Each patron appeared to work under a different set of rules. One person might walk freely into the stacks of documents or photocopy at will, another waved cheery hellos and goodbyes, while such newcomers as us timidly sought his mercy and permission at every step of the way. But his trust in us, and our understanding of him, slowly increased—hence so did our privileges as well. An early point of tension was our desire to make photocopies, which speeded our work but threatened the ancient copy machine and the uniqueness of the archive. More than once did he tell us, "that's it, no more copies, it's finished." Yet in the end he settled on an arrangement that proved more helpful to us than anything we experienced in any other archive.

A more serious tension was our uncertainty of exactly how many documents there were on our subject (and in what collections) and how many requests for documents we might make in a day. Ordinarily we told him our subject for the day, he went behind a door, and then returned with what he thought we needed. Unlike our first visit, Constant now brought us only a few at once, saying, "If you're good, then you'll get more." Being "good" meant working long (at least one hour) with what we had, asking for only a bit at a time, never misplacing or reordering documents (a sin that prompted mutterings that perhaps the archive shouldn't be open to the public), and trusting him to bring what mattered. His absolute control over the dispensing of documents was due largely, as mentioned earlier, to justifiable fears of theft from the archive, but at the time it was to us unnerving—especially when at the end of each summer's negotiations he bade farewell to Craig by saying, "There are many more documents you haven't seen yet, and if you're good I'll show them to you next year." At times it seemed almost a challenge for him to keep some things back. Yet in the end he proved true to his word: we ended up seeing far more relevant documents than we ever could have imagined or expected in most other settings, largely because he began, through his unparalleled knowledge of the archive, to volunteer leads that we hadn't previously considered.

Most important, Constant began to offer parts of his inventory. By now we had learned that portions of his inventory had already been published in various journals. When we arrived at the archive with these partial inventories, and asked for a specifically numbered document, he looked at us with admiration, as if to congratulate us for winning that round. But most of the inventory was still in preparation, and thus even more valuable to us when he benevolently set the typescript on our table. What we saw helped us to realize that the rumors of the archive's disorder were more true for the past than the present: the only things in disorder now were those very few collections that the busy Constant had not yet gotten around to inspecting—and these would be finished soon. This inventory also helped us to gain a whole new respect for the man, especially when we realized that he had learned and performed this task quite on his own, without formal training, and without pay. Here was another reason, besides the sheer size of the project, why the inventory took so long: Constant was new at this task, and wanted to be sure it was right before the public saw it. Whatever one's criticisms of the inventory might be, it enabled one to find what lay in almost any box in that archive.

Over time we inevitably gained more respect for the person of Constant as well, which made him far more human. He had begun his priestly studies, he told us, at this very seminary where the archive now rested, at a time when three hundred seminarians roamed the halls. He told us where he ate lunch on his days at the archive: with the brothers of a nearby convent. He told us about his sister in Texas. He spoke most fondly of his annual trips to Zaire, where he offered courses in canon law to prospective priests. One day we met his cousin Joanna, unfortunately at the hospital, after Constant had fainted in the archive from overwork and had to be rushed for care. Another day he even asked Eddy whether he might be interested in one day succeeding him at the archive. For all his apparent gruffness, he proved to have, as cousin Joanna said, "a heart of gingerbread."

And so the summers went—filled with stress, excitement, tedium, terrific discoveries, subtle negotiations, and improved relations in Mechelen. Of course we visited other interesting archives as well. We found the Vatican archive in Rome as idiosyncratic as most other private archives, and pickpockets on Rome's streets were suffered, but certainly it lived up to its reputation: documents were plentiful, it exuded charm, and it provided a fascinating array of scholars from all over the world, whom one could meet over the liberally provided sandwiches and drinks offered daily at eleven, in the garden that lies between the archive and library. We drove up to some diocesan archives in Belgium and the Netherlands to discover that they were closed far more often than they were open, or that their papers had been transferred to the state archives. We corresponded with archivists in France and Belgium in search of Mathias Hovius' correspondence. We ate an unforgettable lunch at one monastery, during a visit to its well-ordered reading room. We watched at one archive as the whole place went into an uproar whenever we requested a document, which usually provoked a personal visit from the head archivist who emerged cigar in hand before the no-smoking sign and asked just exactly what it was that we wanted. We listened with alarm as another archivist, upon being transferred, explained that in his absence one of his two assistants would be very helpful and kind, but the other could be dangerous, so "watch out." Sometimes we were quite alone in archives, and at other times every seat at every table was filled. Sometimes archives contained the latest, most sophisticated equipment, and sometimes we worked in the midst of no heat and dim lighting or excessive heat and bright lighting. Still, there were inevitably more lasting memories in idiosyncratic places than in the well-run, efficient sort of archives. What was difficult to obtain proved to be far more memorable than what was thrown in our laps.

These are some of the people with whom we spent many of our summers and winters trying to discover the mysteries and routines of Mathias Hovius, and without whom none of our discoveries would have been possible. Despite our uncovering an abundance of documents around much of western Europe, we surely did not find everything. Yet what we did find was so much that even together we could not hope to tell about it all: there are certainly other aspects of the story of Mathias Hovius, even whole other versions, that might be told.

As we finish writing our version, we can say happily that the archive of the archdiocese of Mechelen, and the seminary of which it is part, are in better shape today than they were more than a decade ago. Most of the sprawling building has been repainted, recarpeted, and remodeled. Guests may stay several nights in simple but neat rooms. Seminarians again walk the halls, if in fewer numbers than the three hundred who were at school with Constant during the 1940s. Constant himself has retired: whether due to retirement, or the process of time, he seems far more content and restful. Perhaps it was because just before retiring he at last published his inventories of the archive. The timing was perfect: he had fulfilled his responsibility there but now would not have to deal with the increased numbers of eager patrons sure to result from the publishing of the inventories. More than once had he said, perhaps half-jokingly: "Why should I publish an inventory? Then people will come to the archive." Or was he finished after all? Just recently he said to us with a twinkle in his eye, "I have one more inventory they don't know about: do you think I should publish it?" We laughed, but were not surprised, and urged him to publish away.

Constant's inventories now sit conveniently on a shelf in the reading room for all to consult. Their easy availability and the amiability of his successors have made the whole enterprise infinitely simpler than it was when we first arrived at the archive of Mechelen thirteen years ago, when Constant reigned supreme. Virtually nothing is off-limits or unknown any more. All of which has increased efficiency and openness. And all of which has made things far less romantic than the day we found Mathias.

Glossary

✢

ALB—An ankle-length white tunic, worn by priests or lesser clergy for liturgical purposes.

BANNS—The announcements, in church, of a couple's intent to marry.

BEGUINAGE—Usually a walled area, within a town, for beguines, women who wished to lead a pious life in community but who were less than nuns; beguines took a vow of chastity while inside the community, but no vow of poverty.

BENEFICE—An ecclesiastical position that guaranteed a specific income.

CANON—A title given to certain orders of monks, such as Augustinians, but in this book it refers especially to elite priests attached to cathedral or collegiate chapters. Their task was to sing the divine office and celebrate Masses.

CHAPTER—In this book especially a group of canons attached to a cathedral, or to one of the major (collegiate) churches of a diocese.

CHASUBLE—The outer vestment worn at Mass by the presiding priest.

CHOIR—The area of the church in which the office was sung, which contained the high altar, and which the clergy regarded as its own.

CHRISM—Olive oil mixed with perfume used in anointing, confirming, ordaining, and consecrating. It was blessed yearly by the bishop, then distributed among the clergy.

CHURCH FABRIC—Dutch *kerkfabriek,* usually anglicized to "vestry." The word had two meanings: first, the assets belonging to the local parish church, including lands, the church building itself, liturgical ornaments, vestments, and so forth; and second, the laypeople who, in consultation with the parish clergy, administered the assets. The latter were also called "church wardens."

CHURCH WARDEN. See *Church fabric*

COADJUTOR (or, for females, *coadjutrice*)—An assistant, such as an assistant abbess or bishop.

COMPLINE. See *Divine office*

CONFRATERNITY—A group of laypeople, usually organized within a parish, dedicated to pious works or worship, often around a particular patron saint or theme (for example, the confraternity of the Blessed Rosary).

COPE—A ceremonial silken cloak, worn over the shoulders and extending to the ankles, by bishops or certain priests during processions and other ceremonies; it usually replaced the chasuble.

DEAN, OF A CHAPTER—Leader of a collegiate or cathedral chapter, in charge of discipline among the canons.

DEAN, OF A GUILD—Leader of a craft or merchant guild.

DEAN, RURAL—A bishop's delegate over a designated number of usually rural parishes; in the archdiocese of Mechelen, there were eleven rural deaneries of about forty parishes each.

DIOCESAN COURT (or *ecclesiastical court*, or *church court*, or *bishop's court*)—A bishop's juridical arm, consisting at least of a judge (official), prosecutor, other attorneys (including defenders), clerks, and bailiffs. There was no jury in such courts but merely the decision of the official. Over time secular courts came to claim more and more areas of jurisdiction once claimed solely by church courts, such as marriage.

DIVINE OFFICE—Daily prayers and songs, often consisting of psalms, read or sung usually by religious communities or individual clergy at eight different times of the day, which came to be called Matins, Lauds (usually sung with Matins), Prime, Terce, Sext, None, Vespers, and Compline.

FULLERS—Craftsmen who cleaned and prepared wool for dyeing, first by rubbing it with special clay that removed grease, and then cleaning it in water.

KERMIS—A fair, often taking place in the summer, usually in conjunction with the anniversary of the consecration of the local church.

MITER—A triangular hat worn by bishops and some abbots during official rites.

MONSTRANCE—A liturgical object, usually made of silver or gold, designed to display the Eucharistic host; from the Latin word *monstrare*, to show. A common type placed the host in a small window, surrounded by a metallic starburst.

NAVE—The central part of the church, in front of the choir, usually regarded, along with the aisles, as the laity's area.

OFFICIAL—The title given to the judge of the diocesan court, who was a priest with degrees in law, often both civil and canon.

PALL—A dark piece of cloth that covered a coffin or tomb.

POOR TABLE (Holy Ghost Table)—A parish institution, controlled by lay parishioners, to support the poor and needy.

PREBEND—The stipend attached to a position in a cathedral church.

PROTONOTARY (apostolic)—In the strict sense a papal official who notarized certain types of documents, but the title was also given to priests whom the pope wished to honor. These honors included special robes and symbols to signify their status, and such tangible privileges as immunity from local ecclesiastical courts.

RECTORY—The home of the parish priest, an unsatisfactory English rendition of the Dutch word *pastorie*.

RELIQUARY—A vessel, often made of gold or silver, meant to contain relics.

ROOD SCREEN—A wall that divided the nave from the choir, and thus the high altar, meant to intensify the sacredness of the choir. *Rood* was an English word for "cross," as a cross often was prominent in the decoration of this wall.

SACRISTAN—The caretaker of a church.

SCHOLASTER—An office in chapters empowering the holder with some kind of supervision over local education, especially during the Middle Ages.

STOLE—Narrow piece of fabric worn over the shoulders by all sorts of priests, including bishops.

SURPLICE—A white outer garment worn by priests over the cassock, usually in choir or for special occasions.

TONSURE—A rite of initiation for the clergy, which involved shaving the crown of the head.

TRANSEPT—The section of a church that runs at a right angle to the nave and choir, dividing them.

TRIPTYCH—Three panels side by side, usually depicting paintings or carvings, and usually placed above altars.

VESPERS. See *Divine office*

Sources

✠

Abbreviations of Archives and Libraries

AAM	Archive of the Archdiocese of Mechelen-Brussels	
	K	Kloosters
	A	Archiepiscopalia
	M	Mechliniensia
	O	Officialiteit
	P	Parochialia
	V	Vicariaat
	DV	Dekenale Visitatieverslagen
Agenda	AAM, A, Hovius, 10	
ARA	State Archive of Belgium, Brussels	
	GRS	Geheime Raad (Spanish Period)
	KAB	Kerkarchief Brabant
	MD	Manuscrits Divers
	OFRB	Officie-Fiscaal van de Raad van Brabant
	RSA	Raad van State en Audiëntie
	SJ, FB	Jezuïeten, Provincia Flandro-Belgica
ASPP	Archive of the Parish of St. Peter's and Paul's, Mechelen	
ASV	Rome, Archivio Segreto Vaticano	
	NF	Nunziatura di Fiandra
	FB	Fondo Borghese
	MA	Miscellanea Armadia
	SC	Sacra Congregazione del Concilio, Relationes Visitationum ad limina
BAA	Archive of the Diocese of Antwerp	
BAB	Archive of the Diocese of Brugge	
BV	Rome, Bibliotheca Vaticana	
	BL	Barberini Latina
	BC	Buoncompagni

KAM   Archive of the Chapter of St. Rombout's
       A   Archiepiscopalia
KB   Royal Albert I Library, Brussels
Manuale AAM, Mechliniensia, Register 10, Journal of Mathias Hovius
OBC   State Archive of Utrecht, Oud-Bisschoppelijke Clerezij
RAA   State Archive of Antwerp
RAGM   State Archive of Gent, Fonds Bisdom Mechelen
SAM   Municipal Archive of Mechelen
       CA   Chronologische Aenwijzer

Abbreviations of Periodicals and Reference Works

AGN   *Algemene Geschiedenis der Nederlanden*
ARG   *Archive for Reformation History/Archiv für Reformationsgeschichte*
ASEB   *Annales de la Société d'émulation de Bruges*
BG   *Bijdragen tot de Geschiedenis, bijzonderlijk van het aloude Hertogdom
         Brabant*
BIHBR   *Bulletin de l'Institut historique belge de Rome*
BMGN   *Bijdragen en Mededelingen Betreffende de Geschiedenis der Nederlanden*
CBG   *Collationes Brugenses et Gandauenses*
CHR   *Catholic Historical Review*
CM   *Collectanea Mechliniensia*
HKKM   *Handelingen van de Koninklijke Kring voor Oudheidkunde, Letteren en
         Kunst van Mechelen*
JEH   *Journal of Ecclesiastical History*
NAGN   *(Nieuwe) Algemene Geschiedenis der Nederlanden*
NRT   *Nouvelle Revue Théologique*
RHE   *Revue d'Histoire Ecclésiastique*
ROPB   *Recueil des ordonnances des Pays-Bas*
SCJ   *Sixteenth Century Journal*
TG   *Tijdschrift voor Geschiedenis*

The first two headings below provide an overview of works that, in a general way, influenced our approach and thinking. More complete lists for these and other topics are available in plenty of bibliographical databases for the period of the Reformation. After this overview, we note the specific sources used for each chapter.

Approaches to Early Modern Religion and Culture

T. Brady, "Social History," in *Reformation Europe: A Guide to Research,* ed. S. Ozment (St. Louis, 1982).

G. Le Bras, *Introduction à l'histoire de la pratique religieuse en France,* 2 vols. (Paris, 1942–45).

R. Brentano, *Two Churches: England and Italy in the Thirteenth Century* (Berkeley, 1988).

P. Burke, *The Historical Anthropology of Early Modern Italy* (Cambridge, 1987).

R. Chartier, *Cultural History* (Ithaca, N.Y., 1988).

P. Mack Crew, *Calvinist Preaching and Iconoclasm in the Netherlands, 1544–1569* (Cambridge, 1978).

R. Darnton, *The Great Cat Massacre* (New York, 1984).

N. Davis, *Fiction in the Archives* (Stanford, 1987), *Society and Culture in Early Modern France* (Stanford, 1975), and "From 'Popular Religion' to Religious Cultures," in *Reformation Europe,* ed. S. Ozment.

B. Diefendorf and C. Hesse, eds., *Culture and Identity in Early Modern Europe, 1500–1800: Essays in Honor of Natalie Zemon Davis* (Ann Arbor, 1993).

W. Frijhoff, "Van Histoire de l'Eglise naar Histoire religieuse: De invloed van de Annales-groep op de ontwikkeling van de Kerkgeschiedenis in Frankrijk en de perspectieven daarvan voor Nederland," *Nederlands Archief voor Kerkgeschiedenis* 61 (1981): 113–53.

C. Ginzburg, *The Cheese and the Worms* (Baltimore, 1980).

L. Hunt, ed., *The New Cultural History* (Berkeley, 1989).

E. Muir and G. Ruggiero, eds., *Microhistory and the Lost Peoples of Europe* (Baltimore, 1991), and E. Muir and G. Ruggiero, eds., *Sex and Gender in Historical Perspective* (Baltimore, 1990).

J. Obelkevich, ed., *Religion and the People, 800–1700* (Chapel Hill, 1979).

S. Ozment, ed., *Religion and Culture in the Renaissance and Reformation* (Kirksville, Mo., 1989), and the already cited *Reformation Europe.*

D. Sabean, *Power in the Blood* (Cambridge, 1984).

R. Scribner, *For the Sake of Simple Folk: Popular Propaganda for the German Reformation* (Cambridge, 1981).

K. Thomas, *Religion and the Decline of Magic* (New York, 1971), to be read with E. Duffy, *The Stripping of the Altars* (New Haven, 1992).

C. Trinkaus and H. Oberman, eds., *The Pursuit of Holiness in Late Medieval and Renaissance Religion* (Leiden, 1974).

K. von Greyerz, ed., *Religion and Society in Early Modern Europe, 1500–1800* (London, 1984).

Early Modern Catholicism and the Problem of Reform
Some General Studies

J. Bossy, *Christianity in the West, 1400–1700* (Oxford, 1985), and "The Counter-Reformation and the People of Catholic Europe," *Past and Present* 47 (1970): 51–70.

J. Delumeau, *Le Catholicisme entre Luther et Voltaire* (Paris, 1971), published in English as *Catholicism Between Luther and Voltaire: A New View of the Counter-Reformation* (London and Philadelphia, 1977; first French edition, Paris, 1971).

H. O. Evennett, *The Spirit of the Counter-Reformation* (Cambridge, 1968).

C. Harline, "Official Religion—Popular Religion in Recent Historiography of the Catholic Reformation," *ARG* 81 (1990): 239–62.

R. Po-chia Hsia, *The World of Catholic Renewal* (Cambridge, 1998).

H. Jedin, *Geschichte des Konzils von Trient*, 4 vols. (Freiburg i/Br., 1949–75), published in English as *History of the Council of Trent*, 2 vols. (London, 1957–61).

R. Muchembled, *Popular Culture and Elite Culture in France, 1400–1750* (Baton Rouge and London, 1985; first French edition Paris, 1978), to be read with J. Wirth, "Against the Acculturation Thesis," in *Religion and Society*, ed. Greyerz, 66–78.

M. O'Connell, *The Counter Reformation* (New York, 1974).

J. O'Malley, ed., *Catholicism in Early Modern History: A Guide to Research* (St. Louis, 1988); and J. O'Malley, "Was Ignatius Loyola a Church Reformer? How to Look at Early Modern Catholicism," *CHR* 77/2 (April 1991): 177–93; *The First Jesuits* (Cambridge, Mass., 1993).

S. Ozment, ed., *Reformation Europe.*

V. Press, "Stadt und Territoriale Konfessionsbildung," in *Kirche und Gesellschaftlicher Wandel in deutschen und niederländischen Städten der Werdenden Neuzeit*, ed. F. Petri (Cologne and Vienna, 1980), 251–96.

W. Reinhard, "Gegenreformation als Modernisierung? Prolegomena zu einer theorie des konfessionellen Zeitalters," *ARG* 68 (1977): 226–52, and "Zwang zur Konfessionalisierung? Prolegomena zu einer theorie des konfessionellen Zeitalters," *Zeitschrift für historische Forschung* 10 (1983): 257–77.

Some Specialized Studies of Reform and Bishops
Outside the Spanish Netherlands
(Still other specialized studies are mentioned in notes to each chapter.)

A. Balducci, *Girolamo Seripando: Arcivescovo di Salerno, 1554–1563* (Salerno, 1963).

F. J. Baumgartner, *Change and Continuity in the French Episcopate: The Bishops and the Wars of Religion, 1547–1610* (Durham, N.C., 1986).

P. Benedict, *Rouen During the Wars of Religion* (Cambridge, 1981).

J. Bergin, *The Making of the French Episcopate, 1589–1661* (New Haven, 1996), and *Cardinal de la Rochefoucauld: Leadership and Reform in the French Church* (New Haven, 1987).

J. Bilinkoff, *The Avila of St. Teresa* (Ithaca, N.Y., 1989).

R. Bireley, *Religion and Politics in the Age of the Counter-Reformation* (Chapel Hill, 1981).

W. Bouwsma, *Venice and the Defense of Republican Liberty: Renaissance Values in the Age of the Counter-Reformation* (Berkeley, 1968).

P. Broutin, *La Réforme Pastorale en France au XVIIe siècle*, 2 vols. (Paris, 1956), *L'évêque dans la tradition pastorale du XVIe siècle* (Bruges, 1953; French adaptation of H. Jedin, *Das Bischofsideal der Katholischen Reformation*), and "Les visites pastorales d'un évêque au XVIIe siècle," *NRT* 71 (1949): 937–49.

W. Christian, *Local Religion in Sixteenth Century Spain* (Princeton, 1981), and *Apparitions in Late Medieval and Renaissance Spain* (Princeton, 1981).

E. Cochrane, *Florence in the Forgotten Centuries, 1527–1800* (Chicago, 1973), and "New Light on Post-Tridentine Italy: A Note on Recent Counter-Reformation Scholarship," *CHR* 56 (1970): 291–319.

S. Ditchfield, *Liturgy, Sanctity, and History in Tridentine Italy* (Cambridge, 1995).

D. Fenlon, *Heresy and Obedience in Tridentine Italy: Cardinal Pole and the Counter Reformation* (Cambridge, 1972).

J. Ferté, *La vie religieuse dans les campagnes parisiennes, 1622–1695* (Paris, 1962).

M. Forster, *The Counter-Reformation in the Villages: Religion and Reform in the Bishopric of Speyer, 1560–1720* (Ithaca, N.Y., 1992).

A. N. Galpern, *The Religion of the People in Sixteenth-Century Champagne* (Cambridge, Mass., 1976).

E. Gleason, *Gasparo Contarini: Venice, Rome, and Reform* (Berkeley, 1993).

J. Headley and J. Tomaro, eds., *San Carlo Borromeo: Catholic Reform and Ecclesiastical Politics in the Second Half of the Sixteenth Century* (Cranbury, N.J., 1988).

P. T. Hoffmann, *Church and Community in the Diocese of Lyon, 1500–1789* (New Haven, 1984).

R. Po-chia Hsia, *Society and Religion in Münster, 1535–1618* (New Haven, 1984).

W. V. Hudon, *Marcello Cervini and Ecclesiastical Government in Tridentine Italy* (DeKalb, Ill., 1992).

H. Kamen, *The Phoenix and the Flame: Catalonia and the Counter Reformation* (New Haven, 1993).

K. Luria, *Territories of Grace: Cultural Change in the Seventeenth-Century Diocese of Grenoble* (Berkeley, 1991).

A. Morticone, "L'applicazione a Roma del Concilio di Trento: Le visite del 1564–1566," *Rivista di storia della Chiesa in Italia* 7 (1953): 225–50.

W. D. Myers, *"Poor Sinning Folk": Confession and Conscience in Counter-Reformation Germany* (Ithaca, N.Y., 1996).

S. Nalle, *God in La Mancha: Religious Reform and the People of Cuenca, 1500–1650* (Baltimore, 1992).

M. Peronnet, *Les évêques de l'ancienne France,* 2 vols. (Paris, 1978).

A. Poska, *Regulating the People: The Catholic Reformation in Seventeenth Century Spain* (Leiden, 1998).

L. J. Rogier, *Geschiedenis van het Katholicisme in Noord-Nederland in de 16e en de 17e eeuw,* 3 vols., 2d edition (Amsterdam, 1947).

G. Rooijakkers, *Rituele repertoires: Volkscultuur in oostelijk Noord-Brabant, 1559–1853* (Nijmegen, 1994).

T. M. Safley, *Let No Man Put Asunder: The Control of Marriage in the German Southwest* (Kirksville, Mo., 1984).

R. Sauzet, *Contre-Réforme et Réforme Catholique en Bas Languedoc* (Leuven, 1979), and *Les visites pastorales dans le diocèse de Chartres pendant la première moitié du XVIIe siècle: Essai de sociologie religieuse* (Rome, 1975).

T. Tackett, *Priest and Parish in Eighteenth-Century France* (Princeton, 1977).

M. Venard, *L'église d'Avignon au XVIe siècle,* 5 vols. (Lille, 1981).

B. Vogler, *Vie religieuse en pays rhénan dans la seconde moitié du XVIe siècle, 1556–1619,* 3 vols. (Lille, 1974).

M. Wingens, *Over de grens: De bedevaart van katholieke Nederlanders in de zeventiende en achttiende eeuw* (Nijmegen, 1994).

Works with Focus on the Spanish Netherlands

Surveys of Literature: More titles than those given below are included in a recent historiographical summary in M. Cloet and F. Daelemans, eds., *Godsdienst, Mentaliteit en Dagelijks Leven: Religieuze geschiedenis in België sinds 1970* (Brussels, 1988); also M. Cloet, "Een kwarteeuw historische produktie in België betreffende de religieuze geschiedenis van de Nieuwe Tijd," *Trajecta* 4 (1995): 198–223; and J. Tracy, "With and Without the Counter-Reformation: The Catholic Church in the Spanish Netherlands and the Dutch Republic, 1580–1650," *CHR* 71 (1985): 547–75.

Surveys: J. Toussaert, *Le sentiment religieux en Flandre à la fin du Moyen Age* (Paris, 1960); E. de Moreau, *Histoire de l'église en Belgique,* 5 vols. (Brussels, 1945–52); F. Willocx, *L'introduction des décrets du Concile de Trente dans les Pays-Bas et dans la principauté de Liège* (Leuven, 1929); A. Pasture, *La Restauration Religieuse aux Pays-Bas sous les Archiducs Albert et Isabelle, 1596–1633* (Leuven, 1925); H. J. Elias, *Kerk en Staat in de Zuidelijke Nederlanden onder de Regeering der Aartshertogen Albrecht en Isabella, 1598–1621* (Leuven, 1931).

Specialized Studies (a sample): K. Bergé, *Kerkelijk leven in de landelijke dekenij*

Deinze, 1661–1762 (Leuven, 1981); L. Braeken, *De dekenij Herentals, 1603–1669: Bijdrage tot de studie van het godsdienstig leven in het Bisdom Antwerpen* (Leuven, 1982); R. Castelain, *Kinderen en hun Opvoeding in de Kasselrij Oudenaarde, 1500–1800* (Oudenaarde, 1979); P. Claessens, *Histoire des Archevêques de Malines*, 2 vols. (Leuven, 1881); C. de Clercq, *Cinq archevêques de Malines*, 2 vols. (Paris, 1974); M. Cloet, *Het kerkelijk leven in een landelijke dekenij van Vlaanderen tijdens de XVIIe eeuw: Tielt van 1609 tot 1700* (Leuven, 1968), condensed as "Religious Life in a Rural Deanery in Flanders During the Seventeenth Century: Tielt from 1609 to 1700," *Acta Historica Neerlandica* 5 (1971): 135–58; M. Cloet, "Antoon Triest, prototype van een contrareformatorische bisschop, op bezoek in zijn Gentse diocees, 1622–1657," *BMGN* 91/3 (1976): 394–405; M. Cloet, *Karel Filips van Rodoan en het Bisdom Brugge tijdens zijn Episcopaat, 1602–1616* (Brussels, 1970); C. Harline and E. Put, "A Bishop in the Cloisters: The Visitations of Mathias Hovius, Malines, 1596–1620," *SCJ* 22 (1991): 611–39; and C. Harline and E. Put, "Dagboek van een aartsbisschop: Een portretstudie van Matthias Hovius, 1542–1620," *Trajecta* 3 (1994): 19–33; T. B. W. Kok, *Dekenaat in de steigers: Kerkelijk opbouwwerk in het Gentse dekenaat Hulst, 1596–1648* (Tilburg, 1971); A. Lottin, *Lille: Citadelle de la Contre-Réforme? 1598–1668* (Paris, 1984); M.-J. Marinus, *Laevinus Torrentius als tweede bisschop van Antwerpen, 1587–1595* (Brussels, 1989); T. Morren, *Het dekenaat Diest, 1599–1700: Bijdrage tot de studie van de Katholieke Hervorming in het aartsbisdom Mechelen* (Leuven, 1993); F. Penders, *De dekenij Herentals, 1670–1773: Bijdrage tot de studie van het kerkelijk leven in het bisdom Antwerpen* (Leuven, 1993); J. De Potter, *De dekenij Ninove op 't einde der XVIe eeuw* (Gent, 1945); K. de Raeymaker, *Het Godsdienstig Leven in de Landdekenij Antwerpen, 1610–1650* (Leuven, 1977); J. Schoenaerts, *Kerk en gelovigen in de dekenij Waas tijdens de XVIIIe eeuw* (Leuven, 1979); M. Therry, *De religieuze beleving bij de leken in het 17de-eeuwse bisdom Brugge, 1609–1706* (Brussels, 1988).

The single most important collection of primary sources is in P. F. X. de Ram and J. F. Van de Velde, eds., *Synodicon belgicum: Sive acta omnium ecclesiarum belgii a celebrato concilio tridentino usque ad concordatum anni 1801*, 4 vols. (Leuven, 1828, 1829, 1839, 1858).

Chapter 1: The Canon's New Clothes
An Old World

Inside St. Rombout's: J. Laenen, *Histoire de l'église métropolitaine de Saint Rombaut à Malines*, 2 vols. (Mechelen, 1919–20), especially vol. 1; also KAM, Statutes of the chapter of St. Rombout's, undated, but probably 1600.

Discussion at the Weekly Meeting: KAM, Acta Capitularia, 8 April 1580, reveals that the main topic of business was fines owed the chapter by non-resident canons—a common topic, even in chapters not threatened by invasion.

Hovius' Preparations for Bed: Inferred from his later ownership of an expensive nightgown, worth sixty-one florins, and other items listed in inventories of his "sterfhuis," or estate.

An English Fury

Events of 9 April and First Days of the Calvinist Regime: G. Marnef, *Het Calvinistisch Bewind te Mechelen, 1580–1585* (Kortrijk, 1987); E. van Autenboer, "Mechelen in de 16de eeuw: Schade wordt toegebracht en hersteld," *HKKM* 89 (1985), 197–242; E. van Autenboer, "De Hervorming te Mechelen, 1566–1585," *Noordgouw* 19–20 (1979–83): 47–62; F. A. Berlemont, *Mechelse Kronieken van het jaar 1 tot 1945* (Brussels, 1975); SAM, CA (a series of registers containing copies of documents in the archive); ASPP, Box 172, Chronicles.

Nicolas Vanderlaan: SAM, CA, assorted documents from 1580.

Conjecture About Disguises of Clergy: Anna van Roy, a beguine, thought immediately of dressing as a laywoman; KAM, 325, depositions regarding the relics of St. Rombout, 23 November 1585 (reviewed in Chapter 11). V. M. A. Heyndrikx, "Maximiliaan Morillon, 1517–1586: Medewerker van kardinaal Granvelle" (Licentiaatsverhandeling, Leuven, 1993), 130, describes people who would shelter fleeing nuns, even relatives, only if they were disguised as laypeople. F. Baumgartner, *Change and Continuity*, 151, recounts how, in 1561, Bishop Arthur de Cossé de Brissac of Coutances escaped by disguising himself as a miller.

Hovius' Flight and the Rectory of St. Peter's and Paul's: It is unclear whether there was a rectory, but if so it would have been located near the Nekkerspoel gate. No documents state that Mathias Hovius tried to get out the Nekkerspoel gate before it closed; but it was the exit of choice during the early moments of the Fury, the Palace of Hoogstraten was right next to the gate, and Hovius hid in that palace for several days. The scenario of his trying to exit and falling short is, therefore, conjecture.

Peter De Wolf: E. van Autenboer, "Petrus De Wolf: Carmeliet en Predikant, Verdediger van Mechelen, Geloofsgetuige," *Carmel* 1 (1948): 109–39, also contains details on the palace of Hoogstraten. Other fighting priests are noted in Baumgartner, *Change and Continuity*, 150.

The Death of Jan Hovius: P. Claessens, *Histoire des archevêques*, 1:212.

Hovius and the Wardrobe: The oldest account is L. Beyerlinck, *Oratio in Funere Illustriss. ac Reverendiss. D. Matthiae Hovii . . .* (Antwerp, 1620), 22, a eulogy delivered soon after Hovius' death. Beyerlinck apparently had the story from Hovius himself.

Composing Clever Recantations: Discussed in S. Wabuda, "Equivocation and Recantation During the English Reformation: The 'Subtle Shadows' of Dr. Edward Crome," *JEH* 44/2 (April 1993): 224.

Inside the Wardrobe

Mechelen's Glorious Past: E. van Autenboer, *Volksfeesten en Rederijkers te Mechelen, 1400–1600* (Gent, 1962).

Mechelen's Population: No one knows for sure, but see Marnef, *Bewind,* 69–72; J. Verbeemen, "De demografische evolutie van Mechelen, 1370–1800," *HKKM* 57 (1953): 63–97; and M. Kocken, "De Bevolkingscijfers van Mechelen," *HKKM* 77 (1973): 174–77.

Explosion of the Zand Gate: R. Foncke, "Vlugschriften van de Tijd over het Springen van de Mechelsche Zandpoort, 1546," *HKKM* (1932): 42–65.

Famine: Berlemont, *Kronieken,* 1546, 1556.

Taxes: SAM, *Inventaris,* 4:117, requests made from 8 May 1542, 12 October 1543, and more in 1544.

Poverty and Decline: M. Van der Auwera, "Armoede en sociale politiek te Mechelen in de 16e en de 18e eeuw," *BG* (1976): 227–48.

Outlines of the Dutch Revolt, Especially the 1570s: G. Parker, *The Dutch Revolt* (London, 1985; revised edition), through 198; Marnef, *Bewind;* G. Marnef, "Mechelen en de opstand: Van beeldenstorm (1566) tot reconciliatie (1585)," *HKKM* 88 (1984): 49–63.

Examples of Violence: Moreau, *Histoire de l'église,* 5:43, 172–205, which puts the number of Catholic clergy murdered during the Troubles at 130.

The Spanish Fury in Mechelen: ASPP, Box 172, Chronicles, among others that of Azevedo, which includes Hovius' own declaration of his encounter with the soldiers, and also one from the Parish of St. Jan's, on the details of 2 October 1572. See also Van Autenboer, "Schade wordt toegebracht," 200–204, and KAM, A, Hovius, Bewind, miscellaneous biographical notes.

Hovius' Political Sensibilities: One clue in M. Delcourt and J. Hoyoux, eds., *Laevinus Torrentius Correspondance,* 3 vols. (Paris, 1950–54), 3:279–81, in which Hovius complains to Bishop Torrentius of the impossibility in Philip's dominions of being politically neutral and strongly Catholic. On the sale of precious objects to pay for defenses, see G. Van Caster, "Festivités en l'honneur de S. Rumold," *HKKM* 13 (1903): 261.

A Blesséd Smock

Mechelen After the English Fury: Van Autenboer, "Schade wordt toegebracht," 206.

The Bells of St. Rombout's: Laenen, *Histoire de l'église métropolitaine.*

Scriptural Allusions: Lamentations; Joel 2,3; Isaiah 13:13–16; Revelations 11:7, 13:1–7.

The Anonymous Chronicler: In KAM, A, Hovius, Bewind, miscellaneous notes on Hovius, "eductus ex civitate in vestri rustico, magnus defensor fidei et Inimicus haereticorum."

Chapter 2: The Third Man
A Roman Deliberation

The Quirinal Palace and Hill: P. Partner, *The Pope's Men* (Oxford, 1990); L. Partridge, *The Art of Renaissance Rome, 1400–1600* (New York, 1996); and C. L. Stinger, *The Renaissance in Rome* (Bloomington, Ind., 1985).

The Congregation of Cardinals, and Scrutinies: L. Jadin, "Procès d'information pour la nomination des évêques et abbés des Pays-Bas, de Liège et de Franche-Comté d'après les Archives de la Congrégation Consistoriale, 1564–1637," *BIHBR* (1928): 5–263; and J. Paquay, *Les préconisations des évêques des provinces belges au Consistoire (1559–1853) d'après les archives de la Consistoriale rattachées aux Archives Vaticanes* (Lummen, 1930). The dossier of Hovius is not preserved in Rome, though drafts and notes are in AAM, A, Hovius, 1. Hovius' chaplaincy in St. Rombout's to supplement his meager income as pastor of St. Peter's and Paul's, in SAM, CA, 28 February 1596. The various documents recording his tonsure and ordination between 1563 and 1566 are in AAM, A, Hovius, 1.

Qualifications of Bishops: Session 7 of the Council of Trent included not only legitimate birth but being "endowed with gravity of manners, and skill in letters." A well-known English version is J. Waterworth, *The Canons and Decrees of the Sacred and Oecumenical Council of Trent* (London, 1848).

Philip's Letter of Nomination, and the Difficulties of Naming a New Archbishop: The letter, in ARA, RSA, 938, 20 April 1595, implies that the see was vacant simply because Cardinal Allen recently died. Details on the efforts to name Allen and Torrentius are in J. Lefèvre, "La nomination des archevêques de Malines sous l'Ancien Régime," *HKKM* 63 (1959): 75–92; M. A. Nauwelaerts, "De kandidatuur van Laevinus Torrentius voor de aartsbisschoppelijke zetel van Mechelen," *HKKM* 60 (1956): 120–29; and Marinus, *Torrentius,* 185–88. In L. P. Gachard and J. Lefèvre, eds., *Correspondance de Philippe II sur les affaires des Pays-Bas,* 4 vols. (Brussels, 1848–1960), 4:23, 22 February 1592, Allen wrote that he considered himself a Netherlander.

Characterizations of Torrentius: Partly from Moreau, *Histoire de l'église,* 5:47, and Marinus, *Torrentius,* 47, passim.

Hauchinus' Melancholy: KAM, A, Hovius, Bewind, a document titled "Reservatio mensium apostolicorum et alternativa pro Episcopis residentibus."

Pleas to Philip to Name an Archbishop: ARA, RSA, Zendbrieven, 1944/1, 8 December 1594, chapter of Rombout's to Philip II, and Lefèvre, *Correspondance*

Philippe II, 4:279, 28 January 1595, in which Governor-General Ernst Mansfeld states his preference for Hovius, "already mentioned for the sees of Antwerp and Gent."

Allen's Death: Lefèvre, *Correspondance Philippe II*, 4:248; dated 11 July 1594. Reconsideration of Torrentius in Delcourt and Hoyoux, eds., *Torrentius Correspondance*, 3:574, 27 June 1594.

Exile and Return

Hovius in Liège: Information is sparse, but see Claessens, *Histoire des archevêques*, which drew heavily on Beyerlinck, *Oratio*, as we assume did J. Baetens, *Verzameling van Naamrollen betrekkelijk de kerkgeschiedenis van Mechelen*, 3 vols. (Mechelen, 1881), and J. Schoeffer, "Archidiaconorum Ecclesiae Metropolitanae Mechliniensis Notitia Chronologica" (Ms. 1845 in the AAM). Willem van Pamele (Privy Council) to the Bishop of Middelburg, dated 1582, in A. Miraeus and J. F. Foppens, *Diplomatum Belgicorum Nova Collectio . . .* (Brussels, 1734), 3:489–90, mentions the offer of the pastorship in Breda, and that Hovius had served long in Mechelen "cum summa laude."

Mechelen's Population in 1585: Estimated by J. Briels, "De emigratie uit Mechelen naar de Noordelijke Nederlanden omstreeks 1572–1630," *HKKM*, 89 (1985): 251.

Various Destructions in Mechelen: The stained glass window of St. Peter's and Paul's in ASPP, Box 172, Chronicles. Hovius' lament on morals in RAGM, B3886, 1/2/3, 9 September 1591, to Bishop Damant of Gent. Empty and ruined parishes in J. De Brouwer, *Bijdrage tot de Geschiedenis van het Godsdienstig Leven en de Kerkelijke Instellingen in het Land van Aalst tussen 1550 en 1621 volgens de verslagen van de Dekenale Bezoeken* (Aalst, 1961), 148, 161; P. Dupont, G. Lemaire, and A. Vanderborght, "L'Etat des campagnes Brabançonnes a la fin du XVIe siècle et au début du XVIIe, d'après les rapports des visites decanales de l'archevêché de Malines," in *Annales du XLIIe Congrès de la fédération archéologique, historique et folklorique de Belgique, 1972*, no. 2 (Malmédy, 1974): 77–98; and A. Cosemans, "Het uitzicht van Brabant op het einde der 16de eeuw," *BG* 27 (1936): 285–351. The state of St. Rombout's in Laenen, *Histoire de l'église métropolitaine*, 2:121–78, 279.

Faith-Promoting Stories: Laenen, *Histoire de l'église métropolitaine*, 2:160; Berlemont, *Kronieken*, 1579, regarding a brewery called Den Zeeridder; H. de Backer, "Het Arme Clarenklooster te Mechelen, vanaf 1500 tot de opheffing in 1966" (Licentiaatsverhandeling, Leuven, 1977), 17; Van Autenboer, "Schade wordt toegebracht," 207. The regathering of the relics of St. Rombout in Van Caster, "Festivités en l'honneur de S. Rumold;" Laenen, *Histoire de l'église métropolitaine*, 1:39; Van Autenboer, "Schade wordt toegebracht," 214; and the primary source in KAM, 325, depositions, 23 November 1585. Hauchinus' activities in Mechelen from Laenen, *Histoire de l'église métropolitaine*, 1:259; SAM, CA, 30 September 1587; Van Autenboer, "Schade wordt toegebracht," 214; and Berlemont, *Kronieken*, 3 January 1588.

Hovius as Vicar-General *Sede Vacante:* KAM, Manuscript by Van Helmont, 27, 40, and AAM, M, register 2, various acta, which reflect the extent of Hovius' activities during these years. He also worked to organize the rural deans, in AAM, DV; for the best introduction to the deans and their visitations, see M. Cloet, N. Bostyn, and K. de Vreese, eds., *Repertorium van dekenale visitatieverslagen betreffende de Mechelse kerkprovincie, 1559–1801* (Leuven, 1989), 153–251. Hovius also called in bishops to perform rituals he could not: AAM, M, register 2, 223v, 230v–231, 232, 269v, on requests for confirmations and consecrations.

Disputes Between Town and Clergy: Often these were over the question of clerical exemptions from taxation, as reflected in KAM, Cartularium, F VI, 1, 15 November 1585.

The Equalizer

Hovius' Family and Early Religious Life: Claessens, *Histoire des archevêques,* says Andreas Hovius was eventually dean of the guild. For one recent portrait of the overwhelming sensory images and reminders available to Catholics young and old, Duffy, *Stripping of the Altars.*

Formal Schooling: Parker, *Dutch Revolt,* 21, notes 150 schools in Antwerp alone by the mid–sixteenth century, while Gent had 40, Tournai 11, and Poperinge 7. Mechelen was part of this trend. The late-medieval curriculum in elementary education in E. Frutsaert, *De Rooms-Katholieke Catechisatie in Vlaams-België vanaf het Concilie van Trente* (Leuven, 1934), 34–68, 174–91, and E. Put, *De Cleijne Schoolen: Het volksonderwijs in het hertogdom Brabant tussen Katholieke Reformatie en Verlichting, eind 16de eeuw–1795* (Leuven, 1990), 73–92, 182–257. The Standonck curriculum in J. Laenen, *Geschiedenis van het seminarie van Mechelen* (Mechelen, 1930), 26, and Claessens, *Histoire des archevêques,* 247.

Student in Leuven: KAM, A, Hovius, Bewind, miscellaneous anonymous notes about Hovius states that he moved to Leuven thanks to exhortations from his sister.

The Regime of the Standonck Colleges: Laenen, *Seminarie,* 43, calls Erasmus an "ungrateful insolent fellow" for all his venom against hardships in the Collège de Montaigu in Paris, which was of the same cloth as the Standonck College.

The University of Leuven: *De Universiteit te Leuven, 1425–1985* (Leuven, 1986); R. Guelley, "L'évolution des méthodes théologiques à Louvain d'Erasme a Jansénius," *RHE* 37 (1941): 31–144. Context and wider trends of theological training in J. K. Farge, *Orthodoxy and Reform in Early Reformation France: The Faculty of Theology of Paris, 1500–1543* (Leiden, 1985); J. Pelikan, *The Christian Tradition: A History of the Development of Doctrine,* vol. 4, *Reformation of Church and Dogma, 1300–1700* (Chicago, 1984); E. Rummel, "The Importance of Being Doctor: The Quarrel over Competency

Between Humanists and Theologians in the Renaissance," *CHR* 82/2 (April 1996): 187–203. Bergin, *French Episcopate*, 233, discusses the respective difficulties of law and theology at universities.

Duties of Priests: From the *Pastorale ad usum romanum accomodatum, canones et ritus ecclesiasticos . . . complectens: Ioannis Hauchini . . . iussu olim editum . . . Matthiae Hovii . . .* (Antwerp, 1598 and 1607). Though published well after Hovius became a priest, it adequately reflects the tasks that were being done even before. On the Pastorale, see L. Malherbe, "Le Pastorale de Malines: Son histoire," *CM* 28 (1939): 369–88. Also J. Laenen, *Introduction à l'histoire paroissiale du diocèse de Malines: Les institutions* (Brussels, 1924).

Hovius and the Great: Evidence of his unease is impressionistic, from his stumbling at the Joyous Entry of Albert and Isabella (discussed in Chapter 3), and his apologies, early in his episcopacy, for poor knowledge of French, the language of the court, in ARA, RSA, Zendbrieven, 1944/1, 23 June 1603.

Non-Noble Bishops: Over the next two decades, thirty-nine of the forty new Netherlandish bishops were non-nobles—in contrast to earlier days when a noble pedigree was prerequisite. The trend would revert to nobles after the 1620s.

Bishop at Last

Granvelle: SAM, CA, 29 March 1590, letters of legitimation for Granvelle's son; see also R. Tambuyser, "Antoine Perrenot de Granvelle, premier archevêque de Malines," *CM* 46 (1961): 243–63; M. van Durme, "Een figuur van Europees formaat: Kardinaal de Granvelle, Eerste Aartsbisschop van Mechelen, Besançon 1517–Madrid 1586," *HKKM* 65 (1961): 44–61.

Jan van der Burch: Jadin, "Procès d'information," 64, and Claessens, *Histoire des archevêques*, 216.

Fees and Symbols of Appointment: AAM, A, Hovius, 1, letter requesting dispensation dated July 19, 1595. Also ARA, RSA, 437, 22 July 1595, addressed to the ambassador in Rome, and 30 September and 21 October. Other documents on his appointment in AAM, A, Hovius, 10, 18 July 1595, and KAM, A, Hovius, Bewind, dated 26 November 1595.

The Election Scene with Cardinal Avila: L. Von Pastor, *History of the Popes,* 40 vols. (London, 1932–50), 25:16–17.

Hovius' Consecration: The scene is inferred from the ceremonies surrounding his successor Jacob Boonen, in AAM, A, Boonen, 143, 26 November 1621, and those of Matthias Lambrecht of Brugge in August 1596, whose consecration Hovius performed, in BAB, B252. KAM, A, Hovius, Bewind, 18 February 1596, reveals that Petrus Simons, bishop of Ieper, consecrated Hovius, assisted by Petrus Damant of Gent and John Lesley, exiled bishop from Ireland (identified in AAM, M, 2, fol. 230v).

The first document mentions the dignified crowd, "and many other prelates of the church and other ecclesiastical and secular and distinguished men."

Mottos: The motto close to Hovius' is Jacob Sturm's, in T. Brady, *The Politics of the Reformation in Germany: Jacob Sturm (1489–1553) of Strasbourg* (Atlantic Highlands, N.J., 1997), 95.

Chapter 3: Isabella's Dowry

The Archbishop's New Chapel in Rombout's: Laenen, *Histoire de l'église métropolitaine*, 2:255; or KB, ms. 16527, f. 6, 1 June 1596.

The Archbishop's Hierarchy: See numerous early entries in AAM, M, registers 2–8, for the offices filled.

The Spanish Road

The Journey over the Alps, and Albert and Isabella: Drawn from H. Van der Wee and R. Van Humbeek, "Les Alpes, paradis ou enfer des voyageurs aux temps modernes?" in *Quand la Montagne aussi a une Histoire: Mélanges offerts à Jean-François Bergier,* ed. M. Körner and F. Walter (Stuttgart, 1996), 279–92; M. de Villermont, *L'Infante Isabella, Gouvernante des Pays-Bas* (Paris, 1912); C. Terlinden, *Aartshertogin Isabella* (Antwerp, 1943); L. Klingenstein, *The Great Infanta Isabel, Sovereign of the Netherlands* (New York, 1910); V. Brants, *Albert et Isabelle: Etudes d'histoire politique et sociale* (Leuven and Paris, 1910); P. Callaey, "Albert et Isabelle: Souverains de Belgique, 1598–1621," *BIHBR* (1924): 31–42; G. Parker, *Philip II* (Boston, 1978); P. Pierson, *Philip II of Spain* (London, 1975); H. Kamen, *Philip of Spain* (New Haven, 1997); A. Pasture, *La Restauration Religieuse;* Elias, *Kerk en Staat;* W. Thomas and L. Duerloo, eds., *Albrecht en Isabella, 1598–1621: Catalogus en Essais* (Brussels, 1998). Both Albert and Isabella are in need of new biographies.

Criticism of Philip for Keeping Isabella Unmarried: R. Kagan, *Lucrecia's Dreams: Politics and Prophecy in Sixteenth-Century Spain* (Berkeley, 1990), 31.

Ceremony of the Act of Cession: L. P. Gachard, *Collection de documents inédits concernant l'histoire de la Belgique* (Brussels, 1833), 1:460–96; also ARA, RSA, 1191/21, *Relation des particularitez et ceremonies . . . ;* and R. Wellens, "Les Etats Généraux de Bruxelles en 1598 et la cession des Pays-Bas aux archiducs Albert et Isabelle," *Cahiers Bruxellois* 23 (1978–81): 23–34.

Anna and a Thousand Others

The story of Anna Utenhove relies on F. Van Dijk, "Het laatste ketterproces in de Nederlanden," *Gereformeerd theologisch tijdschrift* (1949): 219–31, plus archival documents in ARA, OFRB, port. 1194, ARA, RSA, 1398/2, and the Dutch martyrologies cited below. On martyrs and heresy (including Anna), see a brilliant new study by Brad Gregory, *Salvation at Stake: Christian Martyrdom in Early Modern Europe* (Cambridge, Mass., 1999).

The Family of Love and Anabaptists: A. Hamilton, *The Family of Love* (Cambridge, 1981), and J. Dietz Moss, *"Godded with God": Hendrik Niclaes and His Family of Love* (Philadelphia, 1981). The Rampart sisters were from Antwerp, where the Family was centered, and in 1585 moved to Brussels, where they attended church, participated in the sacraments, and heard sermons, all typical of Family members. As for Anna, she was quite poor, refused to take an oath, and refused to attend Mass, all more typical of Anabaptists.

The Possibility of Anna's Recanting: Inferred from decisions of the recent past in AAM, M, registers 2–8, under Hovius, which let people go if they recanted in time.

Penalties for Female Heretics: *ROPB*, 2de reeks, 6 (Brussels, 1922): 110–18.

Hovius' Attitude Toward Anna: Letter to Albert, 7 April 1597, in ARA, RSA, 1398/2. Albert sought Hovius' advice in March 1597, in ARA, RSA, 1854/1. See also Albert to Council of Brabant, 28 May 1597, ARA, Raad van Brabant, 4886. Albert hints that King Philip took the initiative: "estant l'intention du Roy monseigneur et la notre que l'on ne souffre telles plus, . . . qu'ils soient exemplairement puniz en termes de droict excusant touttefois le feu."

Dutch Martyrologies About Anna: P. Leendertz, *Het geuzenliedboek, naar de oude drukken uit de nalatenschap van Dr. E. T. Kuiper* (Zutphen, 1925), 2:47–52; *Théâtre des martyrs, Depuis la mort de J. Christ jusqu'à présent; représenté en très belles tailles-douces par le célèbre graveur Iean Luyken* (Leiden, n.d.), copy in ARA, Topografisch-Historische Atlas 711/103; T. J. Van Braght, *Het Bloedig Tooneel of Martelaersspiegel der doops-gesinde of weerelose christenen . . .* (Amsterdam, 1685), 792–94; A. C. Van Haemstede, *De historie der martelaren die om het getuygenisse der Evangelischer waerheyt haer bloet gestort hebben, van de tijden Christi onses Salighmakers af tot den jare sesthien hondert vijf-en-vijftig toe* (Amsterdam, 1671), f. 466v–467.

Other-Believers Before and Just After Anna: AAM, DV, Ronse (Dikkelvenne), 1592; De Brouwer, *Land van Aalst*, 183; Dupont, Lemaire, and Vanderborght, "L'Etat des campagnes Brabançonnes," 98; AAM, M, 3, fols. 71–73, 10 September 1597; AAM, M, 3, f. 93 (Rumoldus a Lin, 19 December 1597), f. 140 (Catharina Wannemaker, 27 May 1598), f. 180 (Windelina Brems, 10 December 1598).

The Softening of the Archdukes: H. Grotius, *Annales et histoires des troubles du Pays-Bas* (Amsterdam, 1662), 344–45, claims that Albert was more careful after Anna;

L. Maes, *Heksenprocessen* (Antwerp, 1977), 409; H. J. Elias, "De ketterij in de Zuide-lijke Nederlanden onder Albrecht en Isabella," *ASEB* 61 (1926): 367–87. See AAM, M, 4, f. 4v. (Hiëronymus Diercx); AAM, DV, Betekom 1600, where just a year before a suspected heretic had fled to Holland.

A Joyous Entry

Assorted Entries: J. Bochius, *Historica narratio profectionis et inaugurationis serenissimorum Belgii principum Alberti et Isabellae, Austriae archiducum . . .* (Antwerp, 1602), 110 ff.; M. Soenen, "Fêtes et cérémonies publiques à Bruxelles aux Temps Mod-ernes," *BG* 68 (1985): 60–61; Grotius, *Annales,* 452; H. Soly, "Plechtige intochten in de steden van de Zuidelijke Nederlanden tijdens de overgang van Middeleeuwen naar Nieuwe Tijd: Communicatie, propaganda, spektakel," *TG* 97 (1984): 341–61.

The Entry in Mechelen: SAM, CA, 5 December 1599, describing the general festivities and the church festivities in particular; Bochius, *Historica narratio,* 163–70; H. Coninckx, "La joyeuse entrée des Seigneurs de Malines," *HKKM* 6 (1896): 220–27, 273–78; F. de Reiffenberg, *Itinéraire de l'archiduc Albert, de la reine d'Espagne Marguerite d'Autriche et de l'infante Isabelle en 1599 et 1600* (Brussels, 1841).

The States General of 1600: L. P. Gachard, ed., "Les actes des états généraux de 1600," in *Collection de documents sur les anciennes assemblées nationales de la Belgique* (Brussels, 1849).

Isabella's Humor: J. Verberckmoes, "The Archdukes in Their Humour," in *Albrecht en Isabella,* ed. Thomas and Duerloo, 137–44.

Chapter 4: Mathias' Pence
An Old, Old Quarrel

Conflict Between Affligem and Mathias Hovius: The most important second-ary source is W. Verleyen, "De Affligemse monniken in het Keizershof te Mechelen, 1595–1605: Het conflict met aartsbisschop Hovius," in *Mechliniensia in honorem Prof. em. Dr. Constantini Van de Wiel septuagenarii,* ed. R. de Smedt (1994), 93–117. For more background, see W. Verleyen, *Negen eeuwen Affligem* (Affligem, 1983), and *Dom Benedictus van Haeften, Proost van Affligem, 1588–1648: Bijdrage tot de studie van het kloosterleven in de Zuidelijke Nederlanden* (Brussels, 1983). Also Moreau, *Histoire de l'église,* 5:207–9. Primary sources in AAM, K, Affligem; KAM, Affligem; ASV, FB; and the Archive of the Abbey of Affligem itself.

The Bulls of Incorporation: A. Miraeus and J. Foppens, *Opera diplomatica et historica . . .* (Leuven, 1723–48), 2:1092–93. The best study of the new bishoprics is M. Dierickx, *De Oprichting der nieuwe bisdommen in de Nederlanden onder Filips II,*

1559–1570 (Antwerp, 1950). Abbeys that undid incorporation were Tongerlo, attached to Den Bosch, and St. Bernard's, attached to Antwerp. For French examples of bishops using monasteries, see Baumgartner, *Change and Continuity,* 63.

Mobilizing Saints: P. Geary, *Furta Sacra* (Princeton, 1990), 20–21. M. Bax, "Saint Gerard's Wrath: Religious Power-Politics in a Dutch Community," *Anthropological Quarterly* 65/4 (October 1992): 177–86.

Hovius' Visitation to Affligem (as Vicar-General): KAM, 84, 27 February 1595. The Bursfeld visit is in the same folder, as is Hovius' counter-visitation on 23 April— three days after he was nominated as archbishop.

The Memory of Hauchinus: Both monks and Hovius refer to him; letter to Cardinal Borghese, 5 January 1601, ASV, FB, III98D, 106; and 4 January 1601, III6A, 108, and 109.

Livinus Mulder in Bethanie: AAM, K, Bethanie Brussels, visitation of March 1590. A February 1592 visitation repeated the stories about Linken, and added more. Hovius wrote to Mulder in 1590 and warned him to stop seeing Sister Linken; Archive of the Abbey of Dendermonde, Acta Capituli, I, f. 399–402, which also mentions the prior's visits to Grand Bigard.

Hovius' Correspondence with Mulder in Vlierbeek: AAM, K, Affligem, 3, including 10 September 1598, 15 November 1598, 20 June 1599, 26 October 1599, and an undated letter.

The Anonymous Letter in Rome: Reported to Frangipani by the papal secretary of state Aldobrandini, 31 July 1599; L. van der Essen and A. Louant, *Correspondance d'Ottavio Mirto Frangipani, premier nonce de Flandre, 1596–1606,* 3 vols. (Rome, 1924–42), 3:65, with Frangipani's answer of 27 August 1599 in *Frangipani,* 3:52.

Other Illnesses Supposedly Caused by Hovius: AAM, K, Roosendaal, Chronology, f. 68, recounts that Hovius rebuked a mother superior for the frivolous behavior of two nuns, who turned out not to be hers; still, she was so thunderstruck that she returned home affected in her throat, lay down without speaking, and died the same day.

The Mediator from Naples

Complaints from Affligem: The nuncio Frangipani to Aldobrandini, 9 February 1602, in Van der Essen and Louant, *Frangipani,* 3:303.

Clash Between Local Reform and Papal Authority: Another example is how Rome, despite the decrees of Trent, supported the claim of St. Peter's in Leuven to be exempt from episcopal authority, in J. Paquet, "L'exemption du chapitre Saint-Pierre de Louvain et la visite de la Collégiale par le nonce Morra, 1617–1619," *BIHBR* 38 (1967): 233–70. The best example, however, is that of all the abbeys attached to new bishoprics in Brabant only Affligem remained so.

Trent's Potential to Undermine Papal Authority: The inspiration for our interpretation was J. Roegiers, "Jansenisme en katholieke hervorming in de Nederlanden," in *Geloven in het verleden: Studies over het godsdienstig leven in de vroegmoderne tijd, aangeboden aan Michel Cloet,* ed. E. Put, M. J. Marinus, and H. Storme, (Leuven, 1996), 43–64. Examples of dispensations to concubining clergymen from Roegiers, 53–55, and Balducci, *Seripando,* 55–57. See also G. Alberigo, "The Council of Trent," in *Catholicism in Early Modern History,* ed. O'Malley, 211–26; and J. Tomaro, "San Carlo Borromeo and the Implementation of the Council of Trent," in *San Carlo Borromeo,* ed. Headley and Tomaro, especially 73–77. W. Bouwsma, *Venice and the Defense of Republican Liberty,* devotes much attention to the Venetian Paolo Sarpi, whose famous *History of the Council of Trent* alleged, among other things, that Rome would not enhance episcopal authority to perform the task of reform properly (581–83). That local churches were not merely a carbon copy of Trent or each other is discussed in Cochrane, "New Light on Post-Tridentine Italy," and P. Prodi, "The Application of the Tridentine Decrees: The Organization of the Diocese of Bologna During the Episcopate of Cardinal Gabriele Paleotti," in *The Late Italian Renaissance, 1525–1630,* ed. E. Cochrane (New York, 1970), 226–43. M. Pacaut, "Naissance et fonctionnement des Réseaux Monastiques et Canoniaux: Réflexion sur le Bilan d'un Colloque," *Cahiers d'Histoire* 31 (1986): 41–52, shows that in monastic life specifically, as in religious life more broadly, reform was always more successful if those charged with implementing reform covered a limited geographical area.

Sketch of Frangipani: Especially from Van der Essen and Louant, *Frangipani,* 3, introduction.

Mulder's Complaints About Hovius: AAM, K, Affligem, 3, 26 October 1599, to Frangipani. The monks' sixty points in ASV, FB, III98D1, f. 99, 15 January 1601.

Hovius' Self-Defense: To Secretary Aldobrandini, ASV, FB, III98D, f. 106, 5 January 1601. Testimonials from other bishops AAM, A, Hovius, 2, letters dated 18–28 Februari 1601. Hovius' defense to Frangipani in ASV, FB, III98D, f. 91, undated. Hovius' argument that Hauchinus wanted to remove Mulder was actually made to Mulder himself; see above at "Hovius' Correspondence with Mulder."

Frangipani Weary of Affligem: Letter to Hovius, 9 September 1597, Van der Essen and Louant, *Frangipani,* 2:207–11. Verleyen, "De Affligemse monniken," places Frangipani's sentiments in favor of the archbishop from mid-1599, even though the nuncio remained sympathetic to some of the monks' complaints.

Rumors About the Bishop Snubbed in Rome: Van der Essen and Louant, *Frangipani,* 3:86, 15 January 1600; 644, 5 February 1600; J. D. M. Cornelissen, *Romeinsche bronnen voor den kerkelijken toestand der Nederlanden onder de apostolische vicarissen, 1592–1727* (The Hague, 1932), 1:73, 75, letters from 5 February 1600, 13 April 1600.

Una Bella Concordia

Episcopal Income: More than a third of bishoprics in France took in over 24,000 livres; Baumgartner, *Change and Continuity,* 62; also Moreau, *Histoire de l'église,* 5:284–87.

Frangipani's Supporting the Subjection of Affligem: To Aldobrandini, in Van der Essen and Louant, *Frangipani,* 3:231–43, 2 May 1601. When Frangipani begins to recount the entire history of incorporation, Aldobrandini's marginal note is to the effect that "the holy father doesn't need to know all this." Aldobrandini's response in Phalesius, Archive of the Abbey of Affligem, f. 197.

On the Sense of a National Church: Pasture, *La Restauration Religieuse,* and Elias, *Kerk en Staat.* Archbishops on Albert's Council of State in J. Houssiau, "L'Archevêque de Malines, conseiller d'Etat au XVIIe s.," in *Mechliniensia in honorem Prof. em. Dr. Constantini Van de Wiel,* ed. De Smedt, 81–92. Hovius apologizes for his lack of French, and Spanish, in ARA, RSA, Zendbrieven, 1944/1, 23 June 1603.

Relationship Between Rome and the Archdukes: Van der Essen and Louant, *Frangipani,* introduction, notes that one of the chief papal goals in the Low Countries was to promote good relations with the archdukes. Concern over this is explicit in Frangipani's justification of the agreement to Rome, in Van der Essen and Louant, *Frangipani,* 3:231–43.

Picnic in Affligem: Discussed by Phalesius, and Frangipani's letter to Aldobrandini, 12 May 1601, Van der Essen and Louant, *Frangipani,* 3:244. See Verleyen, "De Affligemse monniken," 112.

The Final Meeting: Verleyen says this occurred on 9 February, but the 19th makes more sense, because "four days" later, on the 23rd, the monks signed.

Costerius: F. Prims, "Onze 'plebaan' Henricus Costerius, de wonderdoener (+1618)," "Henricus Costerius, Frans poeet," "Henricus Costerius, historicus," "Henricus Costerius en St.-Jan Baptist," "Costerius: Over wolven en weerwolven, 1588," "Henricus Costerius over toverij, oorlog en hongersnood, 1588," all in *Antwerpiensia.* Also E.-H.-J. Reusens, in *Biographie nationale* (Brussel, 1876), 5:col. 19–21; Van der Essen and Louant, *Frangipani,* 3: introduction; and M. Gastout, "Un aspect de la diplomatie du nonce Frangipani," in *Miscellanea Historica in honorem Leonis Van der Essen* (Brussels and Paris, 1947), 1:781–98. Costerius' criticism of the Netherlandish church is in a document he titled "Miser et deplorandus status ecclesiae belgicae," undated, ASV, MA, II, 147. That Costerius was gossiping in Rome about Hovius and Frangipani is suggested in Van der Essen and Louant, *Frangipani,* 1:264 and 3:cxxv.

Affligem's Lingering Hopes to Undo Incorporation: Frangipani to Aldobrandini, 9 February 1602, Van der Essen and Louant, *Frangipani,* 3:303.

Costerius' Harsh Treatment of the Monks: Mentioned in only one source, the manuscript history of Affligem by one of its monks, Beda Regaeus, *Hafflighemum*

Illustratum, in the Archive of Affligem itself. But it is not unlike other behavior that Costerius exhibited later. The text of the "agreement," and some details of the meeting at Hovius' residence in Brussels, in ARA, RSA, 596, 26 February 1602.

Frangipani's Feeling Neglected: To Aldobrandini, 8 March 1602, Van der Essen and Louant, *Frangipani,* 3:305–7.

Rebuilding the Abbey: Restorations in Affligem were begun at Hovius' (belated) order in May 1601, according to Phalesius, f. 192.

None of the Old Monks Returned: Livinus Mulder died in 1605, in Leuven. Wolfran Coen, the only monk who refused to sign the forced agreement of 1602, even moved to a Cistercian abbey rather than accept a lesser status at Affligem's priory.

Chapter 5: Rumor Mill

The chief documents for this chapter are in KAM, A, Hovius, Processen Algemeen, which contains thick folders on the entire case. In citing these documents below, we give only the dates and other identifying materials.

Testimony on the Attempted Suicide: 14 September 1601 (Pauwel Villix) and 20 September 1601 (Ludolph vande Bossche, Promotor). A document dated 15 September 1601, signed by vande Bossche, Joannes van Eynde, and Nicolas Oudaert, recounts their interview with Pussius on the following day, treated in the last section of this chapter.

Calling on Devils: Paul stated in his testimony that he doubted Canon Pussius did such a thing, but several other witnesses swore that the canon did after the suicide attempt.

"O Archbishop": In fact the canon said "O Bishop," not "O Archbishop," but we use "Archbishop" here to avoid confusion: it was clearly Hovius whom he meant; testimony Vande Bossche.

The Man in the Garters

The chronology of events is drawn largely from a document beginning "Coram Vobis," exhibited 24 September 1601. This is a long brief by the prosecution that summarizes the entire episode of Canon Pussius. The canon confirmed, in later questioning, virtually all these events, but added nuance or justification.

Pussius' Accusations Against Hovius: Letter of Pussius, October 1598, and article 26 of the "Coram Vobis" brief.

The Forged Confession: There are at least two copies. Both say the same thing, all in capital letters, but one adds more details than the other. We offer here an amalgamation of the two:

I Mathias Hovius declare to all that my manservant Andreas was, in most harmful fashion and against all justice and equity, recalled home by his parents (that he might be placed in my household) from the household of the reverend canon Pussius, unknown to him and completely against his will and certainly meriting protest, since the boy was obligated to [Pussius], and a short time before departing had been fully provided with clothing, indeed a whole year's worth or more, and with a brand new cloak, under the assumption that he was going to stay a long while, as his parents daily assured, yet once the clothing was ready they immediately, uncivilly, and with all injustice removed him from his lord, which I permitted to be done and as if I played an active role—wrongly persuaded, I admit, by some ranting talkers (who in the common tongue are called *potbaginen,* a species of most ambidextrous men), whom I believed too much, and to whom I paid more heed than to my brother priest, and I did great injury to him, especially since I had discussed the removal of the boy for more than three months with the parents, who meanwhile hid all things deceitfully from the same lord Pussius, acting as if the boy would stay with him for several years (indeed he wished to keep the boy), and persuading him by word and deed that they agreed to this, and this one, walking in simplicity, knew nothing of the matter, until the moment the boy was seized.

The document was sealed clumsily and signed at the archbishop's palace, 16 April.

Grammatical Errors: Pointed out in article 45 of the "Coram Vobis" brief, "libellus vocat famulam pedissequum vocabulo quo rarius invenitur in masculino usus eodem verbo famulum designans."

Profile in Patience

Hovius' Restraint: Noted in article 15 of "Coram Vobis," composed by the chapter's lawyers and thus sympathetic toward Hovius, but his actions were indeed few and slow, for the moment.

Examples of Punishments for Forgery: Julio Honetto was chained in prison; SAM, CA, 9 August 1603. In 1533 Jan de Coeyere was placed bareheaded on a scaffold, had three false seals hung around his neck, was led around the market, was lashed until he bled, and was branded on the cheek; Berlemont, *Kronieken,* 6 September 1533. An Erasmus Mersia was convicted of forging dispensations for marriage in 1614, and Archbishop Hovius even reduced the fine from two thousand florins to one thousand; see ASV, FB, II99, f. 223, 19 April 1614; II106, f. 207–8, 23 March 1615; II116, f. 104, 8 August 1615.

Background on Chapters: Moreau, *Histoire de l'église*, vol. 5; A. Pasture, *Les chapitres séculiers pendant le règne des archiducs, 1596–1633* (Liège, 1926), and A. Pasture, "La réforme des chapitres séculiers pendant le règne des archiducs, 1596–1633," *BIHBR* (1925): 5–50; R. Mols, "De seculiere clerus in de 17de eeuw," *NAGN* 8, 369–82. There were around seventy-five chapters in all the Spanish Netherlands; the archdiocese of Mechelen had thirteen. Collegiate chapters were usually a bit smaller than cathedral chapters, with some as small as eight, and cathedral as large as fifty. See more on "chapters" in Chapter 14 below.

Cathedral Chapters and Bishops: The bull of incorporation required the canons of Rombout's to assist the archbishop and accept office in the diocesan hierarchy, but other cathedral chapters resisted, believing this hurt their independence. See Dierickx, *De Oprichting der nieuwe bisdommen*, appended documents, and G. Rolin, "L'esprit du concile de Trente dans le statut organique de l'archeveché de Malines," in *Miscellanea Historica in honorem Leonis Van der Essen* (Brussels and Paris, 1947), 1: 881–94.

Pussius' Tantrums in Choir, Now and in the Next Several Days: "Furiose clamando, caput agitando, manus et brachia iactando," article 50 in "Coram Vobis." Also a deposition dated 12 July 1599, beginning "Feria 3, post festo S. Trinitatis," a deposition from 10 June 1599, by Van den Eynde and De Mol, and a deposition of July 1599, by Peter du Pont, standard-bearer of St. Rombout's.

Pussius' Mental State: Noted in a short, undated chronology of four points, attested to by Dean Henri van der Burch and Joannes Vanden Eynde, and another deposition dated 10 July 1599, signed by the same two men.

Five Days That Shook a World

Hovius' Speech to the Chapter: In articles 53 and 54 of the "Coram Vobis" brief; also inferred from an undated document, beginning "Domine Confrater." Internal evidence puts the speech at July 1599. Another brief of 1601, signed by F. Bernartius, and beginning "Venerabiles Domini," also mentions the incident, in article 10.

The Shackling of Pussius: Articles 72, 77, 80 of "Coram Vobis," and also Pussius' claims 8 August 1599, letter to Hovius. Finally 14 July 1599, notarized document by Lescuyer, in which the dean claimed that the superior of the Cell brothers insisted on the shackling, while the Pussius family insisted it was the dean's doing.

Pussius' Threats: Article 89, "dat hyer twee oft dry saude ombringhen ende syn selven oock."

The Eternal City

Pussius' Letters: To Hovius, 23 July 1599, 2 August 1599, 8 August 1599; to Dean van der Burch, 13 Kal. August (thus 19 July) 1599, Nono Kal. August 1599 (thus 23 July), 13 August 1599, and undated.

Conditions of Penance: Hovius to Pussius, 22 July 1599, also an undated confession, drawn up in Hovius' hand, beginning "Ego N. ut reparem coram deo et hominibus gravem lapsum linguae meae."

Hovius' Heavy Hand: Article 39 of "Coram Vobis," "quod in aliis est leve in Rev[erendissi]me est grave."

Reputation of the Cell Brothers: Moreau, *Histoire de l'église*, vol. 5, words of Bishop Antoon Triest of Gent; notarized document by Lescuyer, 14 July 1599.

The Dean's Alleged Accusations: About the nuncio, see Pussius' long letter to Hovius of 8 August 1599. The supposed charge of carnal relations between Pussius and Andreas is in an undated letter from Pussius to the chapter, but other briefs mention the charge occurring in 1599.

Denials that the Dean Accused Pussius of Carnal Intents: Canons W. Vuesels, October 1599, Van den Eynde, and A. Sucquet, plus a similar deposition from 4 October 1599.

Ecclesiastical Approaches to Sexual Scandal: For instance, in one set of interviews each canon was asked two questions about statements the dean had made—one regarding the canon's right to hear confession, the other regarding Pussius' carnal relations with Andreas. Except in one instance, the interviewer noted only the responses on confession. See also the case of Henri Joos, confessor of a convent in Leuven, in C. Harline, *The Burdens of Sister Margaret* (New York, 1994), books 1 and 3.

Pussius Embracing a Woman in the Chapel: A letter signed D. P. F. B., in the same hand as the forgery, addressed to the chapter.

Nuns of Thabor: Deposition of 17 July 1599 by the Mother Superior.

The Desire to Solve the Case Quietly: Pussius to Dean Van der Burch, 19 July 1599.

Pussius' Trips: KAM, Acta Capitularia, 1597–99, 23 July 1599, 6 August 1599; also Acta 1600–1615, in which he's listed as absent for most of 1601, and Pussius to Dean Van der Burch, 19 July 1599. The trip to Rome in Pussius to Dean and chapter, undated, but contents suggest 1600, and the chapter's responses, attached.

Death of Adrian Pussius: Article 103 of "Coram Vobis," and confirmed as 12 April 1601, in L. Stroobant, "Le magistrat . . . ," *Annales de l'académie d'Archéologie de Belgique* (1903), 5th series, 4:483–615.

Fall of an Enfant Terrible

Pussius' Return to Mechelen: It was supposed to be before St. Remigius' day, 1 October 1601; KAM, Acta Capitularia, Register 1600–1615, lists him present at chapter meetings on 20 and 27 July 1601.

Pussius' Confession: KAM, Acta Capitularia, 1600–15, meeting of 17 September 1601; also 13 September 1601, apparently Ludolph van den Bossche to the chapter.

Pussius' Refusal to Confess Before Others: Noted in a brief by Bernaerts and three others, undated, not easily legible, but some of the first lines are "de confessione praedicti francisci, dicto domino reverendissimo et domino decano decima huius mensis ante prandium facta."

Pussius' Rumor-Spreading: Quoted in article 45 of interview of 15 September 1601, the day after his attempted suicide, carried out by N. Oudaert, J. Van de Eynde, Jean de Froidmont, and Ludolphus vande Bossche.

The Scene of Pussius' Arrest: From Vande Bossche's testimony of events after the attempted suicide, cited above, and the actual warrant of 13 September 1601.

Threats from De Vulder to Countersue: Letter from Pussius to chapter, beginning "Omni qua decet reverentia exponit Franciscus Pussius quod hodie expiret tempus ad respondendum," received on 22 October.

The Final Agreement: Contained in various documents, including the permutation of Pussius' benefice on 30 January 1602, which noted that he would shortly vacate in favor of Dismas Briamont; also KAM, Acta Capitularia, 1600–1615, from which the canon disappears after January 1601; on 8 August 1602, the man who took Pussius' place, Dismas Briamont, resigned in favor of Nicolas Smeyers and mentioned that the pension of 150 florins to Pussius was for life. Kalendis February 1602, De Vuldere promised to pay the expenses of the trial. Pussius' confession is dated the same day.

Stereotype of the Canon: The saying, whose origins are of unknown date, goes in Latin, "Amplitudo ventris, falsitudo vocis, dementia mentis," which literally translated is "ample of stomach, false of voice, demented of mind."

Chapter 6: Our Dear Lady on the Sharp Hill
Sister Catharina

A commission from Hovius mentions that the archbishop has heard the stories for fifteen of sixteen months; KAM, A, Hovius, Bewind, undated, but from 1603.

Catharina's Story: P. Numan, *Historie vande Miraculen die onlancx In grooten getale ghebeurt zyn, door die intercessie ende voorbidden van die Heylighe Maget* (Leuven, 1604). Hovius did have an audience with her, but the scene we portray is based on the assumption that he asked her to tell what happened.

Cloister: The archbishop could be quite strict about this himself, and he refused leave to many other nuns, even those who sought to care for lonely, dying parents, in Manuale, 29 June 1618, and also 16 November 1619.

Frangipani's Report to Rome: To Aldobrandini, in Van der Essen and Louant, *Frangipani*, 3:437.

The Legend and Its Keepers

Background on the Sharp Hill: A. Boni, *Scherpenheuvel: Basiliek en gemeente in het kader van de vaderlandse geschiedenis* (Antwerp, 1953); T. Morren, "Bastion op de 'scherpenheuvel,' " in *Spectrum Atlas van Historische Plaatsen in de Lage Landen,* ed. A. F. Manning and M. de Vroede (Utrecht and Antwerp, 1981); T. J. Gerits, "Een onbekend getuigenis over Scherpenheuvel," *Oost-Brabant* 7/1 (1970): 30–32; H. Hechtermans and G. Humblé, "Mirakelen te Scherpenheuvel," *Vlaamse Stam* 8 (1972): 617–25, and 9 (1973): 32–40, 289–95; and Numan, *Historie.*

Stories of Images in Oaks: Wingens, *Over de Grens,* 67–68. Christian, *Local Religion,* on grace and place. C. Ginzburg, *Night Battles: Witchcraft and Agrarian Cults in the Sixteenth and Seventeenth Centuries* (Baltimore, 1984), on the effort to conquer medieval worship of Diana.

Tienwinckel's Account of Tragedies in Zichem: KB, Handschriftenkabinet, 3549, *Het belt met een cort verhael van onze Lieven Vrouwe ten Scherpenheuvel,* summarized in Boni, *Scherpenheuvel.* For more on Tienwinkel, and Hovius' questions about him, see AAM, DV, Dekenij Diest, Parochie Zichem, 1600 through 1613.

Why the Virgin Chose the Sharp Hill: Numan, *Historie,* 14–19. Isabella's sending of bark from the oak to King Philip III in A. Rodriguez Villa, *Correspondencia de la Infanta Archiduquesa Dona Isabel Clara Eugenia de Austria con el duque de Lerma y otros personajes* (Madrid, 1906), 217.

Two Crowning Miracles

Hans Clemens: Numan, *Historie,* devotes twenty-three pages to the story, the longest in the book. Numan notes that Protestants attributed the healing of Hans to a skillful barber-surgeon, but he challenges them to produce the man.

A Proper Shrine

Church Authorities and Shrines: Wingens, *Over de Grens,* 12. See 13, 25, 26, on the "instrumental" qualities of shrines, and the role of Jesuits in promoting them.

Condemned Techniques of Otherworldly Power: At great length in AAM, V,V,

Belezingen en Exorcismen, 3. See also the meeting of the deans in 1612, in De Ram, *Synodicon belgicum*, 2, and Toussaert, *Le sentiment religieux.*

Organization of the Shrine: First guidelines in AAM, K, Scherpenheuvel Oratorium, 6, undated decree by Hovius (certainly before 1604), 18 October 1603, and bundles 12–16, 19 June 1604, "Ordonnantien gemaect deur den Eerw. ende doorluchstigen heere Aertsbisschop van Mechelen, ende magistraet van Zichem." Inventories of jewels in AAM, K, Scherpenheuvel Oratorium, 8, 22 December 1603, "Inventaris van al den Iuwelen van ons L. Vrouwen Scherpenheuvel," and bundle 6, 12 January 1604. Gifts in kind in AAM, P, Scherpenheuvel, the first accounting, of 9 January 1604; also AAM, K, Scherpenheuvel Oratorium, 12–16, 19 June 1604, "Instructie voir Mr. Jan Lintermans." Instructions for priests in AAM, K, Scherpenheuvel Oratorium, 12–16, 19 June 1604, "Instructie voor de Priesters opden Scherpenheuvel."

Marionette Makers: Referred to by Joost Bouckaert in ARA, RSA, 1947/2, Bundle Montaigu, July 1613; Hovius names specific people to the task of watching sales in his instructions in AAM, K, Scherpenheuvel Oratorium, 12–16. "Memoire van seker observancen diemen sal sien tonderhauwe tot beter directie." Instructions for confessors and exorcists in ARA, KAB, 23350, statutes for the church of Scherpenheuvel, by Hovius, 16 December 1616.

Missing Only One Audit: Hovius mentions that he missed one audit in AAM, K, Scherpenheuvel Oratorium, 2, 2 February 1604, letter to Magistrates of Zichem.

Tienwinkel's Leadership of the Shrine: AAM, K, Scherpenheuvel Oratorium, 6, 12 January 1604, "Specificatie van alle de beeldekens." The auditors' unfavorable comments about Tienwinkel are in the first accounting, op. cit. The release of Tienwinkel from the Sharp Hill in AAM, K, Scherpenheuvel Oratorium, 2, 2 February 1604, letter from Hovius to the magistrates of Zichem. Also in bundle 6, letter from Hovius to Tienwinckel, 2 February 1604, praising his good will but noting the impediments to his careful supervision over the hill.

Numan's Appointment as Historian: AAM, Fonds Steenackers, Inventaire des Lettres, etc. des Archevêques de Malines, Bundel Hovius, 35, 18 October 1604.

The Council of Trent on Images: Session 25. The archbishop would reiterate the ideas there in the upcoming Provincial and Diocesan Councils, in De Ram, *Synodicon belgicum*, 2: Titulus XIV, De Imaginibus et Sanctorum Reliquiis.

Discouraged Practices at Shrines: Wingens, *Over de Grens*, 34, 103; J. Sumption, *Pilgrimage: An Image of Mediaeval Religion* (Totowa, N.J., 1975), 82; carving images from oaks in AAM, M, 6, fol. 244v, 4 March 1609, parish of Volkegem; also AAM, K, Aarschot St. Niklaasberg, 19, 13 May 1617.

The Archdukes and the Sharp Hill: J. M. Plantenga, *L'architecture religieuse dans l'ancien duché de Brabant depuis le règne des Archiducs jusqu'au gouvernement autrichien, 1598–1713* (The Hague, 1926). Also L. Duerloo, "Archducal Piety and Habsburg Power," in *Albrecht en Isabella*, ed. Thomas and Duerloo, 267–84.

Chapter 7: Pulling Up Tares
An Everlasting Council

Many events of the council are contained in the huge collection of published sources by De Ram, *Synodicon belgicum*, vol. 1. These can be supplemented by Willocx, *L'introduction des décrets du Concile de Trente,* Claessens, *Histoire des archevêques,* and other general works cited in the introductory note above.

Opening Procession: Inferred from the ceremonial protocol in De Ram, *Synodicon belgicum,* 1:269–70.

Provincial Councils Every Three Years: One exceptional church province that held regular councils was that of Tarragona, in Spain; Kamen, *The Phoenix and the Flame,* 77–78.

Letter of Convocation: De Ram, 1:239–41, 28 February 1607.

Hovius' Invoking the Holy Spirit: Inferred from Costerius' letter to Cardinal Borghese, in which the protonotary highlights his objection. Significantly, the invocation of the Holy Spirit was scratched from the council's final record, suggesting that the protonotary was right after all. ASV, FB, 107EF, 260, 30 June 1607.

Hovius' Speech: The actual text was twice as long as what is presented here, and probably took forty-five minutes to deliver; De Ram, 1:281–89. We offer a condensed version of the speech, but without ellipses, brackets, and diversions for ease of reading. Thus some transitions have been added, some parts have been excluded altogether, and some sentences and thoughts have been condensed into simpler form. This violates various rules of citation, but we found it more important to try to convey the spirit of the archbishop's speech than every single word.

Plenary Sessions: The order for offering amendments proceeded from bishops to cathedral chapters to abbeys to collegiate chapters and finally to pastors.

A Troubled Council

Arguments over Order of Participants: De Ram, *Synodicon belgicum,* 1:271–78, especially the chapters of Gent, Antwerp, and Brugge.

The Absent: Inferred from De Ram's list of the present. See also Willocx, *L'introduction des décrets du Concile de Trente,* 284. Restrictive instructions from chapters in Gent, Antwerp, and Den Bosch given in De Ram, *Synodicon belgicum,* 1:264.

The Preliminary Meeting of Bishops: Willocx, *L'introduction des décrets du Concile de Trente,* 285, and De Ram, *Synodicon belgicum,* 1:291–92. For one typical example of chapters resisting councils universal and provincial, see R. de Almeida Rolo, "L'application de la réforme du Concile de Trente à Braga," in *Il Concilio di Trento e la Riforma Tridentina* (Rome, 1965), 2:555–76.

Tensions with Rome over Councils: General context from Roegiers, "Jansenisme en katholieke hervorming"; specific evidence from letters telling the nuncio to have nothing to do with it, in L. van Meerbeeck, *Correspondance du Nonce Decio Carafa, Archevêque de Damas, 1606–1607. Analecta Vaticano-Belgica, tweede reeks: Nonciature de Flandre* (Brussels, 1979), 72, 24 March 1607, Carafa to Borghese; also 77, 14 April 1607, Borghese to Carafa. According to Elias, *Kerk en Staat*, the nuncio Bentivoglio arrived in Brussels only on 9 August 1607. See also Pasture, "La réforme des chapitres séculiers," 9–10, and Willocx, *L'introduction des décrets du Concile de Trente*.

Costerius' Protests to Proposed Decrees: De Ram, *Synodicon belgicum*, 1:310–22.

Fall of a Purple One

Costerius: Above, especially Prims, "Onze 'plebaan,'" etc., op. cit.; Reusens, *Biographie nationale* (Brussels, 1876), 5:col. 19–21; Van der Essen and Louant, *Frangipani*, 3: introduction.

Costerius' Seminary: Clement VIII to Costerius, BV, BL, 1992, 20 November 1601; Frangipani to Hovius, ARA, MD 200 C, 4 December 1602; Frangipani to the magistrates of Brussels, ARA, MD 200 C, 4 December 1602; AAM, Steenackers, H, 22.

Bogards: ARA, MD, 200 C, 18 February 1603, Frangipani to Hovius, rejoices that the archbishop will reform the Bogards.

Frangipani's Letter of Purgation for Costerius: ARA, Archief kapittel van St. Goedele, 3806, 4 August 1603.

Costerius' Complaints About Hovius: Inferred from a letter that appears to be by the new nuncio Bentivoglio; ASV, FB, III45C, 49, undated. This same letter also mentions the "appeal" Costerius sent to Hovius and calls it more a "libel," given all its insults.

Councilor Liebaert at the Council: De Ram, *Synodicon belgicum*, 1:302, 303, 306. Costerius' imprisonment is mentioned in a letter from Bentivoglio to Borghese, 18 August 1607, ASV, FB, II100, 172.

Finale

Hovius' Dry Response to the Complaints of the Chapters: De Ram, *Synodicon belgicum*, 1:298–99. The policy of the Bishop of Cuenca, in Nalle, *God in La Mancha*, 48.

Sudden End of Trient: Jedin, *Geschichte des Konzils von Trient*, and Roegiers, "Jansenisme en katholieke hervorming."

Final Meetings: Monasteries didn't like the tax levied on all ecclesiastical institutions to support diocesan seminaries. Parish clergy didn't like the requirement that they actually touch dying victims of the plague when administering last sacraments. See De Ram, *Synodicon belgicum,* 1:320 ff., 20 July 1607.

Christophori in Rome: De Ram, *Synodicon belgicum,* 1:349–58. The comparison with Borromeo's efforts to ratify his provincial decrees is in Tomaro, "San Carlo Borromeo," 78.

Brussels and the Decrees: The archbishop's efforts in De Ram, *Synodicon belgicum,* 1:329–37.

Borghese's Urging Bentivoglio to Assume Control over Costerius: ASV, FB, II100, 183, 1 September 1607.

Costerius' Meeting in the Crypt of St. Peter's: Archivio Capitolino, Fondo notarile, refiti originale, 776, libro VI: Alexander de Wisse uit Duisburg, notaris, ff. 13–15. It begins, "Henricus Costerius, Prot. apostolicus, Praelatus [Sacri] Palatii." Thanks to Bart de Groof for this reference, and the next.

Costerius' Broken Reputation in Rome: KB, Handschriftenkabinet II, 71666, later printed as F. Hachez, *Voyage de François Vinchant en France et en Italie du 19 septembre 1609 au 18 février 1610* (Brussels, 1897). On fo. 76 in the manuscript, pp. 96–97 in the printed work, a priest named Vinchant, from Mons, says that the cemetery of S. Lucina in S. Paolo (the catacombs) now required formal permission to remove any relics, because Costerius claimed that his false relics came from there. For more on frauds and the catacombs, see T. Johnson, "Holy Fabrications: The Catacomb Saints and the Counter-Reformation in Bavaria," *JEH* 47/2 (April 1996): 274–97.

The Sexual Overtones of Costerius' Exorcisms: Prims, "Onze 'plebaan,'" 69, 90. Sodomy is mentioned in the brief by three councilors of the Council of State, namely Adriani, Rosa, and Van Varick, in AAM, Amatus Coriache, 12, fol. 7, 18 July 1608.

Reading of the Verdict: Hovius to the Council of State, ARA, RSA, 1944/2, 4 July 1608. The verdict itself in AAM, Amatus Coriache, 12, 5, 29 July 1608.

Hovius on the "State of War": ARA, RSA, 1944/2, also referenced above.

Costerius' Spreading Tracts from Prison: Hovius to the Council of State, ARA, RSA 1944/3, 14 September 1608. Also the decree of the nuncio in AAM, M, 140, f. 147 r-v, 26 September 1608.

Chapter 8: Three Pastors

Anxieties of Early Years: KAM, Acta Capituli, 10 Februari 1589, adds another example in which Hovius, then vicar-general, asks the chapter for assurances that they will ransom him if he's captured while traveling on business for the diocese.

The Quality of Netherlandish Priests: ASV, SC, 506A, 9 September 1606, Hovius' *ad limina* report. Later observers include Laenen, *Geschiedenis van het semi-*

narie, 5; Moreau, *Histoire de l'église,* 5:323. Yet early in his episcopacy, Hovius composed a document for the archdukes on the preservation and promotion of the true religion: fifteen of its twenty points are devoted to improving pastors; AAM, A, Hovius, 8, 12 January 1600.

The Prince of Tithes

The Importance of Tithes in the Income of Rural Pastors: M.-J. Marinus, "De financiering van de contrareformatie te Antwerpen, 1585–1700," in *Geloven in het verleden,* ed. Put, Marinus, and Storme, 239–52, shows that urban parishes relied on subsidies from town governments, alms, and tax exemptions. A. Tihon, "Les revenus et les dépenses des curés en 1787: Le doyenné de Jodoigne," in *Geloven in het verleden,* ed. Put, Marinus, and Storme, 301–12, shows that arrangements in the countryside could vary greatly: of twenty-six parishes, eight relied heavily on tithes for the pastor's income, but some not at all.

Pastor Heynot: Early years in J. Lindemans, *Geschiedenis van Opwijk* (Brussels, 1937), 104–7. The testimony and accounts of Heynot's later activities are all in the bundle in AAM, P, Opwijk. The allusion to robbing God is from Malachi.

Scoundrel: Testimony of Willem Correman, age sixty-six, 21 October 1611.

Refusal of Absolution: Testimony of Jaspar de Houwere, 21 October 1611; the pastor told the man he would have to seek absolution from the Jesuits, in Brussels or "somewhere else."

Pastor's Book of Accounts: Testimony of Andries Goeman, 21 October 1611.

The Pastor's Father: Testimony of Persoons Robert.

Throwing Sheaves over the Hedge: Testimony of Andries Goeman.

Flax: Testimony of Jan Coorremans, 29 December 1611, and Amelberge Smets.

Pigs and Excise Taxes: Testimony of Jan van Hoorenbeke, 21 October 1611.

Cutting Trees: Testimony of Hendrik Verspecht, and Willem de Voldere, 2 and 10 March 1612.

Testament: Testimony of Reynier van Praet, 25 May 1612.

Schoolmaster's Wife: Testimony of Jacques Cappe, 22 May 1610.

New Year's Sermon: For general background see H. Storme, "Zedenlessen in geschenkverpakking: Opmerkelijke nieuwjaarspreken uit de zeventiende en de achttiende eeuw," *Trajecta* 2 (1993): 204–27; also testimonies of Cornelis vande Broecke, Hendrik Verspecht, Jacques vander Hulst, 2 January 1612.

Cheating on Lambs: Testimony of Jan Vermeire, 25 May 1612.

The System of Tithes: Especially A. Pasture, *Les anciennes dîmes dans l'administration paroissiale* (Wetteren, 1938); R. de Keyser, M. Cloet, and L. Preneel, "Geschiedenis van de parochie vanaf het onstaan tot aan het Concilie van Trente," *Dynamiek en Inertie van de Parochie* (December 1965): 121–42; M. Cloet, "Kerkelijke instellingen en het belang ervan voor de plaatselijke geschiedenis, XVIde–XVIIIde eeuw," *De Leiegouw* 25 (1983): 3–31; M. Cloet, "Pastoors op het Platteland," *De Roede van Tielt* 2/1 (1971): 3–14.

Financial Pressures on Parishioners: Forster, *The Counter-Reformation in the Villages,* for German dioceses; Nalle, *God in La Mancha,* 28, 36, and especially Kamen, *The Phoenix and the Flame,* for Spain. See also M. Therry, "Het Goede Doel: Bedeltoelatingen verleend door de Brugse en Gentse Bisschoppen in de 17de eeuw als spiegel van een samenleving," *Collationes* (June 1988): 153–76. Paying ransoms to free pastors in AAM, M, 4, fol. 3, June 1597, Sint-Pieters-Leeuw.

Hovius Aiding Parishes Against Titheholders: AAM, M, 5, fol. 117, 3 March 1605, the pastor and church wardens of Wambeek receive Hovius' support against the titheholder, Peter vande Velde, canon of Anderlecht; Manuale, 20 May 1618, Hovius takes action against a Domina de Marcke, titheholder, after complaints from a pastor.

Trent and Local Councils on Tithes: Trent warned against "begrudging the servants of God" their due and encouraged bishops and titheholders to reach "amiable agreements" on the local share; Session 25, chapter 12, and Session 24, chapter 13, also Pasture, *Les anciennes dîmes,* 173–74. The provincial council of 1607 stipulated that pastors should receive 300 florins a year in small villages, 500 in larger, and 750 in urban parishes. On bishops rendering verdicts against titheholders and the nuncio reversing them, see Pasture, *Les anciennes dîmes,* 178, 199, 214. Pasture discusses developments generally, but specifies that efforts to sue titheholders in civil courts began in the years of Hovius' episcopacy, especially after 1613.

The Archbishop's High Standards for Pastors: KAM, A, Hovius, Bewind, miscellaneous notes mention that he "offended many" by refusing to accept unfit priests as chaplains in the army.

The Church's Exclusive Claim to Discipline Priests: AAM, P, Opwijk, 23 June 1612, Hovius to the notables of the parish.

Deans About Heynot: Lindemans, *Geschiedenis van Opwijk,* 106; Hovius' "insufferable" comment in Manuale, 23 February 1618.

Letting Magistrates Collect Tithes: Pasture, *Les anciennes dîmes,* 183. The salary agreed to for Heynot was 396 florins—less than the 500 mandated for large rural parishes, and above the 300 for small ones; see also Cloet, "Kerkelijke Instellingen," 10.

Heynot's Resignation: Manuale, 3 April 1618. The successor in Lindemans, *Geschiedenis van Opwijk,* 107.

The Poor Priest of Laar

Desolation: Villages around Leuven had lost more than half their houses to war, and everywhere were catastrophic losses of population; Dupont, Lemaire, and

Vanderborght, "L'Etat des campagnes Brabançonnes"; Cosemans, "Het uitzicht van Brabant"; Morren, *Diest,* 51.

The Parish: No descriptions of this church in Laar remain; the current church was built in the eighteenth century on the previous foundation, but the current tower was part of the earlier building; see *Aanteekeningen op het Parochiaal bestuur der pastoors van Laar, bij Landen* (St. Truiden, 1889), 12–15. Selling altar stones and the Mass of six florins in AAM, M, 3, fol. 261, 1 December 1599. Also AAM, M, 6, fol. 140, 4 October 1604.

Pastor van Schagen's Activities: Documents for this case are in AAM, O, 7. Testimony of villagers regarding these activities in the depositions of 1, 2, and 8 October 1610. Also AAM, DV, Zoutleeuw 2, the pastor's 1598 description of the parish. Van Schagen was aggressive in taking rented land from Gordt Coenen, Geertruyt Smets, Aleydis Theunis, and Gordt van Dienant.

Spiritual Ills Caused by Small Incomes: A pastor hiring a woman of ill repute, AAM, DV, Zoutleeuw, Op-Dormaal, 1601. Pasture, *Les anciennes dîmes,* 172, on whether Protestant conversions resulted from poor priestly salaries.

Chaplaincies as Supplemental Income: AAM, P, Asse, 21 December 1611, Masses and the income attached; RAGM, 6, visitations of Aalst, 1595, parish of Erembodegem, where the pastor had a chapel inside the church; RAGM, 81, Meerbeek, 11 July 1608, Hovius agrees to a union of chaplaincies for the pastor; AAM, P, St. Rombout's, 132b, 3 June 1611, Hovius united the next vacancy among the Zellars, a group of lesser canons, to the pastorship of St. Rombout's, since income was insufficient— thus even a great church might not pay its pastor enough.

Deservitors: AAM, DV, Brussels, 1594, the deservitor of Meerbeke served four parishes; RAGM, 58, Haaltert, 26 July 1608, the pastor of Haaltert serves as deservitor of Kerksken to "supplement his living."

Hovius' Subsidies to Pastors: Manuale, 5 May 1619, alms to a priest of Tienen; 7 August 1619 to the deservitor of Kiezegem; 21 February 1618 to the pastor of Zellik; AAM, P, Leefdaal, 7 June 1595, Hovius gives the deservitor of Leefdaal and Vossem one hundred florins a year.

Village Subsidies: The archbishop himself received a municipal supplement when he was pastor of St. Peter's and Paul's; SAM, CA, 10 October 1595.

Ruin of Rectories: This was not merely from war and age, as in P. Chrispeels, "Kerkelijk leven in de dekenij Sint-Pieters-Leeuw, 1573–1795" (Licentiaatsverhandeling, Leuven, 1972), 198, where the pastor of Ruisbroek in 1595 burned his house down while drunk.

Arrangements to Pay for Rectories: Pasture, *Les anciennes dîmes,* 160.

Desire for Own Pastors: AAM, M, 2, fol. 192v, 1591, parishioners of Molenbeek; also fol. 279v, pastor of St. Nicholas' in Brussels. Manuale, 22 November 1618, shows Hovius keeping a deservitor in a village rather than a permanent pastor until the populace builds a rectory.

Pastors and Lucre: AAM, M, 6, fol. 29v, 21 October 1601, to Simon Molanus, pastor of Moerbeke, who was warned against trading and selling.

Possessions of Pastors: AAM, P, Natten-Haasdonk, inventory of the sterfhuis of Pastor Wauter vande Maude, who died 10 August 1621; he owned a black robe, black coat, hat, two cassocks, two pair of underwear, two pair of shoes, six shirts, a cap, a bed, two sheets, three blankets, three napkins, three wooden chairs, one chest, two candlestands, two pots of beer, one small kettle, one waterpot, four glasses, one lead inkpot, three tin plates, one pen knife, one wicker basket, one salt container, and seventeen books of sermons, decrees, catechisms, and pastoral instruction. The Pastor of Butsel had an empty beer barrel, a pig, a few mean tables, a few chairs, an old pillow, a "mean" reading-stand, an "old chest," a few books, a full churn of butter, and a small barn full of grain; AAM, P, Butsel, inventory of the sterfhuis of Guilliam Aubert.

Future Events in Laar: AAM, DV, Deanery of Tienen, 1626 through 1634.

The Carnal Priest of Etterbeek

The Women from Etterbeek: Details from Hovius' Agenda, AAM, A, Hovius, and Manuale, entries from April to June 1619.

The Good Shepherd

Pastors as Models: Trent, Session 25; AAM, M, 6, fol. 29v. The pastor as God from Bouwsma, *Venice and the Defense of Republican Liberty,* 315. The later example of the diligent Henri Calenus in M. Lemmens, "Hendrik Calenus, 1583–1653: Contra-reformist en Jansenist," *Ascania* 23 (1985): 31–84.

Residence: Manuale, 22 May 1618, 23 May 1618 for examples of many; RAGM, 7, Aalst, 1610 in Appels, and 1613; a wandering priest condemned in AAM, M, 4, fols. 39v, 43, 13 October 1599.

Heresy: AAM, M, 2, fol. 167, 1590, testimony of orthodoxy; also 218v bis, 31 July 1594.

Study: Manuale, 20 December 1617, the pastor of Kerkom required to study further; 23 August 1619, a stammering pastor; AAM, P, Natten-Haasdonk, the sterfhuis of the pastor of Haasdonk, in 1621, included a library of seventeen books.

Preaching: RAGM, 6, Haaltert, 1595; RAGM, 7, Lede, 1613; the last examples from Hovius' contemporary Antoon Triest of Gent, in M. Cloet, ed., *Itinerarium visitationum Antonii Triest, episcopi gandavensis, 1623–1654: De visitatieverslagen van bisschop Triest* (Leuven, 1976), Melsele, September 1626, Wakken, September 1624, Heusden, April 1626.

Confession and Confessionals: *Brevis ac Dilucida Instructio Minus exercitatorum Pastorum & Confessorum, quorum opera in hac Sacerdotum raritate est necessaria Ecclesiae Belgicae* (Brussels, 1607), contains the archbishop's imprimatur. RAGM, 7, the dean of Aalst notes in 1619 that there were confessionals "everywhere." Also A. Jansen, "Het zeventiende-eeuws kerkelijk meubilair," *HKKM* 69 (1965): 93–218. On deaf priests: H. Geets, "Het kerkelijk leven in de Landdekenij Mechelen volgens de visitatieverslagen van deken Antonius De Mol, 1599–1616" (Licentiaatsverhandeling, Leuven, 1960), 89.

Drinking: AAM, DV, in every deanery, contain plenty of examples. On botching a baptism, and doing it again, Morren, *Diest*, 185.

Chastity: RAGM, 7, Aalst, 1613, parish of Impe, Pastor Joannes Alboom claims that his housekeeper, recently delivered of a baby girl, is his sister, causing the visitor to make the snide remark about Sarah. Manuale, 29 December 1619, Simon Brouwer claims his beautiful maid is his sister. RAGM, 7, Aalst, 1616, Buggenhout, on the altarpiece. The unseemly pastor at the shrine was from Laken; he had an illicit relationship with his god-daughter. Perhaps the example of lowest morals are the sadomasochistic priests described in Spain by W. Thomas, "De contrareformatie en het probleem van de seksualiteitsbeleving van de katholieke geestelijkheid in het 17de-eeuwse Spanje," in *Geloven in het verleden,* ed. Put, Marinus, and Storme, 147–62.

Priorities of Bishops and Villages: An example of villagers making up stories of sexual improprieties in A. Barnes, "The Social Transformation of the French Parish Clergy, 1500–1800," in *Culture and Identity in Early Modern Europe,* ed. Diefendorf and Hesse, 139–58, which draws on J. Bossy, "Blood and Baptism: Kinship in Western Europe from the Fourteenth to the Seventeenth Centuries," in *Studies in Church History,* ed. D. Baker (Oxford, 1973), 10:129–43.

Rural Deans as Select Men: *Ad limina* of 1606, op. cit.

The Size of Dioceses: Bergin, *French Episcopate,* 30.

The Archbishop's Right of Nomination: AAM, M, 140, fols. 114–16, shows that thirty-eight of the sixty-seven positions he controlled were thanks to his position as abbot of Affligem, not archbishop. The kings of Spain, like the archdukes and other princes, insisted as well on their rights of clerical patronage; Nalle, *God in La Mancha,* 82.

Relations Between Pastors and Patrons: Moreau, *Histoire de l'église,* 5:314, 315.

Parishes Having Own Pastors: In the deanery of Mechelen, thirty-five of forty-four parishes had their own pastors by 1620. But things were much worse elsewhere: in the diocese of Brugge less than half the parishes were served by permanent pastors, and in Roermond and Den Bosch still fewer.

Hovius' Ordinations: Manuale, 14 April 1618; AAM, K, Blijdenberg, Victorinnen, Reg. 72, records his totals as well.

Jacobus à Castro: Morren, *Diest,* 58, 64.

Training Boys Early: See AAM, P, Merchtem, case from 1609, in which the archbishop appropriated the resources of a hostel for the seminary and explained why.

Seminaries: J. A. O'Donohoe, "The Seminary Legislation of the Council of Trent," in *Il Concilio di Trento e la Riforma Tridentina* (Rome, 1965), 1:157–72; T. Deutscher, "Seminaries and the Education of Novarese Parish Priests, 1593–1627," *JEH* 32 (1981): 303–19; J. Roegiers, *De oprichting en de beginjaren van het bisschoppelijk seminarie te Gent, 1569–1623* (Gent, 1974); P. De Clerck, "De diocesane priesteropleiding na Trente, 1563–1789," *CBG* 13 (1967): 373–89, "De priesteropleiding in het bisdom Ieper, 1565–1626," *ASEB* 100 (1963): 7–67, "De priesteropleiding in de Mechelse kerkprovincie na Trente, 1564–1796," *CBG* 13 (1967): 487–517, and 14 (1968): 82–102, "Het seminariedecreet van Trente," *CBG* 11 (1965): 3–41; L. Le Clerq, "Het Antwerpsch Seminarie," *CM* 25 (1936): 19–41; A. C. de Schrevel, *Histoire du séminaire de Bruges*, 2 vols. (Brugge, 1895); and of course J. Laenen, *Geschiedenis van het seminarie van Mechelen*.

Expenses of the Mechelen Seminary: The expense account for 1613 shows that the largest single expense was food; AAM, Groot Seminarie, AI.4. Wages and construction were significant as well.

Appropriating Pious Funds for Seminaries: AAM, P, St. Rombout's, 637a, a lawsuit concerning the estate of Petrus de Greve, which Hovius wished to have for the seminary; the archbishop also reinterpreted the charter of the old Standonck school, where he was a student as a boy, and used its endowment for the seminary. He seized the properties and incomes of at least three defunct convents and hospitals in Merchtem, Kalfort, and Humelgem, with much protest.

Fining Sinners: AAM, M, regs. 4, 7 contain plenty of such fines; also KAM, Hovius, Bewind, 4 July 1618, an adulterer, and AAM, O, 1, bundel I/6, 14 March 1608.

Recruiting Donors: Manuale, 8 February 1618, 23 January 1619, 27 March 1619.

Number of Seminarians: Account sheet for 1613, AAM, Groot Seminarie, AI.4.

Quality of Priests: Von Pastor, *History of the Popes*, vol. 24, chapter 5, on Clement VIII, and on Bishop Triest, S. Vanden Broecke, "Seculiere geestelijken in het 17de-eeuwse bisdom Gent: een prosopografie," *Trajecta* 3 (1994): 200.

Comment to Henri Geerts: Manuale, 1 November 1618.

Hovius Rooting Out Sinning Priests: See the list of questions prepared for the *ad limina* report of 1606, in ASV, SC, 506A, 2 December 1606.

Hovius' Occasional Toleration of Bad Priests: AAM, DV, Zoutleeuw, Z1, 1600; Manuale, 6 February 1619.

Parishioners Tolerating More: Kerksken, AAM, DV, Aalst, 1606; Kobbegem, AAM, DV, Sint-Pieters-Leeuw, P2, 1595.

Failure to Get Good Priests in Place: Assessment is by Haymo Timmermans, the good friend of the archbishop, just before Timmermans died; AAM, DV, Diest, addendum, dated 28 July 1618.

Chapter 9: The Trouble with Peace
Scabby Sheep

Sacrament Procession: It's not clear from Van Autenboer, *Volksfeesten en Rede-rijkers,* exactly which of Mechelen's many processions was involved, but it was probably the Sacrament Procession, given the events and date. It was also probable that Hovius carried the sacrament, but this is not stated in documents.

Incident with the Sheriff: From SAM, CA, 18 June 1610, two documents, and SAM, inventory, 6:308, number 30.

Henri IV's Final Love: Among others, see P. Henrard, *Henri IV et la princesse de Condé, 1609–1610: Précis historique, suivi de la correspondance diplomatique de Pecquius et autres documents inédits* (Brussels, 1870). The allusion to the Homeric war is Spinola's; though various historians have concluded that Henri's infatuation played no major role in the political crisis of Cleves-Julich, Isabella and Spinola believed otherwise.

Worries About the Land Returning to Spain: Elias, *Kerk en Staat,* 17; also L. Pirenne, "Petrus Peckius, dienaar der aartshertogen," in *Voor Rogier: Een bundel opstellen van oud-leerlingen de hoogleraar bij zijn afscheid aangeboden* (Hilversum-Antwerp, 1964): 81–96.

Concessions to the Dutch: H. De Schepper, "De katholieke Nederlanden van 1585 tot 1609," in *NAGN* 6 (Haarlem, 1979): 279–97.

Religious Toleration After Peace: Albert's edict of 1609 in ARA, *ROPB,* dl. 2, 10; also A. Pasture, "Le placard d'hérésie du 31 décembre 1609, sa portée juridique et son application pendant le règne des archiducs Albert et Isabelle, 1609–1633," in *Mélanges Moeller* (Leuven-Paris, 1914), 2:301–30. On tolerance in the Dutch Republic there is a multitude of studies, beginning with H. A. Enno van Gelder, *Getemperde Vrijheid* (Groningen, 1972). Other violations of Albert's decree noted in Manuale, 5 January 1618, 8 September 1618, 6–7 April 1619; M. J. Marinus, "De protestanten te Antwerpen, 1585–1700," *Trajecta* 2 (1993): 329–30; Malderus to Hovius, 30 November 1613, in De Ram, *Synodicon belgicum,* 3:369; M. Therry, "Geloven in de kroeg: God, Kerk en eer in de herbergen van het 17de-eeuwse bisdom Brugge," in *Geloven in het verleden,* ed. Put, Marinus, and Storme, 163–88; De Brouwer, *Land van Aalst,* 178, 183; L. Maes, *Vijf eeuwen stedelijk strafrecht: Bijdrage tot de rechts- en cultuurgeschiedenis der Nederlanden* (Antwerp and The Hague, 1947), 156.

Print Propaganda from the North: De Ram, *Synodicon belgicum,* 1:338–43; Van der Essen and Louant, *Frangipani,* 3:435–37, Frangipani to Terranova, 11 October 1603; Wingens, *Over de Grens,* 27, 32; J. van Haver, "Het refereyn van Scherpen-Heuvels Droom," in *Cultuurhistorische caleidoscoop aangeboden aan Prof. Dr. Willy L. Braekman* (Gent, 1992), 549–60; P. Leendertz, *Het Geuzenliedboek* (Zutphen, 1925), 2:112–14; W. J. C. Buitendijk, *Het calvinisme in de spiegel van de Zuidnederlandse Literatuur der*

Contra-Reformatie (Groningen, 1942), 199–201. The death of the bishop of Antwerp in L. P. Gachard, "Le cardinal Bentivoglio: Sa nonciature à Bruxelles," *BARB,* 2d series, 38 (1874): 204.

Excommunication: De Ram, *Synodicon belgicum;* AAM, O, 1, 1/6, 1 January 1610; and the archbishop's letter during the trial of Anna Utenhove, above in Chapter 3.

Hovius' Attitude Toward Heretics: Letter to the Council of State, 8 October 1611, ARA, RSA, 1944/3; 30 September 1611; 15 October 1613. Sabina Golsius in Hovius to Chancellor of Brabant, 13 May 1614, ARA, OFRB, port. 2323; also Manuale, 30 June 1619, where she is still convinced of her beliefs. Also H. Lonchay and J. Cuvelier, eds., *Correspondance de la cour d'Espagne sur les affaires des Pays-Bas au XVIIe siècle,* vol. 1, *Précis de la correspondance de Philippe III, 1598–1621* (Brussels, 1923), 1:395. On the drowned woman, see *Een Waerachtighe Jammerlijcke ende droeve gheschiedenisse, dewelcke geschiet is binnen Bruessel in Brabant, van een schamele Vrouwe met twee onnoosele kinderen . . . gheschiet den 15. Februarius 1615* (Dordrecht, P. Verhaghen, n.d.) (Knuttel catalogue, in the State Archives of The Hague, number 2138). Eventually Hovius and other bishops would conclude that all Anabaptists should be expelled, while Calvinists would be expelled only if they caused scandal. Worries about reprisals from the Dutch Republic are discussed, among other places, in *Correspondance,* ed. Lonchay and Cuvelier, 1:347, letter from Brizuela to Philip III, 20 February 1610. Hovius' own worries on this score in a letter to the Council of State, 15 October 1613, ARA, RSA 1944/3.

Enhancing Powers of Church Courts: Bentivoglio to Borghese, 18 January 1614, ASV, FB, II99, 39. Carlo Borromeo's idea in B. Lenman, "The Limits of Godly Discipline in the Early Modern Period with Particular Reference to England and Scotland," in *Religion and Society,* ed. Greyerz, 127.

Albert's Repetition of Decrees: Pasture, *La Restauration Religieuse,* 38, 39; Pasture, "Le placard d'hérésie du 31 décembre 1609," 308; also AAM, M, 140, fols. 191v–192 (published in *ROPB,* 2:221–22).

Found Sheep

Hovius' Rumored Death: Correspondence between Bentivoglio and Borghese, BV, BL, 6808, 268, 29 June 1613; ASV, FB I, 914, 595, 20 July 1613; and ASV, FB, I, 914, 598, 27 July 1613.

Catholics from the Dutch Republic: De Villermont, *L'Infante Isabella,* 503; Bentivoglio to Borghese, 27 June 1609, BV, BC, 62E, 228; Gachard, "Le cardinal Bentivoglio," 163. For more on Bentivoglio, R. Belvederi, *Guido Bentivoglio e la politica Europea del suo tempo, 1607–1621* (Padua, 1962).

Frans Boels: E. Steenackers, "Le Chanoine Jean de Froidmont: Bienfaiteur de Saint Jean Berchmans," *HKKM* 34 (1929): 19–63. Original documents in ARA, RSA

1894/4. We assume Hovius confirmed the new convert, about whom he wrote to the Archdukes; ARA, RSA 1894/4.

Bickering Shepherds

Catholics in the Dutch Republic: A whole string of documents on Dutch Catholics can be found in the correspondence of Vosmeer, OBC, 270, 21 April 1591; OBC 277, 2 October 1607; OBC 278, 23 August 1608; OBC 279, 20 December 1609, and so forth. Also AAM, M, 5, fol. 65, 14 February 1602; Van der Essen and Louant, *Frangipani*, 3:322, 324, 365; Frangipani to Aldobrandini, 21 June 1602, Cornelissen, *Romeinsche Bronnen*, 90; ARA, MD 200 C, Frangipani to Hovius, 18 February 1603, and many more. Background on the general dispute in M. Spiertz, "Priest and Layman in a Minority Church: The Roman Catholic Church in the Northern Netherlands, 1592–1686," in *The Ministry Clerical and Lay* (*Studies in Church History*, vol. 27, 1989), ed. W. J. Sheily; and M. Spiertz, "Pastorale praktijk in de Hollandse Zending," in *De Jezuïeten in de Nederlanden en het prinsbisdom Luik*, ed. E. Put and M. Wijnants, (Brussels, 1991), 87–99. The vagueness of papal instructions to the Apostolic Vicar didn't help the situation, as recounted in Rogier, *Geschiedenis van het katholicisme*, 2:20.

The Vicar and the Dutch Clergy: Earlier disputes in Von Pastor, *History of the Popes*, 24:4. The figure of seventy pastors under the vicar from C. Kooi, "Popish Impudence: The Perseverance of the Roman Catholic Faithful in Calvinist Holland, 1572–1620," *SCJ* 26 (spring 1995): 75–86, but other sources suggest even more.

The Vicar and the Jesuits: Bentivoglio, October or November 1611, Cornelissen, *Romeinsche Bronnen*, 175.

Jansonius: L. Ceyssens, "Autour de Jacques Jansonius, professeur à Louvain, 1547–1625," *Augustiniana* 22 (1972): 356–97.

Conclusion that Jesuits and the Apostolic Vicar Were Both at Fault: Hovius, letter to Vosmeer, 25 April 1611, OBC 281.

The Conferences: Hovius to Vosmeer, 13 August 1613, OBC 281; Bentivoglio to Borghese, 15 October 1611, BV, BL, 6805, 170, and 29 October 1611, 5 November 1611, Cornelissen, *Romeinsche Bronnen*, 168–69. Vosmeer's last letter to Hovius was on 3 December 1613, OBC 324. The plan for yet another conference in Borghese to Bentivoglio, 19 November 1614, ASV, NF, 137A, 253–4; and 20 December 1614, Cornelissen, *Romeinsche Bronnen*, 204–5.

Intra-Faith Debates in Public: Damage discussed in Borghese to Morra, 7 November 1617, Morra to Borghese, 2 December 1617 and 9 February 1619, and Bentivoglio to Borghese, 16 May 1615, in Cornelissen, *Romeinsche Bronnen*, 222, 224–25, 253, and 207–8.

Hovius' Trip to Den Bosch: Bentivoglio to Borghese, 23 May 1615, Cornelissen, *Romeinsche Bronnen*, 208–9.

Chapter 10: A Schoolboy from Diest

Life of Jan Berchmans: Major published sources for the events depicted here are A. de Laet, "De Heilige Joannes Berchmans bij den Landdeken te Diest," *CM* 29 (1940): 121–39, 245–70; and the same author's reconsideration of his conclusions in "De Heilige Joannes Berchmans: Zijn leven te Diest opgehelderd en rechtgezet," *CM* 31 (1946): 480–504, 577–606. Also A. Poncelet, "Documents inédits sur Saint Jean Berchmans," *Analecta Bollandiana* 34–35 (1915–16): 1–227. There are a host of hagiographically inclined works on the saint.

Friendship Between Hovius and Timmermans: Poncelet, "Documents inédits," interview of Walter van Stiphout; Manuale, 16 May 1619, notes that Hovius accepted to the seminary Timmermans' nephew, then on 30 May 1619 invited this nephew to dinner in Mechelen. That Hovius actually stayed with Timmermans is De Laet's guess, but highly plausible, since during visitations the archbishop often stayed with clerical hosts, and in Diest there was no one he knew better. Moreover, in AAM, P, Diest St. Sulpitius, II, 10 July 1615, Jan vanden Brule received a commission from Hovius "in the home of the pastor of the beguinage." See also the 1618 document in which Timmermans suggested several reforms that were taken up at the archbishop's next annual meeting with all the deans: AAM, DV, D3, end of the 1618 visitation by Timmermans.

Layout of the Rectory: See the De Laet articles, above.

Bentivoglio: He left Brussels in late 1615 to become nuncio of France.

Timmerman's Assistance to Hovius: Because Timmermans accompanied the archbishop during the visitation of the chapter, one of the most sensitive places to visit, it's plausible that he was along for others as well.

State of the Chapter of St. Sulpitius': Among many documents AAM, P, St. Sulpitius, visitation decrees of 6 July 1615. Also Chapter 14 below.

Table Talk in Diest: What the two men discussed is supposition, based on our sense of why Hovius was in Diest at this particular time. Although he toured the archdiocese regularly, we think it no coincidence that he went to Diest just after Berchmans entered the Jesuit School of Mechelen.

Stolen Once

Father Berchmans: According to De Laet, the elder Berchmans, as an alderman, received an invitation to the pastor's annual dinner for civic leaders; that the pastor and he knew each other is inferred from this fact, and the presence of Jan's two aunts in the beguinage.

Jan's Early Schooling: While attending the Latin School, Jan lived for a time in its residential college but moved into the attic of a Pastor van Emmerick in 1608 or 1609. There is some debate as to how long Jan stayed there: some say he moved to Pastor Timmermans' in fall 1612, meaning that his stay there was only about six months (until January 1613). De Laet eventually concludes, however, that Jan lived with Timmermans starting in fall 1611 — or for eighteen months rather than six. One witness, Poncelet, "Documents inédits," 60, said that Jan moved in at "about age 11 or 12." Either way, Jan was at least six months with Timmermans, and perhaps eighteen. One must ask why Groenendonk didn't take Jan in himself. Perhaps he had enough servant boys, or perhaps he wasn't yet the main influence on the family. Either way, patronage did not necessarily mean living with the patron.

"That Boy Is an Angel": Poncelet, "Documents inédits," 120–21, interview of Walter van Stiphout ("iste puellus angelus est").

Father Berchmans and Frans Groenendonk: That Jan's father put more trust in Groenendonk is inferred from the father's eventual actions in the canon's favor. Groenendonk as the family's "best benefactor" is from De Laet, 601–3.

Frans Groenendonk: From both De Laet and archival documents, especially Hovius' visitations to St. Sulpitius in 1608, 1612, and 1615: AAM, P, St. Sulpitius.

Local Schools and Scholasters: G. Huppert, *Public Schools in Renaissance France* (Urbana, Ill., 1984), especially chapters 1 and 2.

Stiphout and Berchmans: De Laet, 600–601. The rector's broken heart from his testimony in Poncelet, "Documents inédits," 118–21. See Poncelet, "Documents inédits," 60, testimony of Jacques Wyns and Zegerus Susius, on how upset Timmermans was, and how at odds with Groenendonk.

Jan's Arrival in Mechelen: De Laet, 601–3.

Stolen Twice

Jan Berchmans' Influence on Frans Boels: Poncelet, "Documents inédits," 41, 70.

Jean de Froidmont: E. Steenackers, "Le Chanoine Jean de Froidmont: Bienfaiteur de Saint Jean Berchmans," *HKKM* 34 (1929): 19–63, as well as De Laet. That Froidmont wished to become ecclesiastical councilor is Steenacker's argument.

The Cantor's Income: Froidmont told Hovius that he got 40 florins a year as cantor, plus a double daily distribution. His income as canon was probably between 150 and 300 florins a year.

Froidmont's Witness: Steenackers speculates that the servant Froidmont sent to testify on his behalf was Berchmans, because from Poncelet it's clear that Berchmans went on a trip to Leuven on his master's errand, and that Froidmont sent "a servant" to Leuven on his behalf to testify.

Jan's Virtues: Poncelet, "Documents inédits," every witness.

Hovius' Concern for Schools Generally: AAM, Archiepiscopalia, Hovius, 8,

12 January 1600, memorandum to the archdukes on steps to restore Catholicism. The inclinations of youth by Dean Calenus, writing to the magistrates of Brussels on schools, AAM, Fonds Catechismus, IV, 2, 1623.

Hovius' Concern for the Latin School and Seminary: Frequent entries in the Manuale. Good articles on the Mechelen Latin School are E. Steenackers, "La grande école à Malines, 1450–1630," *HKKM* 26 (1921): 21–104, and E. Steenackers, "A propos de Saint Jean Berchmans," *CM* (1921): 81–91. Hovius lauding his graduates in ARA, SJ, FB 782, undated, addressed to magistrates of Mechelen. Fears about the demise of the Latin School and seminary are most clearly expressed here.

Jesuits in the Low Countries: Put and Wijnants, eds., *De Jezuïeten in de Nederlanden*. ARA, MD 5415, 29 May 1598, Hovius to rural pastors, urging them to cooperate with Jesuits. ARA, SJ, FB 986, Hovius at the consecration of the novice house. The stone quarries in ARA, RSA 1944/3, 26 June 1615, Hovius' bookkeeper to the Jesuits of Brussels and Antwerp. De Sailly delivered Hovius' *ad limina* once, and appeared regularly in the Manuale. On Jesuits and the archbishop's catechism, E. Frutsaert, *De Rooms-Katholieke Catechisatie in Vlaams-België vanaf het Concilie van Trente* (Leuven, 1934). Hovius' reservations about Jesuits, Manuale, 13 March 1619.

Jesuits Arguing with Local Schools: One example from elsewhere is in Benedict, *Rouen.*

Agreement Between Jesuits and Magistrates: R. van Aerde, "Les Jésuites à Malines, 1611 à 1773: L'Installation du Noviciat," *HKKM* 34 (1929): 87–102; ARA, SJ, FB, 986, the house history; Steenackers, "La grande école," 81.

Hovius' Return from Den Bosch: ARA, SJ, FB, 782, Hovius to the magistrates, undated.

The Archdukes and the Jesuits: The Jesuit novitiate in Mechelen was in a palace of the archdukes, who granted the order permanent use; Steenackers, "La grande école," 82. Also AAM, P, St. Rombout's, 1010, no date.

The Spread of Free Education: Huppert, *Public Schools,* chapters 2 and 3, as well as resistance to Jesuits in France, chapter 8.

Hovius' Threat to Move: L. Brouwers, *Carolus Scribani S.J., 1561–1629: Een groot man van de Contra-Reformatie in de Nederlanden* (Antwerp, 1961), 214; also ARA, SJ FB 986, the house history, though perhaps this was Brouwers' source.

Hovius and Jesuits Arguing over Berchmans: A. Poncelet, *Histoire de la Compagnie de Jésus dans les Anciens Pays-Bas,* 2 vols. (Brussels, 1927–28), 502, claims that Hovius feared the Jesuits would take the brightest students from the Latin School. Steenackers, "A Propos," 85, and ARA, SJ, FB 986, on the chasm and "tempest." Steenackers, "La grande école," 87, and Poncelet, "Documents inédits," 108–9, suggest that Hovius directly and specifically opposed the transfer of Berchmans to the Jesuit School. From the latter: "et in eo mirabatur providentiam divinam quod, omnibus quibus obstringebatur obnitentibus (etiam ipso fortassis archiepiscopo Mechliniensi, qui de ipso, ut in scholis suis degente, plurima sperabat) ad scholas Societatis esset translatus." One other tantalizing bit of evidence is from a register of the vicariate requiring an unspecified fine, for an unspecified transgression, of one "Jan Berckmans," at the very time the debate was raging and the transfer made. Was this a fine levied in response to his switching schools? AAM, M, 7, fol. 101, 27 May 1615.

Froidmont and Jan's Transfer: K. Schoeters, *Jan Berchmans van Diest, 1599–1621* (Kasterlee, n.d.), 49, was one of the first to allege that Froidmont was behind Berchman's transfer to the Jesuit School.

Partings

Hovius' Decree to St. Sulpitius: AAM, P, St. Sulpitius, 10 July 1615.

House Arrest of Groenendonk: De Laet, "De heilige Joannes Berchmans," 128–31.

Van den Brule and the Decrees: AAM, P, St. Sulpitius, 10 July 1615.

Hovius Back in Mechelen: Steenackers, "La grande école," 83–86; and AAM, P, St. Rombout's, 19 October 1615, agreement between Latin School and Jesuit college. R. van Aerde, "Het Schooldrama bij de P.P. Jezuieten," *HKKM* 40 (1935): 44–119, on the plays of the Jesuit School. Hovius also celebrated among the Jesuits to promote an indulgence for the forty hours, Manuale, December 1619. Hovius' criticism of a play at the Latin School in Manuale, 7 February 1619. The Manuale records frequent visits to Hovius from officials of the Latin School, and rare visits from Jesuits (except for Sailly).

Hovius' Continued Complaints About the Jesuits: AAM, P, St. Rombout's, 1014, 14 April 1617, on the looming decline of Gregorian chant, now overshadowed by polyphonic music (for more on this tradition see T. F. Kelly, *Plainsong in the Age of Polyphony* [Cambridge, 1992]). Hovius' letter to the magistrates of Leuven, AAM, P, St. Rombout's, 1004, 16 November 1615. Manuale, 13 March 1619, on now suspecting "all intentions" of the Jesuits.

Jan's Entry into the Jesuits: Poncelet, "Documents inédits," 143, and testimony of Josse van Suercx, who says Jan's father sent a Capuchin cousin to talk Jan out of entering the Jesuits, but Jan always refused.

Father Berchmans as Priest: Mother Berchmans died in December 1617, Jan senior took the tonsure in January, became a canon of Sulpitius' a few days later, then was ordained a priest in April 1618—all unusually fast, and suggesting friends in high places. He died in October 1618.

Hovius' Jubilee: Foppens, *Notae pro historia Archiepiscopatus Mechliniensis,* KB, Handschriften II, 1275, fol. 226v, and KAM, A, Hovius, Bewind, "Conceptus ordinis et rituum in celebratione Jubilei Illustrissimi ac Reverendissimi Domini Archiepiscopi Mechliniensis observandum."

Chapter 11: Table Talk

Robes for the Image on the Sharp Hill: Isabella, for instance, gave numerous robes, evident in inventories of jewels and precious objects in AAM, K, Scherpenheuvel Oratorium, 8, 22 December 1603, and bundle 6, 12 January 1604.

Liturgical Objects in Gold or Silver: Hovius' visit to Kumtich on 24 August 1614, included a scene in which he broke some "contemptible" ornaments on the spot, just as Bishop Triest regularly did during his tours of parishes; AAM, DV, Tienen, 3.

Hovius' Dinners and Household: See the Manuale for his frequent dining invitations. On his material life, see his accounts, especially AAM, A, Hovius, 6, performed by Jacob van Sassegem for 1610. Also a string of documents in KAM, A, Hovius, Sterfhuis, listing food and items at the end of his life, the accounts of Robert Meynaertz, Anthonius De Mol, and Nicolaus Smeyers as executors of the estate, accounts of food delivered by Hendrik Caers, accounts of Rombaut Croone for deliveries, accounts of the pharmicist Jan Vander Strepen for deliveries, a list of furniture the archbishop's successor, Jacob Boonen, purchased, a list of funeral expenses, and similar accounts. Materials on the house in Hofstade from AAM, Seminarie, III C 17. For more extended treatment of these sources see E. Put, "Geen geld, geen hervorming? Het financieel beleid van de Mechelse aartsbisschop Mathias Hovius, 1596–1620," in *Geloven in het verleden,* ed. Put, Marinus, and Storme, 271–84; and E. Put and C. Harline, "Sterven als aartsbisschop: Omtrent overlijden en begrafenis van Matthias Hovius, 1620," in *Mechliniensia in honorem Prof. em. Dr. Constantini Van de Wiel,* ed. De Smedt, 119–40.

Idle Conversations: Isabella and wine, Manuale, 7 May 1619, a Doctor Pas. On the diver, 23 October 1618, told by three Hollanders and a Doctor Coginam.

The Bishop of Grenoble: Luria, *Territories of Grace,* 53.

The Miller's Sabbath

There is no direct evidence that this particular story, or the other two in this chapter, were discussed at the archbishop's table. But there is a mountain of evidence that such conversations, on these same topics, occurred often at table. We use these three because they were recorded in good detail.

Diocesan Court: Promotors probably ate more often with Hovius than bailiffs, according to the Manuale. The best single account of a legal life on the road is AAM, O, 1, containing expenses and anecdotes of a promotor for 1637, which are very similar to earlier, spottier records. For more on bailiffs, and their stories of peril, see X. Lesage, *Den Duerwaerder: Geschiedenis van het gerechtsdeurwaardersambt* (Kapellen, 1993).

Joris de Buel: In the archbishop's Agenda, 8 June 1617.

Aert Goosens: AAM, O, 1, I/6, includes a list of ten names brought to court for violating the Sabbath decree of 1598; Aert's case is the only one given at length. It began on 2 December 1601, but the problem was common throughout the period.

Hovius' Request for State Assistance: De Ram, *Synodicon belgicum,* 1:330–37.

More on the Sabbath: J. Verberckmoes, "De catechismusmop tijdens de katholieke hervorming," in *Geloven in het verleden,* ed. Put, Marinus, and Storme, 189–202, includes an eighteenth-century example of a perplexed bishop stopping to watch all the drinking and singing on a feast day.

The State's Interest in Limiting Feast Days: Luria, *Territories of Grace,* 96, has local authorities citing the "advantage of the public" in supporting economic activities on feast days. A miller in Oosterzele, forbidden by the dean to work on Sundays, took his case to a secular court and won; J. de Brouwer, *De kerkelijke rechtspraak en haar evolutie in de bisdommen Antwerpen, Gent en Mechelen tussen 1570 en 1795,* 2 vols. (Tielt, 1971–72), 2:56.

Cantankerous Butchers and Brewers: AAM, O, 1, I/6.

Rivalry Between Bailiffs of State and Church: The bailiff Willem Pottiers of Brugge, around 1630, ridiculed the church's bailiffs with obscene and blasphemous jokes in a café; Therry, "Geloven in de kroeg," 175–76.

Sabbath Decree of 1598: Available in many sources, including De Ram, *Synodicon belgicum,* 2:335–41; 9 September 1598.

Hovius Getting His Way: During the visit to Kumtich, for instance, he chastised the caretaker for sleeping inside the church with his wife, or concubine, and the woman left immediately—though of course she might have returned; AAM, DV, Tienen, 3, 1614.

The Women of Limal

The best sources of this story are in AAM, P, Basse-Wavre, testimonies from 1611. For background on this shrine, see *Précis historique de Notre-Dame de Basse-Wavre* (Neerwaver and Leuven, 1947).

Marie de l'Hospital: ARA, OFRB 1195, 6 August 1601.

Special Shrines for Children: In France, believers commonly sought out shrines that specialized in bringing infants briefly to life so they might be baptized, even when bishops were skeptical of them; Luria, *Territories of Grace,* 6, 161. Also J. Gélis, *History of Childbirth: Fertility, Pregnancy, and Birth in Early Modern Europe* (Cambridge, 1991). H. Platelle, *Les Chrétiens face au Miracle: Lille au XVIIe siècle* (Paris, 1968), 48–52, regarding the miracle of baptizing revived infants, speaks of "la méfiance des autorités ecclésiastiques," yet the practice continued. R. Finucane, *The Rescue of the Innocents: Endangered Children in Medieval Miracles* (New York, 1997), notes the strong emotions attending the emergence of a stillborn child; he also argues that Christian parents had been placing such children on altars to revive them since the time of Augustine. The development of the idea of limbo, which removed the physical torments of unbaptized children but still kept them from the presence of God, obviously wasn't enough to console parents.

Bones of a Saint

Plans for the New Reliquary: SAM, CA, 4 December 1617; ARA, GRS, 1116, December 1617; Manuale, 5–7, 9 February 1618, 3 April 1619. The request to the archdukes asked to cheapen the silver to 48 stivers an ounce, for a total of 4,000 ounces—this would be something less than 200,000 stivers, or 10,000 florins.

Gathering the Bones: The story is taken from various sources, including ASPP, Kronieken, Azevedo, Petrus Seré (1738), and an anonymous author. Also Van Autenboer, "Mechelen in de 16de eeuw," 214; Marnef, *Bewind;* Laenen, *Histoire de l'église métropolitaine,* 39. Primary sources are in KAM, 325, testimony regarding the gathering of the relics on 27 October 1585 (the announcement) and the inspection (3 November) in the chapel of St. Martin.

The Number of People with Relics: Witnesses identified sixty-five people with portions of Rombout who had not actually gone inside the church to gather them. Fourteen others said they had gone inside Rombout's themselves. Finally, eighteen others were named who claimed to have been inside, and who then passed along pieces of the relics. This is nearly one hundred people who were involved, and they were not all.

Van der Burch on Saintly Odors: Jadin, "Procès d'information," 150. But the testimony of Marie Oyvaers shows that laypeople knew the smell test too: "She thinks from the color and smell that they are from the holy martyr St. Rombout." Barbara van Straeten, a beguine, also thought the bones simply smelled right.

The Bones Deemed Authentic: That they were kept in the chapel of Mathias Hovius when he became bishop is in Laenen, *Histoire de l'église métropolitaine,* 2:255, with the original in KB, Handschriften, 16527, fol. 6. The two pious daughters were named Strickaert and Van den Hove (virgines); Van den Hove was not an uncommon name, but the archbishop had various nieces who would have been likely candidates for the task.

Archdukes' Decree that Clergy Carry Reliquary: ARA, GRS, 1116, December 1617. The archbishop's lament at the temerity of magistrates in busying themselves with the relics in Manuale, 3 April 1619.

Chapter 12: Ladies of the Garden
Walls of Jericho

Cloister: One typical ordinance says, "Especially female convents are to remove themselves from all worldly friendships"; see AAM, M, 183, fol. 138v, visitation of Jericho, in Brussels, June 1609. Also AAM, M, 8, fol. 130. For more on the tradition of cloister, see Harline, *The Burdens of Sister Margaret,* chapter 12, and the related bibliographical note; plus De Ram, *Synodicon belgicum,* 1:254, De Clausura Monialium. Many churchmen believed that the vow of chastity implied a vow of cloister, as reflected in the bull of Pius V, Circa pastoralis, of 1566; see P. Ranft, *Women and the Religious Life in Premodern Europe* (New York, 1996), 104.

Convents Eager for Cloister: These included Blijdenberg (Manuale, 2 January 1618), Kortenberg (Pasture, *La Restauration Religieuse,* 316, plus AAM, K, Kortenberg, 2, Register, fol. 350, and Manuale, 18 and 20 November 1617), Vorst (Manuale, 6 December 1617, 17 and 22 February 1618), and Marcigny (Ranft, *Women and the Religious Life,* 40).

Convents Less Eager: Refusing the archbishop's loan was the convent of Cabbeke, in Manuale, 18 September 1619. Convents resisting cloister in AAM, K, Algemeen, 36, 19 August 1619, Hovius to the nuncio.

Other Topics of Reforms in Convents: E. Pieters, "Het pastoraal beleid van Antoon Triest, 5e bisschop van Brugge, 1616–1620," *Het Land van Beveren* (1982): 5–63, notes that the most common topics of visitations were cloister, silence, and factionalism. Harline and Put, "A Bishop in the Cloisters," emphasizes the attention ecclesiastical visitors paid to factionalism. Lottin, *Lille,* chapter 7, states that the most frequent problems were factionalism, little silence, and too much attention to temporal matters. Also Moreau, *Histoire de l'église,* 5:64–65.

Holdovers: The other convent besides Grand Bigard that would not accept strict cloister was Zichem; Manuale, 16 and 31 December 1618.

The Name Grand Bigard: This is one case in which we use the French version of the name rather than the original Dutch, Groot Bijgaarden, simply because the original is such a mouthful. J. Mansion, *De Voornaamste Bestanddeelen der Vlaamsche Plaatsnamen* (Brussels, 1935), 21, notes that *bijgaarden* is from medieval Dutch, and comparable to *biloke,* which means an enclosed place, more specifically a prison or a cloister. There is even a convent called "Biloke," in Gent. Thus "Groot Bijgaarden" is most likely rooted in the enclosed convent than in the other possibility, a *bijengaard,* or beehive. Another related root is *gaerde* or *gaarde,* which referred usually to a garden, or also to the guard or watch. The enclosed garden was a favorite motif in this time, especially for religious women.

Previous Transgressions in Grand Bigard: AAM, K, Grand Bigard, 3, visitations, including 1616, and especially Hovius to the nuncio, in the same bundle,

23 March 1617. All references to primary documents in this chapter are from this same file, unless otherwise indicated.

Compelling New Nuns to Accept Cloister: See also AAM, M, 140, fol. 190v, 203v, for Bethanie in Brussels, where Hovius instituted a new profession formula to include a promise of cloister. He would follow the same scheme in Zichem in 1618; Manuale, 16 December 1618.

Refusing Absolution: The visit of 9 December 1616 included his decision. Nuns appealed this decision to Albert in L. Van Meerbeeck, *Correspondance des Nonces Gesualdo, Morra, Sanseverino avec la Secrétairerie d'état Pontificale, 1615–1621. Analecta Vaticano-Belgica, tweede reeks: Nonciature de Flandre* (Brussels, 1937), 30 January 1616, a letter from Gesualdo to Borghese. On Italian generalizations about cloister, see R. De Ganck, "Marginalia to Visitation Cards for Cistercian Nuns in Belgium," *Cîteaux* 40 (1989): 236–37. The nuncio's support of cloister is also mentioned in the archbishop's letter to the nuncio of 23 March 1617.

The Nuns' "Crying and Shouting": Kerremans to Hovius, 10 June 1617. Hovius' decision to compromise is inferred from a letter by the nuns of 24 October 1617, and by the compromise of 30 November 1617 itself, recorded in the Manuale.

Albert's Strictness: Inferred from an appeal by the sisters to the archbishop, on 28 November 1617, in which they ask that Hovius not speak with the archdukes, but deal directly with them.

Walking Outside the Convent: Such a practice was also occasionally allowed to another privileged institution, Jericho in Brussels; AAM, K, Jericho Brussels, 1628 interview summaries, which mention Hovius, who by this time was dead.

More on the Compromise: Also in AAM, M, 8, 128v, as well as assorted loose papers of the convent in AAM, K, Grand Bigard.

Reluctance to Go from One Extreme to Another: In Hovius' letter to the nuncio of 23 March 1617.

Madam Boisot

Albert's Delight at Hovius' Success: Manuale, 5 December 1617.

Hovius' Conversation with Boisot: Manuale, 1 December 1617.

Difficulties of Cloistering Netherlandish Nuns: E. Puteanus, *Relationi Fatte Dall' Illustrissimo e Reverendissimo Signor Cardinal Bentivoglio. In tempo delle sue Nuntiature di Fiandra, e di Francia* (Antwerp, 1629, first published 1611), especially 160–63.

Workers and Financial Affairs of the Convent: Gathered from the convent's accounts, available in transcription at the archive of the Brothers of La Salle, which sits on the site once occupied by Grand Bigard; also in ARA, KAB.

Joanna's Request to Collect Money: Manuale, 1 January 1618. Her request to care for her ill relative in Manuale, 25 February 1618. Investigations by the doctor in Manuale, 25 and 27 February 1618, 19 July 1619.

Joanna's Excommunication: It happened after her trip of February 1618 and before June 1618, when the excommunication was lifted; AAM, M, 8, fols. 150–51, idus tertio July. See also Manuale, 23 June 1618, which suggests that the relaxation was brought back from Rome by Karel Masius, president of the Council of State, and thus that people of the highest rank were in Joanna's camp. But compare to Manuale, 18 August 1618, where she tells Hovius that she's been reinstated by Rome but doesn't yet have official papers.

Joanna's Claim of Invalid Vows: Manuale, 10 October 1618. The archbishop's court charging her with contempt, Manuale, 15 October 1618.

Luncheon: Manuale, 3 November 1618.

Father Kerremans

Confessor in Grand Bigard: AAM, K, Celestines Heverlee, 2, a whole bundle on Kerremans, reveals that he began in Bigard around 1608, and sometime after 1600 as prior of Heverlee. That he was also steward emerges from later documents of Bigard.

Disorder in Heverlee: Morra to Borghese, 11 August 1618, Van Meerbeeck, *Correspondance des Nonces Morra, Gesualdo, Sanseverino*, 302. Farge, *Orthodoxy and Reform*, 193, notes that Paris consulted Heverlee often between 1520 and 1540.

Morra's Efforts to Dismiss Kerremans: Manuale, 12, 18 August, 2, 9 September 1618; Van Meerbeeck, *Correspondance des Nonces Morra, Gesualdo, Sanseverino*, 1 September 1618, 310–11, and 8 September, p. 312. The latter letter, plus another from 15 September, show that Hovius' doubts about the nuncio's jurisdiction were confirmed by Henri van der Burch, now archbishop of Cambrai; see also Manuale, 21 September 1618. Morra's negative judgment of Hovius in two letters to Borghese on 22 September 1618, also in Van Meerbeeck, *Correspondance des Nonces Morra, Gesualdo, Sanseverino*, 313–14, 317. Manuale, 14–15 November 1617, suggests Hovius was concerned that the nuncio was offended at not being invited to the jubilee. See further the Manuale, 2, 5, 6 September 1618, for hints of their cool relationship.

Kerremans' Trip to France: Morra's letter of 1 September 1618. The offer to resign as prior and remain confessor in the letter of 8 September. The nuncio's anger with the plan in Manuale, 9 September 1618. Hovius' hesitation to release Kerremans in Morra's letter of 15 September. Morra's order to dismiss Kerremans, Manuale, 4, 5 October 1618.

Kerremans' Dismissal: Morra to Borghese, Van Meerbeeck, *Correspondance des Nonces Morra, Gesualdo, Sanseverino*, 321, 6 October 1618.

Hovius Turns Against Kerremans: The nuncio's blaming of Hovius in Morra to Borghese, 22 September 1618, Van Meerbeeck, *Correspondance des Nonces Morra,*

Gesualdo, Sanseverino, 317. Hovius still hesitating to act against Kerremans in Manuale, 25 September 1618, but on 14 January and 31 January 1619 he's clearly against him, and resents the need to "purge" his reputation among the great. Kerremans' insistence that he was exempt from the nuncio in Morra to Borghese, 6 October 1618, Van Meerbeeck, *Correspondance des Nonces Morra, Gesualdo, Sanseverino,* 321, and Manuale, 3 November 1618.

Reports by Calenus: Material damage in Hovius to Calenus(?), 31 January 1619, AAM, K, Grand Bigard, and Manuale, 31 January 1619. Information on Michel Kerremans in Manuale, 27 July 1619. That Michel continued to orchestrate things comes from various documents after 1620 in the Grand Bigard bundle.

Scandals in Convents: Harline, *The Burdens of Sister Margaret,* chapters 2–4, and Harline and Put, "A Bishop in the Cloisters," based on Hovius' Agenda, 30 December 1618, testimony of Gertrudis Spina.

Nuns Going to Heverlee: Catharina Martigny, Johanna Heresim, and Joanna Boisot all left shortly after the archbishop's ban; Manuale, 17 January 1619.

Kerremans Hiding in Bigard: Manuale, 18 March 1619. On one visit to Grand Bigard, the councilor Fourneau, distinguished father of one of the nuns (he had even been held at his baptism by Charles V), tried to summon Kerremans and chastise him for ignoring the archbishop's order, but Kerremans secretly left the convent first; Manuale, 27 April 1619.

Hovius' Farewell Audience with Morra: Manuale, 21 July 1619. That Kerremans had a lover is from a later letter of Calenus to Hovius' successor, Jacob Boonen, in AAM, K, Grand Bigard, 30 January 1622. Calenus also mentions the longtime role of Margaret Kerremans, the ex-confessor's niece or cousin, in the convent, especially with Joanna Boisot. Maria Boiselli is in Manuale, 24 February 1620, and AAM, K, Grand Bigard, 3, visitation of April and May 1630, interviews with Maria Tiry, Catharina Meert, and Anna Tambuyser. Wivina Tserclaes in Manuale, 18 February 1620, and letter to Calenus, 24 February 1620. Maria D'Ombre in AAM, M, 8, fols. 152–53, visitation decrees for Grand Bigard.

Kerremans Insisting on Innocence: Letter to Calenus, 1 or 7 February 1619.

A New Abbess for the Garden

Anna's Coat of Arms: Visible on the gravestone of Anna D'Ittre, on the site of the old monastery of Grand Bigard.

A Coadjutrice: Manuale, 16 April 1619, 12–29 June 1619, 1, 11 July 1619, 11 August 1619. Also dossier in ARA, RSA 926, 13 July 1619, regarding the election.

Catherina's Elevation: Manuale, 21 November 1619, and especially 16, 17 February 1620.

Triumph: Manuale, 19 December 1619, has Hovius writing to Bishop Boonen of Gent, and to the nuncio, exulting. Congratulations to Hovius on the election in Manuale, 21 July 1619, from the nuncio Morra.

Joanna Asking to Leave Again: The very day of the elevation of Catherina, Manuale, 16 February 1620. Her other requests to quit the religious life, Manuale, 16 and 17 November 1618, 23 and 24 December 1618, 4 March 1619.

Sealed Letters: The problem was mentioned in the visitation of 1619, interview of Catherina Martigny.

Afterward: Manuale, 2 December 1619. Kerremans' further visits in the nuncio Sanseverino to Borghese, 27 July 1619, Van Meerbeeck, *Correspondance des Nonces Gesualdo, Morra, Sanseverino*, 393–4, and 7 September, 405. The new nuncio's complaints to Hovius, in Manuale, 22 July 1619. Imprisoning Boisot, Manuale, 17 December 1619. Taking away the Eucharist, Manuale, 30 March 1620.

Chapter 13: Sisters of the World
The Tavernkeeper's Gold

The main source for Cornelia's story is AAM, K, Zwarte Zusters Leuven, 35, testimonies. Also included are letters from Gertrude van Bierbeek and other interested parties. Documents range from January through April 1619.

Number of Black Sisters in Leuven: At a 1585 visit, there were more than twenty; in Mechelen there were seventeen by 1618.

Visiting the Sick: The statutes in Leuven, like those of most houses, decreed that sisters should return home each evening except in extraordinary illnesses or circumstances. The maid Margaret did sleep in the house.

Hendrik's Death Scene: This is conjecture, based on practices of the time, as prescribed in C. Leutbrewer, OFM, *Gulde biecht-konste om op den tijdt vanmin als twee uren sich te bereyden tot een generale biechte van heel syn leven, sonder peryckel van eenighe doodt-sonden achter te laten* (Brussels, 1646), or J. van Gorcum, *Troost der Siecken* (Antwerp, 1644), and also on the fact that he didn't die suddenly—hence there was time to round everyone up for a final goodbye.

Active Female Religious in the Low Countries: C. Harline, "Actives and Contemplatives: The Female Religious of the Low Countries Before and After Trent," *CHR* 81/4 (October 1995): 541–67. On Black Sisters, F. van der Berghe, J. van den Heuvel, and G. Verhelst, *De Zwartzusters van Brugge, Diksmuide, Oostende, Veurne, en Brazilië* (Brugge, 1986); K. Baert and J. Dauwe, *Zwarte Zusters van Sint-Augustinus te Aalst* (Aalst, 1975); L. van Buyten, "Kwantitatieve bijdrage tot de studie van de 'Kloosterdemografie' in het Leuvense: De priorij 's-Hertogeneiland te Gempe, het zwartzusterskloster en de communauteit van het Groot-Ziekengasthuis te Leuven, 16de-18de eeuw," *Arca Lovaniensis* (1976): 241–76; G. Vanden Bosch, *Monasticon van zwartzusters-augustinessen in Belgie: Bibliografische inleiding tot de Belgische kloosterge-*

schiedenis voor 1796, 18 (Brussels, 1998). Hospital sisters are reviewed in the section below on that topic.

The Nuncio on Cloister for All: Van Meerbeeck, *Correspondance des Nonces Gesualdo, Morra, Sanseverino,* 307, 25 August, 1618, Morra to Borghese; Pasture, *La Restauration Religieuse,* 322, on bishops insisting that Black Sisters at least go out two by two rather than alone.

Medical Activities of Nuns: See E. Arenal and S. Schlau, *Untold Sisters: Hispanic Nuns in Their Own Words* (Albuquerque, 1989). On their spiritual services, see statutes, including those for Leuven, in AAM, M, 8, fol. 35, Leges Nigrarum Sororum Lovaniensium.

Hovius' Respective Visits to Active and Contemplative Houses: Harline and Put, "A Bishop in the Cloisters."

Characteristics of Nursing Sisters: AAM, M, 8, fol. 35, statutes for the Black Sisters of Leuven.

Paludanus: He was actually the underpastor of St. Peter's, serving under the direction of the chapter.

Hovius' May Visits in Leuven: Manuale, 23, 26 May 1619; "after lunch I went to the Black Sisters for the negotiations on Cornelia Vande Vinne."

Rich and Poor: M. Therry, "De religieuze duiding en beleving van de kloof tussen arm en rijk in de 17de-eeuwse Zuidelijke Nederlanden," *Archief- en Bibliotheekwezen in België* 62 (1991): 491–520.

A Godly Hospital

The Archbishop's Visitations: These are inferred from various sources about how he proceeded, including comments in his Manuale about his coach, 29 March 1618, and comments ad nauseam about his health, including 16–20 July 1619 on his dizziness. For more specifics on the procedure of visitation, see Harline and Put, "A Bishop in the Cloisters," and Harline, *The Burdens of Sister Margaret,* chapters 10 and 15. Tasks awaiting him in Diest are inferred from Manuale, 23 September to 10 October 1619. Manuale, 3 May 1619, Hovius was already trying to appoint a replacement for Timmermans in the beguinage.

Hospitals in Diest: Diest held within its walls at least four such institutions, including the hospital of the Gray Sisters (or Cell sisters), the house of the Cell brothers, the Plague House adjoining the Gray Sisters' hospital, and the town hospital whose reform was at stake. For an excellent survey of Hospital Sisters, see J. Ockeley, *De gasthuiszusters en hun ziekenzorg in het aartsbisdom Mechelen* (Brussels, 1992), and for Diest, M. van der Eycken, *Ziekenzorg te Diest van de 12e tot de 18e eeuw* (Diest, 1979).

Hovius to Baron of Boelaere: 29 August 1616, AAM, A, Hovius, 4.

Examples of Asse, Landen, Geraardsbergen: AAM, A, Hovius, 7, "Exempl

inconvenientium et abusuum . . . ," undated, and "Articuli ex actis visitationis deca-
natuum archiepiscopatus Mechliniensis . . . ," also undated. Church-state relations
at the local level are discussed generally in J. de Kempeneer, "Bevoegdheidsconflicten
tussen aartsbisschop Hovius en de plaatselijke heren in het Land van Aalst," *Het Land
van Aalst* 46 (1993): 209–15.

The Archdukes' Decree of 1606 on Poor Tables and Hospitals: In numerous
places, including AAM, A, Hovius, 4, 17 March 1606. Correspondence between archbishop and archdukes in the same file, plus ARA, RSA, 1944/2; ARA, MD 5434.

The State of the Hospital of Diest: AAM, M, 8, fol. 198, undated, but from
contents 1618. Hovius' letter to the magistrates is implied in AAM, M, 8, fol. 201,
magistrates to Hovius, in which they repeat what Hovius' letter contained. Hovius'
visit to Albert, Manuale, 21 March 1619. Hovius' draft for Albert in RSA, 1944/4,
25 March 1619, to Council of State.

The Archdukes in Diest: RSA, 1944/4, Archdukes to magistrates of Diest,
29 March 1619. That Hovius went to Diest as well in Manuale, 2 May 1619.

Opposition of Magistrates to Hovius' Reforms: AAM, M, 8, fol. 198; and
Manuale, 4 May 1619. The delegation of magistrates who came to Hovius in Manuale,
3, 7 May 1619. Anthony de Jonge in AAM, M, 8, fol. 209; and Manuale, 4 May 1619.

Help from the Council of State for Hovius: RSA 1944/4, 21 May 1619, Hovius
to Council of State. Manuale, 21 May 1619; see also AAM, M, 8, fol. 207, 9 May 1619.

Hovius and the Magistrates of Diest: Telling them to submit in AAM, M, 8,
fol. 204, undated, but we think from the summer of 1619. On accounts, Manuale,
26 September 1619. The sheriff's promise to help, and the ensuing farce, Manuale,
24–26, 30 September, and 1 October 1619.

Final Proclamation of the Agreement: AAM, Fonds Amatus Coriache, 5, fol.
28, 30 October 1619. The sisters moving from Tienen in Manuale, 4 October 1619. Recommendation for Anthony de Jonge in Manuale, 27 September 1619, 9 October 1619.

Magistrates Attacking Tax-Exempt Status: AAM, K, Gasthuis Diest, 6,
Bouckaert to Boonen, 4 January 1623.

Chapter 14: The Sportsman's Mass

The chapter's title is an adaptation of the label some inhabitants of Diest gave
to "The Dean's Mass": the "missa venatoris," or literally, the Hunter's Mass. Sportsman is a better choice to describe his all-around interests, however, because there were
more complaints about his fishing than his hunting.

Frans van Groenendonk in 1619: By this time he had begun to show signs of
reconciliation with Mathias Hovius. In Manuale, 4 May, he asks the archbishop for instructions on doing his accounts, and even promises to report any rumors of drinking
or gambling by Dean Wiggers or Arnold Cryters.

Jan Coen: testimony by his vicar, Martin Aegidius, on 13 July 1615, in AAM, P, Diest St. Sulpitius, II, and the visitation of 6 July 1615, in the same bundle. The provost, by the way, was always a monk of nearby Tongerlo, which was no doubt one reason why the canons regularly feuded with him. After being released as provost, Jan Coen went on to become abbot of Tongerlo! See Morren, *Diest*, 149, as well. On the provost's vicars, see the 1615 visitation below, testimony of Canon de Weerdt. The new provost in AAM, M, 5, fol. 126v, 24 October 1615.

Soulmates

The portraits of Wiggers and Cryters are drawn from the visitation reports of 1612, 1615, 1617, in AAM, P, Diest St. Sulpitius, II; a letter from Hovius to the chapter, in the same file, 2 December 1608; a letter from several canons to Hovius, 8 January 1618; the visitation of 1608, in AAM, M, 183, fol. 134–36.

Wiggers' Age: AAM, P, St. Sulpitius II, visitation June 1621, by Boonen, says he's fifty.

Rabelais: The fictional religious community was the Abbey of Thélème, in *Gargantua and Pantagruel.*

Canons Halting Their Singing: This sort of industrial action in the visitation ordinances of 1615, in AAM, P, St. Sulpitius Diest, II.

Choir: About a third of each canon's income was tied to attendance at choir. Some clever canons therefore arrived in time for the start, left, then returned in time for the ending, thus claiming attendance and the day's income. See De Ram, *Synodicon belgicum,* vol. 1, decrees of provincial synod (365–410), Titulus XII. Other standards of behavior for canons are also contained in this section of the decrees. Teachers of the local Latin School were so mad about disputes in choir with the canons that one reportedly said, "I'd like to go fetch some wood and burn all those long-robes"; testimony from one of the canons, named De Weerdt, in the visitation of 1615.

Changing Henri

Chapters: In addition to Pasture, *Les chapitres séculiers,* and "La réforme des chapitres séculiers," see Baumgartner, *Change and Continuity,* 100, and Moreau, *Histoire de l'église,* 5:310. The judgment about canons enjoying an "easy life" quoted in R. Bireley, "Early Modern Germany," in *Catholicism in Early Modern History,* ed. O'Malley, 18.

Cathedral and Collegiate Chapters: The cathedral chapter of Tournai, however, refused to accept any office at all in the bishop's diocesan hierarchy, lest it be perceived as subject to him; Pasture, *Les chapitres séculiers,* 12, 17. Especially Halkin,

AGN, 5:289, criticizes chapters for their "selfish" behavior and insists that they should have been more active in pastoral concerns.

Gifts of Rams by Nearby Abbots: Manuale, 29 and 30 September 1619.

Hovius' Early Meeting with Wiggers: Manuale, 24 September 1619.

Jerome's Words: Quoted by canons in their appeal to Hovius against Dean Wiggers and Arnold Cryters, 8 January 1618, cited above.

Arnold Cortenbosch of Aarschot: Visitation of the chapter, 24 May 1618, in AAM, P, Aarschot, III. Also Morren, *Diest,* 131–33; and especially AAM, P, Aarschot, II, document of 1627 summarizing Cortenbosch's misdeeds. Also Manuale, 24–26 April 1618.

Lindanus of Zoutleeuw: Manuale, 29 July 1619, among others.

Ronse: Hovius' Agenda, 6 August 1619; RAGM, 232, 7 September 1592, notes of a secretary, as well as other documents in the same file from 1606, 1607, and 1615. Also Manuale, 18 December, 29 December 1617, 31 January, 1 February, 26 March, 26 and 27 April, 18 and 20 June, 5 and 29 September, 21 October, 5 December 1619, 10 January 1620, Hovius' talks with a Canon Mulder, who reported the misdeeds of his confreres.

Canon Hartius: The father's letter in AAM, O, 3, dated 30 March 1617. Various entries in Manuale, November 1617, as well.

Decrees for St. Sulpitius in 1619: AAM, M, 8, fol. 214.

Passages of Scripture: These appear on the back of RAGM, 232, an agreement with the chapter of Ronse. It is a list, in Hovius' hand, of scriptures that would have been relevant to the sins against the priestly state. The scriptural texts cited are Leviticus 4, Joel 2, Malachi 2, II Corinthians 6, and still others.

Hovius' Stormy Interview with Wiggers: Manuale, 6 October 1619. Earlier threat to call the nuncio in Manuale, 16, 17 March 1618.

Joannes Wiggers' Intervention: Manuale, 7 October 1619.

Final Interviews with Henri: Manuale, 8 October 1619, and AAM, M, 8, fol. 217.

Hovius Helping Other Bishops Against Chapters: Manuale, 25 August 1618, 27 September 1618, 1 November 1618, among others.

The "Policy of Inertia": Pasture, *Les chapitres séculiers,* 42. For a similarly pessimistic picture of chapters, Nalle, *God in La Mancha,* 74–80, and Forster, *The Counter-Reformation in the Villages,* 39–57, among many others.

Chapter 15: Almost Eternity

The main source for the chapter is the Manuale. Supplementary documents only are listed below.

13 February: Documents in Put, "Geen geld, geen hervorming." On Francis de

Sales, F. Trochu, *Saint François de Sales, Evêque et prince de Genève . . .* , 2 vols. (Paris, 1942), 2:532.

Late March: See the Manuale first of all, but also De Villermont, *L'Infante Isabelle,* 2:33–35; De Ram, *Synodicon belgicum,* provincial council of 1607, title VII, chapter 5. Negligent communers in De Brouwer, *De kerkelijke rechtspraak,* 2:32, among others. The scene with Pater Zoes in Manuale, 31 March 1619.

15 April: P. Burke, "How To Be a Counter-Reformation Saint," in *Religion and Society,* ed. Greyerz, 45–55. W. Vroom, "De martelaren van Gorcum," in *Waar de blanke top der duinen en andere vaderlandse herinneringen,* ed. N. C. F. Van Sas (Amsterdam, Antwerp, 1996), 107–17, and *In tumultu gosico, Over relieken en geuzen in woelige tijden* (Nijmegen, 1992), 24–30; Manuale, 18 October 1618, 15–17 April 1619, 10 June 1619, 23, 24 July 1619; Van Meerbeeck, *Correspondance des Nonces Morra, Gesualdo, Sanseverino,* 397, 401, 554–56; AAM, M, 5, fols. 130–31; G. Estius, *Historia martyrum Gorcomiensium* (Antwerp, 1603); J. Reusens, *Historia beatorum martyrum Gorcomiensium* (Leuven, 1867), 276–84; W. Lampen, "De vergadering te Leiden (24 mei 1628) betreffende de zaligverklaring van de martelaren van Gorcum," *Bijdragen voor de Geschiedenis van de provincie der Minderbroeders in de Nederlanden* 14 (1953): 169–77.

14 June: AAM, O, 3, 14 June 1611. De Brouwer, *De kerkelijke rechtspraak,* says eight of ten cases before the ecclesiastical court involved marriage or sexual matters, the Sabbath, and the supernatural. Children born out of wedlock in AAM, O, 1, bundle I/6, 14 March 1608, short proclamation signed by Hovius. Request for financial support from departed spouses in AAM, O, 1, bundle 7, 1612 cases. Return of a husband thought dead in AAM, M, 6, fol. 263, 9 December 1609. Dispensations from banns and degrees of relations in Manuale, 24 September 1618, as an example. Disputed engagements in AAM, O, 4, bundle 1, 1618 case of Maria Cornelis and Aert Mutsaerts, which followed the classic formula, for Maria claimed that Adrian had pursued her for years, that she yielded to him only after a promise of marriage, and that she became pregnant, while Adrian counterclaimed that he made no such promise, and that Maria was promiscuous, hence who was the true father? Abuse of spouses in Manuale, 20 October 1619, Hovius grants separation to a woman.

26 July: Manuale, 23 May, 26 May 1619, 26 July 1619, 12 October 1619, for times the two ate together in Leuven. 30 April 1619, Hovius visits the sick Jansonius. L. Ceyssens, "Autour de Jacques Jansonius, professeur à Louvain, 1547–1625," *Augustiniana* 22 (1972): 356–97, especially 377.

18 August: *Pastorale ad usum romanum accomodatum.* Also the diocesan synod of Mechelen, of 1609, mentions the headband worn by children. Hovius to pastor of Overijse, announcing he will arrive to confirm people, undated, KAM, A, Hovius, Bewind. Background information from M. Cloet, "Het vormsel in Vlaanderen van ca. 1600 tot ca. 1800: Een verwaarloosd sacrament," in *Levensrituelen, Het vormsel* (KADOC-studies 12), ed. K. Dobbelaere, L. Leijsen, and M. Cloet (Leuven, 1991), 16.

KAM, A, Hovius, Bewind, anonymous biographical notes. Manuale, 18 September 1618, 28 October 1618, are two examples of confirmation. AAM, DV, Sint-Pieters-Leeuw, P1, 1610, Gooik, where bailiff said his son did not need confirmation.

21 September: Roegiers, *Het bisschoppelijk seminarie,* 105. Also Pasture, *La Restauration Religieuse,* 220–24. AAM, K, Blijdenberg, Victorinnen Mechelen, 72, fols. 72–73, notes the total of his ordinations. See also Van den Broecke, "Seculiere geestelijken," 199. On the number of regulars ordained by Hovius see for example A. M. Bogaerts, *De Dominikanen in de wijdingsregisters van het Aartsbisdom Mechelen* (Brussels, 1965).

November: AAM, K, Algemeen, contains several documents, one dated October 1614, but the entire case was apparently handled within a couple of months. Genoveva was forty-nine at the time of the dispute; that she was a grandmother is plausible, given her statement about raising numerous children. A precedent for release from vows in AAM, M, 5, 71v. That Genoveva won is inferred from eighteenth-century writing on the back of her documents: "the case of a woman released from her vows."

5 December: Most of the information in this section comes from Stadsarchief Antwerpen, Notariaat, 3539, f. 26 r-v and 37, provided by Marie-Juliette Marinus, plus background from the Manuale, 5, 6, 14 December 1617, 13, 14, 21 January, 10, 13 February, 15, 16, 18, 19 March, 14 May, 23, 24, 26 August, 1 September, 20, 21, 24, 26, 30 November, 8, 12, 14 December 1618, 1, 5, 9, 17, 29 January, 6 March, 1, 12 August, 1 October 1619, 19 March 1620. Also J. Materné, "The Officina Plantiniana and the Dynamics of the Counter-Reformation, 1590–1650," in *Produzione e commercio della carta e del libro secc. XIII–XVIII, Istituto Internazionale di Storia Economica 'F. Datini' Prato,* Seri II, 23 (Florence, 1992), 482. Manuale, 9 March 1619. F. Donnet, *Les imprimeurs Trognaesius et leur famille* (Antwerp, 1919); A. K. L. Thijs, *Van geuzenstad tot katholiek bolwerk: Maatschappelijke betekenis van de Kerk in contrareformatorisch Antwerpen* (Turnhout, 1990), 105.

Chapter 16: Mathias at Rest

The main source of the chapter is E. Put and C. Harline, "Sterven als aartsbisschop," which lists the various accountings and reports that give clues of proceedings. Also KAM, Cartularium (1736), F VI/2, 331–34, notes of Antonius de Mol on Hovius' death. Also Beyerlinck, *Oratio.* Hovius' will in KAM, A, Hovius, 72; Archief van het Grootseminarie, A I, 21 a and A, IV, 6; and SAM, Varia, 550; SAM, *Lettres* Missives, reg. II, 72; Claessens, *Histoire des archevêques,* 1:235. The text from Isaiah is 3:24.

Hovius Preparing His Papers: Manuale, 8–11 January 1619. His experiment with cupping in Manuale, 31 July, 2 August 1619.

Masses for the Dead: G. Bousset, "Brusselse kanunniken en kapelaans in de spiegel van hun testamenten, 1600–1650," *Trajecta* 1 (1992): 366; and J. Chiffoleau,

"Sur l'usage obsessionel de la messe pour les morts à la fin du Moyen Age," in *Faire croire: Modalités de la diffusion et de la réception des messages religieux du XIIe au XVe siècle*, ed. A. Vauchez (Rome, 1981): 235–56. Ch. Potvin, *Albert et Isabelle: Fragments sur leur règne* (Paris and Brussels, 1861), 1:190.

Preparing the Corpse, and Other Customs of Burial: AAM, A, Hovius, 1, anonymous notes, and the notes by Antonius de Mol, cited above. For context, Ph. Ariès, *L'homme devant la mort* (Paris, 1977), 172; M. Soenen, "Fêtes et cérémonies publiques à Bruxelles aux Temps Modernes," *BG* 68 (1985): 70; P. Chaunu, *La mort à Paris* (Paris, 1978), 357.

Choir Organ: Jadin, "Procès d'information," 150.

Manuale: Beyerlinck noted in his speech that Hovius always had it nearby.

Jansonius' Speech: *Oratio funebris in obitum Ill. ac Rev. Domini, Matthiae Hovii, archiepiscopi Mechliniensis . . .* (Leuven, 1620).

Hovius' Sister Catharina: ASV, FB, III98D, 91, shows that she was sixty-six in 1602 during talks with Affligem; she was named in the accounts of 1610, when she was thus seventy-four, but she disappeared by 1620.

The secretary's note on Hovius' death comes at the end of his register of ordinations, in AAM, H.

Costerius' Fast: Manuale, 4 March 1618.

Laar: "Kerk en Kerkhof," *Heemkundig Landen*, typescript, p. 7, in the church of Laar.

Bentivoglio: Bergin, *French Episcopate*, 83.

Kerremans: Calenus to Boonen, AAM, K, Grand Bigard, 30 January 1622.

A Word After

Examples of older studies of bishops (not listed in the first note above) include, from the Netherlands alone:

O. Bled, *Les évêques de Saint-Omer, depuis la chute de Thérouanne*, vol. 1, *1553–1610* (St. Omer, 1898).

E. Cortyl, *Un évêque du XVIe siècle: Pierre Pintaflour, évêque de Tournai de 1575 à 1580* (Lille, 1893).

G. Dansaert, *Monseigneur de Baillencourt, évêque de Bruges, 1610–1681* (Brussels and Paris, 1927).

E. Debout, *Vie de Matthieu Moulart, évêque d'Arras* (Paris and Arras, 1901).

L. Duflot, *Un orateur du XVIe siècle: François Richardot, évêque d'Arras* (Arras and Paris, 1897).

A. de Leyn, *Esquisse biographique de Pierre de Corte (Curtius), premier évêque de Bruges* (Leuven, 1863).

A. Possoz, *Vie de Monseigneur Van der Burch, archevêque, duc de Cambrai, prince du Saint-Empire, comte de Cambrésis* (Cambrai, 1861).

New books about bishops, most influenced by the new religious history, are certainly written, especially for Germany and Italy, as evidenced at the beginning of the notes, under works on the Catholic Reformation, and by several works added here. This is not to mention a number of unpublished theses and dissertations, diocesan studies, and other general studies of the Age of Reformation that include bishops.

C. Cairns, *Domenico Bollani, Bishop of Brescia* (Nieuwkoop, 1976).

W. Hudon, *Marcello Cevini and Ecclesiastical Government in Tridentine Italy* (DeKalb, Ill., 1992).

M. Becker-Huberti, *Die tridentinische Reform im Bistum Münster unter Fürstbischof Bernhard von Galen 1650 bis 1678* (Münster, 1978).

K. Hengst, *Kirchliche Reformen im Fürstbistum Paderborn unter Dietrich von Fürstenberg, 1585–1618 . . .* (München-Paderborn-Wenen, 1974).

B. Kirchgässner, W. Baer, *Stadt und Bisschof, Arbeitstagung in Augsburg, 15.–17. November 1985* (Sigmaringen, 1988).

H. G. Molitor, *Kirchliche reformversuche der Kurfürsten und Erzbischöfe von Trier im Zeitalter der Gegenreformation* (Wiesbaden, 1967).

P. H. Verhoeven, *Maarten van Riethoven, eerste Bisschop van Ieper* (Wetteren, 1961).

C. de Clercq, *Cinq archevêques de Malines*, 2 vols. (Paris, 1974).

There is no full-length study of Hovius. The closest thing is a chapter in Claessens, *Histoire des archevêques*. And his assessment follows the usual stereotype of "the" Counter-Reformation bishop: an active and able administrator who promoted ecclesiastical discipline, good morals, and piety. Not that these judgments are wholly wrong, but they fail to tell the whole story. Also E. Put and C. Harline, "Hovius (Mathias)," in *Dictionnaire d'Histoire et de Géographie Ecclésiastiques* (Paris, 1993), 24: cols. 1297–99. Hovius further plays a role in Harline, *The Burdens of Sister Margaret,* chapters 3 and 4.

H. E. Midelfort's comment is in "Witchcraft, Magic, and the Occult," in *Reformation Europe: A Guide to Research,* 183–209.

Acknowledgments

✦

Collaboration not only takes twice as long but affords us the pleasant task of thanking twice as many people.

We must begin in the archives and libraries which made our work possible, most especially with Constant van de Wiel of the Archive of the Archdiocese of Mechelen-Brussels, who with unusual diligence over several decades brought more order to this great treasure than it had ever known before, and who literally made our book possible. We thank as well his most helpful successor, Aloysius Jans. Also valuable were the Vatican Archives and Library in Rome, the Algemeen Rijksarchief in Brussels, the Provincial Archives of Gent and Antwerp, the Royal Albert I Library in Brussels, the Library and Archive of the Katholieke Universiteit Leuven, the Municipal Archive of Mechelen, the Diocesan Archives of Brugge and Antwerp, the Archive and Library of the Abbey of Affligem, the Archive of the Abbey of Dendermonde, the Archive of the Abbey of Averbode, the Archive of the Abbey of Parc, Brother Jacques Palmans of the Brothers of LaSalle in Grand Bigard, the Provincial Archive of the Franciscans in St. Truiden, the parish staff of St. Peter's and Paul's in Mechelen, the Provincial Archives of Utrecht (Netherlands), and the Diocesan Archive of Den Bosch (Netherlands).

It's impossible to name all those individuals who over the years have helped shape this book in one way or another. Both of us owe unpayable debts to Michel Cloet, who guided Eddy as a graduate student and who introduced Craig, as a green foreigner, to the archives of Belgium—besides his many personal kindnesses, it was he who first suggested Mathias Hovius as a possible topic of study. We owe further intellectual and personal debts to Jan Roegiers and Herman and Monique Van der Wee. Marc Therry, Megan Armstrong, Robert Kenney, and Paula Kelly graciously read and commented on earlier versions of this work. Plenty of others read parts of the work or contributed in still other ways, including Marie-Juliette Marinus, Guido Marnef, Walter Prevenier, Erika Rummel, Thomas Brady, James Tracy, Jodi Bilinkoff, Theodore Rabb, Maurice Lee, James Fisher, Louis Perraud, Wyger Velema, Kevin Kenner, Kent Hackmann, Carlos Schwantes, and Kendall Brown. Herbert Rowen, who died before the final version appeared, was also a great inspiration. Thanks as well to research assistants Paola Benedetti, Karen Carter, Maria Cummado, Jeff Jacklin, and Bekki Richards, plus Julie Radle, Shawny Grover, Spencer Davis, and Leah Sherry.

Various institutions supported our work financially. A research trip by Eddy to the Archivio Segreto Vaticano was made possible by the Belgian Historical Institute in Rome, the Algemeen Rijksarchief (Belgian State Archives), and the Belgian Fund for Academic Research. Both of us were supported in various ways by the Katholieke Universiteit Leuven—especially the History Department, the Research Fellows Program (namely Ignace Bossuyt), and the International Housing Office. Thanks in the United States to the National Endowment for the Humanities, the American Council of Learned Societies, the American Philosophical Society, the University of Idaho Research Council, the Idaho State Board of Education, and the History Department, Kennedy Center, and College of Social Sciences at Brigham Young University.

Thanks to John Ware for his efforts to find the manuscript a good home, and to Charles Grench, Philip King, and others at Yale for their enthusiasm and expertise in shaping the manuscript into a book.

And thanks above all to our families for tangible and emotional support over the years. Craig's parents, Lloyd and Kay Harline, have offered decades of encouragement, while Paula, Andrew, Jonathan, and Kate have enjoyed but also endured distant trips and what must have seemed an unusual amount of arcane talk. Eddy's wife, Maria, and their children Liesbeth, Pieter-Jan, and Kathelijne have suffered, thanks to our long years of collaboration, more evenings lost to research sessions than can rightly be expected. Yet collaboration also brought to all of us not only new ideas and interests but the pleasure of new friendships.

Index

✦

Page numbers in italic type refer to illustrations.

384